The memory of catastrophe

Published in our
centenary year
2004
MANCHESTER
UNIVERSITY
PRESS

The memory of catastrophe

edited by
Peter Gray and Kendrick Oliver

Manchester University Press

Manchester and New York

distributed exclusively in the USA by Palgrave

Published by Manchester University Press
Oxford Road, Manchester M13 9NR, UK
and Room 400, 175 Fifth Avenue, New York, NY 10010, USA
www.manchesteruniversitypress.co.uk

Distributed in the United States exclusively by
Palgrave Macmillan, 175 Fifth Avenue,
New York, NY 10010, USA

Distributed in Canada exclusively by
UBC Press, University of British Columbia, 2029 West Mall,
Vancouver, BC, Canada V6T 1Z2

British Library Cataloguing-in-Publication Data is available

Library of Congress Cataloging-in-Publication Data is available

ISBN 978 0 7190 6345 9 paperback

First published by Manchester University Press in hardback 2004

This paperback edition first published 2012

The publisher has no responsibility for the persistence or accuracy of URLs for any external or third-party internet websites referred to in this book, and does not guarantee that any content on such websites is, or will remain, accurate or appropriate.

Printed by Lightning Source

In Memoriam
Timothy Reuter (1947–2002)

Contents

List of contributors

Carol Acton is Assistant Professor of English at St Jerome's University (federated with the University of Waterloo) Ontario, Canada. Since she completed a PhD thesis on combatant poetry of the First World War, her research has focused primarily on women and war experience, particularly the First World War and the Vietnam War. Her comparative discussion of women's writing from both wars will be published in a forthcoming issue of *War, Literature, and the Arts*. She has also published on Vera Brittain's life-writing as part of ongoing research in the Vera Brittain archives at McMaster University, Ontario. The Brittain research and the chapter in this collection are part of a larger project on the relationship between grief, mourning, and cultural contexts in wartime.

Donald Bloxham lectures in history at the University of Edinburgh. He received his PhD from the University of Southampton, before serving as Research Director of the Holocaust Education Trust in 1998–2000, and as a Leverhulme Special Research Fellow at Southampton University in 2000–2, studying the Armenian genocide. His first book, *The Holocaust on Trial: War Crimes Trials and the Formation of History and Memory*, was published by Oxford University Press in 2001.

P.A. Cramer is a doctoral student of rhetoric in the Department of English at Carnegie Mellon University. His research interests include aesthetics and politics, discourse ethics, and American political discourse. He is particularly interested in the role of public space as a precondition for argumentation and as a traditional domain of rhetoric. Before moving to Pittsburgh, Pennsylvania, he lived and worked in Charleston, South Carolina.

Peter Gray is Senior Lecturer in History at the University of Southampton, and was formerly a British Academy Research Fellow at Downing College, Cambridge. He has published extensively on the history of the Great Irish Famine, including *The Irish Famine* (Thames and Hudson, 1995) and *Famine, Land and Politics: British Government and Irish Society 1843–1850* (Irish Academic Press, 1999). He is currently working on studies of the Irish Poor Law and of nineteenth-century British-Irish relations, and is director of the EPPI project to digitise nineteenth-century Irish official publications.

James Guimond is Professor of English at Rider University, New Jersey. He is the author of *The Art of William Carlos Williams: A Discovery and Possession of America* (University of Illinois Press, 1968) and *American Photography and the American Dream* (University of North Carolina Press, 1991). He is currently completing a book with Katherine Maynard on narrative theory and justice, and will then begin a project on the cultural and historical contexts of disaster narratives.

Edgar Jones is Reader in the History of Medicine and Psychiatry at King's College Medical School, London, where he is currently researching the treatment of post-combat syndromes from the Boer War to the present. He originally trained as an economic and social historian at Nuffield College, Oxford, and subsequently completed a doctorate in psychopathology at Guy's Hospital. He has written on the history of military psychiatry and the symptomatology of post-combat syndromes; his history of Glaxo, *The Business of Medicine*, was published in 2001.

Lisa A. Kirschenbaum is Associate Professor of History at West Chester University, Pennsylvania. She received her PhD from the University of California, Berkeley, in 1993, and is the author of a number of articles and essays on the Soviet kindergarten and private life in Soviet Russia. Her first book, *Small Comrades: Revolutionizing Childhood in Soviet Russia, 1917–1932*, was published by Routledge in 2001.

Glen D. Kuecker is Assistant Professor of History at DePauw University, Greencastle, Indiana. He received his PhD in Latin American and Global History from Rutgers University in 1998. He is currently writing a book entitled *Through the Prism of Modern Spaces: An Urban Geography of Modern Tampico*.

Tony Kushner is Marcus Sieff Professor of Jewish/Non-Jewish Relations in the History Department of the University of Southampton. He is the author or editor of eleven books, including *The Holocaust and the Liberal Imagination* (Blackwell, 1994) and, with Katharine Knox, *Refugees in an Age of Genocide* (Frank Cass, 1999). His research interests are in the areas of Jewish history; the Holocaust; the history of racism; ethnic and minority studies; and history, heritage, and memory.

Rose Lindsey received her PhD from the University of Southampton. She has been a research fellow at Reading and Bristol Universities, where she worked on a Home Office-funded project examining the English inquest system and its impact on bereaved families. She is the author of 'From atrocity to data: historiographies of rape in former Yugoslavia and the gendering of genocide', *Patterns of Prejudice* (2002), and is currently a Research Officer at King Alfred's University College, Winchester.

Kendrick Oliver is Senior Lecturer in American History at the University of Southampton. He is the author of *Kennedy, Macmillan and the Nuclear Test-Ban Debate, 1961–1963* (Macmillan, 1998), and is currently writing a book for Manchester University Press on the massacre at My Lai in American history and memory.

Andrea Reiter is a Lecturer in the School of Modern Languages, University of Southampton, and a fellow of the Parkes Institute. She received her PhD from the University of Salzburg and held a teaching position there and also at the National

University of Ireland and the University of Frankfurt. Her publications include *Narrating the Holocaust* (Continuum, 2000) and articles on Holocaust literature, contemporary Austrian and East German writers, and music and literature.

Kathinka Sinha-Kerkhoff is Senior Fellow at the Asian Development Research Institute, Patna, India, and is affiliated to the International Institute of Social History, Amsterdam. She received her PhD from the Centre for Asian Studies, Amsterdam, in 1995. Since then, she has been carrying out research in the fields of gender and youth studies and globalisation and refugee studies in a South Asian context, and is presently involved in research on the Hindu minority in Bangladesh and the Muslim minority in India after the Partition of British India. She is also involved in a research project on the relation between the government of India and people of Indian origin in Mauritius, Surinam, and the Netherlands. She has published *Save Ourselves and the Girls! Girlhood in Calcutta under the Raj* (Extravert, 1995), and articles in edited books and international academic journals.

Mark Stoyle is Senior Lecturer in Early Modern History at the University of Southampton. He is author of several books, including *West Britons: Cornish Identities and the Early Modern British State* (Exeter University Press, 2002) and *From Deliverance to Destruction: Rebellion and Civil War in an English City* (Exeter University Press, 1996). He is currently working on the ethnic dimensions of the English Civil Wars.

Acknowledgements

We have incurred many substantial debts since this project was first conceived, during its evolution from two hot words thrown out into the ether to see whether they would elicit an interesting response, through the organisation of a major international conference at Southampton in 2000, and onto the publication of this volume. Our own understanding of what we were trying to achieve has been frequently reformed during that time, and we are grateful for all those who kept faith with the project as it passed from intellectual adolescence into maturity.

We have reason to be grateful to our families, particularly, in Peter's case, Sara, Niall, and Aisling, and, in Kendrick's case, Patricia Morandini – for their love and support and for not reading too much into our preoccupation with the catastrophic. We would like to thank our contributors for the quality of their essays and for the timeliness of their submissions, and Alison Welsby and Jonathan Bevan of Manchester University Press for both their enthusiasm and their patience.

Among our colleagues at Southampton, we appreciate the willingness of Nils Roemer and Tony Kushner to read and comment upon drafts of the Introduction. If the volume as a whole turns out to be well received, the responsibility is entirely ours; if not, we would like to emphasise that the fault is most probably theirs. For diverse reasons, we also have cause to be grateful to Neil Gregor, Waltraud Ernst, Joan Tumblety, Chris Woolgar, Jo Reilly, Patrick Geary, Peter Furtado, James Murrell, Sara Bonadio, Shirley Matthews, and the members of the Cavaliers Cricket Club.

Finally, we would like to acknowledge the contribution made to this project by Professor Timothy Reuter, who died suddenly of a brain tumour in the autumn of 2002. Though he may not have realised it, Tim was the person who converted *The memory of catastrophe* from a timid thought into a concrete enterprise, by applying both institutional and intellectual support when it most mattered, and by encouraging colleagues to think across national and chronological boundaries and to consider the interests that they had in common. We hope that something of Tim's critical but always compassionate spirit is represented in this volume. We dedicate it to him.

Introduction

We are writing on the first anniversary of the terrorist attacks on the World Trade Center in New York, after a year in which images of the catastrophe have been endlessly replayed on our television screens and many times too, perhaps, in our private imaginations. The policy responses of the American government to the horrors of that day still dominate news headlines and public debate. The destruction of the twin towers set forth vibrations that continue to radiate around the world.

Yet it did not take the events of 11 September 2001 to sensitise contemporary culture to the themes of disaster and ruin. For some time now, there has been evident an inclination – not least within Western scholarly circles – to identify the modern age (variously defined) as one peculiarly afflicted and affected by the experience of extremity and cataclysm. In the early 1990s, one cultural critic wrote assuredly of 'our own catastrophic era' dating back about twenty years, during which time, she asserted, wars and other disastrous events had been occurring with increasing frequency.[1] Following a series of technological calamities – including the massive emissions of poisonous gas from the Union Carbide chemical plant in Bhopal in 1984 and radioactive particles from a nuclear reactor at Chernobyl in 1986 – the 1980s were described as a 'decade of disaster'.[2] To the sociologist Kai Erickson, toxic emergencies of this kind, and other catastrophes with discernible human authors, were 'one of the social and psychological signatures of our time'. They amounted to 'a new species of trouble', which was first apparent in the form of the Holocaust and the bombings of Hiroshima and Nagasaki.[3] For James Berger, meanwhile, this catastrophic sensibility had become so embedded in late twentieth-century culture that it was virtually structural, virtually routine: 'The conclusive catastrophe has already occurred, the crisis is over (perhaps we were not aware of exactly when it transpired), and the ceaseless activity of our time – the news with its procession of almost indistinguishable disasters – is only a complex form of stasis.'[4]

Historians might cast a rather sceptical eye over the tendency of cultural critics to identify their own times as uniquely or exceptionally 'catastrophic'. A present- and Western-centred narcissism may risk blinding commentators to the place of catastrophe and its remembrance in much of human history. Moments of acute and devastating mass mortality, from the Black Death pandemic of mid-fourteenth-century

Europe to the worldwide famine crisis of the 1870s (characterised by one historian as an imperially engendered 'late-Victorian holocaust'), have had profound social and cultural effects prior to the twentieth century.[5] Ecological catastrophes, often the consequence of human activities such as deforestation, unsustainable land use, and pathogen-bearing migration, are by no means unique to 'our age'.[6] Even if the bourgeois European and American elites of the nineteenth and early twentieth centuries were relatively insulated from the catastrophic experiences that frequently shaped the consciousness of their inferiors – from enslaved blacks to famine-stricken Irish and Indians – they could not be wholly immune. As P.A. Cramer reminds us in this volume, anticipated and feared catastrophe, whether slave insurrection or class-based revolution, haunted the elites. Such catastrophic phantoms could be rendered material by the experience of humiliating defeat or pyrrhic victory in the great wars of 1861–65 and 1914–18.

Against the image of an unmitigated catastrophic present, other stories have been told: the 1990s were read by some as an era of 'catastrophe avoided' – with the threat of imminent nuclear annihilation apparently lifted, and 'peace processes' (however flawed) seeming to offer an end to the destabilising violence of South Africa, the Middle East, and Northern Ireland. The assertion was made that, following the undoubted horrors of the first half of the twentieth century, human history had in fact embarked upon a more benign and hopeful course. While it was certainly true that 'large and grave events' continued to occur, the real story of the recent past lay not in humankind's submission to Berger's catastrophic sensibility, but rather in the progress that they had made towards a universal condition of political liberty and economic prosperity, the end (in both senses of the word) of history.[7] Whatever else is to be made of this thesis, it does not seem to have effected a permanent restoration of teleological momentum to our understanding of historical development. Both popular culture and scholarly endeavour over the course of the last two decades have been marked by their preoccupation, not with the promise of the present or the prospects for a virtuous and contented future, but with the past. The trajectory of attention has been backwards, not forwards. Historical consciousness and cultural optimism can certainly be reconciled, most obviously in the truism that a resource for social improvement lies in the knowledge of past mistakes. Nevertheless, when contrasted with the search of earlier societies for a usable past, the current enthusiasm for thinking in the pluperfect seems to evince an excess of enchantment over utility; and the perception that this excess is not quite historical in the sense of being disciplined above all by the desire for accuracy has encouraged many commentators to employ an alternative term to capture the phenomenon: 'memory'.[8]

As Nancy Wood has observed, 'Memory is decidedly in fashion.'[9] Just as contemporary culture is reportedly fixated upon catastrophe, so, too, does it appear 'addicted' to memory.[10] This is not a condition confined to the West. 'Over the last twenty or twenty-five years,' asserts Pierre Nora, 'every country, every social, ethnic or family group, has undergone a profound change in the relationship it traditionally enjoyed with the past.' Responsible in part is what Nora terms 'the acceleration of history' – the increasing velocity with which life circumstances, for individuals and for groups, are formed and transformed in the modern world. As a consequence, we lose traction both upon our place in historical time and upon who we really are; in communing with the past, we seek to address this deficit of identity by reconstructing a memory of ourselves. The 'current upsurge in memory' may also be related, in Nora's view, to the process of decolonisation and the wave of regime changes in Eastern Europe, Latin America, and Africa during the 1980s and 1990s. These developments established across much of the world a more permissive political environment for the creative articulation of communal histories, as did – within Western societies – the liberation of groups previously excluded from the public sphere on grounds of gender, race, religion, class, provinciality, and sexual orientation.[11] Many of the precedents for the practice of collective memory were instituted by nation states in the nineteenth and early twentieth centuries, but that context no longer fully holds. Memory creation is presently a decentred, pluralist enterprise, with its practitioners sometimes exhibiting an antagonism not just towards state-sponsored renditions of the past, but also towards the prefectorial reflex of academic authorities to mistrust any assertion which has not been or cannot be tested against the historical grain.[12]

If an affective engagement with the past and a catastrophic sensibility are both integral elements of contemporary culture, it may be instructive to consider in what ways they are related. That the two frequently converge in practice is hardly a remarkable revelation. When the state and state-affiliated institutions engage in commemorative activities, often the focus of their efforts will have the status of catastrophe. Recent examples include the attempt of the Lower Manhattan Development Corporation to integrate a space for a memorial to the victims of the 11 September attacks into proposed designs for rebuilding on the site of the twin towers, and, in Britain, the inauguration in 2001 of an annual Holocaust Memorial Day and the opening of a new exhibit in the Imperial War Museum dedicated to the Holocaust. Academic output on the subject of memory reveals a similar gravitation towards the catastrophic, and particularly towards the experience of war. As Patrick Finney has observed, research into the memory of war 'has lain at the heart of the broader memory project, focusing initially on the unparalleled traumas of the two world wars and the Holocaust but increasingly enfolding a wider range of conflicts within its purview'.[13]

The memory initiatives discharged by the processes of decolonisation and democratisation, meanwhile, have often been driven by a desire for the recognition and reparation of earlier wrongs, including instances of genocide and other episodes of collective violence. Thus, the inauguration of a democratic government in Argentina in 1983, following seven years of brutal military dictatorship, led to the establishment of a 'commission of notables' to receive testimony from the relatives of those who had 'disappeared' during the regime and from the survivors of its clandestine detention camps.[14] Where the horrors of catastrophe do not overwhelm the human capacity to describe what has happened, the writing of memory can function as a means of restoring what was in danger of being lost for good: in particular, a sense both of agency and of continuity with the past. In Jewish literature, a common response to the experience of catastrophe was the creative invocation of a tradition of remembrance linking recent and current vicissitudes to earlier Jewish catastrophes, thereby sustaining a narrative of community resistance and survival.[15] The first Jewish book printed in Nazi-occupied Warsaw was a 101-page anthology called *Suffering and Heroism in the Jewish Past in Light of the Present*, including materials documenting the persecutions of the crusades and the massacres of Jews in the Ukraine in 1648–49. David Roskies comments: 'Without this profound historical awareness, there could not have been a last stand in the ghetto.'[16]

If memory and catastrophe are identified so often as sharing the same cultural space, however, this may reflect the intellectual promiscuity of each concept as much as an essential affinity. The rise to prominence of memory in academic and popular discourses over the last decade has occurred despite (or perhaps because of) its resistance to definition. With regard to two aspects of its use in particular – its relationship to history and its existence at the level of the collectivity – the concept of memory has threatened to escape the reach of secular critical enquiry. Almost from the inception of memory as a subject for academic investigation, there was an inclination among its students to antithesise history and memory by attributing to the latter an archaic, organic, almost spiritual quality that distinguished it from the analytical practices of the former. For Pierre Nora, in his influential 1984 essay, 'Between memory and history', memory 'installs remembrance within the sacred; history, always prosaic, releases it again.'[17] As Kerwin Lee Klein has noted, this attribution of an occult dimension to memory can still be detected in even some of the most thoughtful recent contributions to its study.[18] Dominick LaCapra, for example, judges the critical role of history towards memory to be an essential and desirable component of their relationship; at the same time, however, he contends that, when dealing with events that test the limits of human fathomability, historical writing may embody an act of mourning and legitimately appeal therefore 'to ritual as well as to scientific and aesthetic criteria'.[19] In the absence of a single disciplinary home and evoking as it does a variety of beguiling, mystical associations, memory is permitted to stick to anything.

Similarly, rather too many historical studies have been willing to use the term 'collective memory' as if it was entirely unproblematic, as if social modes of remembering were effectively analogous to the operations of the individual mind. It is certainly the case, as Nancy Wood has observed, that remembering, both at the individual and collective level, incorporates mechanisms of selection, narrativisation, repression, displacement, and denial.[20] It would be unsustainable, moreover, to assert a discrete, pristine separation between individual memory and the processes by which wider social groupings engage with the past: for collective expressions of memory to occur, individuals must participate; the memories of individuals, in turn, are structured and influenced by the memory practices of the community to which they belong and by the exchange of memory content with other members of that community.[21] But there is no enduring repository of memory beyond that extant within the minds of individuals; there is no such thing as a group mind. The existence of a capacity for the cultural transmission of memory is not equivalent to the existence of a shared cultural consciousness.

For Jay Winter and Emmanuel Sivan, memory is collective only in the sense that members of a group may engage in communal memory practices. It is for this reason that they privilege the term 'collective remembrance' over 'collective memory' as a description of their subject, for it directs attention to acts and practices rather than to the chimera of the *mentalité* or *Geist*.[22] Ranging from formal commemorative rituals to informal conversations about the past, these practices of remembrance may allow components of individual memory to intersect and 'create a kind of pattern with an existence of its own'.[23] In the event that they also become a central element of the group's cultural tradition, these practices may help sustain the impression of a permanent and unified memory community, especially if they are transcribed into physical ritual and are thus rendered less vulnerable to critical questioning.[24] Despite the persistence of many commemorative rituals, they remain constantly subject to the possibility of change, precisely because they are the outcome of an ongoing negotiation between the individual members of the group, for whom participation is ultimately dependent upon its continued relevance to their own personal memories and needs. Though inevitably shaped by the environment that surrounds it, memory – in the view of Winter and Sivan – is not socially determined.[25] A multitude of private motivations are usually at play in the public practices of memory, and to impose the adjective 'collective' upon the fluctuating, multifarious contents of the latter may simply function, in many instances, to homogenise and ultimately abstract the real complexity of a group's engagements with its past. To the extent that aggregations of remembrance do occur within a culture, however, it is unlikely that an explanatory model which does not preserve some role for the interventions of the state and the cultural operations of power within civil society will be sufficient; to the extent, moreover, that those aggregations manifest convergences of content as well as practices, the term 'memory' may retain a basic conceptual usefulness and validity.[26] It is the attribution of qualities of spiritual or cultural transcendence to 'memory' which most effectively limits the capacity of the critical method to gain purchase upon its historical operations.

A similar challenge to the conventional intellectual defences against mystification – the processes of representation, investigation, and explanation – has also been evident within recent formulations of 'the catastrophic'. In simple – probably oversimple – terms, the experience of catastrophe is held to have collapsed the Enlightenment. Although reasonable claims have also been advanced for the paradigm-shattering effects of the First World War, it is the Holocaust which is most often asserted to lie at the core of this crisis of historicisation.[27] With respect to no other event in the modern era, it is argued, do the preparatory reflexes of historical enquiry – the questions 'what happened and why?' – seem quite so insufficient a response. For many Western scholars, Saul Friedländer has suggested, there exists a painful tension between 'the obligation to bear witness and record' the extermination of the Jews of Europe and the almost paralysing concern that 'this record should not be distorted or banalised by grossly inadequate representations.'[28] In 1992, he contended that no German or Jewish scholar had yet produced

> an overall history of the extermination of the Jews in Europe that is not a mere textbook presentation, an analysis of the internal cogs and wheels of the destruction machinery or a compendium of separate monographs. The 'Final Solution' in its epoch has not yet found its historian.[29]

In addition, the resistance of the Holocaust to narration and other practices of historical sense-making provoked a broader intellectual deconstruction of the established modes by which meaning could be imposed upon human affairs. The subjective, ideological bases of discourses previously asserted to have had universal salience – nature, progress, truth – were exposed, along with the hope that society would subsequently realise a more democratic, pluralistic model of cultural and intellectual production. Thus, the Holocaust, in Jean-François Lyotard's metaphor, was like an earthquake that destroyed all existing instruments of measurement.[30] As Friedländer notes, it encouraged postmodernist thinkers in particular 'to question the validity of any totalising view of history, of any reference to a definable metadiscourse, thus opening the way for a multiplicity of equally valid approaches'.[31]

Many of the most influential intellectual writings of the late twentieth century, then, exhibited a pronounced scepticism about the power of empirical research and critical analysis to yield anything more insightful about their subjects than local and provisional truths. Yet the alternatives that they offered were in many respects no more satisfactory, not least because the event that had provoked their disillusionment with the positivist conceits of the Enlightenment was itself in danger of being dissolved by the relativism to which those conceits had now given way. The Holocaust seemed to haunt the post-war intellectual world, precipitating thoughts that proved to have unbearable implications when they eventually came back round to consider the Holocaust as their subject. It is in this sense, as well as in the sense of the radical scale of the crimes committed, that Saul Friedländer and Dominick LaCapra assert the Holocaust to have been a 'limit event', resistant to normalisation and final resolution, and likely always to maintain an opacity that even the most inventive historical reckonings cannot dispel.[32] Such classifications, however, may ultimately – and ironically, given its impact upon other totalising discourses – elevate the Holocaust to the status of a totalising presence within contemporary culture, an intellectual move that, as David Roskies has argued, 'succeeds only in robbing the dead of the fullness of their lives and inviting the abstraction of the survivor into Everyman, the Holocaust into Everything'.[33] The extension of what Peter Novick has called 'Holocaust consciousness' may indeed have been facilitated by the passing of years and the natural attrition of survivors, for with fewer and fewer individuals able to claim a position more 'privileged' than any other in terms of first-hand experience of the camps, the Holocaust, as James Berger observes, 'has become open for universal appropriation'.[34] It is possible, moreover, that in the attribution of 'limit' status and through the insistence that something of its meaning can never be disclosed, the Holocaust may be projected into the category of the sublime, evoking a kind of elation in those who reflect upon it and precipitating thereby the very reverse of a moral and historical education.[35]

Catastrophes are ultimately defined by what is said about them, and – even with regard to the most radical of historical cataclysms – saying too much may produce hazards as compelling as those that result from saying too little. This is not to assert that the operations of language, in some unfettered, arbitrary fashion, determine whether or not a particular event is accorded the status of catastrophe, for those operations are themselves affected by the contexts in which they occur. The human and material consequences of the event are inevitably influential in the sense that the more dramatic they are in scale, the more likely it is that, effectively or not, language will be brought to bear on the experience. What sort of language that is, moreover, will be informed by earlier precedents of catastrophic discourse and the prevailing conditions of politics and culture. Nevertheless, to remind ourselves that, whatever the historical event they describe, words retain a transformative power is to caution against naturalising the classification and subsequent memory of even the most apparently intractable catastrophe. After all, the understandings of the Holocaust current in Western Europe and the United States did not spring forth spontaneously from the liberation of the camps in 1945 and the revelation of the horrors that lay within. The legal proceedings against Nazi leaders in the immediate post-war period – often claimed to have been the mechanism through which knowledge of the crimes against the Jews was codified and disseminated to a wider audience – actually served, in Donald Bloxham's view, to draw attention 'away from the victims of Nazi genocide and onto much more ambiguous symbols of suffering'.[36] Only with the trial of Adolf Eichmann in 1962 and the evolving perception, following the Six-Day War of 1967 and the Yom Kippur War of 1973, that another Jewish catastrophe was not impossible, was the Holocaust propelled towards the centre of modern Jewish-American identity, thereafter to begin its movement into the mainstream cultural consciousness of the American people as a whole.[37] Catastrophic memories can be subject to dramatic mutations; if they were not, we could safely ignore the likes of David Irving.

There is, therefore, no essential relationship between the definition of a particular event as catastrophic, and the sustaining of that definition within memory, and the quantum of human suffering that it produced. The arithmetic of a catastrophe does not determine the pattern of its reception and subsequent remembrance. It was not the Australian forces at Gallipoli that suffered the most casualties in that disastrous campaign, but it was only in Australia that the memory of Gallipoli engendered a new national consciousness.[38] The fact that in 1822 the planned slave insurrection in Charleston never actually occurred, as P.A. Cramer argues in this volume, did not prevent its designation as a catastrophe by the city's white population. In the view of Alan Mintz, the quantifiable aspects of a destructive event are an insufficient index of its catastrophic status, which inheres instead in its 'power to shatter existing paradigms of meaning'.[39] Thus, despite all the terrible material waste generated by the fall of Jerusalem in 587 BCE, it was in the resulting 'cognitive disorientation', in the interpretation of the experience as marking the end of the relationship between God and Israel, that its catastrophic quality lay.[40]

The essential characteristic of catastrophe, then, is not any particular level of physical suffering, though it is rare for that to be entirely irrelevant, but the aggregate realisation of a profound sense of cultural disruption across the members of the affected community. The catastrophe is precipitated by the new knowledge that radical historical circumstances present to that community about itself, and to its members about themselves: about the pertinence and tenacity of their values, about their social cohesiveness, about their ability to perform their expected functions, about their capacity for violence or their vulnerability to physical harm, about their assumptions of progress, about the power and purposes of their governing institutions, and about the power and constancy of their gods. Often evident in the responses of communities which have experienced severe disasters, asserts Kai Erickson,

> is an understanding that the laws by which the natural world has always been governed as well as the decencies by which the human world has always been governed are now suspended – or were never active to begin with. They look out at the world through different lenses. And in that sense they may be said to have experienced not only (a) a *changed sense of self* and (b) a *changed way of relating to others* but (c) a *changed world view* altogether.[41]

To take acute cultural rupture as the identifying mark of the catastrophic is to invite the possibility that connections will be made across a wide range of historical phenomena, between 'natural' catastrophes and those with discernible human authors; between civil wars and global conflicts; between localised disasters and genocides. It is also to place the processes of memory at the very core of catastrophe studies, for those processes are concomitant with the mechanisms by which the new knowledge presented by extremity is integrated into (or voided from) the usable pasts of the individuals who experienced it and the communities to which they belong.

If this conceptualisation of catastrophe is to be intellectually productive, however, it must admit creative application while maintaining certain broad parameters of legitimate interpretation and use. As a category of comparative analysis, cultural disruption registers the intensity of effect within a given community, and implies no equivalence with respect to the historical scale or moral dimensions of the precipitating event. Like all such categories of analysis, its function is not to enforce the assertion of analogies, but to clarify points of contrast as well as comparison between what for the most part will have been singular and distinct catastrophic experiences. Moreover, it is a definition of catastrophe that may be held to exclude some broad historical developments with undoubtedly fateful and malignant effects, such as structural poverty and global climate change. This is because a sense of profound disruption requires a keen and affective if not necessarily first-hand consciousness of what had been before, and with phenomena the originating conditions of which either lie in the distant past or coalesced gradually over generations, that precatastrophe consciousness is likely to be weak: catastrophes are structured by the presence of memory.[42]

Further qualifications apply. Not every instance of radical destruction need inevitably be catastrophic for all those that it affects. The experience of war, for example, may reaffirm rather than dramatically reorder the value systems and identity claims of certain communities, while the witnessing of and involvement in acts of slaughter can often be quite easily reconciled with an individual's sense of self.[43] Even when the catastrophic status of an event is uncontentious, that event may produce a diverse range of disruptive effects within the various social groups affected. As Slavos Žižek writes, the great transatlantic liners of the Edwardian era were seen as symbols of affluence and technological progress, and, in the well-defined class distinctions observed on board, also of a stable and coherent social structure; the sinking of the *Titanic* therefore became a story 'in which society lived the experience of its own death'.[44] The cultural resonances of the catastrophe, however, were just so much white noise in the streets of Northam and St Mary's – the districts of Southampton that were home to most of the ship's crew – where the loss was registered in the personal and material form of children without fathers and families without a means of financial support.[45] Marked disparities of impact are perhaps most likely to be evident in instances of catastrophe where the categories of perpetrator, victim, collaborator, and bystander apply and where those categories, pluralised, are reflected in the self-identifications of the communities concerned. Identities, in addition, are not necessarily exclusive or inflexible; a catastrophe may resonate differently for those with a high degree of psychological investment in the status quo ante than for those with a more improvisable set of cultural affinities or a resource of alternative identifications beyond the affected collectivity.

It is rare, moreover, for catastrophic ruptures to be entirely obliterative of the old order. The term 'rupture' indeed implies damage but not quite disintegration, discontinuity but not quite a definite end. Very often, the radical new knowledge that is the mark of the catastrophic enters into a negotiation with the cultural logics of the past, and over time the dissonances may be resolved. In the view of Jay Winter, such a negotiation was evident even in the wake of the First World War; contrary to representations of the conflict as the mortal crisis of European 'civilisation', continuities were as marked as radical innovation.[46]

Among Jewish communities in Palestine and, subsequently, the state of Israel, the Holocaust was interpreted as a tragic confirmation of well-established Zionist teachings that they were not safe as a diasporic people and that their security could be ensured only through the creation of a separate Jewish state. Indeed, as Idith Zertal has argued, the Zionist movement exhibited a profound ambivalence towards the victims of the Holocaust, even as – in the immediate post-war period – it endeavoured to transport survivors to Palestine against British opposition. Though regarded with undoubted pity, the sufferings of these survivors were also ascribed in part to their past delusions of diasporic emancipation. As a result, they were now expected to convert to Zionist goals. Zertal concludes: 'the Holocaust, its victims, and its survivors all played their crucial historical and political roles according to the Zionist script'.[47] The Western democracies, meanwhile, retained much of their conventional allegiance to liberal and Christian universalisms in the wake of the Holocaust, an allegiance that in the immediate post-war decades actually mediated against a full understanding of and accounting for the Nazi genocide. Liberal universalism, in presenting the concentration camps as a crime against humanity, engaged often uneasily and sometimes not at all with the particular fate of the Jews, while Christian universalism encouraged a resistance to memorial activities on the grounds that they might impede moves towards international reconciliation and forgiveness.[48]

Although the terms 'rupture' and 'disruption' appear regularly in popular and scholarly literatures of catastrophe, their conceptual status remains rather undefined; they often seem simply to be used as secondary level synonyms for 'trauma'. It is the discourse of trauma that currently dominates the field of catastrophe studies. Having received clinical validation in 1980 in the form of the American Psychiatric

Association's (APA) recognition of post-traumatic stress disorder (PTSD) as a diag-
nosable psychological condition, trauma's association with therapeutic practice may
have made it an attractive concept to students of the humanities seeking to re-
establish an ethical and empathetic position vis-à-vis their subjects amidst the intellectual debris of liberal universalism and doctrines of scholarly objectivity, and
increasing unease about the relativist implications of postmodernist thought.[49] To
reflect upon trauma is to become intimately acquainted with the unstable, discontin-
uous, often treacherous character of human experience, but also to sustain the possibility that meaningful moral and imaginative connections can be drawn across that
troubled, fragmented terrain. It is perhaps ultimately to suggest, as Cathy Caruth
does, 'that history, like trauma, is never simply one's own, that history is precisely the
way we are implicated in each other's traumas'.[50] While owing, then, a significant debt
to the endorsements of clinical authority, trauma studies creatively exploit the ambiguity that still surrounds the condition to extend its application well beyond the
realms of clinical practice and, in a few of the more expansive meditations upon the
subject, even to invite the promise of a new historical cosmology.[51]

As Mark S. Micale and Paul Lerner have indicated, the passage of trauma to its
current diagnostic status conforms hardly at all to conventional narratives of the progressive advance of medical understanding and practice.[52] Mind wounds, nerve pros-
tration, railway spine, traumatic neurasthenia, shell shock, war neurosis, and so on:
the exotic portfolio of terms used by clinicians during the nineteenth and twentieth
centuries to describe the various mental disorders that they witnessed in their patients
is eloquently expressive of their inability to fashion a common concept of what trauma
is and what trauma does. In 1959, the American psychiatrist Abram Kardiner
reviewed the current state of psychiatric understanding with regard to traumatic neuroses and concluded: 'there is a vast store of data available on these neuroses, but it is
hard to find a province of psychiatry in which there is less discipline than in this one.
There is practically no continuity to be found anywhere, and the literature can only
be characterised as anarchic.'[53] The situation had not markedly improved by the time
that PTSD claimed its place in the APA's diagnostic manual, a development which
reflected not so much verifiable advances in clinical research, as the lobbying efforts
of American veterans of the Vietnam War to secure official acknowledgement that the
psychological problems many of them had suffered in the years since may have been
connected to their service experience.[54] Indeed, it was only after it had attained formal
diagnostic status that serious resources were mobilised to promote research into the
disorder and to fund its treatment. As Allan Young has argued, however, these
resources have served in turn to create a whole series of institutional and ideological
investments in the diagnosis of the condition, even in individuals whose experiences
and symptoms are inconsistent with existing clinical definitions.[55] The passage of
PTSD into the formal medical literature, therefore, has served to further obscure
rather than clarify what one person's trauma might have in common with the trauma
of somebody else.

The danger of trauma theory is that it implicates us all in an undifferentiated world
of hurt. Over the last two decades, as Lerner and Micale observe, 'the idea of post-

traumatic psychopathology has spread far beyond combat-related stress to include natural disasters, work accidents, domestic abuse, and all manner of emotionally trying experiences.'[56] The diagnosis of PTSD, moreover, is no longer dependent upon the already fairly ambiguous condition that the patient had been personally present at an event 'outside the range of usual human experience'. Revised in 1994, the APA's diagnostic manual now allows that '*accounts* of death or injury (in contrast to direct encounters) can be sufficient to constitute traumatic stressors'.[57] The clinical definition of trauma thus licenses us to identify its transference to and pathological presence within any individual or community exposed to narratives of potentially traumatising events, regardless of the trials that they themselves have actually endured. Given this definition and the ever-extending reach of global communications, as well as the persistence of more organic patterns of social and cultural interaction, there may be few individuals who could not now lay claim to the status of trauma victim.

To retain a scepticism about the validity of such definitions and the permissiveness of their application is not to assert that the psychological and emotional pain that often afflicts the victims of catastrophe is not real, or that it is entirely incommunicable. That catastrophes are frequently accompanied by acute mental suffering among those who directly experience them is empirically undeniable. It may well be the case, as Allan Young suggests, that PTSD 'is glued together by the practices, technologies and narratives with which it is diagnosed, studied, treated, and represented and by the various interests, institutions, and moral arguments that mobilised these efforts and resources'; this does not mean, however, that the ordeals of those diagnosed with the condition are necessarily inauthentic, and undeserving of attention, care, and sympathy.[58] There is little doubt, moreover, that a catastrophe can have adverse impact upon the well-being not just of its immediate victims, but also of those to whom they are close, in the form of personal bereavement or through the burdens of intimate interaction with the physical and psychological sufferings of the survivor.[59] In addition, it is quite reasonable to declare, as Dominick LaCapra does, that a catastrophe can create 'problems of identity' for individuals and communities well beyond its circumference of material destruction, 'insofar as it unsettles narcissistic investments and desired self-images, including – especially with respect to the Shoah – the image of Western civilisation itself as the bastion of elevated values if not the high point in the evolution of humanity'.[60]

Our ambivalence does not apply to assertions such as these, but rather to the manner in which the term 'trauma' is often employed to confer a quasi-clinical authority upon a particular set of critical interpretations, and to the way in which this usage implies and serves to reinforce the impression that a coherent and unified framework of trauma theory actually exists. The association with clinical doctrine promises a precision, stability, and universality of application that trauma theory in most if not all instances remains unable to deliver. Even within the field of medical history, as Lerner and Micale observe, there seems little immediate prospect that theoreticians can develop 'a single, uniform, transhistorically valid concept of psychological trauma'.[61] In the absence of such a model, however, scholarly enquiries into the memory of catastrophe need not simply dissolve into an intellectually arid assortment of incommensurable and individuated case studies. The adoption of conceptual language with a more modest categorising effect upon the historical circumstances to which it is applied is likely to offer a productive alternative; to speak of 'rupture' and 'disruption' in the terms that we have described may better respect the balance that must obtain between excavating the irreducible specificities of each catastrophic experience and illuminating what that experience may have in common with others.

The essays in this volume explore the themes of catastrophe, memory, and trauma through a chronologically ordered series of historical case studies. Inevitably, given the multifaceted character of these themes, the authors – historians, sociologists, and literary critics – deploy a variety of methodologies appropriate to their study. The approaches range from sharply focused investigations of the construction of official and unofficial memories contemporary with the event, through longitudinal studies of shifts in commemorative discourse and practice over decades or centuries, to detailed analysis of individual memorialising texts. The sources utilised include participant observation, oral histories, folklore, memoirs, archive documents, and the mass media. What unites all is a set of core questions: how have these varied 'catastrophes' – wars, genocides, massacres, rebellions, famines, expulsions, and nautical and ecological disasters – been conceptualised, memorialised, and remembered? How have certain memories come to acquire precedence over others, and how have such hegemonies been challenged over time? What should be the critical relationship between the academic commentator (especially the historian) and the authenticity claims of memorial forms?

Longitudinal surveys feature in a number of the essays, but are particularly developed in two essays tracing the shifting patterns of the memory of pre-twentieth-century catastrophes: the mid-seventeenth-century English Civil Wars, and the Great Irish Famine of the 1840s. Mark Stoyle traces how recalling the 'double catastrophe' of the Civil Wars was first politically contested and subsequently embedded in English linguistic and folkloric forms which long outlived the traumatised participants in the conflict. In contrast, Peter Gray questions the linearity of Irish Famine memory, drawing attention to the discontinuities between modern and 'early' memorial constructions, and relating these fluctuations in time and space to changing political and social contexts in Ireland and the Irish diaspora. In considering the 'sites of memory' created during the sesquicentenary commemorations in the 1990s, Gray employs the theoretical insights of Pierre Nora, and discusses the role of the historian in critiquing or contributing to a process that appears to lie more in the realm of heritage than of academic history.

A number of studies consider the processes by which memories were consciously or unconsciously formed and shaped during or in the wake of disastrous events by states, elites, the media, and ordinary witnesses. P.A. Cramer's essay on the abortive Charleston slave insurrection of 1822 analyses how the imagined catastrophe was interpreted and memorialised by members of the white elite, who employed the discourses of providentialism and paternalism to depoliticise and domesticate the threatened rupture of their social world. Glen D. Kuecker also considers the imposition of memorial structures from above, in this case the means whereby Mexican elites asserted a hegemonic collective memory of the ecologically disastrous Dos Bocas oil fire of 1908, marginalising the diversity of contemporary non-elite responses and recasting the event as an emblem of scientific progress.

Such top-down structurings of memory can sometimes be the inadvertent consequences of the pursuit of political objectives rather than acts of deliberate misrepresentation. Donald Bloxham traces here how the predominant Anglo-American cultural memory of the Holocaust was formed by the Nuremberg war crimes trials of 1945–46. While seeking to reconstruct German society and to punish guilty leaders, the prosecutors employed investigatory techniques and analytical categories that tended to downplay the Jewish ethnicity of the victims, and to erase from the record the *Aktion Reinhard* extermination camps in the east – lacunae which were to prove long-lasting. The role of legal processes and their reportage in shaping 'bystander' memory is also stressed in Kendrick Oliver's essay on the impact of the My Lai massacre of 1968 on American consciousness. Examining public reactions from the initial revelation of the massacre to the end of the court martial of Lieutenant William Calley – one of the key perpetrators – Oliver traces the interplay of institutional, social, and cultural forces which led to the erasure of the victims' perspectives from the national debate, allowing a point of apparent 'closure' to be reached.

Non-elite victims and witnesses frequently struggle to preserve and validate their own memories under the weight of state and elite impositions. Occasionally, however, spaces may be found in which collective memories can be articulated and shaped, even in the most catastrophic of circumstances. Lisa A. Kirschenbaum's essay describes how, during the horrific siege of Leningrad in 1941–44, women workers at the city's library self-consciously accumulated an archival record of popular experience, intertwining the public narratives and private memories of the event. Though the end of the war witnessed the reimposition of more overt state control over memorial space, Kirschenbaum stresses the importance of active memory-work as a survival strategy in appalling circumstances, and as a legacy to future generations. Subaltern memories are also the subject of Kathinka Sinha-Kerkhoff's study, based largely on interviews with Bengali refugees and their descendants living in Bihar, of the legacy of the Partition of Bengal. Half a century on from the division of India and the mass forced migrations that ensued, the Partition remains a force in contemporary life – its memorialisation continuing to act as a source of communal cohesion and differentiation, simultaneously empowering and disempowering. Catastrophic memory, in this case, remains socially relevant and therefore potent, although capable of some modulation in the face of changing times and circumstances.

Trauma is a theme common to many of these essays, but two look explicitly at the traumatic memories of medical professionals – at once witnesses and victims themselves – caught up in two catastrophic conflicts. Edgar Jones considers the experience of those British doctors thrown into the front-line treatment of 'shell shock' disorders in the First World War – an experience which produced profound disillusionment in many, and which received little support or recognition from the medical and military establishments. Carol Acton discusses the parallel experiences of female American nurses in and after the Vietnam War, and how they sought to disrupt official attempts at rationalising and regulating grief, initially through their memoirs and poetry, and latterly through the public representation exhibited in the Vietnam nurses memorial in Washington, DC.

In modern society, memory is suffused with conceptions of authenticity and authority; yet, it can be, and frequently is, also commodified and rendered into the forms of popular culture and mass entertainment. The sinking of the *Titanic* in 1912 has assumed, as James Guimond describes, the status of an iconic disaster. From the immediate aftermath of the event to the present, it has been made to carry symbolic and metaphorical meanings of various kinds, often embodied in forms of cultural commodification. Guimond's essay analyses several cinematic representations of the disaster as snapshots of changing cultural contexts and dramatic appropriations of collective memory. In her essay, Andrea Reiter considers the Binjamin Wilkomirski case, in which the apparent memoirs of a Holocaust camp survivor – a great literary success of the mid-1990s – were subsequently revealed to be the fictive product of a non-Jewish Swiss writer. Reiter analyses questions of literary, historical, and ethical authenticity thrown up by the case, and poses the problem of the relationship between the academic critic and the carrier of personal 'memory'.

The two concluding essays in the collection address the political instrumentalisation of memory in relation to the Balkan conflicts of the 1990s. Rose Lindsey provides a case study of the way in which the dominant reading of an event can quite swiftly change public perceptions and collective memories of that event, while forcing private, cultural, and contested memories underground. Her study describes the political usage by the Tudjman regime of the memory of the 1991 fall of Vukovar in the construction of a Croatian national myth, and the subsequent disintegration of that official version in the wake of the regime change in 2000. Tony Kushner's essay investigates British responses to both the war crimes trials and the Kosovo conflict of 1999, as read through the prism of memories of the Second World War. In contrast to the post-war situation described by Donald Bloxham, by the 1990s the Holocaust had for many in Britain become an ethical measuring rod for the modern world – a fact witnessed in the failure of appeals to older, more domesticated images of the war in the defence case of the war criminal Anthony Sawoniuk. At the same time, the specificity of Holocaust memory, powerful as it is, poses problems of application in contemporary world affairs. Memory serves as a potent ethical force, but is not without its limitations and blind spots.

Notes

1 Cathy Caruth, 'Unclaimed experience: trauma and the possibility of history', *Yale French Studies*, 79 (1991), 181–2.
2 Ann Larabee, *Decade of Disaster* (Urbana, IL: University of Illinois Press, 2000).
3 Kai Erickson, *A New Species of Trouble: Explorations in Disaster, Trauma, and Community* (New York: Norton, 1994), p. 240.
4 James Berger, *After the End: Representations of Post-Apocalypse* (London: University of Minnesota Press, 1999), p. xiii.

5 Mike Davis, *Late Victorian Holocausts: El Niño Famines and the Making of the Third World* (London: Verso, 2001).

6 Alfred W. Crosby, *Ecological Imperialism: The Biological Expansion of Europe, 900–1900* (Cambridge: Cambridge University Press, 1986). It is, however, obvious that a late twentieth-century ecological catastrophism has sensitised Western audiences to the history of ecological disaster; for a popular example see Clive Ponting, *A Green History of the World* (London: Penguin, 1991).

7 Francis Fukuyama, *The End of History and the Last Man* (New York: Avon Books, 1992), p. xii.

8 Kerwin Lee Klein, 'On the emergence of *memory* in historical discourse', *Representations*, 69 (Winter 2000), 127–50.

9 Nancy Wood, *Vectors of Memory: Legacies of Trauma in Postwar Europe* (Oxford: Berg, 1999), p. 1.

10 Charles S. Maier, 'A surfeit of memory? Reflections on history, melancholy and denial', *History and Memory*, 5 (1993), 140.

11 Pierre Nora, 'The reasons for the current upsurge in memory', www.iwm.at/t-22txt3.htm (accessed September 2002). See also Nora, 'Between memory and history: *les lieux de mémoire*', *Representations*, 26 (Spring 1989), 7–25.

12 Peter Gray and Kendrick Oliver, 'The memory of catastrophe', *History Today*, 51:2 (February 2001), 9–15.

13 Patrick Finney, 'On memory, identity and war', *Rethinking History*, 6:1 (2002), 5–6. Key studies of the memory of war include T.G. Ashplant, Graham Dawson, and Michael Roper (eds), *The Politics of War Memory and Commemoration* (London: Routledge, 2000); Martin Evans and Ken Lunn (eds), *War and Memory in the Twentieth Century* (Oxford: Berg, 1997); Jay Winter and Emmanuel Sivan (eds), *War and Remembrance in the Twentieth Century* (Cambridge: Cambridge University Press, 1999).

14 Elizabeth Jelin and Susana G. Kaufman, 'Layers of memories: twenty years after in Argentina', in David E. Lorey and William H. Beezley (eds), *Genocide, Collective Violence and Popular Memory: The Politics of Remembrance in the Twentieth Century* (Wilmington, DE: Scholarly Resources Inc., 2002), pp. 31–52.

15 Alan Mintz, *Hurban: Responses to Catastrophe in Hebrew Literature* (New York: Columbia University Press, 1984); David G. Roskies, *Against the Apocalypse: Responses to Catastrophe in Modern Jewish Culture* (London: Harvard University Press, 1984).

16 Roskies, *Against the Apocalypse*, p. 14.

17 Nora, 'Between history and memory', p. 9.

18 Klein, 'On the emergence of *memory* in historical discourse'.

19 Dominick LaCapra, *History and Memory After Auschwitz* (London: Cornell University Press, 1998), p. 20.

20 Wood, *Vectors of Memory*, p. 2.

21 Winter and Sivan (eds), *War and Remembrance*, pp. 19–29.

22 *Ibid.*, p. 9.

23 *Ibid.*, p. 28.

24 Paul Connerton, *How Societies Remember* (Cambridge: Cambridge University Press, 1989), pp. 102–3.

25 Winter and Sivan (eds), *War and Remembrance*, p. 10.

26 Ashplant, Dawson and Roper (eds), *The Politics of War Memory*, pp. 7–12.

27 Paul Fussell, for example, comments: 'the drift of modern history domesticates the fantastic and normalises the unspeakable. And the catastrophe that begins it is the Great War' in

Paul Fussell, *The Great War and Modern Memory* (London: Oxford University Press, 1975), p. 74. See also Modris Eksteins, *Rites of Spring: The Great War and the Birth of the Modern Age* (London: Bantam Press, 1989), p. 211. For Michael Bibby, the conditions of postmodernity were not finally in place until the later years of the Vietnam War: 'The Post-Vietnam condition', in M. Bibby (ed.), *The Vietnam War and Postmodernity* (Amherst, MA: University of Massachusetts Press, 1999), pp. 143–71.

28 Saul Friedlander, 'Introduction', in S. Friedländer (ed.), *Probing the Limits of Representation: Nazism and the 'Final Solution'* (London: Harvard University Press, 1992), p. 3.

29 Saul Friedländer, 'Trauma, transference and "working through" in writing the history of the Shoah', *History and Memory*, 4 (1992), 50.

30 Jean-François Lyotard, *The Differend: Phrases in Dispute* (Minneapolis, MN: University of Minnesota Press, 1988), pp. 56–8.

31 Friedländer, *Probing the Limits of Representation*, p. 5.

32 *Ibid.*, pp. 2–6; Friedländer, 'Trauma, transference and "working through"'; LaCapra, *History and Memory after Auschwitz*, pp. 6–7, 26–7.

33 Roskies, *Against the Apocalypse*, p. 9.

34 Peter Novick, *The Holocaust and Collective Memory* (London: Bloomsbury, 2000), p. 3; Berger, *After the End*, p. xvi.

35 LaCapra, *History and Memory After Auschwitz*, pp. 27–40.

36 Donald Bloxham, *Genocide on Trial: War Crimes Trials and the Formation of Holocaust History and Memory* (Oxford: Oxford University Press, 2001), p. 2. See also Dr Bloxham's essay in this volume.

37 Novick, *The Holocaust and Collective Memory*, pp. 127–69, 207–14.

38 For casualty figures at Gallipoli, see Ian Turner, '1914–19', in F.K. Crowley (ed.), *A New History of Australia* (Melbourne: William Heinemann, 1974), p. 324, and Alan Moorehead, *Gallipoli* (London: Hamish Hamilton, 1956), p. 361. For an analysis of Gallipoli's changing place in Australian memory, see Alistair Thomson, *Anzac Memories: Living with the Legend* (Melbourne: Oxford University Press, 1994).

39 Mintz, *Hurban*, p. x.

40 *Ibid.*, pp. 19–21.

41 Erickson, *A New Species of Trouble*, p. 241. Emphasis in original.

42 For Kai Erickson, 'chronic conditions' like homelessness and poverty may induce 'trauma' just as readily as 'acute events'. The testimonies that Erickson produces to support this proposition often suggest, however, that the 'traumatic' nature of poverty depends upon an awareness that a profound change has occurred in life circumstances: 'When one realises where one is, the result can be a panic that borders on disorientation and disbelief. Most of these people have lived near the edge of poverty before, so they know something of deprivation and want. But this new world is a grotesque wonderland where nothing can be taken for granted and the rules of everyday life seem inverted'; Erickson, *A New Species of Trouble*, pp. 21, 173–4.

43 Joanna Bourke, *An Intimate History of Killing: Face-to-Face Killing in Twentieth Century Warfare* (London: Granta Books, 1999).

44 Slavos Žižek, *The Sublime Object of Ideology* (London: Verso, 1989), p. 70.

45 Donald Hyslop, Alastair Forsyth and Sheila Jemina, *Titanic Voices: The Story of the White Star Line, Titanic and Southampton* (Southampton: Oral History, City Heritage, Southampton City Council, 1994).

46 Jay Winter, *Sites of Memory, Sites of Mourning: The Great War in European Cultural History* (Cambridge: Cambridge University Press, 1996), p. 3.

47 Idith Zertal, *From Catastrophe to Power: Holocaust Survivors and the Emergence of Israel* (Berkeley, CA: University of California Press, 1998), p. 274. For a discussion of how similar Zionist interpretations of the Holocaust were evident in Israeli history textbooks at least until the 1970s, see Ruth Firer, 'Israel: the Holocaust in history textbooks', in Randolph L. Braham (ed.), *The Treatment of the Holocaust in Textbooks: The Federal Republic of Germany, Israel, The United States of America* (Boulder, CO and New York: Social Science Monographs and the Institute for Holocaust Studies of the City University of New York, 1987), pp. 177–92.

48 Tony Kushner, *The Holocaust and the Liberal Imagination: A Social and Cultural History* (Oxford: Blackwell, 1994), pp. 205–69.

49 On the return of humanities to a concern with ethics, see Marjorie Garber, Beatrice Hansen, and Rebecca L. Walkowitz (eds), *The Turn to Ethics* (London: Routledge, 2000); Jennifer L. Geddes (ed.); *Evil After Postmodernism: Histories, Narratives, Ethics* (London: Routledge, 2001); and Howard Marchitello (ed.), *What Happens to History: The Renewal of Ethics in Contemporary Thought* (London: Routledge, 2001). See also Dominick LaCapra, 'Conclusion: psychoanalysis, memory, and the ethical turn', in D. LaCapra, *History and Memory after Auschwitz*, pp. 180–210.

50 Cathy Caruth, *Unclaimed Experience: Trauma, Narrative, and History* (London: The Johns Hopkins University Press, 1996), p. 24.

51 In Caruth's view, trauma – in its latency, in the opacity of the traumatic experience, and in the way in which the return (never complete) of that experience to memory depends upon the stimulation provided by subsequent, exterior forces and therefore upon the connections made with other pasts – offers a conception of history 'which is no longer straightforwardly referential (that is, no longer based on simple models of experience and reference).' She asserts: 'For history to be a history of trauma means that it is referential precisely to the extent that it is not fully perceived as it occurs; or to put it somewhat differently, that a history can be grasped only in the very inaccessibility of its occurrence'; Caruth, 'Unclaimed experience', pp. 182, 187.

52 Paul Lerner and Mark S. Micale, 'Trauma, psychiatry, and history: a conceptual and historiographical introduction', in P. Micale and M.S. Lerner (eds), *Traumatic Pasts: History, Psychiatry, and Trauma in the Modern Age, 1870–1930* (Cambridge: Cambridge University Press, 2001), pp. 24–5.

53 Quoted in Allan Young, *The Harmony of Illusions: Inventing Post-Traumatic Stress Disorder* (Princeton, NJ: Princeton University Press, 1995), p. 93.

54 Most unusually, the six-member working group organised to find evidence to support the inclusion of PTSD in the third edition of the APA's *Diagnostic and Statistical Manual of Mental Disorders* comprised not just two psychiatrists who had close relationships with Vietnam veterans, but also the head of a veterans' advocacy group, who possessed no clinical qualifications whatsoever, *ibid.*, p. 110.

55 *Ibid.*, pp. 174–5.

56 Lerner and Micale, 'Trauma, psychiatry, and history', p. 2.

57 Young, *The Harmony of Illusions*, p. 289. Emphasis in original.

58 *Ibid.*, pp. 5–6, 10.

59 For interpretations which emphasise the capacity of trauma to travel down generations, see Martin S. Bergmann and Milton E. Jucovy (eds), *Generations of the Holocaust* (New York: Basic Books, 1982); Aphrodite Matsakis, *Vietnam Wives: Women and Children Surviving Life with Veterans Suffering Post-Traumatic Stress Disorder* (Kensington, MD: Woodbine House, 1988); and Dina Wardi, *Memorial Candles: Children of the Holocaust* (London:

Routledge, 1992). For more agnostic and conditional readings, see Dan Bar-on, *Fear and Hope: Three Generations of the Holocaust* (London: Harvard University Press, 1995); Howard Cooper, 'The second generation "syndrome"', *Journal of Holocaust Education*, 4:2 (Winter 1995), 131–46; and John J. Sigal and Morton Weinfeld, *Trauma and Rebirth: Intergenerational Effects of the Holocaust* (New York: Praeger, 1989).
60 LaCapra, *History and Memory After Auschwitz*, p. 9.
61 Lerner and Micale, 'Trauma, psychiatry, and history', p. 25.

Remembering the English Civil Wars

Over 350 years after the Civil Wars of the mid-seventeenth century finally came to an end, they continue to exert a tenacious grip on the English historical imagination. Charles I standing on the scaffold; Charles II hiding in an oak tree; sombre-looking men interrogating uncomfortable-looking children as to the whereabouts of their fathers: such images form part of the collective subconscious of the English.[1] Why should the memory of this particular conflict have stayed so green, when that of scores of others has faded away? The answer is surely because the Civil Wars had a deeper, more profound effect upon English society than any other conflict before or since.

When Charles I raised his standard at Nottingham in August 1642, he unwittingly raised the curtain on a national catastrophe. The internecine struggle which ensued – and which was to continue, on and off, for the next nine years – was to prove the greatest disaster visited upon the English people since the coming of the Black Death. A very large proportion of the country's adult male inhabitants was forced to serve in arms between 1642 and 1651.[2] Nor were they the only ones to suffer, for the Civil Wars were fought on English soil and thus affected women and children as well as men. Recent estimates suggest that almost 200,000 people – some 3.6 per cent of England's total population – perished as a direct result of the fighting. The wars were thus, as Charles Carlton has observed, 'the bloodiest conflict in relative terms in English history'.[3]

The Civil Wars were not only remarkable for their duration and their impact – they also saw the accustomed mental universe of the English people turned upside down. For centuries they had been taught to revere their kings and to see Parliament as merely a part of royal government (albeit an important one). Then, in 1642, a majority of the House of Commons, together with many of the Lords, came out in open defiance of the reigning monarch and appealed to the country for support. Forced to choose between king and Parliament, Englishmen found themselves in a position for which nothing in their previous history had prepared them. Soon both Charles I and his Parliamentarian opponents had raised powerful armies, and, after four years of conflict, the king was defeated and imprisoned. Finally, in 1649, he was tried and executed, an event which sent shock waves throughout all of Europe. Further staggering developments were still to come. Immediately after the king's death, a republican government was established in England, something which would once have seemed impossible. The country then witnessed, in rapid succession, an attempt by the dead king's son, Charles, to reclaim the crown, his defeat at the battle of Worcester in 1651 (followed by his sojourn in the oak tree and subsequent flight abroad), the establishment of an immensely strong military regime under Oliver Cromwell, Cromwell's installation as Lord Protector in 1653, his death in 1658, and, finally – as a result of popular longing to return to the old ways – the restoration of the monarchy in the person of Charles II, who returned triumphantly from France in 1660. The period between 1642 and 1660 witnessed a truly unprecedented series of events. How were these events to be remembered over the next 300 years?

Clearly, such a vast and infinitely complex question cannot be fully resolved within the constraints of a single essay. Instead, the present discussion restricts itself to the consideration of three central themes: firstly, how those who lived through the Civil Wars subsequently looked back on their wartime experiences; secondly, the processes by which memories of the Civil Wars became inextricably tied up with later political conflicts; and thirdly, how images of the Civil Wars continued to live on in English folk memory, even after all those who had taken part in the conflict were dead. These are subjects about which little has yet been written by scholars, so this essay explores what is still very much uncharted territory.[4] If it helps to stimulate further work into the neglected 'afterlife' of England's Civil Wars, then it will have served its primary purpose.

First-hand memories

The most terrible memories of the Civil Wars were probably those of the combatants themselves. For the men who had taken part in the fighting, the conflict would always be associated with hardship, with pain, and with death. After 1660, many ex-Royalist soldiers wrote to the county authorities asking for pensions to support themselves in their old age. Their letters convey a vivid impression of how they remembered their wartime experiences. As one would expect, the most dominant theme is that of wounding: of 'great harms', 'great hurts', and 'great bruises'; of bullets lodged in heads, limbs, and bodies; of arms, legs, and hands cut off; of eyes 'scalded and blasted . . . with gunpowder'.[5] Such physical reminders of the wars remained with the veterans for the rest of their lives. During the post-Restoration period, one ex-soldier from Devon complained that he had 'divers wounds which now doe very much grieve & disable him'. Another lamented that he 'is [now] sixty three yeares of age, and his labour is all most don by reason of the badnes of his sight, having a great ruhm [weeping] in his eyes by reason of [a musket] shote' in his head. A third deposed that he was 'utterly disabled to gett his livelyhood' as a result of wounds inflicted during the Civil Wars.[6] Tens of thousands of other ex-soldiers nursed similarly bitter memories of being crippled in the service of king or Parliament.

What of the other hardships which were endured by Civil War soldiers? Many who had been captured during the fighting later shuddered to recall their treatment in enemy prisons. After the Restoration, one ex-Royalist testified that, in 1645, he had been imprisoned by the Parliamentarians in Plymouth, where 'hee remained . . . longe in great misery & suffered much hardshipp'.[7] As late as 1717, a Welshman, who had fought for the king as a young man and had been captured by the Parliamentarians at Gloucester, recounted how he and his fellow captives had been herded into a church and kept there for days on end with nothing to eat but 'turnip-tops [and] cabbage leaves'.[8] Other soldiers later remembered the weariness of long marches, the discomfort of sleeping in the open fields at night, the 'excessive cold', the lack of pay, the ravages of disease, and the fact that they had sometimes been forced to eat horseflesh simply in order to survive. Finally – though this was not so often spoken of, perhaps because the wounds ran too deep – the veterans recalled the pain of seeing their comrades die.[9] In all of these ways, the war inflicted deep mental scars, and – unsurprisingly – some of the former combatants were unable to cope with the memory of what they had been through. Several Civil War veterans are known to have become mentally ill as a result of their wartime experiences. Victims of what would today be called 'combat fatigue', such men were described at the time as 'disabled . . . in . . . [their] senses', or, more expressively still, as 'fallen lunatick'.[10]

Nor were ex-soldiers the only ones to shoulder a heavy mental burden. Civilians had not been insulated from the realities of this conflict, for the wars had been fought on everyone's doorsteps, and many non-combatants, too, were haunted by the horrors of what they had seen. One poor serving-maid – who had been wounded during the storming of Hopton Castle on the Welsh Marches, and then forced to watch as her fellow servants were put to death – 'was ever after distracted from the fright'.[11] Obviously, such peculiarly horrific experiences – and such extreme reactions to them – were rare, but few who had witnessed violent death during the Civil Wars were ever able to exorcise it from their memories. The Shropshire yeoman Richard Gough, who, as a boy, saw a Royalist cavalryman being fatally wounded in the village street, was still able to give a minutely detailed account of the affair half a century later: recalling how he and his neighbours had sat at the dying man's bedside and watched 'much blood running along the floore'.[12] The killing had clearly scorched itself into his brain – and many similar examples could be given.

Almost everybody who had lived through the conflict remembered its horrors. But this was by no means all that was recalled, for many thousands of people also remembered the wrongs which had been done to them during the Civil Wars. Such grudges were nursed at every level of English society, by those who had been impressed for military service against their will, by those who had suffered at the hands of the soldiery, by those who had seen their property destroyed, and – perhaps most importantly of all – by those who had been jeered at, beaten up, denounced, or imprisoned, simply because they had chosen to support a different side from their neighbours. The experience of war split some English communities from top to bottom, while it turned other communities against their neighbours, stoking up bitter feuds between those towns and villages which had supported the Parliament, and those which had supported the king.[13] Usually such feuds remained at the verbal rather than at the physical level, but sometimes they flared up into actual violence. During the 1650s, for example, an Exeter man was accused of having murdered a former Parliamentarian soldier whom he believed to have killed his brother during the wars.[14]

The generation which had witnessed the Civil Wars took many years to pass away, and it was not until the end of the century that those who could remember the conflict started to become genuinely thin on the ground. By 1690 or thereabouts, such individuals were beginning to become figures of interest in their own right, keenly sought after by antiquarians and others who enjoyed listening to their wartime reminiscences. One veteran who found an appreciative audience for his recollections was Sir William Neale, who died in 1691, and was (wrongly) believed by John Aubrey to be the last surviving Royalist field officer.[15] Another was 'Welsh Thomas', the ex-Royalist foot soldier who related his wartime experiences to a Gloucestershire antiquary as late as 1717.[16] Welsh Thomas – then well into his nineties – may be regarded as one of the last confirmed veterans of the Civil Wars, but other alleged 'survivors' continued to come forward for years to come. Indeed, the last of these men, a certain William Walker, lived on until 1736![17] Throughout the late seventeenth and early eighteenth centuries, then, such unusually long-lived individuals continued to provide the generations which had grown up after 1660 with a direct link to the Civil Wars. Yet it should not be thought that memories of the conflict remained preserved in amber as a result. Long before they died, the surviving eyewitnesses were already customising their own recollections (albeit often subconsciously), picking out the best bits, as it were, in order to make their reminiscences sound more exciting, and to make their own wartime conduct seem more creditable than it had really been. Their testimony should not always be taken at face value, leaving aside the increasing tendency of recollections of the Civil Wars to become politicised during the post-Restoration period.

The politics of memory

The restoration of Charles II in 1660 was intended to bring an end to the divisions which had been caused by the Civil Wars. This was what almost everybody wanted, of course. The immediate post-war years had been supremely uncomfortable ones for most people, forced as they had been to live cheek-by-jowl with neighbours against whom they had only recently fought, and whose political and religious views they still found abhorrent. In order to make day-to-day life bearable in the divided communities of post-Civil War England, the enmities of the past had to be brushed over as far as possible. Euphemistic language became commonplace. Most people avoided speaking about the war in public, and when forced to do so, resorted to carefully neutral formulations. They did not speak of the conflict as 'the rebellion', for example – a term which would have implied criticism of the former rebels – but referred delicately instead to 'the late warres', 'the late unhappy times', 'the troublesome times', or just 'the troubles'.[18] We should note the parallel with contemporary Northern Ireland here; precisely the same term, 'the troubles', is used by many Northern Irish people to refer to the sectarian conflict which raged in that unhappy province from 1969, and for precisely the same reasons – it acknowledges the fact of conflict, but throws no blame on any particular party.

The restored monarchy of 1660 could not afford to be so generous. Charles II was unwilling to perpetuate the divisions of the past, but the fact remained that his restoration signified the final triumph of the Royalist party – and he and his supporters were determined to expunge the memory of the republican regime which had executed his father. Even before Charles II had been formally crowned, all visual reminders of the previous government had begun to be destroyed. The republic had possessed its own coat of arms, copies of which had been set up in public places. These were taken down and burnt in 1660, and replaced with the royal arms.[19] The republic had issued coins, decorated with its own insignia. These were recalled, melted down, and replaced with new issues featuring the king's portrait.[20] The republic had named its warships after the great Parliamentarian victories of the Civil Wars: *Naseby*, *Langport* and *Winceby*, for example. These ships were given new names in 1660: respectively, *Royal Charles*, *Henrietta* (after Charles II's mother), and most tellingly of all, *Happy Return*, to signify the 'happy return' of the monarchy.[21]

Even the memory of dead republicans was not spared. Gravestones and monuments which had been erected to Parliamentarian leaders during the interregnum, and which had stressed their military service against the Crown, were defaced, removed, or destroyed.[22] Yet such desecration pales into insignificance when compared with the treatment which Charles II's regime meted out to the remains of Oliver Cromwell and two other especially prominent Parliamentarians who had died before 1660 and been interred in Westminster Abbey. Not only were the funerary monuments of these men destroyed, but, in January 1661, their very graves were dug up so that their mouldering corpses could be drawn forth, flung into an open cart, drawn through the streets of the capital in obscene public show, and finally strung up upon the common gallows at Tyburn.[23] The sight of these poor bodies, exposed in their various states of decomposition to the mockery and ridicule of every passer-by, testified to the new government's determination to heap shame and ignominy on the memory of those who had made war against Charles I. Once the shrivelled cadavers had finally been cut down, their heads were hacked off and the remains cast into unmarked graves. The Restoration regime was acutely conscious of the potential power of the dead.

Sweeping away every last public symbol of the republican era was one way for Charles II and his supporters to 'gain control of the past' – to influence the way in which the Civil Wars would be remembered by later generations of Englishmen and women. However, it was not enough simply to erase the visible memorials of the Parliamentarian regime. In this war over memory, the supporters of the restored monarchy had to construct, as well as destroy – to make sure that Charles I and the Royalist cause were remembered in a favourable way, just as they tried to make sure that Cromwell and his supporters were condemned to everlasting opprobrium. Accordingly, in 1660, it was decreed that the anniversary of Charles I's execution (30 January) should henceforth be 'for ever set apart to be kept and observed in all . . . churches . . . as an anniversary day of fasting and humiliation, to implore the mercy of God' on this nation for the impious 'sins' which had been committed during the late Civil Wars (most notably, of course, against the sacred person of Charles I himself). Thereafter, sermons vaunting 'the late King's' memory and condemning the heinous sin of rebellion were regularly preached in churches across the realm every year.[24]

As well as solemnly commemorating the execution of Charles I, after 1660 the bulk of the English people also celebrated the accession of Charles II. The anniversary of Charles II's restoration (29 May) was set aside as a day of public rejoicing, and thereafter became one of the high points of the English festive calendar.[25] Every 29 May, in towns and villages across the country, bells pealed out from the church towers while young men and women got up early and made their way into the woods, partly in order to do what young men and women have always done in woods, but chiefly in order to cut down great boughs of oak wood.[26] These were then brought back in triumph by the revellers, and used to decorate the front doors of their own houses, the parish church, and almost every other building of communal significance.[27] The branches signified the oak tree in which Charles II had hidden after his escape from the battle of Worcester, and it was considered a sign of loyalty to pin oak leaves, or oak-apples, to one's clothes for the rest of the day. This custom persisted well into the twentieth century, not just among children, but among adults too. As late as 1914, the porters at Paddington Station habitually wore oak leaves in their lapels on 29 May, and the Chelsea pensioners continue to do so to this day.[28]

Because of the adoption of the oak-tree imagery, 29 May quickly became known as Royal Oak Day. But it had another, much more curious, name too. Well into the last century, Royal Oak Day continued to be popularly known as 'Shig Shag Day' or 'Shick Shack Day' throughout much of rural England.[29] The origins of this name have always been regarded as obscure.[30] Yet there are good grounds for thinking that, in its earliest incarnation at least, the alternative name for Royal Oak Day may well have been 'Shit Sack Day'.[31] Why should such an unappealing term have been applied to 29 May? The answer takes us back to the spiteful world of Restoration politics. As we have seen, the custom of wearing oak leaves was intended to demonstrate loyalty. But it could also be used as a crude means of identifying those who were disloyal. There were many in Restoration England who did not subscribe to the official view of the past, had not mourned the death of Charles I, had not been glad to see the back of Cromwell, and had not welcomed the return of Charles II. For these individuals, the 'Old Oliverians'[32] – many of them ex-Parliamentarian soldiers and their families – to have donned the oak leaves would have been to have betrayed the principles for which they had fought and suffered in the past. Yet, by refusing to adopt the emblems of loyalty, they identified themselves as political deviants, and opened themselves up to the hatred of their neighbours. And just as the 'treacherous' miners who returned to work during the British coal strike of the mid-1980s were vilified by the other members of their communities as 'scabs' – a vile, loathsome name, signifying utter contempt – so those seventeenth-century Englishmen and women who refused to wear the oak leaves on 29 May were vilified by the loyal majority as 'shit sacks'.[33]

Later evidence shows that children who refused – or simply forgot – to wear the oak leaves on Royal Oak Day were, variously, pinched, drenched with water, pelted with eggs, stung with nettles, or spat at by their peers as a result.[34] An alternative punishment for the same offence was to be grabbed, to have one's head thrust into a sack, and then to be vigorously punched while the surrounding mob chanted 'Shig-shag, penny a rag, bang his head in Croomwell's Bag!'[35] Those who refused to decorate their houses with oak branches ran the risk of having their windows smashed. Long after

1660, in other words, Royal Oak Day was used as an excuse to rekindle the rivalries of the Civil Wars. In the Dartmoor town of Tavistock, rival groups 'intended to represent the republican and monarchial parties' continued to engage in mock street battles on 29 May until well into the nineteenth century.[36]

The fact that there were enough Oliverians in Tavistock to engage the loyalists on equal terms reminds us that the heirs to the republican tradition were not always the victims. In some towns, indeed – those which had been strongly Parliamentarian during the Civil Wars – it was the supporters of the Restoration, rather than its opponents, who were in the minority. And just as the Crown used the anniversaries of Charles I's death and Charles II's restoration to reaffirm support for its cause, so the 'Oliverians' used the anniversaries of local Parliamentary victories during the Civil Wars to reaffirm support for theirs. At Barnstaple, Gloucester, Lyme Regis, Nantwich, Taunton, and Plymouth (all towns which had resisted long Royalist sieges during the First Civil War), the anniversaries of the dates on which those sieges had been raised were regularly celebrated by huge crowds until well into the eighteenth century.[37] As local loyalists were only too well aware, such practices were deeply subversive, for, by celebrating Parliament's former victories, the townsfolk were openly questioning the legitimacy of the restored monarchy.[38] Nor was this the only way in which those who looked back with nostalgia to what they termed the 'Good Old Cause' were rumoured to express their political preferences. During the eighteenth century, members of a secret society known as the 'Calves' Head Club' were said to meet behind closed doors every 30 January in order to celebrate the anniversary of Charles I's execution by dining off the head of a calf.[39]

The Civil Wars were commemorated in different ways by different factions, and this in turn ensured that the political traditions which had grown up during the conflict would continue to endure for decades to come. Thus, the 'Royalist party' of the 1640s gradually transmogrified itself into the 'Loyal party' of the 1660s, and later still into the 'Tory party' of the 1700s, while the 'Parliamentarian party' of the 1640s transformed itself into the 'Oliverian party' of the 1660s, and later still into the 'Whig party' of the 1700s. As a result, Charles I and Cromwell remained powerful political icons even after all those who had lived through the Civil Wars were dead. The final part of this chapter will explore the different ways in which these two pivotal figures of the 1640s were remembered in English folklore.

The 'White King' and Old Noll

The image of Charles I which was transmitted to posterity was primarily the construction of Restoration propagandists. We have already seen how crucial 'the late King's' memory was in underpinning the authority of the restored monarchy, and from 1660 onwards Charles II's supporters pulled out all the stops to ensure that that memory was a positive one. A perfect torrent of publications poured off the London presses between 1660 and 1670, all of them depicting Charles I as the best of kings and the most wronged of men, and many of them containing powerful visual images to the same effect. Meanwhile, ministers of the established Church did all they could to reinforce the same

message.[40] Playwrights and poets, anxious for royal patronage, added their contributions to the swelling tide of praise. In addition, former Royalist soldiers waxed lyrical
about 'the late King of happie memory', knowing full well that, as the stock of Charles
I rose in the public estimation, so would that of the men who had fought for him.[41]

The result of all this was the effective beatification of Charles I, as a martyr king,
or 'White King', who had died for his people's sins.[42] Indeed, as time went by, Charles
came increasingly to be equated with Christ. Items associated with the late king,
however trivial or mundane – a glove, a jug, a snuffbox, and a map-book, for example
– were cherished as sacred relics.[43] Houses in which he was known to have stayed
became virtual shrines, like the mansion in Welshpool, where the bedroom in which
Charles had slept was later decorated with 'the initials C.R. and the regal crown'.[44]
His wanderings during the First Civil War came to be regarded as a kind of Via
Dolorosa, with the king's halts on the way to the scaffold being compared to those of
Christ on the way to the cross. Huge copies of the engraving of Charles which had
appeared as the frontispiece to the *Eikon Basilike* were painted in oils and hung up in
several London churches.[45] People wore silver lockets featuring the king's portrait next
to their hearts.[46] As the years slipped by and actual memories of the Civil Wars faded,
so – when viewed through the roseate spectacles so thoughtfully provided by church
and state – the popular image of Charles I gradually became that of an impossibly
good and incorruptible figure, who had been wantonly murdered by evil 'rebels'.

If Charles I was to be allocated the role of Christ in this 'authorised version' of the
past, then there was only one role which could possibly be given to Oliver Cromwell:
that of the Devil. And from the early 1650s onwards, it was in precisely this role that
Royalist propagandists began to cast him. Even before Cromwell was dead, it was being
claimed that he had made a pact with Satan, that he had sold his soul to Beelzebub in
return for infernal assistance against his enemies. The fact that a huge storm struck
southern England shortly before Cromwell's death in 1658 was taken by Royalists as
proof positive that the Devil had come to fetch away his own.[47] For decades afterwards,
the storm was referred to as 'Oliver's Wind' and, in Herefordshire, it was believed that
a line of fallen trees in Brampton Bryan Park marked the route along which the Lord
Protector had been dragged away to hell.[48] At the time of the Restoration, it was as the
Devil's servant that Cromwell was usually portrayed by his detractors. As time went
by, however, and as Charles I assumed an ever more Christ-like image in the popular
imagination, Cromwell came to be increasingly identified with the Devil himself.

Supernatural powers were attributed to him: his horse was said to have burnt its
hoof prints into a rock in Wales, for instance.[49] Children in the New Forest were
taught to curse his name on Sundays, while mothers all over England warned their
toddlers that, if they didn't behave, 'old Oliver Crummell'll have 'ee'.[50] Ruins every-
where were ascribed to the malice of 'Crummell', 'the Destroyer'. In 1852, a visitor
to a crumbling castle in the Scilly Isles wrote that 'here, as elsewhere, I was met by the
ghost of the stern old Protector', and added that, 'the spirit of old Oliver comes to
brood wherever death has been, grim, ghostly, impalpable, a principle rather than a
real corporeal existence, seated always amid destruction'.[51] Particularly significant is
the fact that forbidding features in the physical landscape which had once been named

after the Devil, were often, from 1660 onwards, renamed after Cromwell. There are probably more physical features named after Cromwell in England than after any other historical figure: for example, Cromwell's Arch, Cromwell's Bridge, 'Oliver's Castle', and Cromwell's Court.[52] As belief in the Devil as a real presence began to fade during the nineteenth century, Cromwell was frequently conflated with that other great villain of the day: Napoleon Bonaparte.[53]

In the dominant strand of national memory, then, Cromwell appeared as the Devil incarnate. But there are many different ways of remembering the past, and, despite the best efforts of the restored monarchy, a pro-Cromwellian counter-tradition always survived beneath the surface – a vision of the Lord Protector as a champion of England's liberties and a stern upholder of the Protestant faith which was particularly cherished by religious nonconformists. The idea of Cromwell as a friend to the poor and as an enemy of privilege also lingered on among labouring men, some of whom continued to believe that everything had been better 'in Oliver's Days'.[54] During the later nineteenth century, moreover, a confident, god-fearing Victorian society took 'God's Englishman' to its collective bosom, and Cromwell's image was rehabilitated. In 1899, the tercentenary of his birth was widely celebrated, and a statue of him was unveiled in Old Palace Yard, facing Parliament Square, in London.[55] A further statue was erected to Cromwell in St Ives, Cambridgeshire, in 1901, and over the following decade many streets were named after him. Several public houses were even named 'The Oliver Cromwell',[56] though it is hard to know what Oliver himself would have made of this particular accolade. Today, Cromwell is perhaps more popular with the English political establishment than he has ever been, a point well illustrated by the fact that, when the Blair government came to power in 1997, several New Labour ministers requested portraits of the old Protector to grace their newly acquired offices.

The twists and turns of Oliver Cromwell's posthumous reputation – from saint to sinner and back again – provide a fitting conclusion to the present chapter. Historians have recently developed a much more sophisticated understanding of the ways in which Cromwell has been remembered at all levels of English society over the past 350 years.[57] Yet, the myriad ways in which the wider conflict in which he fought have been remembered by the English people over that same period remain largely unexplored. This discussion has indicated a few of the avenues along which future research into popular memories of the English Civil Wars might possibly proceed. Not until we have pressed much further down these routes of enquiry – and, indeed, down many others like them – will we be able fully to judge how the catastrophe which engulfed the nation between 1642 and 1660 was viewed in retrospect by ordinary Englishmen and women.

Notes

1 A point well illustrated in W.C. Sellar and R.J. Yeatman, *1066 and All That* (London: Magnum Books, 1980), pp. 74–7.
2 J. Morrill, 'Introduction', in J. Morrill (ed.), *Reactions to the English Civil War, 1642–49* (London: Macmillan, 1982), p. 17.

3   C. Carlton, 'The impact of the fighting', in J. Morrill (ed.), *The Impact of the English Civil War* (London: Collins & Brown, 1991), p. 20.

4   This is beginning to change; see C. Carlton, *Going to the Wars: The Experience of the British Civil Wars* (London: Routledge, 1992), pp. 339–50; D. Rollison, *The Local Origins of Modern Society: Gloucestershire, 1500–1800* (London: Routledge, 1992), pp. 171–6; G. Foard, *Naseby: The Decisive Campaign* (Whitstable: Pryor Publications, 1995), pp. 343–82; L. Glassey, 'Introduction', in L. Glassey (ed.), *The Reigns of Charles II and James VII & II* (Basingstoke: Macmillan, 1997), pp. 1–11; J. Miller, *After the Civil Wars: English Politics and Government in the Reign of Charles II* (Harlow: Pearson Education, 2000); B. Worden, *Roundhead Reputations: The English Civil Wars and the Passions of Posterity* (London: Allen Lane, 2001); M. Stoyle, *West Britons: Cornish Identities and the Early Modern British State* (Exeter: Exeter University Press, 2002), pp. 157–80.

5   See, for example, Devon Record Office, Exeter (hereafter DRO), QS/128 (Maimed Soldiers' Petitions), 1–147, *passim*.

6   DRO, QS/128, petitions of Israell Tucker, Christopher Berry, and Hugh Sexon.

7   *Ibid.*, petition of Simon Morey.

8   J. Washbourn, *Bibliotheca Gloucestrensis: A Collection of . . . Tracts Relating to the Country and City of Gloucester Illustrative of and Published during the Civil War* (3 vols, Gloucester: Washbourn and Son, 1825), III, p. 372.

9   See DRO, QS/128, nos 1–147, *passim*.

10 DRO, QS/128, certificate relating to Philip Luccombe; O.M. Moger (ed.), 'Devonshire Quarter Sessions Petitions, 1642–85' (two typescript volumes, 1983, copies held in West Country Studies Library, Exeter), II, p. 365.

11 J. Webb and T.W. Webb, *Memorials of the Civil War Between King Charles I and the Parliament of England, As It affected Herefordshire and the Adjacent Counties* (2 vols, London: Longmans, Green, and Co., 1879), I, p. 389.

12 D. Hey (ed.), *The History of Myddle* (Harmondsworth: Penguin, 1981), pp. 73–4.

13 See M. Stoyle, *Loyalty and Locality: Popular Allegiance in Devon During the English Civil War* (Exeter: Exeter University Press, 1994), p. 75.

14 R. Bush, 'The Civil War and interregnum in Exeter', *Devon and Cornwall Notes and Queries*, 29 (1962), 134.

15 Aubrey was wrong; see P. Young, *Edgehill 1642: The Campaign and the Battle*, (Kineton: Roundwood Press, 1967), p. 154.

16 Washbourn, *Bibliotheca Gloucestrensis*, III, pp. 372–3.

17 See Young, *Edgehill*, p. 154; R. Ollard, *This War Without an Enemy: A History of the English Civil Wars* (London: Hodder and Stoughton, 1976), p. 75.

18 A. Clark (ed.), *Aubrey's Brief Lives* (2 vols, Oxford: Clarendon Press, 1898), I, p. 309; DRO, Exeter Chamber Act Book, 1663–83 (unpaginated), entry of 10 November 1663; Clarke, *Aubrey*, I, p. 403; DRO, Exeter Chamber Act Book, 1/10 (1652–63), f.73r.

19 R. Latham and W. Matthews (eds), *The Diary of Samuel Pepys* (11 vols, London: G. Bell, 1970), I, p. 133. The arms of the Commonwealth were also burnt in a number of provincial towns; see D. Underdown, *Revel, Riot and Rebellion: Popular Politics and Culture in England, 1603–60* (Oxford: Clarendon Press, 1985), p. 271.

20 E. Besly, *Coins and Medals of the English Civil War* (London: Seaby, 1990), pp. 102–3.

21 Latham and Matthews (eds), *Diary of Samuel Pepys*, I, p. 154.

22 Webb, *Memorials*, p. 429; M. Atkin, *Gloucester and the Civil War: A City Under Siege* (Stroud: Alan Sutton, 1992), pp. 139–40.

23 R. Latham (ed.), *The Shorter Pepys* (London: Penguin, 1987), p. 115. The two other bodies

disinterred at this time were those of Ireton and Bradshaw, and the body of Cromwell's mother was also exhumed; see J. Morrill (ed.), *Revolution and Restoration: England in the 1650s* (London: Collins & Brown, 1992); B. Coward, *Oliver Cromwell* (Harlow: Longman, 1991), p. 176.

24 B.S. Stewart, 'The cult of the royal martyr', *Church History*, 38 (1969), 175–87; D. Cressy, *Bonfires and Bells: National Memory and the Protestant Calendar in Elizabethan and Stuart England* (London: Weidenfeld and Nicolson, 1989), pp. 171–2.

25 Latham and Matthews (eds), *Diary of Samuel Pepys*, I, p. 166; R. Hutton, *The Stations of the Sun: A History of the Ritual Year in Britain* (Oxford: Oxford University Press, 1996), pp. 288–94.

26 For general discussion of Royal Oak Day customs, see H. Ellis (ed.), *Observations on the Popular Antiquities of Great Britain, by John Brand* (3 vols, London: Henry G. Bohn, 1890–3), I, pp. 273–6; Cressy, *Bonfires and Bells*, pp. 64–6, 171–4, 186–7; Hutton, *Stations of the Sun*, pp. 288–94.

27 T.F. Thiselton-Dyer, *British Popular Customs, Present and Past* (London: Bell, 1876), p. 305; J.S. Udall, *Dorsetshire Folklore* (Hertford, 1922), p. 43; E.M. Leather, *The Folklore of Herefordshire* (Wakefield, 1970), p. 102.

28 W. Plomer (ed.), *Kilvert's Diary: Selections from the Diary of the Rev. Francis Kilvert* (2 vols, London: Cape, 1960), II, p. 202; C. Hole, *A Dictionary of British Folk Customs* (London: Paladin, 1978), p. 221.

29 See, for example, Thiselton-Dyer, *British Popular Customs*, p. 305; Udall, *Dorsetshire Folklore*, p. 44; M. Dacombe, *Dorset Up Along and Down Along* (3rd edn, Dorchester: Longmans, 1951), p. 24.

30 I.H. Evans (ed.), *Brewer's Dictionary of Phrase and Fable* (14th edn, London: Cassell, 1990), p. 1011; Hutton, *Stations of the Sun*, p. 292.

31 See *Oxford English Dictionary* (hereafter *OED*) (2nd edn, Oxford: Oxford University Press, 1989), XV, p. 251. The term 'shit sacks' long remained current in Wiltshire and Berkshire; see C. Hole, *English Custom and Usage* (3rd edn, London: Batsford, 1950), p. 101.

32 This term was in common usage; see, for example, *Calendar of State Papers, Domestic* (hereafter *CSPD*) *1682*, p. 493.

33 For the use of the term 'scab' to signify a strike-breaker, or blackleg, see *Shorter OED* (3rd edn, Oxford: Oxford University Press, 1987), II, p. 1893.

34 See E. Porter, *Cambridgeshire Customs and Folklore* (London: Routledge and Kegan Paul, 1969), p. 118; J. Edgar Mann, *Hampshire Customs, Curiosities and Country Lore* (Southampton: Ensign, 1994), p. 49; Leather, *Folklore of Herefordshire*, p. 102; Udall, *Dorsetshire Folklore*, p. 43; J. Harvey-Bloom, *Folklore, Old Customs and Superstitions in Shakespeare Land* (London: Mitchell, Hughes and Clarke, 1929), p. 124; Thiselton-Dyer, *British Popular Customs*, pp. 302, 306. Children in the Devon parishes of Brixham and Silverton were still accustomed to sting each other with nettles on 29 May as late as the mid-twentieth century. I owe this point to Messrs Graham Parnell and Jack Tree of the Thorverton History Society.

35 Mann, *Hampshire Customs*, p. 49; Thiselton-Dyer, *British Popular Customs*, p. 305; Leather, *Folklore of Herefordshire*, p. 103.

36 J.R.W. Coxhead, *Old Devon Customs* (Exmouth: Raleigh Press, 1957), pp. 88–9.

37 On Barnstaple, see R.W. Cotton, *Barnstaple and the Northern Part of Devonshire During the Great Civil War* (London, 1889), pp. 265–9 and J. Gribble, *Memorials of Barnstaple* (Barnstaple: J. Avery, 1830), p. 80; on Gloucester, see R. Sherwood, *Civil Strife in the Midlands, 1642–51* (Chichester: Phillimore, 1974), pp. 86–7; on Lyme, see A.R. Bayley,

The Great Civil War in Dorset, 1642–60 (Taunton: Barnicott & Pearce, 1910), p. 190; on Nantwich, see J.R. Phillips, *Memoirs of the Civil Wars in Wales and the Marches* (2 vols, London: Longmans, Green, & Co., 1874), I, p. 195; on Taunton, see J. Toulmin, *The History of the Town of Taunton* (Taunton: T. Norris, 1791), pp. 422–3 and Underdown, *Revel, Riot and Rebellion*, pp. 289–90; on Plymouth, see C. Bracken, *A History of Plymouth* (Plymouth: Underhill, 1931), pp. 132–5. I am currently writing a paper on these neglected celebrations.

38 See *CSPD, 1682*, p. 208.

39 J.P.D. Dunbabin, 'Oliver Cromwell's popular image in nineteenth-century England', in J.S. Bromley and E.H. Kossmann (eds), *Britain and the Netherlands: V* (The Hague: Nijhoff, 1975), p. 146; A. Smith, 'The image of Cromwell in folklore and tradition', *Folklore*, 79 (1968), 19.

40 For detailed discussion of this subject, see Stewart, 'Cult of the royal martyr'.

41 See, for example, DRO, QS/128, petition of Robert Ware.

42 Webb, *Memorials*, II, p. 317.

43 Atkin, *Gloucester*, p. 119; Webb, *Memorials*, II, pp. 198, 383; J. Willis-Bund, *The Civil War in Worcestershire* (Birmingham: Midland Educational Company, 1905), p. 158.

44 G.S. and M.C.J., 'Herbertiana', *Montgomeryshire Collections*, V (1872), p. 176. See also G. Gomme (ed.), *The Gentleman's Magazine Library: English Topography, Part III* (Boston, MA: Houghton, Mifflin, 1893), p. 142; Webb, *Memorials*, II, pp. 223, 232.

45 *Notes and Queries*, I (1849–50), 137, 184.

46 Gomme, *English Topography, Part III*, p. 165.

47 See C. Hill, *God's Englishman: Oliver Cromwell and the English Revolution* (London: Penguin, 1988), pp. 182–3; D. Underdown, *A Freeborn People: Politics and the Nation in Seventeenth Century England* (Oxford: Clarendon Press, 1996), pp. 101, 106; R.C. Richardson (ed.), *Images of Oliver Cromwell* (Manchester: Manchester University Press, 1993), p. 43; Smith, 'Image of Cromwell', p. 36.

48 Webb, *Memorials*, II, p. 329; Leather, *Folklore of Herefordshire*, p. 42; P. Gaunt, *The Cromwellian Gazetteer: An Illustrated Guide to Britain in the Civil War and Commonwealth* (Stroud: Sutton, 1987), p. 79.

49 E. Hamer, 'A parochial account of Llangurig', *Montgomeryshire Collections*, II (1869), p. 229.

50 Edgar-Mann, *Hampshire Customs*, p. 49; F. Thompson, *Lark Rise to Candleford* (London: Penguin, 1988), p. 215.

51 H. Whitfield, *Scilly and Its Legends* (Penzance: F.T. Vibert, 1852), p. 55. Cf. Smith, 'Image of Cromwell', pp. 23–7.

52 L.V. Grinsell, *Folklore of Prehistoric Sites in Britain* (Newton Abbot: David and Charles, 1976), p. 118; Gaunt, *Gazetteer*, pp. 13, 40 and 97.

53 I. and P. Opie, *The Oxford Dictionary of Nursery Rhymes* (Oxford: Oxford University Press, 1969), p. 59; Dunbabin, 'Cromwell's popular image', p. 146; Smith 'Image of Cromwell', p. 32.

54 Dunbabin, 'Cromwell's popular image', pp. 143–5; Smith, 'Image of Cromwell', p. 20.

55 *Ibid.*, p. 159; B. Worden, 'The Victorians and Oliver Cromwell', in S. Collini, R. Whatmore, and B. Young (eds), *History, Religion and Culture: British Intellectual History, 1750–1950* (Cambridge: Cambridge University Press, 2000), pp. 112–35. See also Gaunt, *Gazetteer*, p. 70.

56 At Bovey Tracey, in Devon, for example: see Gaunt, *Gazetteer*, p. 41.

57 See, most notably, Smith, 'Image of Cromwell'; Dunbabin, 'Cromwell's popular image'; Richardson, *Images of Oliver Cromwell*; Worden, 'The Victorians and Oliver Cromwell'.

'Diabolical design': the Charleston elite, the 1822 slave insurrection, and the discourse of the supernatural

By the timely discovery of this plot, Carolina has been rescued from the most horrible catastrophe with which it has been threatened, since it has been an independent state. (Magistrates Lionel Kennedy and Thomas Parker, 1822)

[T]his reflection has convinced the writer that, as most of the causes of the late misfortune are beyond our control, the best way to remove the evil is to abolish that which is completely within our power. (Thomas Pinckney, 1822)

On 25 May 1822, near the shipyards of the Cooper River in Charleston, South Carolina, William Paul, a slave owned by John Paul, struck up a conversation with Peter Desverneys, a slave owned by John Prioleau. This would be a crucial moment in the history of American slavery.[1] From subsequent trial records and published accounts, we know that Paul invited Desverneys to join with him, other slaves, and a number of free blacks, in a large and organised military action against the whites in Charleston.[2] He told Desverneys that 'many have joined, and if you go with me, I will show you a man, who has the list of names who will take yours down'. The man to whom Paul referred was Denmark Vesey, a free black resident of Charleston, who was, by all accounts, the chief organiser, recruiter, and visionary behind the plot. Led by Vesey, the rebels planned to overtake the city on the night of 16 June by setting fire to its buildings and killing all of the whites – men, women, and children – that emerged. Once Charleston had been destroyed, they intended to commandeer a ship and sail to Haiti. Founded in 1804 by former slaves who had violently overthrown their white French masters, the Republic of Haiti was believed to be a safe haven for escape. The rebels also believed that Haiti would send troops to support the rebellion.[3]

The insurrection never took place. In response to Paul's appeal, Desverneys asserted that he was 'satisfied . . . [and] wished no change in his condition'.[4] Burdened by knowledge of the plot, Desverneys confided in William Penceel, a free black man, who suggested that Desverneys tell his owner what he knew. Once he was told of the plot, John Prioleau informed the Charleston intendant, James Hamilton, setting into action an investigation and a series of trials of suspected conspirators. These trials, which took place in May, June, July, and August 1822, resulted in the hanging of 34, the banishment of 40, the acquittal and discharge of 15, and the release of 38 prisoners before trial.[5] The court consisted of two magistrates, Lionel Kennedy and Thomas Parker, and five 'Freeholders'. According to the trial transcript, the court was created to try 'sundry Negroes apprehended and charged "with attempting to raise an Insurrection amongst the Blacks against the Whites"'.[6]

Had the rebels been able to execute their plan, it would have been the largest and best-organised slave rebellion in US history.[7] Although it is probably impossible to know the precise extent of the conspiracy, the evidence is suggestive. In his trial testimony, William Paul asserted that one of the plotters had a roster of 9,000 names of people who had signed on with the rebellion.[8] Joe La Roche testified that he had heard from Rolla Bennett, one of the chief rebels, that:

> Mingo [Harth] from James Island was to come over to Charleston with 4000 men, land on South Bay, march up and seize the Arsenal by the Guard House and kill all the City guard – that another body was to seize upon the powder magazine and another body to seize the Arsenal on the neck, then march to town and destroy the inhabitants who could only escape by jumping into the river.[9]

Frank Ferguson testified that 'Gullah' Jack Pritchard had reported that he had 'been in the country around Goose Creek & Dorchester and that he had spoken to 6600 persons who had agreed to join'.[10] Goose Creek and Dorchester are small communities just north of Charleston.

Most of the essays in this volume are concerned with events that few would deny the status of 'catastrophe': the Holocaust, the Irish Famine, and the sinking of the *Titanic*, among other man-made and 'natural' disasters. When an event involves great loss of life and/or the large-scale destruction of property, it is difficult for its horror to escape public attention and public memory either through direct local experience or through media transmission. The case of the attempted slave insurrection in Charleston, however, is different. It lacks what would seem to be the obvious defining characteristics of catastrophe. Without a massive body count or great physical devastation, the insurrection nevertheless provides an illustration of the way in which the catastrophic status of an event can inhere in the challenge that it presents to the dominant cultural assumptions of the group or groups affected. The extant legal documents and news accounts from the time suggest that, for the white elite of Charleston, the simple fact that such an insurrection had been planned qualified as a catastrophe, for it dramatically, if not fatally, ripped open the 'Magnolia Curtain', exposing as a charade southern paternalist constructions of black–white relations under the institution of slavery.

Particular attention will be paid in this essay to the discourse of the supernatural deployed by the white elite in its response to the discovery of the plot and its role in shaping the cultural memory of the event. That memory is limited. Had the conspirators not been intercepted, the story of the Charleston slave insurrection of 1822 would probably have formed a significant chapter of any popular history of racial conflict in the United States. In the event, however, the place of the uprising in American memory, until recently at least, has been marked by silence and suppression. In Charleston, there are two modest memorials to the insurrection, neither reflecting the alarming qualities attributed to the plot or to Vesey by his contemporaries. One, at the Emanuel African Methodist Episcopal Church, is a group of statues depicting children who seem to be listening to a sermon on liberation delivered by Vesey, who does not appear. The other, installed in the lobby of Gaillard Municipal Auditorium in 1976, is a small watercolour painting by Dorothy Wright depicting Vesey, with his back to the viewer, speaking to a group of followers. The painting was stolen just after it was dedicated and was returned anonymously only after an appeal by the mayor of the city.[11] At the time of the dedication, a columnist writing in the *Charleston News and Courier* remarked, 'If black leaders in Charleston had searched for a thousand years, they could not have found a black whose portrait would have been more offensive to many white people.' In a letter to the editor, Vesey was compared to Hitler, Attila the Hun, and Herod.[12]

When scholars have addressed the history of the insurrection, as they have been inclined to do only in the last few decades, they have tended to focus on Denmark Vesey, the organiser and leader, and more broadly on his inner circle – Rolla Bennett, Ned Bennett, Peter Poyas, Monday Gell, and 'Gullah' Jack Pritchard. Accounts such as those provided in recent books by David Robertson and Douglas Egerton have celebrated Vesey as a forgotten hero and illuminated much about the experience of the rebels, and, in doing so, serve usefully to draw public attention to a long-neglected episode in American history.[13] They represent Vesey as an African-American who displayed formidable intellectual and political resistance to the institution of slavery, who spoke out in public against it, and who was fearsome to both his followers and to the white elite. Robertson compares Vesey to Malcolm X. The wider economic and political environments in which the insurrection occurred are not ignored in these narratives, but they are discussed more fully in Edward Pearson's *Designs Against Charleston*, which goes a considerable distance toward placing the planned rebellion into the context of Caribbean politics and the slave trade, and into the context also of nineteenth-century Charleston's civic and economic life.[14]

This essay aims neither to reconstruct the rebel narrative nor to situate the plot in broader historical context, projects capably accomplished in these recent publications. An exercise in rhetorical criticism, it examines a specific discourse feature – the discourse of the supernatural – evident in a number of contemporary texts concerned with the insurrection. It was a feature that, even as it articulated a consciousness of catastrophe, nevertheless had implications for the marginal place of the catastrophe in subsequent cultural memory.

It is probably not the only reason. The voices of the group upon whom the insurrection had the greatest material impact – the black community which suffered the 34 executions and renewed racial hostility – were swiftly eliminated from the public record. The months following the discovery of the plot saw the publication of the trial transcript by Kennedy and Parker entitled *An Official Report of the Trials of Sundry Negroes Charged with an Attempt to Raise an Insurrection in the State of South Carolina*, a narrative of the plot by Intendant Hamilton entitled *An Account of the Late Intended Insurrection*, and policy documents such as Thomas Pinckney's *Reflections, Occasioned by the Late Disturbances in Charleston*.[15] These narratives were all authored, edited, and published by members of the slaveholding elite. Even the 'direct' testimony from the principal rebels during the trials was mediated by this elite. In his introduction to a collection of documents concerning the insurrection, Robert Starobin calls attention to this problem:

> Given the savagery of the white retaliation against the blacks, serious methodological problems arise in assessing the evidence left from the plot, for all of the surviving sources derive either from terrorised blacks or fearful whites. The trial testimony came largely from witnesses who desired to escape death or to direct attention away from themselves. Though two leaders confessed, they did so under extreme duress; the rest of the leadership denied complicity or remained silent. The original court minutes survive, but the whole trial record was edited by the magistrates before publication. In sum, the evidence is inherently biased against the conspirators and must therefore be used with scepticism and caution.[16]

The memory of the insurrection may also have been informed by the fact that it did not occur. Since there were no burned buildings, no dead slaveholders, and no rosters of rebels or tactical maps (these were reportedly burned by Vesey, Poyas, and Gell), the insurrection exists only in text and imagination. All that we know of the plot comes from the trial transcripts, which feature accounts of the plot as narrated by suspects speaking in a jury-less court presided over by the wealthiest and most powerful slaveholders in the city. One historian, Richard Wade, has gone so far as to suggest that the conspiracy, described in the trials as enormous and well organised, was in fact invented by the slaveholding elite as an excuse to persecute free blacks and to restrict the relative latitude that some slaves had been afforded. In 1964, he wrote: 'The "plot" was probably never more than loose talk by aggrieved and bitter men.'[17] A similar argument has been advanced recently by Michael Johnson.[18] Whatever the validity of these theories, the fact that we can have a controversy concerning the very existence of the plot dramatises our primary dependence on narrative and testimony in discussing this event.

Within the available textual evidence of the insurrection, then, must lie both the definition of the event as catastrophe and the seeds of later forgetting. In the absence of dramatic physical harm, the members of the slaveholding elite, whose perspectives dominated contemporary accounts, located the source of the catastrophe in the new and necessary awareness of their own vulnerability. In sentencing ten of the rebels to death, Magistrates Kennedy and Parker expressed surprise at the 'wild and diabolical' plot, at the intentions of men whom they considered to have been 'reared by the hand of kindness, and fostered by a master who assumed many of the duties of a parent'.[19] The plot represented a violation of fundamental beliefs about the prevailing order of social, economic, and political privilege, and a challenge to tacit knowledge of basic differences between people of African and European origins. Although no slaveholders had died and no property had been destroyed, the social order was shaken by the revelations concerning the scope and organisation of the plot as it was described by the rebels in their testimony during the trials.

However, even as members of the slaveholding elite reflected on the insurrection, even as they expressed difficulty in understanding why the slaves and free blacks involved in the plot would want to risk their good position by plotting against whites, they remained disinclined to imagine and meditate upon the historical conditions – the reality of race relations in Charleston – that might have led the rebels to plan such an endeavour. It was a failure that exemplified the discursive limits of southern paternalism and its need to contain knowledge of the tensions within its own cultural system; it was a failure, ultimately, that also had consequences for memory.

William Freehling has characterised Southern white paternalism and slaves' corresponding performance 'as consenting children' as 'the Domestic Charade'.[20] He considers the ways in which the slaveholding elite could distinguish their power from other authoritarian regimes by emphasising its particular venue of coercion: 'With dictators throughout history available to them as models, these titans were drawn to their own homes as exemplar of proper dictatorial sway.'[21] Freehling goes on to explain the charade:

> Paternalists sought to make their own performance as benevolent fathers, their wives' performance as moral matriarchs, and their slaves' performance as consenting children achieve the total verisimilitude that is possible only when actors are one with their act. Parallels in ways of controlling white homes and blacks slaves turned out to be close enough so that charade as reality was sometimes possible.[22]

Following Freehling's characterisation, David Robertson suggests that the complementary roles of whites and blacks during this period were enabled by what he calls the 'Magnolia Curtain' and 'Sable Curtain', respectively. The 'Magnolia Curtain' represents whites' 'shared assumption that slaves *would not* revolt because they knew they were loved as an extended black family'. The 'Sable Curtain', meanwhile, represents blacks 'playing their role of a people who *could not* revolt, whose mature emotions were secretly hidden from harm behind a Sable Curtain of pretended childish incomprehension or simple docility'.[23]

Pearson also describes the fundamental paternalism of whites in their relationship to slaves: 'Many white southerners saw themselves not as murderers but as the protectors of their enslaved property who presided over a benevolent institution.'[24] In sentencing to death the ten rebels, Kennedy and Parker demonstrated the paternalistic stance and the inability to rationalise the rebels' antagonistic position to it:

> In addition to the crime of treason, you have on the present occasion, displayed the vilest ingratitude. It is a melancholy truth, that those servants in whom was reposed the most unlimited confidence, have been the principal actors in this wicked scheme . . . you have realized the fable of the Frozen Serpent, and attempted to destroy the bosom that sheltered and protected you.[25]

Even after discovering the size and organisation of the plot and even after hearing blunt statements such as that of John Horry, who said to his master that he intended 'to kill you, rip open your belly and throw your guts in your face', the slaveholding elite remained dedicated to the terms of the 'domestic charade'.[26]

This dedication speaks to the centrality of the familial analogy in the coercion and punishment of slaves, its importance in a vision of a unified Charleston, and its

necessity in justifying 'the Peculiar Institution', as slavery was called, to the slaveholding elite. The familial analogy, the idea that the slave/master relationship was the same
as the parent/child relationship, lay beyond question; it was an analogy that rested on
the assumptions that Africans were, as Kipling characterised non-Europeans much
later in the nineteenth century in 'The White Man's Burden', 'sullen peoples / half-
devil and half-child'.[27] It also reflected and supported the notions of scientific racism,
such as those offered in the work of Louis Agassiz, a Swiss naturalist, Harvard professor, and dedicated empiricist, who performed research on slaves in Charleston in the
1840s.[28] Agassiz advocated the theory of special creationism which held that God
created each type of organism independently of every other and that therefore continuities between organisms did not exist.[29] Reflecting on seeing a black man – an
American slave – for the first time, Agassiz wrote, 'The more pity I felt at the sight of
this degraded and degenerate race, the more . . . impossible it became for me to repress
the feeling that they are not of the same blood as we are.'[30]

Explanations for the motives behind the plot that did not rest on assumptions consistent with the familial analogy failed to fall 'within the true' for Charleston's slaveholding elite.[31] Kennedy and Parker in their trial transcript, Hamilton in his account
of the plot, and Pinckney in his policy proposal adhere to and reinforce the pre-plot
assumptions about the roles of blacks and whites. Pearson writes, 'Through the use of
the printed word, the city's intellectual community attempted to regain their hold
over a social order that was momentarily placed in jeopardy by Vesey's conspiratorial
designs.'[32] In response to knowledge of the plot, the slaveholding elite was forced to
make explicit what had previously been a predominantly tacit notion. In *The New
Rhetoric*, Chaim Perelman and L. Olbrechts-Tyteca suggest that epideictic discourse,
speech oriented toward praise and blame, tends to reinforce a status quo.[33] They write
that 'the speaker readily converts into universal values, if not eternal truths, that which
has acquired a certain standing through social unanimity.'[34] Although the trial transcripts and other documents announce themselves as expositions, there can be little
question of the epideictic motive, illustrated particularly by Hamilton's introduction,
in which he points the reader to the 'lesson' that can be gained by reading his account.

One of the resources used by the slaveholding elite in the effort to reinforce prevailing assumptions was the discourse of the supernatural. In his discussion of 'god-
terms' in *A Rhetoric of Motives*, Kenneth Burke examines the discursive link between
natural and supernatural explanations for phenomena. By 'god-terms', Burke indicates a host of rarefied abstractions, such as 'nature', 'truth', 'science', and 'freedom',
which operate as 'declared and undeclared synonyms for God' in their ultimate
grounding function and incontestable value. He writes, 'Even if you grant the distinction between natural and supernatural motives, there is still the drastic fact that the
power of rhetoric may arise rather from the *confusion* between the two orders.'[35] Burke
emphasises that an effective ambiguity can be created where motives relating to
natural phenomena are blended with ultimate motives: 'The rhetorical use of religion
as an instrument of politics depends upon this very ambiguity. For the priest identifies some questionable secular faction or cause with a transcendent order held to be
beyond question.'[36] For Burke, both the possibility of rhetoric in general and the spe-

cific effort to find grounds for certain political discourses depend on a relationship between local, secular causes and ultimate, spiritual causes. Burke's god-terms provide a way of understanding the discourse of the supernatural not as an artefact or ornament but as a politically productive strategy for addressing causes.

One of the ways that the slaveholding elite attempted to reinforce the pre-plot notions of social order was to invoke the spirit world both in support of its own notion of justice and against the conspirators. This Manichaean vision was a response to what may have seemed to be, given the dominant familial analogy, an invasion of the sanctity of the home. Often the rebels themselves were singled out as embodiments of evil. The Reverend Richard Furman referred to the rebels as 'Wicked Men' and to the plot as a 'Diabolical Design'.[37] In his account of the plot, Hamilton described Vesey as a man whose 'passions were ungovernable and savage . . . he displayed the haughty and capricious cruelty of an Eastern Bashaw'.[38] In sentencing to death 'Gullah' Jack Pritchard, Kennedy and Parker referred to his 'wicked designs', his efforts to enlist 'all the powers of darkness' and 'the most disgusting mummery and superstition'.[39] In their view, the planned insurrection was 'this wicked scheme', and 'wild and diabolical'. They suggested that the rebels should consider their immanent trials in heaven judged by 'the everliving God, whose holy ordinances you have violated'.[40] This discourse of the supernatural was central to the textual effort of what Starobin calls 'white retaliation'.

The insurrection was considered a threat on the order of a natural disaster. In their narrative of the plot, Kennedy and Parker made the analogy:

> By the timely discovery of this plot, Carolina has been rescued from the most horrible catastrophe with which it has been threatened, since it has been an independent state; for although success could not possibly have attended the conspirators, yet before their suppression, Charleston would probably have been wrapped in flames[41]

On 27 September, after the trials, executions, and banishments had come to an end, a hurricane hit the city. One resident remarked, 'Our city has been most severely scourged this last eight months what with Insurrection and then Storm.'[42] The parallel drawn here evaded the difference in agency between the plot and an 'act of God'. Because of their fundamental paternalism, the response of the slaveholding elite exhibited little if any awareness of blacks, slave or free, as a class with a political consciousness or even a comprehensible political motivation. Comparisons between the plot and natural disasters reinforced this by equating the actions of the rebels with the motions of nature, in which the ultimate agency was a mysterious or spiritual source.[43] The analogy between the insurrection and natural disasters also placed the rebels on the 'nature' side of the nature/culture divide, reinforcing the familial analogy and the assumptions of otherness supported by scientific racism.

In *The Theory of Communicative Action*, Jürgen Habermas notes the role of mythical and magical discourse in the obscuring of agency:

> Myths do not permit a clear, basic, conceptual differentiation between things and persons, between objects that can be manipulated and agents – subjects capable of speaking and acting to whom we attribute linguistic utterances. Thus it is only consistent when

magical practices do not recognize the distinction between teleological and communicative action, between goal-directed, instrumental intervention in objectively given situa-
tions, on the one hand, and the establishment of interpersonal relations, on the other.[44]

Habermas's discussion of these permeable boundaries expands on the nature/culture
dichotomy, highlighting the ways in which it distinguishes motivated subjects from
others. By not recognising a distinction between 'teleological and communicative
action' in the case of the rebels, the slaveholding elite obscured their agency and failed
to acknowledge them as a political voice with a rational motivation.

In his account of the insurrection, the Charleston intendant, James Hamilton,
framed the narrative of the plot in the discourse of the supernatural. In his introduction, where he outlined the motivation for its publication, Hamilton suggested a
moral that can be brought away from the story: 'that there is nothing they are bad
enough to do, that we are not powerful enough to punish'.[45] In his conclusion,
Hamilton reflected on the motives and character of Denmark Vesey:

> Of the motives of Vesey, we cannot sit in judgement; they have been scanned by a power
> who can do higher justice than ourselves. But as they are explained by his character and
> conduct, during the combinations of the plot, they are only to be referred to a malig-
> nant hatred of the whites, and inordinate lust of power and booty.[46]

Here Hamilton invokes God's judgment, identifying it with the judgment of the
court. He begins with the idea that Vesey's motives cannot be judged or understood
by the earthly court, but then goes on to offer an earthly explanation: Vesey's character. This is a way to individualise the plot, to explain it in terms of the peculiar perspective of one man, and to link that interpretation to the authority of 'a power who
can do higher justice'. This resonates with Burke's notion concerning the marshalling
of the supernatural in order to authorise explanations of the natural. Hamilton's final
words of the document reflected a trust in the moral goodness of the work of the slaveholding elite in its response to the plot, and a trust that history would vindicate them
and that God would protect them: 'With little to fear, and nothing to reproach ourselves we may, without shrinking, submit our conduct to the award of posterity, and
ourselves to the protection of the Supreme Ruler of Events.'[47]

What emerges from the trial documents is a picture of the rebels as agents of evil,
acting not as the boldest members of an underclass, but as special individuals whose
motives can be understood only as wild and irrational, and of the slaveholding elite
as holy defenders of order, compelled to punish the rebels for their efforts 'to destroy
the bosom that sheltered and protected' them. Central to this characterisation of the
rebels and the elite is the issue of order and its relationship with civilisation and morality. Also important is the boundary that marks the distinction between the community of Charleston and its enemies.

In *Blessings in Disguise; or, the Morality of Evil*, Jean Starobinski writes:

> A term fraught with sacred content demonizes its antonym. Once the word *civilization*
> ceases to denote a fact subject to judgment and becomes an incontestable value, it enters
> the verbal arsenal of praise and blame. Evaluating the defects and merits of the civiliza-
> tion is no longer the issue. Civilization itself becomes the crucial criterion.[48]

In the terms of Kenneth Burke, 'civilization', for Starobinski, has become a 'god-term', that is, a universal ground for value. When the slaveholding elite accuses the rebels of being motivated by 'inordinate lust for power', or of being 'ungovernable and savage', it is attacking the rebels as uncivilised, as beyond and opposed to the order of culture as an unquestioned ground. Linked with this attack is the characterisation of the rebels as against god itself, as working in concert with 'all the powers of darkness'. In *The Transparency of Evil*, Jean Baudrillard identifies links among disorder, otherness, and evil: 'The principle of Evil is not a moral principle but rather a principle of instability and vertigo, a principle of complexity and foreignness, a principle of seduction, a principle of incompatibility, antagonism and irreducibility.'[49] In the discourse of the slaveholding elite, the rebels have come to represent evil, where, as Baudrillard writes, 'Evil is founded on itself alone, in pure incompatibility.'[50] Ultimately, they must be executed not only because they have broken the laws of the state which prohibit slave insurrections, but because they have dared challenge the social order which is invested with divine significance. Citing the Charleston lawyer Henry DeSaussure, Martha Richardson wrote to James Screven in September 1822, 'The hand of Providence was singularly visible in the discovery and development of the plot and our gratitude should be commensurate with it.'[51]

In Thomas Pinckney's *Reflections*, the discourse of the supernatural takes a different form, as he outlines his plan to address the problems that have led to the plot. Pinckney identifies a number of causes: the example of and encouragement from San Domingo, the influence of Northern notions of 'universal liberty', the leniency of 'proprietors' towards slave permissiveness, the ability of slaves to earn money as craftsmen, and 'the disparity of numbers between the white and black inhabitants' of Charleston. Most of his document is devoted to addressing the final three causes, because they are the most local. Pinckney writes, 'No effort of ours can remove some of these causes, but over others we may exercise control.'[52]

Through his discussion of the problems inherent in the local causes, Pinckney makes a number of references to 'evil' or 'evils'. He uses *evil* as a metonymy, a master trope which functions to characterise the agency behind the causes proposed in the document. In 'The Four Master Tropes', Kenneth Burke characterises metaphor, metonymy, synecdoche, and irony as fundamental in human 'discovery and description of "the truth"'.[53] In highlighting these master tropes, Burke finds himself in a tradition of thinkers who have focused on these tropes, or some subset of them, as particularly primary among the volumes of tropes and figures from classical rhetoric: Aristotle, the Ramists, Giambattista Vico, Friedrich Nietzsche, and Hayden White.[54] He highlights the primacy of these four tropes in all discourse challenging assumptions of *truth* unmediated by language. Burke characterises the application of metonymy as 'reduction' while emphasising both the ways that 'the four tropes shade into one another', and the importance of seeing them not only in 'their purely figurative usage'.[55] I characterise Pinckney's use of 'evil' as metonymic because it stands in a whole/part relationship to a number of causes, reducing them to a single cause.

Burke emphasises the way metonymy states the intangible in terms of the tangible – for example, to 'speak of "the heart" rather than "the emotions"' – and he shows how this particular move is prominent in 'scientific realism' exemplified by behaviourism where bodily movement takes the place of a complex of psychological states.[56] Perhaps because of his particular target, Burke focuses on metonymy as a unidirectional reduction, that is, from the intangible to the tangible, but he adds this qualification:

> Reduction, *as per scientific realism*, would be confined to but one direction. Reduction, that is, as the word is now generally used. But originally, 'reduction' was used in ways that make it closer rather to the margin of its overlap upon 'perspective', as anything considered in terms of anything else could be said to be 'reduced' – or 'brought back' ('referred') – to it, so that the consideration of art in terms of morality, politics, or religion could have been called 'the reduction' of art to morality, or politics, or religion.[57]

It is on this margin that 'evil' operates in Pinckney's policy document. As a term denoting the intangible, 'evil' comes to stand for a series of more tangible local causes of the plot. It provides a superordinate which joins together all of the causes discussed by Pinckney. By suggesting the presence of a large, disembodied, and morally corrupt force within the city, it also serves to cloud the role of human agency in the insurrection.

At a concrete and external level, Pinckney can explain, in pragmatic fashion, the causes of the plot. With regard to the ultimate motivations of the rebels, however, the most that Pinckney can offer – as with Kennedy and Parker's trial transcript and Hamilton's account – is a discussion of external influences. In arguing for his policy to prevent future uprisings, Pinckney claims that he is acting in the interests of the slaves, suggesting that, if successful, his proposal would ensure that 'they could never be again subjected to the horrors and calamities, in which an attempt at insurrection, whether at first successful or not, must inevitably involve them'.[58]

There are many instances of Pinckney using 'evil' in reference to concrete, local concerns. His first use of 'evil' occurs in his discussion of the lax approach to slave ownership among 'proprietors' in Charleston:

> Over the indulgencies which have so pampered the enormous number of domestics, entertained by the inhabitants, the State Laws and City Ordinances may have considerable control; but the execution of these laws may be so frustrated by public inattention, and more by the particular way of thinking and weakness of many proprietors, that it is to be feared this evil will not be effectually checked, particularly as it respects the dangerous instrument of learning, which many of them have acquired . . .[59]

At the end of the same paragraph, 'this evil' refers specifically to education: 'for it is not only impracticable to deprive them of what they have attained, but as it is easily communicated, it is probable that, in spite of all endeavors to the contrary, this evil will rather increase than diminish'.[60]

The next reference to 'evil' occurs in Pinckney's exploration of the disparity of numbers: 'If we examine the last census, and refer to that taken twenty years previous, we shall find that this evil is rapidly increasing; for at the former period the white population of Charleston exceeded the other, while in the last census the black population was to the white nearly as 22 to 14.'[61] He does not make clear whether the evil refers to the disparity between the numbers of whites and blacks in the city or to 'the black population'. Later in the document, Pinckney suggests ways to reduce the numbers of blacks in Charleston, noting that white immigrant workers could replace them, 'but the mere rumor of a conspiracy would occasion distressing alarm, and the attempt, though ultimately unsuccessful, would produce incalculable evils. It would be, therefore, prudent not only to reduce their force below what, upon a fair calculation, would afford no prospect of success to rational persons, but to place it so low as to deprive even the rash and desperate of all hope.'[62]

Having outlined the causes, Pinckney offers solutions to the problems of the disparity of numbers and the money earned by slaves in the city. He offers reasons for reducing the number of slaves in the city, explaining the strategy of slaves who plan revolt: 'this is an intestine enemy, who by availing himself of his advantageous situation, and properly selecting the time of attack, might render it extremely formidable'.[63] Here he uses a bodily metaphor to suggest that for the white population of Charleston, the enemy is internal – inside their homes and businesses – and that this position would make a surprise attack very potent, even after the disparity of numbers was corrected. The bodily metaphor is powerful because, consistent with the familial analogy, it locates the evil inside the most intimate parts of the community/body.

Near the end of his discussion of solutions, Pinckney links 'evil' with 'slavery': 'It is generally admitted, even in these Southern States, that the slavery which here prevails, is an evil entailed upon us by our former British rulers, and difficult to be averted from its extensive influence, being amalgamated with most of the property of the country.'[64] Pinckney links slavery with 'evil' but locates its cause, as he does with many of the causes of the plot, beyond the borders of Charleston. He blames the British, the enemies from the Revolutionary War.

As he concludes his reflections, Pinckney reiterates his argument that Charleston should 'remove the evil' by attacking the most local and manageable problems: 'as most of the causes of the late misfortune are beyond our control, the best way to remove the evil is to abolish that which is completely within our power'.[65] Here 'the evil' is a superordinate which seems to reduce to itself all of the evils discussed in the document. It is this 'evil' that participates most in the discourse of the supernatural, as it seems to stand beyond the local causes, 'that which is completely within our power'. While Pinckney's plan is pragmatic – reduce the numbers of slaves in the city and prohibit the ones who remain from earning any money – his constant reference to the causes as 'this evil' or 'the evil' ultimately suggests a force beyond human agency and control.

In the slaveholding elite's response to the discovery of the plot, the discourse of the supernatural served to reinforce the familial analogy, obscuring the agency of the rebels. Seeing slaves as children in need of protection justified the 'Peculiar Institution'. By attributing the ultimate cause of the plot to a dark force beyond the borders of Charleston, the slaveholding elite willed a consensus which included free and enslaved blacks as members of a common Charleston community threatened by the plot. Rather than emphasise or even recognise the boundary drawn by the rebels, the one between the slaveholding and enslaved, the elite highlighted boundaries between the city and outside agents – Santo Domingo, Britain, the North. Although the 'intestine enemy' was acknowledged, that is, the notion that slaves could represent a threat, the identification of Providence as the protector of the city and Evil as the threat obscured both the tension between the slaveholding and the enslaved, and the agency of both parties in the conflict. The slaves were at once a newly discovered force of opposition which required policy changes such as Pinckney's suggestions for deportation and increase in civil restriction, and, as formerly understood, a class of children who had to be protected from the dangerous persuasions of individuals such as Vesey: free black intellectuals with a political consciousness and imagination that reached beyond the boundaries of Charleston.

To claim that, historically, the South's stance toward what is regarded as alien has been closed and defensive would not be radical. James M. Banner has argued that South Carolina, in particular among Southern states, has, over the course of its history, been extreme in its isolation, its resistance to the Union, its maintenance of a quasi-feudal system, and its resistance to the abolition of slavery.[66] An ongoing controversy during the 1990s regarding the flying of the Confederate battle flag over the statehouse illustrates in a small way this dubious inheritance. South Carolina was the last state to maintain this practice, widely considered racist. The familial analogy still resonates through comments by flag apologists who emphasise the allegiances of blacks to the Confederacy by pointing to their participation in the Civil War on the side of the South.

In the 1820s, it was this analogy, rather than the experience of material losses, that framed white Charleston's identification of the insurrection as a catastrophe, because of the challenge the plot presented to their culture's understanding of itself. Nevertheless, the cultural impact of the catastrophe was eventually contained and its memory cast to the margins of historical consciousness. One of the key means of achieving this was the invocation of the discourse of the supernatural, by which the slaveholding elite elided the agency of the rebels and reinforced the familial analogy. With the plot's ultimate cause located outside the boundaries of the city and embodied only in some supernatural force, the plot took on, in the terms of the dominant narrative, the quality of an 'act of God', a natural disaster. This rhetorical shift accomplished two tasks: first, the distinction between the rebels' motives and the motives of the slaveholding elite was erased. In fact, the possibility that the rebels could have independent agency at all was denied. Second, the terms of the event were shifted from those of a political uprising to those of a natural disaster. In the terms of a natural disaster, the plot can be rendered a minor historical footnote since it did not lead to the material damage typically associated with such catastrophes. If the plot were a hurricane, a parallel that at least one city resident drew in the months following its discovery, then the discourse of the supernatural had converted it successfully into a hurricane that missed the city.[67]

Notes

1 I would like to acknowledge Benjamin Cramer for first bringing this event to my attention and for the helpful conversations he and I have had about it since.

2 Edward Pearson suggests that Vesey and the organisers demonstrated a 'real understanding of urban guerrilla warfare'; see E. Pearson (ed.), *Designs Against Charleston: The Trial Record of the Denmark Vesey Slave Conspiracy of 1822* (Chapel Hil, NC: University of North Carolina Press, 1999), p. 3.

3 *Ibid.*, p. 86.

4 James Hamilton, *An Account of the Late Intended Insurrection Among a Portion of the Blacks of this City, Charleston, S.C.* (Charleston, SC: A.E. Miller, 1822), p. 4.

5 Pearson (ed.), *Designs Against Charleston*, pp. 1–3; Hamilton, *An Account*, p. 28. Hamilton's numbers differ slightly from Pearson's: 'It will be seen . . . that one-hundred and thirty-one were committed: thirty-five have suffered death, and thirty-seven have been sentenced to banishment.'

6 Lionel H. Kennedy and Thomas Parker, *An Official Report of the Trials of Sundry Negroes Charged with an Attempt to Raise an Insurrection in the State of South Carolina*, in Pearson (ed.), *Designs Against Charleston*, p. 165.

7 William Freehling refers to 'The Vesey Conspiracy' as 'the most widespread and cogent insurrection plot uncovered in the nineteenth-century South'; W. Freehling, *The Road to Disunion: Secessionists at Bay 1776–1854* (New York: Oxford University Press, 1990), p. 79. David Robertson refers to the plot as 'the most elaborate and well-planned slave insurrection in the history of the United States'; D. Robertson, *Denmark Vesey: The Buried History of America's Largest Slave Rebellion and the Man Who Led It* (New York: Knopf, 1999), p. 4.

8 Kennedy and Parker, in Pearson (ed.), *Designs Against Charleston*, p. 166.

9 *Ibid.*, p. 170.

10 *Ibid.*, p. 210.

11 Robertson, *Denmark Vesey*, p. 4; Pearson (ed.), *Designs Against Charleston*, pp. 7–8.

12 *Ibid.*, p. 8.

13 *Ibid.*, p. 117; Douglas R. Egerton, *He Shall Go Free: The Lives of Denmark Vesey* (Madison, WI: Madison House, 1999). During the legislative and military battles over slavery in the US in the nineteenth century, Vesey was invoked as both a hero and a villain, though he has been relatively lost to public discourse since. In recruiting soldiers for the Fifty-Fourth Massachusetts Regiment of black volunteers during the Civil War, Frederick Douglass asked them to 'Remember Denmark Vesey of Charleston', see F. Douglass, 'Men of Color to Arms!', in F.M. Holland (ed.), *Frederick Douglass: The Colored Orator* (New York: Haskell House, 1969), pp. 297–8. For other accounts of the insurrection, see John Lofton, *Insurrection in South Carolina: The Turbulent World of Denmark Vesey* (Yellow Springs, OH: Antioch Press, 1964) and Lois A. Walker and Susan R. Silverman (ed.), *A Documented History of Gullah Jack Pritchard and the Denmark Vesey Slave Insurrection of 1822* (Lewiston, NY: E. Mellen Press, 2000). A two-part forum on the insurrection was recently published in the *William and Mary Quarterly*, 58:4 (October 2001), 913–76 and 59:1 (January 2002), 135–202.

14 Pearson (ed.), *Designs Against Charleston*.

15 Thomas Pinckney, *Reflections, Occasioned by the Late Disturbances in Charleston* (Charleston, SC: A.E. Miller, 1822), in *Slave Insurrections: Selected Documents* (Westport, CT: Negro University Press, 1970).

16 Robert S. Starobin, 'Introduction', in R.S. Starobin (ed.), *Denmark Vesey: The Slave Conspiracy of 1822* (Englewood Cliffs, NJ: Prentice-Hall, 1970), p. 7.

17 Richard Wade, 'The Vesey plot: a reconsideration', *Journal of Southern History*, 30 (1964), 160.

18 Michael Johnson, 'Denmark Vesey and his co-conspirators', *William and Mary Quarterly*,

58:4 (October 2001), 915–76. For responses to Johnson's article, see 'Forum: the making of a slave conspiracy, part 2', *William and Mary Quarterly*, 59:1 (January 2002), 135–202.

19 Kennedy and Parker in Pearson (ed.), *Designs Against Charleston*, p. 281.

20 Freehling, *The Road to Disunion*, p. 59.

21 *Ibid.*

22 *Ibid.*, pp. 59–60.

23 Robertson, *Denmark Vesey*, pp. 76–7.

24 Pearson (ed.), *Designs Against Charleston*, p. 102.

25 Kennedy and Parker, in *ibid.*, p. 281.

26 *Ibid.*, p. 341.

27 Rudyard Kipling, 'The White Man's Burden', in *Collected Verse of Rudyard Kipling* (Garden City, NJ: Doubleday, 1907), p. 217.

28 Brian Wallis, 'Black bodies, white science: Louis Agassiz' slave daguerreotypes', *American Art*, 9:2 (Summer 1995), 44–5.

29 Edward Lurie, *Louis Agassiz: A Life in Science* (Chicago, IL: University of Chicago Press, 1960), pp. 255–6.

30 *Ibid.*, p. 257.

31 Michel Foucault writes: 'In short, a proposition must fulfil some onerous and complex conditions before it can be admitted within a discipline; before it can be pronounced true or false it must be, as Monsieur Canguilhem might say, "within the true".' Michael Foucault, *The Archaeology of Knowledge and The Discourse on Language* (New York: Pantheon, 1982), p. 224. Although there was an ongoing debate concerning the institution of slavery itself between representatives of South Carolina and those of the Northern States, this conflict operated on the level of policy. The assumptions of the familial metaphor could be tacit within this debate.

32 Pearson (ed.), *Designs Against Charleston*, p. 159.

33 Aristotle describes epideictic, forensic, and deliberative discourse as the three major forms of speech. Epideictic speech praises and blames, forensic speech addresses issues about past events, and deliberative speech addresses issues that will affect the future. The typical domains of each are ceremonies, court trials, and legislative assemblies, respectively. Aristotle, *On Rhetoric: A Theory of Civic Discourse* (trans. and ed. George A. Kennedy, New York: Oxford University Press, 1991).

34 C.H. Perelman and L. Olbrechts-Tyteca, *The New Rhetoric: A Treatise on Argumentation* (trans. J. Wilkinson and P. Weaver, South Bend, IN: University of Notre Dame Press, 1969), p. 51.

35 Kenneth Burke, *A Rhetoric of Motives* (Berkeley, CA: University of California Press, 1969), p. 299.

36 *Ibid.*

37 Richard Furman to Governor Thomas Bennett, September 1822, in Pearson (ed.), *Designs Against Charleston*, p. 351; see also *ibid.*, p. 158.

38 Hamilton, *An Account*, p. 17.

39 Kennedy and Parker, in Pearson (ed.), *Designs Against Charleston*, p. 280. 'Gullah' Jack Pritchard was known as a spiritual man trained in African tribal religious practice, and many of the conspirators believed that he possessed special powers, such as an inability to be killed. According to the trial record, many of the recruits were highly respectful of his spiritual power.

40 *Ibid.*, pp. 281–2.

41 Kennedy and Parker, 'Narrative of the conspiracy and intended insurrection amongst a

portion of the negroes in the state of South-Carolina, in the year 1822', from Kennedy and Parker, *An Official Report of the Trials of Sundry Negroes Charged with an Attempt to Raise an Insurrection in the State of South Carolina*, in Starobin (ed.), *Denmark Vesey*, p. 119.

42 Pearson (ed.), *Designs Against Charleston*, p. 4.

43 Kenneth Burke notes the importance of the analogical relationship between the terms of the supernatural and 'the empirical realm', especially 'the sweep and power of the natural (of storms, of seas, of mountains)'; K. Burke, *The Rhetoric of Religion* (Boston, MA: Beacon Press, 1961), p. 37.

44 Jürgen Habermas, *The Theory of Communicative Action* (trans. T. McCarthy, Boston, MA: Beacon Press, 1984), p. 48.

45 Hamilton, *An Account*, p. 2.

46 *Ibid.*, p. 29.

47 *Ibid.*, p. 30.

48 Jean Starobinski, *Blessings in Disguise; or, The Morality of Evil* (trans. A. Goldhammer, Cambridge, MA: Harvard University Press, 1993), p. 17. Emphasis added.

49 Jean Baudrillard, *The Transparency of Evil: Essays on Extreme Phenomena* (trans. J. Benedict, New York: Verso, 1993), p. 107.

50 *Ibid.*, p. 139.

51 Quoted in Pearson (ed.), *Designs Against Charleston*, p. 347.

52 Pinckney, *Reflections*, p. 7.

53 Kenneth Burke, 'The four master tropes', in K. Burke, *A Grammar of Motives* (Berkeley, CA: University of California Press, 1969), p. 503. Also see Roman Jakobson and Morris Halle, 'The metaphoric and metonymic poles', in R. Jakobson and M. Halle, *Fundamentals of Language* ('s-Gravenhage: Mouton, 1956), pp. 76–82.

54 F.J. D'Angelo, 'Tropics of arrangement: a theory of *dispositio*', *Journal of American Culture*, 10:1 (1990), 101–2.

55 Burke, 'Four master tropes', p. 503.

56 *Ibid.*, p. 506.

57 *Ibid.*, p. 509. Emphasis added.

58 Pinckney, *Reflections*, p. 25.

59 *Ibid.*, p. 9.

60 *Ibid.*

61 *Ibid*, p. 10.

62 *Ibid.*, p. 11.

63 *Ibid.*

64 *Ibid.*, p. 24.

65 *Ibid.*, p. 27.

66 James M. Banner, 'The problem of South Carolina', in Stanley Elkins and Eric McKitrick (eds), *The Hofstadter Aegis* (New York: Knopf, 1974), pp. 60–93.

67 Pearson (ed.), *Designs Against Charleston*, p. 4.

Memory and the commemoration of the Great Irish Famine

In 1995 a cycle of commemorative activities to memorialise the Great Irish Famine of 1845–50 was initiated in Ireland, North America, Great Britain, and Australia. This transnational phenomenon owed its geographical range to the existence of an Irish diaspora that looked to the Famine for its foundation myth. While the specific forms and meanings of memorialisation varied between geographical contexts, there were some common themes: Irish and Irish-diasporic groupings sought simultane-ously to focus on the meaning of Famine memory for national or ethnic identity, and to extract formal recognition of the historical suffering associated with the event from the British and other governments. This extensive commemorative emphasis on the 1840s catastrophe was largely unprecedented; the vigour and scope of the 1990s com-memorations must be contrasted with the relative indifference that had greeted the centenary of the Famine in the 1940s. The public 'memory' articulated in recent years needs therefore to be interrogated for its contemporary motivations, its areas of con-testation, and its relationship with both historical readings and popular traditions. The key questions posed by the commemorations – why now? and why in this form? – might be regarded as paralleling Peter Novick's interrogation of contemporary American 'Holocaust consciousness'.[1]

The professional historian's role in commenting on these manifestations of 'public history' is not straightforward. Commemorative activities of this description might best be categorised as 'heritage', an arena with its own rules and perspectives fre-quently at odds with the ideals of professional historical practice. David Lowenthal suggests that heritage be regarded as a separate sphere in which the past is approached with a different agenda and focus from academic history, and recommends that his-torians leave it to its own devices.[2] Others are less confident. Eric Hobsbawm agrees that communal memory and forms of public memorialisation are inherently antithet-ical to the universalist ethos and methodological distancing he places at the heart of good historical practice, but argues that the parasitic relationship of heritage to history and the inability of historians to extract themselves from society imposes a duty of critical commentary on heritage forms.[3] In his study of Irish heritage sites, the art his-torian David Brett denies Lowenthal's duality, arguing that 'heritage' is, in effect, a contemporary mode of popular or non-specialist history, insofar as its role is that of communal self-definition through historical self-presentation. Heritage sites (in this case, museums and 'interpretative centres') must, in his view, be subjected to historical and cultural criticism to elucidate and interrogate their public meanings.[4] It follows that other sites where 'history' and 'heritage' intersect – such as the school classroom and the public monument – might equally be subjected to critical scrutiny.

This essay has two points of focus, both reflecting the preoccupations of a professional historian who is also engaged with the political contestations for which the Great Irish Famine stands as a metaphor. One focus is on the history of Famine 'memory' over the intervening century and a half; the second on the validity of the truth claims made about the Famine as part of the process of commemoration and the rhetorical forms through which these are articulated. In considering the latter, I am fully aware (as Lowenthal argues at length) that such claims serve functions far removed from the necessarily limited and conditional readings constructed by historians using critical methodology, but insofar as they also assert historical veracity and impinge on pedagogical processes, I believe heritage claims do lay themselves open to critical historical investigation.

At the same time, simply to dismiss commemorative and heritage-related appropriations of the past as subacademic myth-making is unhelpful. In a recent polemical essay, R.F. Foster gleefully exposed the commemorative excesses of 'Faminism' in 1990s Ireland, at the cost of caricaturing some elements and ignoring others less susceptible to revisionist ironising.[5] A less confrontational approach may throw some illumination both on the past and on its place in the present.

What 'memory' did the Famine leave?

The memory of the Famine has always been a misnomer. Plural 'memories', or, perhaps more accurately, memorial traditions, reflecting the differing social experiences and interpretations of the 1845–50 disaster, were evident from its immediate aftermath. British and elite non-nationalist Irish 'memories' of the Famine – an event seen from a distance but in which the middle-class public as well as the political class was acutely interested – were, from the early 1850s, concerned with rationalising and normalising the crisis. Malthusian, providential, and euphemistic claims integrated it into a narrative of progress in the mid-nineteenth century; Ireland's inevitable modernisation became the underlying interpretation of the Famine inscribed in fiction, travel literature, and economic texts.[6]

The demographic effects of the Famine – forcing 1.8 million into emigration as well as killing around a million – had a profound effect in creating divergent Irish memories of the event. For Famine survivors in Ireland itself, remembering the Famine might serve rather different social functions (and thus take different forms) than for the Irish diaspora and elite groups. Regional and class differences within Ireland further complicate the idea of a uniform national 'memory' based on shared experience. These variations in the 'mental mapping' of the Famine allow for some overlap, but embody significant divergences.

The folk or 'living' memory of the Famine remains a controversial area.

Explanations using such concepts as 'trauma' and 'shame' have been deployed to explain a perceived 'silence' in the folk tradition of Ireland itself. However, as Niall Ó Ciosáin has eloquently stated, the idea of 'silence' is problematic, and of relatively recent provenance.[7] The application of the language of psychoanalysis to national history – advocating the therapeutic and healing power of 'recovering' and 'remembering' a traumatic past – has made some inroads into Irish popular culture,[8] and has unquestionably been widely used in the language of commemoration, usually in such constructions as 'breaking the silence'. As an analytical concept, this is, however, deeply flawed, drawing on Freudian concepts that might be applicable to individual psyches but which pose profound difficulties when applied to the transgenerational imagined community of the 'nation'.[9]

Recent studies of the folklore relating to the Famine have revealed not silence, but a deeply textured and complex web of traditions that largely ignore the national narrative, while drawing together the specificities of locality and the interpretative structure of folk beliefs and practices.[10] Large amounts of folklore relating to the Famine were collected by the newly established Irish Folklore Commission (mostly from the children or grandchildren of survivors) in the late 1930s and mid-1940s. The framework of questioning was explicitly national-historic, and some collectors expressed frustration at the paucity of responses to such queries, but the thousands of pages of transcripts lodged in the archives (and left relatively untouched until recently) suggest not silence but forms of collective memory that had only a limited engagement with the romantic nationalist official ideology of the state or with literate textual constructions of the Famine.[11]

Ó Ciosáin suggests that it was the great increase in academic historical writing about the Famine, especially from the early 1980s, that gave rise to the idea of a 'silence' being broken. The role of academic production is obviously important, and will be returned to later, but there are other reasons why this theme of 'recovered memory' may have become so widespread in the Ireland of the 1990s.

Pierre Nora's theoretical perspectives on *les lieux de mémoire* are of use in constructing an explanation. Late twentieth-century Ireland presents a particularly acute case of what Nora describes as a process of 'memory sites' taking the place of the 'milieux' or 'environments' of memory typical of traditional (often peasant) communities bound together with communal traditions and 'living' memories.[12] The sheer scale and rapidity of Irish economic and social modernisation since the 1960s (accelerating markedly in the 1990s) has transformed it from a largely agrarian and emigration-dominated society on the periphery of Europe into one of the wealthiest and most dynamic economies in the EU, a country of net immigration and one facing social dislocations novel in its modern history. It is hardly coincidental that a society that has seen massive rural depopulation and rapid urbanisation should express consciousness of a loss of its traditional forms of memory (increasingly 'silent' to modern urbanites) at the same time as rushing headlong towards the creation of 'sites of memory' which are intended to capture and stabilise that disappearing past.

The same might be said, although to a lesser extent, of Irish-Americans. In the mid-nineteenth century, Irish Catholic immigrants were at the despised base of the social pyramid in the northern states, crowded into heavily, if not exclusively, Irish urban concentrations. Shared memories of 'the Famine' and 'the crossing' (actual or inherited) contributed to an emerging sense of collective ethnic solidarity, and provided the moral idea of strength through shared suffering. Yet, in the course of the twentieth century, Catholic Irish-Americans have become statistically one of the most wealthy and politically powerful ethnic groups in American society. It is possible to detect in the language of those advocating the creation of Famine memorial sites in the 1990s, including the controversial high-school 'Famine' curricula and numerous high-profile urban monuments, an anxiety about 'loss of memory' as suburbanisation and atomisation appeared to weaken this collective identity and its defining myths.[13] These sites were surely intended by their promoters, in Nora's words, 'to stop time, to block the work of forgetting, to establish a state of things, to immortalize death, to materialize the immaterial'.[14]

Another factor in the novel focus on the Great Famine as a site of commemoration has been the increased uncertainty surrounding the traditional nationalist narrative of Irish history. The place of the Famine in this narrative was established in the decades following the catastrophe, and has been the subject of considerable historical study and criticism.[15] The greatest emphasis has been placed on the writings of exiled Young Irelanders, especially John Mitchel and Charles Gavan Duffy, in moulding the nationalist 'memory' of the Famine as a crime committed by a malevolent British government against the Irish people – indeed, Mitchel's claim that 'a million and a half of men, women and children were carefully, prudently and peacefully *slain* by the English government' is one of the central tenets of the nationalist interpretation.[16] It is sometimes overlooked by critics that this 'Mitchelite' perspective had its roots in the more widespread nationalist critique of Famine policy published in the Irish newspapers in the 1840s, and that it derived its power (especially in the diaspora) from its ability to give a coherent structure of meaning to the often horrific and alienating individual experiences of survivors. Whatever the reasons for its success, its influence from the mid-nineteenth century was considerable; the narrative told a tale of a people subjected to an artificial famine at the whim of a genocidal government, the victims of a great injustice that could only be redeemed through the victory of the nationalist movement in removing British rule in Ireland.[17]

Despite the polemical power of Mitchel's writings, the Famine always played a somewhat subordinate role in the nationalist narrative in both Ireland and Irish America. While the idea of 'undoing the work of the Famine' was employed in the mobilisation of the Irish rural classes during the Land War of 1879–82, the complex conflicts of interest in the countryside, and especially the fact that many Catholic large farmers and graziers had ultimately gained from the Famine's consequences, blunted its effectiveness as a rallying point. The simple fact that the dominant images of the Famine were inherently negative was also problematic. For more militant separatists, the Famine, while a useful 'proof' of British oppression, was unhappily associated with passivity and victimhood (and thus for many with what they regarded as femininity). Fenians and their republican successors preferred to promote and memorialise heroic masculine ideals of Irish militancy drawn from the past.[18] It is thus hardly surprising that while the fiftieth anniversary of the Great Famine in the 1890s passed with little public notice, the centenary of the 1798 rising was the focus of a huge commemorative effort involving both constitutional and separatist nationalists in Ireland and Irish America.[19]

Significantly, the Famine's place in the national narrative remained almost exclusively textual – defined by the works of Mitchel and Canon John O'Rourke, and the poetry of Lady Wilde – and lacked the performative or ritual dimensions which infused other aspects of Irish nationalist expression, and in which Paul Connerton has located the core dynamic of collective memories.[20] As generations passed, individual or family traditions were transmitted orally, but the shared 'memory' of the catastrophe, comprehensible to the literate and Anglophone majorities in both Ireland and Irish America, was continually re-created by engagement with these texts and their derivatives. This points not to 'silence', but to a strongly held, narrow, and instrumentalist public 'memory', which, nevertheless, lacked the emotional resonances of other aspects of the nationalist canon as manifested in processions, pageants and public monuments.

This subordinated, even ambiguous, place of the Famine in the national narrative helps explain the low priority given to publicly commemorating its centenary in the 1940s. Eamon De Valera's government, perhaps unconsciously echoing the existing textual bias of Famine 'memory', commissioned an official volume of essays from professional historians – a troubled project whose history has been traced by Cormac Ó Gráda[21] – but the state's primary interest was in celebrating the centenary of the death of the Young Irelander and cultural nationalist hero Thomas Davis.[22] With independence achieved, and popular sovereignty incorporated into the 1937 constitution, publicly recollecting the poverty and shame of the Famine appeared less desirable than forwarding the drive to create an insular Gaelic and Catholic society in Ireland.

A number of developments in the later twentieth century – the drive for economic and social modernisation, the accession to the EEC in 1972 (and the enthusiastic pro-Europeanism in Ireland that have followed), the complex reaction to the Ulster troubles, and the ascendancy of revisionist historians hostile to nationalist 'myths' from the 1960s – have all served to undermine confidence in the Irish Republic in the previously widely accepted nationalist narrative. The contrast between the largely unreflective celebration of the fiftieth anniversary of the Easter rising in 1966 and the muted and embarrassed seventy-fifth anniversary events of 1991 is well known; the 'recovery' of long-suppressed Irish 'memories' of the First World War probably less so.[23] The 1980s and 1990s have been decades of acute introspection in Irish historical writing and cultural criticism; the past is now vigorously contested territory in both academic and public debate. Despite evidence of an anti- (or post-) revisionist resurgence in academic writing, the nationalist narrative can no longer be simply assumed and reasserted. For Irish governments in particular, an era of Europeanism and cooperation with British governments in seeking joint resolution of the Northern problem, have raised the question of the usefulness of a national myth previously centred on the themes of militant anti-Britishness and insular Gaelic and Catholic identity.

The Famine commemorations in Ireland

I want to turn now to how these ambiguities and themes have worked themselves out in the Great Famine commemorations of 1995–98. Given the sheer scale and variety of forms, this must perforce be merely an overview – I want therefore to sketch out some of the main areas of contestation and to look at a few case studies of 'sites of memory'. This survey is concerned primarily with Ireland, south and north, but is conscious that a complete picture cannot ignore comparisons with the diasporic context (especially in the United States).

The role of academic historiography in moulding the modern memory of the Famine is ambiguous. The neglect of the subject by the post-independence generations of professional historians is notorious; critics of Irish revisionism have denounced this as a deliberate repression of the catastrophic dimension of Irish history.[24] Only two major works on the subject appeared between independence and the 1980s. One, the commissioned collection edited by R.D. Edwards and T.D. Williams, while containing some useful essays, has been criticised for its cool, distant, and unengaged tone. The second, Cecil Woodham-Smith's *The Great Hunger* (1962), was dismissed by the historical establishment as amateur and populist. While deserving neither the exaggerated (and sensationalist) praise of some of its reviewers, nor the hostility of its worst critics (the book is carefully researched, if weak on economics and ideology), *The Great Hunger* had an unparalleled public impact. Never out of print since 1962, it is estimated to have sold more copies than any other work of Irish history. Woodham-Smith's graphic accounts of famine sufferings and careful indictment of administrators and ministers (although she avoids the Mitchelite charge of genocide) have probably done more to remould the 'memory' of the Famine on the part of the Irish reading public over the last four decades than any other source.[25] Indeed, one Irish minister took the trouble to praise it as an 'unvarnished overview' of the Famine in a 1997 statement.[26]

A more general revival of historical writing on the Famine began in the early 1980s. The key text was the American historian Joel Mokyr's *Why Ireland Starved* – an econometric study of the Irish economy in the pre-Famine decades that undermined the paradigm of Malthusian inevitability and stressed the contingency (and the role of human agency) in the catastrophe. Subsequent research in economic history, especially by Cormac Ó Gráda, has taken this theme further, and stimulated historians of emigration, administration, and politics to look again at the crisis. The outpouring of academic writing in the 1990s has been broadly post-revisionist in thrust (and thus to some degree at odds with what is still the dominant tone in Irish historiography). The broader impact of this is difficult to gauge, but the demand for more popular texts informed by this academic revival has demonstrated tremendous interest in the wider public.[27] The broadcasters RTÉ, the BBC, and in America PBS have all broadcast commemorative documentary series drawing on the work of this generation of scholars. At the same time, there has been an explosion of often high-quality local studies by amateur historians and local groups conscious of the recent developments in academic writing.

This academic revival has had some impact on stimulating public consciousness of the Great Famine, but by its very nature it has failed to satisfy some of the very demands thus created. Historians tend to render the narrative of the Famine into complex and sometimes contradictory forms, muddying in the process the simple political and moral message of the nationalist tradition; their conclusions are self-consciously conditional and tentative and hence unsatisfactory for those requiring certain and transcendent 'truths' about the past. Their evidence is fragmentary and often opaque. Individual experience is, at best, caught only in glimpses circumscribed by language and the perspectives of privileged witnesses. Frustration at these limitations in the broader public can produce some interesting phenomena.

One of the oddest affairs in the lead up to the Famine commemorations was the extraordinary publishing success of *Famine Diary: Journey to a New World*. Published in Dublin in 1991, this text purported to be the edited diary of Gerald Keegan, a Sligo schoolteacher who fled the Famine, only to die at the quarantine station of Grosse Île near Quebec in 1847. The book topped the Irish best-seller lists for months, was promoted in the media and by the Irish non-governmental organisations (NGOs), but was exposed in 1992 as a further fictive (indeed Mitchelite) rewriting of a short story in diary form published anonymously by the Canadian writer Robert Sellar in 1895.[28] It remains unclear whether the editor or the Irish publisher was responsible for the impostures implicit in the 1991 edition, but it reveals much about the continuing public demand for unmediated narrative 'voices' of the Famine that can satisfy the need to 'remember' without intellectual complications.[29] It is not unique in this respect. Hans Medick has described how a similarly fictive 'hunger chronicle' relating to the Württemberg famine of 1816–17 became a popular *lieu de mémoire* in south Germany from the 1920s and was incorporated into other commemorative forms.[30]

The commemorative fixation of Ireland in the 1990s might be seen more broadly as a consequence of a reinvention or reconstruction of Irish identity in reaction to the questioning of the traditional nationalist narrative. This can be seen operating at a number of levels in politics, culture, and civil society – reflecting attempts to combine secularising and internationalising (or globalising) trends with the reassertion of a distinct Irish national heritage and moral perspective on the world. This self-presentation drew on some established images (the ideal of Ireland as a neutral 'moral' voice in world affairs can be traced to De Valera's rhetoric in the 1930s; Irish charitable self-images were rooted in attitudes towards missionary activities dating from the nineteenth century), but the emphasis was novel, and the memorial centrality of the Famine emerged as crucial.

The self-image of Ireland playing a characteristically leading role in the international politics of hunger came to prominence in the 1980s. The idea that the Irish had a distinct ability and responsibility to mediate between the rich North and poor South, and that this derived from its own history of colonisation and catastrophe, was increasingly promoted in the decade. The prominence of Irish popular musicians (especially Bob Geldof and U2) in organising and promoting the Live Aid campaign for famine relief and development from 1984, and their continuing role in the debt-relief campaign, Jubilee 2000, appeared to signal the emergence of a new radical urban sense of 'Irishness' that ignored older nationalist pieties. Despite low levels of state overseas aid, the Irish contributed more per capita to such appeals than other European peoples – a cause for some self-congratulation, and, some would warn, a degree of national narcissism. A growing tendency by the 1990s to categorise Ireland (uniquely in Europe) as itself a post-colonial society, while drawing the fury of some academic commentators, added to this sense of redefinition.[31]

This case was enthusiastically taken up by the more radical Irish overseas-development NGOs, especially Concern and AFrI (Action from Ireland). In 1984, AFrI initiated its 'Great "Famine" Project' with the explicit intention of mobilising the 'memory' of the Irish Famine for contemporary charitable and campaigning purposes. Its objectives were to ensure that the 150th anniversary of Ireland's Great 'Famine' was commemorated in a dignified and challenging way, both nationally and internationally; publicly to honour Ireland's several hundred unmarked mass 'Famine' graves with dignity and reverence; and thirdly, to harness the memory of Ireland's Great 'Famine' experience as a window through which the Irish (at home and abroad) could better understand the cause and effect of poverty and hunger on the world's poor today – and to encourage an appropriate response.[32] Concern took on the responsibility of coordinating and publicising the commemorations of 1995–97 and lobbying the state and other official bodies for cooperation.

Both charities have been extremely active in pursuing their objectives in the 1990s, and were first into the field in the creation of monuments and the organisation of events explicitly internationalising the memory of famine (not least by the participation of representatives of oppressed social and ethnic groups as speakers). AFrI's annual 'famine walk' at Doolough in County Mayo (begun in 1988 and later emulated in other localities) has taken on the form of a ritual of re-enactment, memorialising those who died on a vain journey to seek aid from relief officials in March 1849, while at the same time raising consciousness of contemporary injustices.[33] The language employed during many of the local commemorations from 1995 onwards suggests some considerable success on the part of the NGOs in reconstructing the meaning of the Famine and displacing (or at least subsuming) traditional nationalist readings.[34]

It would be churlish to criticise the work of the NGOs in raising consciousness about global injustice and poverty. At a political level, one can only applaud their success in externalising and giving an active meaning to Famine commemoration, particularly in the context of a society that is itself now firmly in the leading group of First World economies. There are, however, problems thrown up by this explicit appropriation of Famine memory for contemporary causes. While praising the NGOs for their efforts, Cormac Ó Gráda has questioned the widespread assumption of an unmediated 'collective memory' of famine as a motivating force in modern commemorations, and has undermined the case for simplistic analogies between the Irish and contemporary world famines.[35]

Don Mullan of Concern responded by arguing that academic historians have no more 'ownership' over the Famine than had the NGOs, a point which might be irrefutable were it not for the fact (to which we will return) that some NGOs have themselves asserted superior ownership claims vis-à-vis both historians and other NGOs.[36] The dispute remains unresolved, but has left its mark in the commemorative record. AFrI in particular has made a point of always problematising the word 'Famine' in its publications and memorials, denying (wrongly, in my opinion) its validity to the Irish crisis of 1845–50. Examples of this and the internationalising agenda can be seen in two AFrI-sponsored memorials erected in 1994. The Doolough memorial (an unfinished stone Celtic cross by the roadside) combines the visual languages of the sublime and the picturesque in form and setting; the Swinford workhouse cemetery memorial is more prosaic, but both carry highly instrumentalist text – the first also memorialising the striking Dunnes Stores workers who unveiled it; the second making explicit connections between anti-imperialist struggle in Ireland and India, and stressing the 'so-called' character of Ireland's 'Famine'.

The politics of naming are important here – it is not accidental that alternatives such as 'The Great Hunger', or 'The Great Starvation', or the Irish form *An Gorta Mór* have frequently been preferred. To question or deny the word 'Famine' is regarded by many as rejecting the inevitability or unavoidability of the catastrophe. This is an area where the traditional Mitchelite line that the Famine was a willed and artificial act of policy intersects uneasily with the radical-globalist case (informed by a popularised and universalised version of Amartya Sen's entitlement theory of famine causation) that all modern famines are the artificial consequences of market systems and unequal economic relationships.[37] Such globalising rhetoric leaves little room for examination of the historical specificities of the Irish case – perhaps legitimate in the polemical enthusiasm of humanitarian campaigning, but problematic with respect to a memorialisation process in which making justifiable truth-claims about the past is seen as essential.

Significant Famine commemorations might have remained restricted to parts of Irish civil society had it not been for an unexpected political development at the beginning of the decade. In 1990, Mary Robinson, a veteran campaigner for women's rights and civil liberties, was elected President as an independent (but decidedly left-wing) candidate. From early in her term of office, she grasped the contemporary importance of Famine commemoration in ways parallel to the NGOs, enthusiastically undertaking the role of patron of the proposed Famine Museum in 1991 at an early point in its gestation and encouraging the work of local historical groups.[38] The President's commitment to connecting the Irish Famine to contemporary famines was solidified by her unprecedented and deeply emotional visits to Somalia in the midst of the 1992 famine and to Rwanda in the wake of the 1994 massacres and threatened famine.[39] The Irish President's executive powers are strictly circumscribed, but Robinson seized the opportunity to exploit her office to set a number of agendas – one of which was an active and high-profile commemoration of the Famine and the internationalisation of its meaning. In a number of major speeches between her visit to Grosse Île in Canada in 1994 (itself suggested by AFrI as part of wider struggle to determine the meaning of that contentious site) and her retirement in 1997, she did her utmost to urge the use of the process of remembrance 'to connect us with the terrible realities of our current world'.[40] To an outsider, this rhetoric might be mistaken for a self-regarding (even maudlin) assertion of ethnic 'mission', but it needs to be interpreted in the context of an increasingly savagely fought battle within the Irish political world over such issues as the rights of asylum seekers and immigrants, the overseas aid budget, and the social exclusion of those marginalised by the 'Celtic tiger' economy of the 1990s. This construction of the 'memory of famine' has become a potent political weapon in Irish political culture – a discursive construction with a grammar only partially cognate with that of academic history.[41]

There is little doubt that the enthusiastic leadership provided by President Robinson helped provide the political climate in which otherwise hesitant Irish governments accepted the need for official acts of commemoration. Much of what the Irish government eventually adopted as its commemoration programme was the outcome of lobbying by the NGOs in 1993–94. When an intergovernmental committee on the commemoration was established under Minister of State Tom Kitt in 1994 (succeeded after the change of government of that year by Avril Doyle), AFrI and other civil society groups, such as the Tullamore-based Great Famine Commemoration Committee, were invited to contribute at national and local level.[42]

The government's official commemorative publication, setting out the policy initiatives for 1995–97, thus did so explicitly in terms of internationalising and instrumentalising the memory of the Famine. Entitled *Ireland's Famine: Commemoration and Awareness*, it was produced in cooperation with the European Community Humanitarian Office and included surveys of Irish and European overseas development objectives alongside essays by historians. Meeting AFrI's demands in part, the government pledged additional expenditure on specific projects, including support for the Ethiopian government's national disaster prevention and preparedness project, a potato and maize seed improvement project in Eritrea, and a water supply project in Lesotho. In Ireland itself, a national memorial would be erected (John Behan's massive *Coffin Ship* bronze would eventually be unveiled at Murrisk in County Mayo in July 1997), and assistance would be provided to commemorative services, concerts, and exhibitions. Absent from the NGO wish-list, but significant to the government, was the expenditure of £115,000 on a historical research project into the local impact of the Famine led by a team of prominent Dublin-based historians. For ministers at least, suitable remembrance required some underpinning from professional historiography.[43]

The government's announcements did not save it from harsh criticism. The Fine Gael–Labour coalition in power from 1994 was attacked for downplaying and delaying the commemorations out of fear of their potentially negative impact on Anglo-Irish relations and concern that the issue could only add to Unionist–nationalist polarisation in Northern Ireland. This was rejected by the minister concerned, who pointed out that many of the events were scheduled for the 150th anniversary of the nadir of the Famine in 1997, but there is little doubt that the calls made for a British 'apology' by both Mary Robinson and the opposition leader Bertie Ahern were found politically embarrassing.[44] It was not until Prime Minister Tony Blair made his unexpected and inspired (if not uncontroversial) statement on historic British responsibility in June 1997 that this political problem was largely resolved.[45]

The occasion for Blair's statement, read alongside addresses by other world leaders during the 'Great Famine Event' at Millstreet, County Cork, itself reveals some of the contentions and uncertainties surrounding the public commemoration of catastrophe. The Millstreet 'Event' will be the first of four Irish case studies in which I will try to flesh these out. The 'Event' was organised collectively by the Great Irish Famine Trust and two Irish NGOs, the Big Issues Social Initiative (working to alleviate homelessness and social exclusion in Ireland) and GORTA (an overseas development charity), but also received financial and political support from the Irish and American governments. The prominence of Mary Robinson was intended to add gravitas – the lighting of a 'candle of remembrance' (echoed through a live video link in Washington, London, and other capitals) was to be the symbolic centre of the proceedings.

The central problem for the 'Event' was its yoking together of two contradictory agendas and their associated languages. The first was the secular ceremony of commemoration – a moment in which the nation and its diaspora would be united in solemnly remembering 'their' Famine dead. The second was a Live Aid style concert that would simultaneously raise money for the charitable organisations and serve (in the unfortunate words of its promoters) as a celebration of the triumph of the 'Irish spirit' over the adversities of Famine and diasporic dispersal. The latter would also, in a particularly unfortunate claim, act as a 'great wake' which would essentially 'bury the ghost' of the Famine. However laudable its intentions, the 'Event' was poorly conceived, and its image was worsened by a rather crass (and not hugely successful) advertising campaign to attract Irish-Americans.[46] Whether it deserved the extremity of reaction from some commentators is another matter. To Joe Murray of AFrI, the Event was 'dancing on the graves of the Famine dead'; to the columnist John Waters, it was evidence of both a depoliticising conspiracy on the part of the government and 'the ultimate betrayal of our sacred history'.[47] The Event was to some degree inadvertently rescued from its critics by the significance of Blair's 'apology' statement, but the controversy over precisely what was being commemorated, the tone in which this should be done, and the limits of instrumentalising memory for contemporary purposes was inflamed. Central to the problem were the difficulties a rapidly secularising (even post-Catholic) society faced in finding a novel language and ritual that would sacralise the memory of the imagined community's dead, while retaining the momentum of the rediscovered moral mission associated with that memory.

An almost identical row blew up in 1998 surrounding the new Dublin Famine monument – Rowan Gillespie's group of seven bronze emaciated figures staggering down Custom House Quay towards the docks and the emigrant ship. Controversy surrounds not the figures themselves, but the broader form and function of the memorial. The memorial was commissioned by the Irish Famine Commemoration Fund, chaired by Norma Smurfit, wife of one of Ireland's wealthiest businessmen and incidentally also chair of the trust responsible for the Millstreet Event. The Dublin memorial was to serve a similar instrumental purpose – the fund would be channelled to charities serving the 'homeless, unemployed and disadvantaged youth of Ireland', and donors contributing over £750 would have their (and their families) names engraved on bronze plaques set into the pavement below the figures. Corporate sponsors would have their names listed nearby. The sculptor described this 'sea of names', through which he intended to represent the continuity of Ireland and its diaspora, as an integral part of his work, although a sceptic might suspect such personal memorialisation of the donor owes less to aesthetic inspiration than to the handbook of professional fund-raisers. Despite the endorsement of the new President Mary McAleese and such Irish dignitaries as Gerry Adams and Jack Charlton, the reaction from AFrI and columnists such as Fintan O'Toole was a predictably savage attack on the affluent of today being encouraged to flaunt their wealth and power on an apparent memorial to the victims of inequality and injustice.[48] This fracas clearly illuminated the limitations of any national 'collective memory', and had the (beneficial) effect of foregrounding questions of class in both the politics of commemoration and the history of the Famine itself.

The range of local commemorations in Ireland is too large to be covered here. Generally speaking, the most successful have been those which have integrated the general history of the Famine into local histories, often focusing on local sites and attempting some reconnection between the local folklore traditions and historical research. Art critics might cavil at the conservatism of the representative forms adopted, but it is unquestionable that these have acquired meaning in their local contexts. A good example is the 1995 memorial facing the site of Ennistymon workhouse in County Clare, which juxtaposes the text of a particularly poignant incident from the Poor Law Union records with a figurative representation of the incident.[49] Other monuments have been erected in collaboration with local authorities, with local historical societies, and, in the case of Kilglass, County Roscommon, at the cemetery site associated with the pioneering Famine-period archaeological dig led by Professor Charles Orser.[50] A bronze plaque depicting an impoverished family by the sculptor Michael Killen was commissioned by the local Historical Society of Cappaghmore, County Limerick, which lost nearly half its population during the Famine. Its unveiling was accompanied by calls for greater attention to 'Third World' hunger.[51]

Local memorialisation in the Republic has largely avoided the controversies attached to some of the national events. One significant exception was an illegally erected monument commissioned by a private donor in Killala, County Mayo, which was rapidly removed after the County and Community councils expressed unhappiness over a text reading: 'The Irish Holocaust. Within here are the graves of victims of the Famine 1846–1849 caused by an uncaring, alien Government. We salute their memory.'[52] The suppression of this explicitly Mitchelite statement attracted the attention of the New York-based Irish Famine/Genocide Committee ('our mission: to promote the truth'), which protested and raised funds for the memorial.[53] The very unusualness of this sort of construction and confrontation in the Republic (in contrast to Irish America) draws attention to the divergences in commemorative emphasis (and function) between the 'domestic' and 'diasporic' contexts. This is not to say that traditionalist readings have disappeared in Ireland – as is clear from some of the more unreconstructed (and, to this historian, deeply frustrating) statements made in the 1997 Irish Senate debate on Famine commemoration – but that these have tended to become increasingly marginalised or sublimated by newer (but not necessarily much more accurate) appropriations of Famine history.[54]

A contrast needs, of course, to be drawn between the Republic and Northern Ireland, where traditionalist nationalist ideology remains much more relevant to republicans. Yet, even here, the coincidence of the first IRA ceasefire in 1994 (and reconsiderations demanded by the 'peace process') and the Famine anniversary produced some shifts in emphasis. The year 1995 saw nationalist mural painters for the first time extend their repertoire to the previously neglected historical subject of the Famine. Several were produced under the auspices of *Féile an Phobail,* the West Belfast Community Festival (and, ironically, partly financed by the Northern Ireland Arts Council). The images are a combination of the original and the received – especially in the use of the December 1849 *Illustrated London News* engraving of Bridget O'Donnell and her children, unnamed here (as in most of the multiple recent uses of this image) and serving as an icon of a famished 'mother Ireland'.[55] The texts, a paraphrase of Mitchel's central argument that the Famine was caused by forced food exports, and an extract from Lady Wilde's well-known poem 'The Famine Year', are examples of the mobilisation of the past for contemporary political use. Not surprisingly, in 1997, the republican paper *An Phoblacht* ran a long series of articles on the Famine under the general title 'The Irish holocaust'.[56] Equally unsurprisingly, leading Unionists rejected the Famine commemorations as alien to their historical tradition.

This polarisation over memory in the north was not, however, as extreme as it at first appeared.[57] Local commemorations of Famine-related sites and library and museum displays were occurring on a non-sectarian basis.[58] Sinn Féin's 1996 motion for a commemorative window in the City Hall to recall the thousands of famine migrants who died in Belfast in 1846–48 may have been lauded in the republican press as a nationalist initiative, and received the expected furious denunciation from Paisleyite Unionist councillors,[59] but was accepted by a broad cross-community majority of members after its historical justification was upheld by the non-aligned and respected historian Jonathan Bardon.[60] A public competition was held in 1998 and the memorial window unveiled on 23 March 1999: it combines a collage of images drawn from the *Illustrated London News* with a view of the Belfast poorhouse, thereby locating iconic representations of the catastrophe within a recognisable local context.

Recent developments have suggested a further appropriation of the Famine as shared history in the North, although this is by no means universal. David Ervine, the leader of the loyalist PUP party, visited Tralee in 1999 to inspect work on one of the longest-running Famine memorial projects, the reconstructed immigrant ship *Jeanie Johnston*. Whatever the commemorative value of the ship (which one might suspect has more to do with heritage spectacle), the political symbolism of bringing equal numbers of trainee shipwrights from north and south together on the government-supported project is clearly present-centred.[61] Showing similar independence of mind, Ervine's colleague Billy Hutchinson attended the Irish Famine/Genocide Committee's 1997 conference in New York to speak on the effect of the Famine on Ulster Protestant communities.[62] This shifting attitude was given a public artistic form in 2000 when the Ballymacarrett Arts and Cultural Society created a new mural in that solidly Protestant part of inner-city Belfast integrating the Famine into a chronological narrative running from St Patrick through the *Titanic* to modern Northern Ireland.[63]

One final case study deserves some mention. The history of the Irish Famine Museum at Strokestown Park House in Roscommon is well known – launched from a private initiative in the late 1980s (again with some input from Irish aid agencies) and promoted by Mary Robinson from 1991, its success was due overwhelmingly to the vision of its founder-curator Luke Dodd, who combined a deep sensitivity to locality with transatlantic museological skills. Opened by the President in 1994 in what was itself one of the first acts of public commemoration, the Museum may prove to be the most long-lasting of the many projects of the decade. Rejecting the 'celebration of victimhood', he identifies with the Washington, DC, Holocaust Museum, and dismissing the idea that Strokestown should serve as some kind of 'memorial to genocide' (a construction he disputes), Dodd has sought to convey the complexity of the factors that create famine and to relate these to the contested interpretations of Irish history.[64] Although criticised by one historian for giving insufficient voice to the victims alongside its interrogation of the voice and gaze of the powerful,[65] the museum has won plaudits from most commentators. In his otherwise savage attack on the ideological underpinnings of recent Irish heritage sites, David Brett has singled out Strokestown as a model of self-critical, emancipatory, and ethically challenging practice in a genre otherwise given over to spectacle or heavy-handed didacticism.[66] I find it hard to disagree. It is in the Famine Museum that commemoration, heritage, and the agenda of post-revisionist historical writing come together most satisfactorily.

By way of conclusion, I want to draw some tentative comparisons with the Irish-American experience of Famine commemoration. Although there have been some significant elements of overlap (not least those provided by Mary Robinson on her peregrinations), the balance has been decidedly different. Rather than seeking to construct a new identity out of Famine memory, Irish America has in general sought to revive a faltering ethnic tradition and inscribe its myth in the official record of American public life. In place of the cautious reassessments associated with the Irish events, the United States has seen public campaigns for the full reassertion of the Mitchelite myth of genocide, and a politically effective drive to have this taught in the nation's high schools alongside the Holocaust and the Middle Passage as comparative genocide or human rights studies.[67] After a process of critique from leading Irish-American historians (and others), two divergent models have now emerged – the New York curriculum, which has incorporated the reservations and insights derived from academic research, and the New Jersey model (adopted by at least five other states), which marginalises this in its undeviating pursuit of 'proof' of British genocide.[68]

To understand why the Famine has been so important to Irish America, and why, now, we need to juxtapose the gradual attenuation of its collective identity with a broader cultural climate that promotes ethnic accentuation and competition. The parallels with Jewish-American reappropriations of 'Holocaust consciousness' are more than striking, and it is difficult not to detect a similar enthusiasm for what

Novick describes as the 'sordid game' of seeking to 'wring an acknowledgment of superior victimisation from another contender'.[69] The negative consequences of this extreme instrumentalist agenda for historical research are obvious, but its political implications are equally disturbing. One leading African-American commentator has warned promoters of the Famine curriculum to be careful what they ask for: 'History is not an exercise in feel-good ethnic cheerleading. It is a cold-hearted examination of this nation's many people at their worst, as well as at their best. The study of the Irish, like any other groups, is going to reopen old wounds on all sides that, for many, have not quite healed.'[70]

This subject leads me back to my point of departure. In Ireland, historical writing on the Famine has both informed and served as a critical mirror to the process of commemoration. At the same time, historians have, I hope, been disabused of the idea that they have some sort of exclusive 'ownership' over the past, while those mobilising images of the Famine for contemporary purposes have been made aware that there are limitations to what can be justified from the evidence available. The Famine commemorations have seen, for the most part, a constructive interchange for those concerned, even if a number of points of friction have not been resolved.[71]

Notes

1 Peter Novick, *The Holocaust and Collective Memory: The American Experience* (London: Bloomsbury, 2000), pp. 1–2.

2 David Lowenthal, *The Heritage Crusade and the Spoils of History* (Cambridge: Cambridge University Press, 1998).

3 Eric J. Hobsbawm, 'The Historian between the quest for the universal and the quest for identity', in François Bédarida (ed.), *The Social Responsibility of the Historian* (Oxford: Berghahn, 1994), pp. 51–64.

4 David Brett, *The Construction of Heritage* (Cork: Cork University Press, 1996), pp. 1–6.

5 R.F. Foster, 'Theme-parks and histories', in *The Irish Story: Telling Tales and Making It Up in Ireland* (London: Allen Lane, 2001), pp. 23–36.

6 For the formation of non-nationalist Irish 'memory', see Peter Gray, 'The making of mid-Victorian Ireland? Political economy and the memory of the Great Famine', in Peter Gray (ed.), *Victoria's Ireland? Irishness and Britishness, 1837–1901* (forthcoming, Dublin: Four Courts Press, 2004); for the modernisation narrative in British writing on Ireland, see Christopher Morash, *Writing the Irish Famine* (Oxford: Oxford University Press, 1995), pp. 11–51.

7 Niall Ó Ciosáin, 'Was there "silence" about the Famine?', *Irish Studies Review,* 13 (1995), 7–10.

8 Sinead O'Connor's song 'Famine' on the 1994 *Universal Mother* album exemplifies the popular use of this idea. For her belief that 'That's the time we lost the memory of what we were before these things happened', see interview in *Irish Times* (28 January 1995).

9 For a recent discussion of the language of trauma in Famine commemoration, see Margaret Kelleher, 'Hunger and history: monuments to the Great Irish Famine', in *Textual Practice,* 16:2 (2002), 249–76.

10 See Cathal Póirtéir, 'Folk memory and the Famine', in Cathal Póirtéir (ed.), *The Great Irish Famine* (Cork: Mercier Press, 1995), pp. 219–31; Cormac Ó Gráda, *Black '47 and Beyond:*

The Great Irish Famine in History, Economy and Memory (Princeton NJ: Princeton University Press, 1999), pp. 194–225; and Cathal Póirtéir (ed.), *Famine Echoes* (Dublin: Gill and Macmillan, 1995).

11 Niall Ó Ciosáin, 'Famine memory and the popular representation of scarcity', in Ian McBride (ed.), *History and Memory in Modern Ireland* (Cambridge: Cambridge University Press, 2001), pp. 95–117.

12 Pierre Nora, 'Between memory and history: *Les lieux de mémoire*', *Representations*, 26 (1989), 7–25.

13 See Morton D. Winsberg, 'The suburbanization of the Irish in Boston, Chicago and New York', *Éire-Ireland*, 21 (1986), 90–104. For anxiety about the loss of the communal memories underpinning ethnic identity, see 'Ethnic clichés evoke anger in Irish eyes', *New York Times* (12 March 1995); 'An ocean away, the mark of tragedy remains', *Boston Globe* (24 August 1997).

14 Nora, 'Between memory and history', p. 19.

15 Patrick O'Farrell, 'Whose reality? The Irish Famine in history and literature', *Historical Studies*, 20 (1982–83), 1–13; James S. Donnelly, 'The construction of the memory of the Famine in Ireland and the Irish Diaspora, 1850–1900', *Éire-Ireland*, 31 (1996), 26–61.

16 John Mitchel, *The Last Conquest of Ireland (Perhaps)* (London: Burns, Oates and Washbourne, n.d.), p. 219.

17 On Mitchel, see Morash, *Writing the Irish Famine*, pp. 52–75; for the role of Famine-era nationalist poetry in shaping its textual memory, see Christopher Morash, 'Introduction', in C. Morash (ed.), *The Hungry Voice: The Poetry of the Irish Famine* (Blackrock: Irish Academic Press, 1989), pp. 15–37.

18 The heroic model of memorialisation can be seen in the cult of the Manchester Martyrs; see Gary Owens, 'Constructing the martyrs: the Manchester executions and the nationalist imagination', in Lawrence W. McBride (ed.), *Images, Icons and the Irish Nationalist Imagination* (Dublin: Four Courts Press, 1999), pp. 18–36.

19 Timothy J. O'Keefe, 'The 1898 efforts to celebrate the United Irishmen: the '98 Centennial', *Éire-Ireland*, 23 (1988), 51–73.

20 Paul Connerton, *How Societies Remember* (Cambridge: Cambridge University Press, 1989).

21 Cormac Ó Gráda, 'Making history in Ireland in the 1940s and 1950s: the saga of *The Great Famine*', *Irish Review*, 12 (1992), 87–107.

22 Judith Hill, *Irish Public Sculpture: A History* (Dublin: Four Courts Press, 1998), p. 157.

23 This uncertainty is reflected in the agonistic essays collected in Máirín Ní Dhonnchadh and Theo Dorgan (eds), *Revising the Rising* (Derry: Field Day, 1991); see also Keith Jeffery, 'The Great War in modern Irish memory', in T.G. Fraser and Keith Jeffery (eds), *Men, Women and War* (Dublin: Lilliput Press, 1993).

24 Brendan Bradshaw, 'Nationalism and historical scholarship in modern Ireland', *Irish Historical Studies*, 26 (1989), 329–51.

25 R. Dudley Edwards and T. Desmond Williams (eds), *The Great Famine: Studies in Irish History 1845–52* (Dublin: Browne and Nolan, 1956); Cecil Woodham-Smith, *The Great Hunger: Ireland 1845–1849* (London: Hamilton, 1962). For recent reassessments of these texts, see Cormac Ó Gráda, *Ireland Before and After the Famine* (Manchester: Manchester University Press 1988), pp. 78–82; James S. Donnelly, 'The Great Famine and its interpreters, old and new', *History Ireland*, 1:3 (1993), 27–33. The academic hostility towards Woodham-Smith owes something to A.J.P. Taylor's provocative review likening Famine Ireland to Belsen in 1945; 'Genocide', in A.J.P. Taylor, *Essays in English History* (Harmondsworth: Penguin, 1976), pp. 73–9.

26 David Andrews, Statement on the 150th Anniversary of the Famine, *Seanad Debates – Official Report*, 27 November 1997.

27 See, for example, Helen Litton, *The Irish Famine: An Illustrated History* (Dublin: Wolfhound Press, 1994); Peter Gray, *The Irish Famine* (London: Thames and Hudson, 1995); Christine Kinealy, *'A Death-Dealing Famine': The Great Hunger in Ireland* (London: Pluto Press, 1997).

28 Jim Jackson, 'Famine Diary – the making of a best Sellar', *Irish Review*, 11 (1991/92), 1–8.

29 A subsequent reissue acknowledged the role of the editor in 'fictionalising' the original edition, but continued to claim it was based on an authentic document and that 'cumulative sum stylometry' analysis had proven Sellar was not the author; James J. Mangan (ed.), *Gerald Keegan's Famine Diary: Journey to a New World* (Dublin: Wolfhound Press, 1999), pp. 6, 12.

30 Hans Medick, 'The so-called Laichingen Hunger Chronicle: an example of the fiction of the factual, the traps of evidence, and the possibilities of proof in the writing of history', in Gerald Sider and Gavin Smith (eds), *Between History and Histories: The Making of Silences and Commemorations* (Toronto: University of Toronto Press, 1997), pp. 284–99.

31 Liam Kennedy, 'Modern Ireland: post-colonial society or post-colonial pretensions?', *Irish Review*, 13 (1992/93), 107–21; Therese Caherty (ed.), *Is Ireland a Third World Country?* (Belfast: Beyond the Pale, 1992).

32 Don Mullan (ed.), *'A Glimmer of Light': An Overview of Great Hunger Commemorative Events in Ireland and Throughout the World* (Dublin: Concern, 1995), pp. 32–4.

33 For AFrI's version of the historical events at Doolough and the Mahatma Gandhi-related theme of the 1994 march, see [AFrI], *A Road to Remember* (n.p., n.d. [Dublin, 1994]).

34 See, for example, the stress on global hunger in the special 'Famine' issue of the Achill Island community magazine *Muintir Acla*, 3 (1996), and the survey produced jointly by Meath County Council and AFrI; Danny Cusack, *The Great Famine in County Meath: A 150th Anniversary Commemoration (1845–1995)* (Navan: Meath County Council, 1996).

35 Cormac Ó Gráda, 'The Great Famine and today's famines', in Póirtéir (ed.), *Great Irish Famine*, pp. 248–58; Cormac Ó Gráda, 'Satisfying a great hunger for guilt and self-pity', *Sunday Tribune* (15 May 1994).

36 Don Mullan, 'The Great "Famine" project', *Peacemaker: AFrI Newsletter* (Summer 1994), pp. 4–5. For AFrI's role in publishing 'popular' histories of the Famine, see Mangan (ed.), *Famine Diary*, pp. 1, 12; John O'Rourke, *The Great Irish Famine* (abridged edn with introduction by Don Mullan, Dublin: Veritas, 1989).

37 See Amartya Sen, *Poverty and Famines: An Essay on Entitlement and Deprivation* (Oxford: Oxford University Press, 1981).

38 Interview with Luke Dodd in Tom Hayden (ed.), *Irish Hunger: Personal Reflections on the Legacy of the Famine* (Dublin: Wolfhound, 1997), pp. 50–1; Frances Madigan, 'President Robinson's visit to Ennistymon' (January 1992), www.clarelibrary.ie/eolas/coclare/history/exhibition_mary_robinson.htm (accessed March 2000).

39 John Horgan, *Mary Robinson: An Independent Voice* (Dublin: O'Brien Press, 1997), pp. 188–9.

40 'Address by the President of Ireland Mary Robinson, Grosse Île, 21 August 1994', in Mullan (ed.), *Glimmer of Light*, pp. 9–13. For the controversy over the development of Grosse Île as a national park, see '"It is hallowed ground": Canada honors victims of Irish Famine' (*Boston Globe*, 2 June 1996).

41 See, for example, Maire Nic Suibhne, 'Fortress Ireland', *Guardian* (3 October 1998).

42 Mullan (ed.), *Glimmer of Light*, pp. 33–4, 45–7.

43 [Famine Commemoration Committee], *Ireland's Famine: Commemoration and Awareness* (Dublin: Government of Ireland, n.d.). For historians' lobbying, see 'Correct approach is vital', *Irish Times* (12 October 1994).

44 'Doyle denies Government caution on remembering the Famine', *Irish Times* (28 June 1995); 'President wants both governments to show shared regret for Great Famine', *Irish Times* (27 October 1995); Letter by Bertie Ahern, *Irish Times* (6 June 1997).

45 Blair's statement, acknowledging that 'those who governed in London at the time failed their people through standing by while a crop failure turned into a massive human tragedy', might be critiqued as a historical understatement, but was widely attacked by conservative commentators in both the UK and Ireland. For the case that the British ministry of 1846–52 may be held responsible for sins of commission as well as omission, but not for intentional genocide, see Peter Gray, 'Ideology and the Famine', in Póirtéir (ed.), *Great Irish Famine*, pp. 86–103.

46 'President's star turn at Famine concert', *Irish Times* (2 June 1997). The overseas marketing director of the 'Event' had previously run the '50th anniversary of D-Day' campaign for the British Tourist Authority in North America; see *Great Irish Famine Event Press Pack: Personnel Profiles.*

47 'Famine dead are offered at the altar of tourism', *Irish Times* (27 May 1997).

48 *Irish Famine Commemoration Fund Press Release* (1998); 'The great and the good join Famine roll-call', *Irish Times* (28 October 1998); 'Turning the Famine into corporate celebration', *ibid.* (16 October 1998); 'Famine initiative seen as offensive', *ibid.* (30 October 1998).

49 This memorial was jointly funded by Clare County Council and the Ancient Order of Hibernians.

50 'Professor Orser and former Taoiseach unveil famine memorial', *Roscommon Herald* (11 August 1999). For examples of local initiatives, see the report on Eamonn O'Doherty's memorial at Enniskillen in *CIRCA*, 78 (1998), 8; Greg Fewer, 'Is there a dearth in our Famine heritage? Conserving the fabric of Waterford city's Famine experience', www.infohwy.com/~gfewer/wfdfamin.htm (accessed March 2000).

51 'Plaque commemorates Famine in Cappaghmore', *Irish Times* (13 October 1997).

52 'Killala's moving memorial', *Connaught Telegraph* (26 February 1997).

53 Irish Famine Genocide Committee website, www.webcom/famine/mission.htm (accessed March 2000).

54 '150th Commemoration of the Famine: Statements', *Seanad Debates – Official Report*, 27 November 1997. The contrast between traditionalist backbench speakers' fondness for the phrase 'Irish holocaust' and the more 'internationalist' official statements of Foreign Minister David Andrews and Avril Doyle are striking; both tied Famine commemoration explicitly to Ireland's contribution to relieving famine in North Korea.

55 Bill Rolston, *Drawing Support 2: Murals of War and Peace* (Belfast: Beyond the Pale, 1995), pp. viii, 57–8; Belfast City Council Arts and Tourism Subcommittee, minutes, 6 June 1995. For the political controversy over more such murals, see Belfast City Council, minutes, 7 May 1997.

56 Aengus Ó Snodaigh, 'The Irish holocaust – An droch shaol', *An Phoblacht/Republican News* (10 July–2 October 1997).

57 For the renewed interest in the history of the Famine in Ulster, see, for example, Christine Kinealy and Gerard MacAtasney, *The Hidden Famine: Hunger, Poverty and Sectarianism in Belfast 1840–50* (London: Pluto Press, 2000).

58 The Belfast Linenhall Library's exhibition was later taken on tour to the Commons Library

at Westminster by SDLP MP Eddie McGrady, 'MPs get close-up of Great Famine', *Irish News* (1 February 1996). See also 'Famine cemetery gets renewal cash', *ibid.* (3 January 1996); 'Closer look at north's Famine past', *ibid.* (3 February 1997).

59 'SF "Famine" window proposal passed', *An Phoblacht* (6 February 1997).

60 Belfast City Council Policy and Resources Committee, minutes of 22 November, 13 December 1996, 24 January 1997; Belfast City Council, minutes of 3 February 1997.

61 'Ceasefires ship shape says Ervine', *The Examiner* (7 August 1999); Ervine also attended the ship's launch, 'Famine-era replica ship sails from Kerry', *Irish Times* (8 May 2000).

62 'Breaking the Silences' symposium, 1–2 November 1997, IFGC website, www.webcom/famine/mission.htm (accessed March 2000).

63 Belfast City Council Arts Subcommittee, minutes, 2 December 1999.

64 Terence Duffy, 'The Museum of the Irish Famine: exhibiting Ireland's tragic history', *Museum International*, 48/2 (1996), 51–4.

65 Niall Ó Ciosáin, 'Hungry grass', *CIRCA*, 68 (1994), 24–7.

66 Brett, *Construction of Heritage*, pp. 139–53; cf. Brett's critique of the Famine exhibition at the Ulster Folk and Transport Museum in 'Exhibiting problems', *Irish Reporter*, 19 (1995), 18–19.

67 For a balanced overview of the curricula campaigns, see Thomas J. Archdeacon, 'The Irish Famine in American school curricula', *Éire-Ireland*, 37:1 & 2 (2002), 130–52; for the political controversy over the New York campaign, see 'New curriculum from Albany: the Irish potato famine, or one view of it', *New York Times* (1 December 1996).

68 This divergence is implicit in the contrasting reports on their respective curricula written by their directors, Maureen Murphy, 'New York State's "Great Famine Curriculum": a report', *Éire-Ireland*, 37:1 & 2 (2002), 109–18; James V. Mullin, 'The New Jersey Famine Curriculum: a report', *ibid.*, pp. 119–29. Mullin has explicitly attacked the New York document for failing to comply with his genocidal interpretation; see 'Famine curriculum stirs spirited debate', 'Co-ordinator of Famine Curriculum defends work', *Irish Echo*, 31 July 2002. The text of the New Jersey Curriculum can be found at 'The Great Irish Famine Curriculum', www.nde.state.ne.us/SS/irish_famine.html (accessed March 2000).

69 Novick, *The Holocaust and Collective Memory*, pp. 9–10.

70 Clarence Page, 'A bittersweet reality for Irish boosters', *Chicago Tribune* (15 March 1998).

71 This paper was first read to the 'Memory of Catastrophe' conference at the University of Southampton in April 2000. My thanks to my co-organiser Kendrick Oliver and the other participants for their critical comments, and to Margaret Kelleher, Niall Ó Ciosáin and Cormac Ó Gráda for sharing their thoughts on Famine commemoration.

'The greatest and the worst': dominant and subaltern memories of the Dos Bocas well fire of 1908

A cement marker stands three feet tall and a foot wide on the banks of a body of water near the town of San Diego del Mar, a small, rural community in the Mexican state of Veracruz. It is painted white with some blue and red, but the paint is weathered by the rains and sun of the semi-tropical region. The paint is faded, but one can tell words were once written on the marker. As if to tease us, those words are not discernible. A local informs me that the marker commemorates an event known as the Dos Bocas well fire of 1908.

An artefact signifying historical memory, the marker is full of contrary yet ambivalent meanings. It signifies an event important enough for commemoration, yet it does not merit maintenance. It stands as a visual clue, strong enough to keep the memory of the event alive. Yet, the faded words represent loss of specific and detailed memory. More pedestrian than many markers of memory, such as the Vietnam Veterans Memorial, the United States Holocaust Memorial Museum and the Jewish Museum in Berlin, this small cement structure nevertheless still invites us to restore its words, to unpack the memory of the well fire, and explore its deeper meanings, both past and present.

This essay examines how the Dos Bocas well fire was a catastrophe, an experience that signified to locals a disruption in the course of their lives. The essay explores how locals and nationals gave meaning to that disruption, and how their understandings of the fire produced distinct proto-memories of the event. The essay illustrates how one proto-memory became dominant, and how it subsumed the alternative narrative. The dominant proto-memory was constructed by national actors, journalists, federal government officials, and scientists. The subsumed narrative was produced by locals. Their discourse perceived the fire to be against their interests, a representation that became a significant subaltern memory.

Moving from analysis of the event and the formation of competing memories, the essay explores how memory became part of the hegemonic discourse about the place of oil in Mexican modernity. This analysis shows how 'official' memory was contested by a subaltern survival of local identity and memory. This analysis focuses upon the nationalisation of oil in 1938 and how the 'heroic myth' of nationalisation further subsumed the subversive local discourse about the pernicious features of the fire.

Finally, the essay offers considerations of what the Dos Bocas catastrophe tells us about the great changes taking place in Mexico today under the influence of neoliberal reforms.

The Dos Bocas well fire started in the morning of 4 July 1908. Its cause was accidental. The well had just erupted, and the gushing crude contacted fires that powered the derrick. The contact caused an explosion which ignited the gushing oil. The fire raged out of control until burning itself out on 30 August 1908.[1] Local authorities forced villages to evacuate, a remarkable event for people conditioned to endure forces of nature, especially summer hurricanes. During the fire's two-month life span, oil flowed at an astounding rate of 90,000 barrels per day.[2] It flooded nearby fields and flowed into the region's swamps, streams, lagoons, and rivers. Officials stopped motorboat traffic because they feared oil floating on the water might ignite.[3] The local economy, dependent on river traffic, collapsed.

Desperate attempts at killing the fire failed. A team of 100 army engineers were sent by the Mexican president, Porfirio Díaz, to help the international teams working to extinguish the fire.[4] They tried to dynamite the well shut.[5] They tunnelled to the well mouth in an attempt at capping it underground.[6] Huge water pumps were futilely used to drown it out.[7] To prevent the fire's spread, they dug huge pits into the ground to store oil. They built walls of earth to contain the fire. The president sent a special scientific commission to study the fire.[8] Despite these efforts, the fire would die only of natural causes, after burning itself out.

Dos Bocas as phenomenon

Soon after the fire started, journalists from around the world descended upon the scene. It was a spectacular event, provoking the imagination and fear of readers and writers alike. Dos Bocas was covered daily, turning the local event into a national story, heavily sensationalised by the newspapers. One Mexico City daily declared the fire 'the greatest and worst' in the republic's history.[9] Another claimed, 'We can assert that in recent times Mexico has not had a fire drama so emotional and sensational.'[10] Reporters dramatised the fire by using supernatural and religious references: 'A Fire that Looks Like the Aurora Borealis', read one headline.[11] Another explained how people living nearby 'have come to see in this rare fire a type of godly punishment, something like the flames of fire that Jehovah made fall upon the cursed cities of the bible'.[12] *El Diario* claimed, 'The column of fire of the Israelites was not even so great' as Dos Bocas.[13] In one paper the event was crowned the 'Dos Bocas phenomenon'.[14]

People in Tampico, 75 miles north of Dos Bocas, spent evenings looking to the horizon, 'contemplating the gigantic illumination'.[15] Sailors and passengers arriving in the port added to speculation with their stories of when the flame's light was first seen. One captain sighted it eighty miles from shore.[16] Another saw it a remarkable two hundred miles away.[17] Sailors' folklore and superstition offered explanations for the unexplained glow in the horizon. *El Diario* explained that they had believed it to be a 'geological cataclysm', perhaps a volcanic eruption: 'Several mariners stopped their vessels, consulted their maps to locate volcanoes, and to observe the movement of the water to see if any geological disturbance had agitated the liquid.' Stories of Atlantis came to their mind. Such fancies must have coloured the seafarers' reports when they landed in Tampico, and added to the nature and extent of the 'phenomenon's' reputation.[18]

Everything about Dos Bocas commanded curiosity, respect, and awe. Observers were quick to emphasise that Dos Bocas was the most prolific well in history. Engineers used statistics about the well's production in attempts to contextualise the phenomenon. One estimated that Dos Bocas produced 20,000 gallons of oil per minute, or 3,500,000 gallons per day.[19] Pearson and Sons, the firm that owned the well, placed the oil's value at 50,000 pesos per day.[20] *La Patria* estimated that the fire consumed 3 million barrels of oil in two months.[21] *El Imparcial* pointed out that daily production was enough to supply the Mexican Central Railroad with its fuel needs for 12 days.[22] The temperature of the fire, according to *El Diario*, reached 2,000 degrees, making it dangerous to get within 200 metres of the fire.[23] People marvelled at the height of the flames. One Mexico City paper claimed it reached eight times the height of the national cathedral.[24] People were amazed by the huge crater caused by the gusher. Dos Bocas appeared to be alive; it grew in diameter from 90 to 150 metres within a week of its birth.[25]

Adding to the phenomenon of Dos Bocas was the naturalist, outdoor, adventurous mentality of turn-of-the-century Mexicans.[26] People from Tampico took day excursions to witness Dos Bocas first-hand.[27] Efrán Reyna, the political boss from the district where Dos Bocas was located, organised tours, 'with the goal of witnessing up-close the fire'. Pearson and Sons gave 'official' updates on the fire, as well as 'scientific' explanations of the phenomenon. Reyna was a favourite of the newspapers because of his exploits during these tours. Once, he made a daring horseback dash around the well, during which he approached within ten metres of the inferno and its intense heat. A reporter commented, 'acts like these are characteristic of Efrán M. Reyna'.[28]

Newspaper coverage of fire-fighting efforts made the story even more exciting. Dos Bocas had a great plot, the struggle of man against nature, the forces of modern industry out of control, and the challenge of extinguishing the fire. An element of competition was added when the government offered a 200,000 peso reward to those able to extinguish the fire. As the story unfolded, Mexicans followed the efforts of foreigners, like 'Shorty' Walker, as they prepared to join the war against the fire.[29] Likewise, Mexicans read about the dispatch of the army engineers to Dos Bocas, and followed their every move from Mexico City to the port of Veracruz to Tampico before arriving at Dos Bocas. Papers detailed how they collaborated with Pearson and Sons to combat the fire. One report related the heroic efforts of Captain Delmotte, and how he suffered convulsions after breathing the fire's toxic fumes; 'He conducted himself like a hero, making himself an example to his subordinates', asserted *El Diario*.[30] Newspapers added to the drama of human sacrifice with opening lines like 'A titanic effort'. In this heroic battle, fighters were pitted against a noble enemy, the 'formidable fire'. Observers framed Dos Bocas as an heroic effort of man against nature. In this narrative, however, the fire defeated the best efforts of engineers, scientists, soldiers, and foreigners.[31]

The formation of local proto-memory

Nested within people's perception of Dos Bocas as a 'phenomenon' was a degree of ambiguity about modernity. For many Mexicans, the fire was a threat. Despite the heroic efforts of people who had otherwise mastered the mysterious forces of modernity, especially the engineers and foreign industrial experts, the fire burned out of control. It was a rebellion of nature against modernity, a lesson about the dangers of messing with the natural world. This perception of Dos Bocas as 'threat' was especially strong among locals.

When the fire started, the first reaction on the local level was alarm. In Tampico, for example, a paper reported that 'alarm continues in this city about what may happen because the light that can be seen from the city is greater today than yesterday'. People were worried about family members working in the oil fields. This concern became stronger because authorities failed to provide information. One paper related, 'a few days previously 1500 workers left from the port to the petroleum fields . . . and because of this, great alarm exists within their families'. As families were 'very desperate for information', we can only imagine what fears were stimulated as the port community speculated about the fire, and as rumours spread free of 'official' confirmation or denial.[32]

Alarm was strongest among communities close to the fire. *El Diario* described the scene: the fire 'has planted wonder and fear throughout the region'.[33] Locals saw its immense power, the ineffectiveness of the authorities to combat it, and endured disruptions to daily life. In Tantoyuca, according to *El Pais*, 'the alarm was extraordinary'. People believed the fire was a sign of the 'coming of the end of the world'.[34] One reporter explained how fear was greatest among the 'indigenous and rural folk', who 'at first believed that Earth was burning from the East'. Apparently, these people 'came running to the houses of nearby *haciendas* [rural estates], demanding explanations of the phenomena that they thought was the end of the world'. The paper's report continued, 'in this state of agitation, they resigned themselves to prayer'.[35] Another reporter described their fear as 'passionate imagination'. Pearson and Sons had trouble keeping 400 peons working at the task of containing the fire. Some workers fled in panic whenever the fire's strength suddenly swelled, or when the wind changed directions. Their stories, undoubtedly, added to the perception of Dos Bocas as a 'threat'.[36]

Dos Bocas also caused people to gossip. They spread rumours that the fire's cause was intentional. The authorities arrested four individuals, 'having been suspected of being the authors of the fire'.[37] People had two explanations for who started the fire and why. The first blamed the rural poor, who rented properties from larger landowners. Presumably, they started the fire as revenge for years of exploitation. The second were those landowners who had grievances with the oil companies over unpaid royalties and broken contracts. These rumours proved false, but serve to illustrate the tension and uncertainty that existed among the local community over the nature and direction of oil development.

The local 'threat' perception of Dos Bocas was also expressed by merchants. They wrote a collective letter to President Díaz, complaining about the fire. The event caused 'grave losses in our persons and interests'. They specified losses due to restrictions on transport, as well as costs for repairing docks and boats damaged by oil floating on the waterways. The merchants complained of dead cattle, destroyed crops, and poisoned fish. They concluded, 'through your good government we have enjoyed years of peace, but today, we are presented with a formidable enemy which is the oil well of Dos Bocas'.[38] In describing Dos Bocas as an 'enemy', the merchants articulated local concerns about the newly formed oil industry, especially how it disrupted their lives and was incompatible with their interests. Their perception was echoed in the press. 'There is great alarm', wrote *El Imparcial*, 'because many have ranches in the area and they fear that damages and great losses will result.'[39]

Local perceptions of Dos Bocas as the 'enemy' contained metaphors of society mobilised for war. Communities organised labour gangs for fire fighting, the digging of tunnels, trenches, and ramparts. They also cleaned up dead and decaying animals poisoned by the catastrophe. The battle even had casualties. Two workers died while fighting the fire. Scores of people became violently ill from the well's noxious fumes. A medical doctor suffered from 'mental disorders' attributed to the stress of attending to the public health crisis. The 'war' image was augmented by people's concern for law and order. Pearson and Son, for example, urgently advised the authorities that 'it is essential that any misdemeanour, drunkenness, or misconduct on this lease, during the fire should be at once punished for the general safety of the public'. In response, a contingent of *rurales* (rural police force) was sent by the Mexican president. Restrictions on commercial trade and forced evacuations further indicate the degree of wartime-style mobilisation during the fire.[40]

Disruption and memory

Dos Bocas was clearly a major disruption of everyday life that historians associate with catastrophe and memory.[41] Disruption, however, went deeper than just the inconvenience of the accident. The catastrophe constituted a significant departure in the meaning of life for local people. It is this departure's meaning that constitutes the core of how their proto-memory of Dos Bocas would become memory.

Dos Bocas was a powerful symbol of change used by people to contest the rapid and sustained development of the petroleum industry. Prior to oil, northeastern Veracruz was an isolated region barely integrated into global capitalism. The oil boom of the early 1900s intensified the pace of modernising change. The building of oil camps, wells, pipelines, and storage tanks transformed the rural region. Workers, landowners, lawyers, merchants, and local political officials all interacted with the new industry. For individuals, the transformation in life was substantial. But, the change was experienced in isolated, individual moments. Isolation meant locals had few opportunities to give collective meaning to the changes. Prior to Dos Bocas, many locals had made land deals with the oil companies, or had a light-gauge railway constructed through their property, or witnessed the building of a derrick. These events were individual interactions with the new industry. They probably only stimulated passing thoughts or small talk within the community about how things were changing. Isolated moments, however, were important precursors to the Dos Bocas event. These contexts were the building-blocks for their perception of the fire as a 'threat'.[42]

When the fire disrupted local life, it became the region's first collective encounter with petroleum. As an event experienced by all, the fire established the necessary mechanism for transforming local proto-memory to a formal memory. It served as reference point or marker that symbolised the previous decade's changes. It created a shared context that allowed people to express the meaning of their past and present individual experiences. The event generated the context for locals to debate the current and future relationships with the oil industry. As a vehicle of memory past, present, and future, Dos Bocas signified to locals that oil had altered all of their lives, that an era had ended and a new one had begun. As newly created memory, however, the local 'threat' perception of Dos Bocas was immediately contested.

Dos Bocas as heroic modernisation: the national perspective

Not all Mexicans were uncomfortable with the nasty side-effects of modernity. One such group was an influential circle of politicians, capitalists, and intellectuals known as the *científicos*. They sought to organise Mexico's development under the 'scientific' political philosophy of positivism. These promoters of modernity most often hailed from Mexico City. They exuded a cosmopolitan élan and an arrogant swagger that gave their projects a distinctive quality of officialdom, authority, and certitude. The blueprints of what they imagined to be a modern nation state were formed from a scientific discourse that was hard to challenge. In their view, the new oil industry had a vital role in the transformation to modernity. In the *científicos'* Mexico, local recalcitrants who saw Dos Bocas as 'threat' were irritating vestiges destined to be swept away by modernity's forces of creative destruction.

The *científico* who led Mexican modernity's assault on the locals' proto-memory was a geologist, Juan Villarello. He headed the commission sent by Mexico's president to study the Dos Bocas phenomenon. Arriving at the scene, Villarello acted quickly to dispel the fire's 'threat' image. He used scientific discourse to convince locals not to be afraid. Villarello focused on the 'facts', in order to combat the 'rumours' and 'exaggerations' which were driving fear. His scientific command of the facts produced the illusion of an authoritative, 'official' meaning of the fire. Villarello's version contested local knowledge about the fire, and subsumed it with a national, modernising discourse. In his final report, Villarello countered the list of Dos Bocas' damage to life and property, arguing that local claims were overstated. He dismissed charges that the fire had destroyed the fishing industry by confidently stating, 'as to the fishing industry in the Tamiauha Lagoon, it is enough to look on the map, in order to become satisfied, that the small quantities of caked *chapapote* [indigenous term for oil], floating within perhaps two kilometres from Dos Bocas, cannot in any manner harm the fish it contains.'[43]

Debunking rumours and wild exaggerations, Villarello created an alternate, modernising discourse about the fire. But his version was selective with the facts. 'Of all the facts, that may already be considered history,' Villarello wrote, 'those which I consider worth recording here, are the following'.[44] He redefined Dos Bocas to make it fit the agenda of the nation state. Instead of being Mexico's enemy, the phenomenon was an ally in the *científicos'* heroic project. 'Money alone,' he stated, 'can settle' the damages caused by the fire. 'All the damage and inconvenience' of Dos Bocas would be 'more than compensated by the advertisement that all the . . . region has received'. Instead of local economic collapse, Villarello saw an economic boom, one defined by petroleum. 'In consequence' of the phenomenon, 'there has been an enormous rise in land values'. Local concerns were misguided. The 'region will receive incalculable benefits from the development of the oil industry'. Dos Bocas was a crucial agent in the region's transformation to modernity. The region's future was with oil, and not the anachronistic past of fishing, farming, and cattle.

Villarello's version of the fire was adopted by the national press. They echoed the modernising discourse about Dos Bocas, and emphasised how petroleum development was not a threat but a friend to Mexico's development. *El Pais*, for example, explained, 'Now that so much has been lost; it is revealed how much has been gained.'[45] The fire was just a temporary setback to the benefits of an oil boom. An *El Diario* editorial maintained, the region 'was a by-passed economic sector before oil'. 'It is a great shame,' the paper claimed, 'that [in] a region so fertile and rich as the Huasteca, where cattle of the best quality abound, and immense variety of precious wood, and which counts a variety of agricultural products . . . there has remained until now a lack of rapid communication. No railroad connects it to the great consumer centres of the Republic.'[46] Petroleum promised to bring transportation and access to markets needed for the region's modernisation. Likewise, *El Imparcial* claimed that with oil 'the future is bright for the Huasteca'. The paper explained that 'The famous fire has called attention to the eyes of capitalists . . . the rich region of the *Huasteca*.'[47] Dos Bocas was to be celebrated not mourned.

The modernisers saw oil as the ticket to modernity. Literally, oil would fuel Mexico's passage to the ranks of industrialisation. The tragedy of Dos Bocas was not the environmental catastrophe and passing of a bygone agricultural world, but rather the loss of the black gold that flowed uncontrollably and unprofitably out of Dos Bocas. The new oil industry, stated *El Diario*, 'has powerfully called the attention of our politicians and men of science who have vainly looked since times immemorial at a truly transcendental problem, which until today has been the problem of fuel in Mexico'. Now that oil had been discovered and proven to be exploitable, the question was how to use it properly for the betterment of all Mexicans. In framing the issue in these terms, the local 'threat' image of Dos Bocas was selfish, short-sighted, and wrong. In sharp contrast, the modernisers' version of Dos Bocas was heroic: 'The industries which are the life of modern society encounter in our Republic the hard obstacle of fuel, and, due only to titanic efforts, Mexico has arrived at the frontiers of industrialisation.'[48] The fire was part of the dramatic story of how Mexican industrialists, engineers, bankers, and statesmen triumphed over previously insurmountable odds in bringing modernity to their nation.

From disintegration to reconstitution

One of the most difficult challenges when addressing the memory of catastrophes is the untangling of multiple layers of contested meanings embedded in the contradictory, mixed, and often incompatible ways people remember the past. Core to this problem is the dialectic of disintegration (catastrophe) and reintegration (memory) that constitutes the deeper meanings of an event's memory. The disintegration caused by Dos Bocas – which ironically translates as 'two mouths' – spawned two distinct proto-memories. One was local. It constructed the event as 'threat'. The second was national. It imagined Dos Bocas as 'heroic modernisation'. The process of reintegration, the way in which one proto-memory becomes the dominant memory, was delayed by the events of Mexico's revolution.

Between 1910 and 1920, Mexico experienced a dual process of elites fighting elites for power, and popular classes fighting elites for social justice. A deep fragmentation of the nation resulted. Regions experienced this process differently as determined by local realities. In northeastern Veracruz, the 'logic of revolution' found communities divided into two factions. Rich landowners worked with foreign oil companies to maintain oil production on their properties. Those left out joined revolutionary armies as they sought to gain control of the region. Oil development continued throughout the revolution, and with it additional catastrophes occurred. Drilling practices caused deforestation, and destroyed the farming, fishing, and cattle economies. Another big well fire occurred in 1914. Oil continued to be stored in pits, and oil spills from wells and pipelines were common. Revolutionary armies marched through the area, blowing up pipelines and derricks in their path. Local hardship included 'taxes' demanded by revolutionaries. The locals' proto-memory of Dos Bocas as 'threat' became further entrenched during the revolution. It turned subaltern, and became nested within the twists and turns of how original meanings become memory.[49]

With the revolution, the *científicos* were thrown from power. A new generation of modernisers sought to wrestle control of the oil industry from foreigners. Their vision of Mexican modernity was expressed in the Constitution of 1917 and its Article 27, which placed the subsoil under state domain. The new modernisers were on a collision course with the foreign oil companies. They sought greater regulation with the goal of conserving Mexico's oil reserves, using it for national industrial development, and guarding against environmental catastrophes. The oil companies and their diplomatic representatives resisted these efforts, which led to a prolonged series of court cases. By the early 1930s, regulation inched closer to the national project envisioned by the revolutionary elite's Article 27.[50]

Despite the *científicos'* displacement, their discourse of heroic modernisation was easily adopted by the revolution's new modernisers. Oil remained Mexico's partner in the new version of modernisation. The process of taming oil to the national interest, however, was even more heroic than the *científicos'* project of building the oil industry. The proto-memory of the *científicos* was malleable enough to morph into the heroic struggle of the new elites' revolutionary nationalism.

When reconstitution happened, it came from 'above', as the national elites battled foreigners for control of Mexico's oil. The consummating act was the nationalisation of the oil industry in 1938. Nationalisation is one of the defining moments in modern Mexican history. It represents the realisation of Article 27, the domination of Mexicans over foreign capital. Nationalisation signifies a major paradigm shift in the Mexican political economy from the foreign-led development model of the *científicos* to the import substitution industrialisation model desired by the revolutionary elite. Under the new model, the oil that flowed from the wells near Dos Bocas would no longer serve foreign interest, but it would literally fuel Mexico's industrial development.

While nationalisation played a central part in the political economy of post-revolutionary Mexico, it also had an important role in the Mexican collective memory. It rests at the core of the great myths constructed by the post-revolutionary elites, which they used to justify their power and to conceal continued patterns of social injustice. The heroic myth of nationalisation is the story of society mobilised to accomplish a larger, national objective by making sacrifices. It is the story of how a great president, Lázaro Cárdenas, inspired millions of Mexicans to sacrifice for the *patria*. It is the story of how all Mexicans – urban and rural, rich and poor, Indian and mestizo, men and women – answered their president's call, put aside their differences, and seized their destiny.[51]

Although nationalisation was a radical departure from the economic plans of the *científicos*, it was not a major deviation from their perception of Dos Bocas. The *científicos'* 'partner' construction of Dos Bocas was highly compatible with the heroic myth of nationalisation. Just as the *científicos* rationalised that Dos Bocas would bring local benefits, the revolutionary elites held that oil would transform Mexico. Nationalisation was the realisation of the oil industry's promise. The new moderners, however, perfected the *científicos'* vision by addressing the locals' potentially subversive proto-memory. Local grievances with oil were erased by the larger political and economic forces driving nationalisation. The heroic myth of nationalisation assured Mexicans that local concerns were resolved, and their interests were consistent with those of the nation. Local memory was supplanted by the revolutionary elite's version of modern Mexico.

Memories in place and time

Understanding the process of reconstitution now requires that we visit the present. We need to unpack local memory of Dos Bocas. In this analysis the interplay between place and time is intertwined with the contestation between subaltern and dominant memories.

Nearly 100 years after the event, Dos Bocas remains an ecological catastrophe. This reality is obvious when visiting the former well site. About a mile from it, the odour of freshly laid asphalt is noticeable. It is within a large deforested area that has been roughly worked over by heavy, land-moving equipment. Even closer, the smell becomes stronger, and the outlines of a body of water take shape. The water is much larger than a pond, but smaller than a lake, and appears man-made. The water actually fills the crater created by the mouth of the 'phenomenon'. The water has two distinct colours. The first is a metallic grey, a reflective colour indicating the presence of heavy metals. The second is jet black, the shiny signature of petroleum floating on water. Near the shore, large clumps of *chapapote* float on the surface. They emerge from the subterranean mouth of the crater. Eerily, almost 100 years after the well caught fire and burned in an uncontrolled rage, the *chapapote* continues to flow from the heart of the 'phenomenon'.

For locals, the place is a permanent reminder of the past. It is a physical scar in their mental mapping, the landscape of their identity and memory. As something they cannot escape, Dos Bocas is part of the historical memory that defines their place in time, especially the narrative of modern Mexican history. All locals can recite the Dos Bocas story. Their narrative is consistent in actors, ordering of events, and emphasis. When asked about the event, locals take a certain pride that it happened in their backyard. It is the response of a people who have something exceptional in their community, the bones of a dinosaur, or the artefacts of a battle fought long ago. The place is a physical reminder, a sensual clue of the catastrophe. Dos Bocas as 'place' means the past will always inform the locals' present.

When I spoke with local people, however, something curious took place. They were impatient with my questions about the fire. They wanted to get to the main event, the real story, the punchline. They all wanted to talk about 1938. They were almost irritated that I did not 'get it', that the story was not about Dos Bocas but nationalisation. The heroic efforts of the Mexican people were far more important than the well fire. Almost every response to my questions led to the same moral of the story, the triumph of nationalisation. Their explanations of 1938 were vibrant: eyes widened, pace quickened, and the narrative became more heroic. The memory of Dos Bocas was subsumed in the story of nationalisation, as if it were nothing but a preface to the real object of their memory.

Locals know their place in the heroic myth of nationalisation. It is their land that the oil comes from. They sacrifice it to the greater good of the nation. It was their labour that built the industry. They take pride in their place within the bigger picture of *Lo Mexicano*, what it means to be Mexican. Their part in the heroic myth of nationalisation is reinforced by the reality of continued oil production in the region. PEMEX, the national company, has wells peppered around Dos Bocas. Pipelines crisscross local pastures. Pumping stations hum '24/7', and company trucks come and go as part of the rhythm of local traffic. Just as the physical remains of the 'phenomenon' keep its memory alive, the presence of today's oil industry serves as a constant visual clue to the heroic myth of modernisation. The two memories, it appears, coexist within the meaning of local identity.

Conclusion: what was written on the marker?

A puzzle remains unanswered: what did the faded letters on the cement marker read? Did they articulate the heroic modernisation memory of Dos Bocas, or the local perception of threat? Does the lack of upkeep reflect a breakdown in the heroic myth?

Or, does it show the subaltern survival of the subversive memory signifying a culture of resistance to elite projects of modernisation?

One approach to the puzzle comes from Herbert Gutman, a pioneer in the history of memory. He liked to tell the story of a woman injured by a textile mill accident. It left a nasty scar on her scalp. As a child, the woman's daughter used to comb the woman's hair, deliberately covering the scar in the process. The combing was a ritual between mother and child. Each time the child would comb, they had conversations, but the child never asked about the cause of the scar. Likewise, mom never talked about it. The child learned of the cause later in life, in her sixties, when a journalist contacted her about her mother's participation in the famous 'Bread and Roses' strike of 1912 when 20,000 workers walked from their jobs at the Lawrence mills. Mom had even stepped forward to testify about the repressive labour conditions before Congress. The daughter never knew of mom's labour activism.

David William Cohen's analysis of the story maintains that, for Gutman, 'the story of two women, mother and daughter, was a story of the repressive mechanisms which destroy historical memory. The suppression of history is, in a sense . . . the suppression of experience, the suppression of dissent and resistance.' Cohen continues, 'Should we recognize that history and memory are as much about repression and suppression as they are about creation and recollection?'[52]

Like the scar on the scalp, the scar of Dos Bocas has a hidden text, a subaltern memory that is repressed. The repressive nature of memory struck me while waiting for a lorry to take me from Dos Bocas back to Tampico. I had just finished interviewing the oldest person in the community. His narration was thick with heroic discourse. He was effusive about 1938 and spoke of President Cárdenas in reverent terms. Was this elder combing over the scar? Locals can talk about Dos Bocas, but, at the same time, not talk about what is under the scar. They talk about Dos Bocas but have to navigate around the subversive meaning of the 'threat' memory to their contemporary reality. In telling the heroic modernisation version of the Dos Bocas story, they repress the reality of environmental degradation, poverty, and health hazards. They artfully comb over the scar of Dos Bocas. Yet the scar, the subaltern memory, remains.

At the lorry stop, I talked with one last group of locals. They offered me a version of what oil meant radically different to that of the old man. These folks were bitter. They explained how they never saw one centavo from all their oil. They lacked work. They had health problems which they blamed on PEMEX's lax environmental practices. They complained of exploitation, and spoke in terms of injustice. So much for the heroic myth of nationalisation; they refused to comb over the scar. Through them emerged the subaltern discourse of Dos Bocas as 'threat'.

I have heard the locals' bitter words before, in places like Guerrero where the newest form of modernisation results in deforestation and desertification of a semi-tropical mountain region. One indigenous women explained, 'We have three options: Live in poverty. Migrate. Or, take to arms.' The subaltern discourse of 'threat' has a more powerful message in Chiapas, where indigenous peoples have rebelled against exploitation and proclaimed, 'Never again a Mexico without us.' For the locals at the lorry stop, the subaltern discourse of Dos Bocas had clearly morphed into a strong critique of the new neoliberal order in Mexico, a critique shared by many marginalised Mexicans.

The question of memory's relation to power lurks within the battle between official and subaltern memories of Dos Bocas. While the two discourses coexist within the identity and memory of locals, that coexistence is unstable, constantly on the cusp of disruption, and perpetually playing the symbiotic game of subversion and domination. Looking at the big structures of history and how they are experienced on the local level reveals that major transitions, paradigm shifts in the structures of power offer opportunities for the latent, subaltern memories to rise through the cracks and become counter-hegemonic. With change comes opportunity to imagine a better world, and to act on that vision.

Since the early 1980s, Mexico has undergone such a shift. The *científicos* have returned, but in the form of technocrats – bureaucrats and businessmen trained at Harvard and the University of Chicago. These technocrats have overturned the nationalist, import-substitution industrialisation plan of the revolutionary elite in favour of a return to the liberal, free-trade policies of the *científicos*. Encapsulated by the North American Free Trade Agreement, the shift focuses on privatisation of the public sector, the break-up of communal land, and a drastic cutback in state spending. The foreigners have been welcomed back.[53]

Exploitation in the rural areas is on the increase, along with popular resistance to the elites' neoliberal agenda. At Dos Bocas, the tensions of the transition are stark. Rural people have trouble subsisting while oil continues to flow from their property. The reality of poverty flies in the face of the heroic myth of nationalisation. It overwhelms the repressive capacity of heroic memory to mask the experience of exploitation. The ability of local people to navigate the contradictions between memories of Dos Bocas is taxed to the limit. Once the limit is reached, the reproduction of official memory might halt. Their ability to ascribe to the heroic memory falters before the jarring realities of poverty, environmental degradation, and poor health. While we do not know what was written on the marker, we do know that the heroic memory of Dos Bocas is dysfunctional. Even if its words were on the marker, the discursive power of the heroic myth has faded into history.

Notes

1 Testimony by Pablo Guzmán, 6 July 1908, 'Incendios', Expediente 'Dos Bocas', Ramo de Gobernación, Caja 1, Archivo General del Estado de Veracruz (hereafter AGEV), Xalapa, Veracruz, Mexico.
2 *El Diario* (21 July 1908); *El Imparcial* (18 July 1908).
3 *El Imparcial* (7 July 1908).
4 *Ibid.* (28 July 1908).
5 *El Diario* (29 July 1908).
6 *El Imparcial* (20 July 1908).
7 *Ibid.* (14 August 1908).
8 *Ibid.* (17 August 1908).

 9 *El Pais* (9 July 1908).
10 *El Imparcial* (8 July 1908).
11 *El Diario* (14 July 1908).
12 *Ibid.* (24 July 1908).
13 *Ibid.* (26 August 1908).
14 *El Pais* (6 July 1908).
15 *El Imparcial* (11 July 1908).
16 *Ibid.* (7 July 1908).
17 *Ibid.* (8 July 1908).
18 *El Diario* (26 August 1908).
19 *Ibid.*
20 *El Imparcial* (20 July 1908).
21 *La Patria* (2 September 1908).
22 *El Imparcial* (4 September 1908).
23 *El Diario* (26 August 1908).
24 *El Imparcial* (17 July 1908).
25 *El Diario* (26 August 1908).
26 See William Beezley, *Judas at the Jockey Club and Other Episodes in Porfirian Mexico* (Lincoln, NB: University of Nebraska Press, 1989), pp. 13–66.
27 *El Imparcial* (11 July 1908).
28 *El Diario* (19 August 1908); *El Pais* (21 August 1908).
29 *La Patria* (29 August 1908).
30 *El Diario* (26 August 1908).
31 *El Imparcial* (14 August 1908); *El Diario* (23 July 1908).
32 *El Imparcial* (4 July 1908, 7 July 1908).
33 *El Diario* (28 July 1908).
34 *El Pais* (15 July 1908).
35 *El Diario* (14 July 1908).
36 *Ibid.* (26 August 1908).
37 *Ibid.* (14 July 1908).
38 Amada Cobos *et al.* to Porfirio Díaz, 26 October 1908, Legajo 33, Caja 37, Coleccíon Porfirio Díaz, Universidad Iberoamericana, Mexico City, Mexico.
39 *El Imparcial* (4 July 1908).
40 Heladio Arellanos to Secretaria de Gobernacion, 12 October 1908, AGEV; John Pollard to Heladio Arellanos, 7 July 1908, AGEV.
41 Peter Gray and Kendrick Oliver, 'The memory of catastrophe', *History Today*, 51:2 (February 2001), pp. 9–15.
42 Jonathan Brown, *Oil and Revolution in Mexico* (Berkeley, CA: University of California Press, 1993).
43 Juan Villarello, 'The Dos Bocas Phenomenon' (February 1909), *National Geological Institute*, Folder 5344, Box 114, DeGolyer Library, Southern Methodist University, Dallas, Texas.
44 *Ibid.*
45 *El Pais* (1 August 1908).
46 *El Diario* (21 July 1908).
47 *El Imparcial* (18 July 1908).
48 *El Diario* (26 August 1908).
49 Brown, *Oil and Revolution,* pp. 253–306.

50 Linda Hall, *Oil, Banks and Politics: The United States and Postrevolutionary Mexico, 1917–1924* (Austin, TX: University of Texas Press, 1995); Lorenzo Meyer, *Mexico y los Estado Unidos en el Conflicto Petrolero, 1917–1942* (Mexico: El Colegio de Mexico, 1981).
51 Esparanza Durán, 'Pemex: The trajectory of a national oil policy', in John D. Wirth (ed.), *Latin American Oil Companies and the Politics of Energy* (Lincoln, NB: University of Nebraska Press, 1985), pp. 145–88.
52 David William Cohen, *The Combing of History* (Chicago: University of Chicago Press, 1985), pp. 3, 6–7.
53 John Warnock, *The Other Mexico: The North American Triangle Completed* (Montreal: Black Rose Books, 1995); Bill Weinberg, *Homage to Chiapas: The New Indigenous Struggle in Mexico* (London: Verso, 2000).

The *Titanic* and the commodification of catastrophe

In 1999, when the humour magazine *The Onion* published its satirical history of the twentieth century, *Our Dumb Century*, its bogus news story for 1912 was the sinking of the *Titanic* under the headline: 'WORLD'S LARGEST METAPHOR HITS ICEBERG. TITANIC, REPRESENTATION OF MAN'S HUBRIS, SINKS IN NORTH ATLANTIC. 1,500 DEAD IN SYMBOLIC TRAGEDY'.[1] But what the *Titanic*'s sinking has meant symbolically and metaphorically has varied; and popular, public memories of the night of 14–15 April 1912 have taken different forms depending on the ways those memories have been commodified and narrated in the mainstream mass media in three eras: the period immediately following the sinking; the 1950s, when Walter Lord's 1955 *A Night to Remember* and the 1958 British film (directed by Roy Baker) based on that best-seller were extremely popular; and then the 1990s, when James Cameron's 1997 film, cookbooks with recipes from the White Star Line's kitchens, and commemorative T-shirts enriched entrepreneurs shrewd enough to profit from Captain E.J. Smith's feckless seamanship.[2]

As Walter Lord commented in his 1986 reprise, *The Night Lives On*, 'The story [of the *Titanic*] has something for everyone'.[3] Much of the *Titanic* narrative's appeal can be explained by the fact that its details are so vast and varied that it provides smaller stories with satisfying closures or fascinating factoids for many audiences. When the *Titanic* sank, conservatives could point with pride to millionaires like John Jacob Astor and Ben Guggenheim who died while women and children were saved. Radicals and social critics could point out that a relatively small percentage of third-class, steerage passengers, including women and children, were survivors – 25 per cent – whereas 60 per cent of the ship's first-class passengers were saved. Protestants had their heroes from America's and Britain's upper classes; Roman Catholics had a heroic priest who led passengers in prayer; Jews had a Macy's executive and his wife, Isidor and Ida Straus, who died together because Mrs Straus would not leave her husband; and everyone could admire the courage of the *Titanic*'s musicians. In addition, racists could sneer at the 'cowardice' allegedly displayed by steerage passengers described as being 'Latin' in appearance. Moralists could deplore the *Titanic*'s 'luxury' and consider it a symptom of decadence, while more recent and scholarly analysts have proclaimed the disaster a key event in the history of modernism or a fertile field for cultural studies because it was 'an event of deep and wide resonance in Edwardian England and Progressive Era America'.[4] However, it is an event that also had resonance for Churchill's Great Britain and for Eisenhower's and Clinton's United States – as the popularity of Lord's book and Baker's and Cameron's films demonstrates.

To understand this pattern of *Titanic* memories better, it is helpful to comment on the commodification process, a process so ubiquitous in this century and the past one that it seems often to evade analysis, despite the important role it can play in determining which events are remembered and re-remembered and which are forgotten. First and most obviously, commodification often relies on establishing an association between a product and persons, experiences, events, or objects that have some sort of charisma or imply some kind of gratification or prestige. In the case of the *Titanic*, this process began before the ship sank, since Lord's *A Night to Remember* is illustrated with an advertisement for Vinolia Otto Toilet Soap, which had been provided for the ship's first-class passengers so they could enjoy 'a higher standard of Toilet Luxury at sea'.

Second, commodification thrives on the ability of media to create images and/or narratives in which persons, events, objects, or settings are dramatically idealised or (the opposite) denigrated as heroes versus villains, Coca-Cola versus Pepsi-Cola, the headache remedy that is 'effective' versus the one that is not. Like related subjects such as war, crime, and terrorism, disasters are inherently dramatic and theatrical. Thus, commodification in the media flourishes not only by promising charisma by association and assorted gratifications, but also by its ability to produce romantic or melodramatic, adversarial narratives with exciting beginnings, middles, and closures. Considered in this context, the *Titanic* story is an excellent subject for commodification because of its huge cast of heroes and victims (some of them celebrities) who can be contrasted with its villains (or incompetents or cowards).

Third, commodification thrives on familiarity, and the *Titanic* story is a prime example of one of the most popular narrative genres, the disaster story. At the present time – along with sports, crime, politics, terrorism, wars, and weather reports – such narratives often dominate newspapers and television news programmes that rarely ignore a major flood, tornado, or aeroplane crash. Mall movies feature asteroids and earthquakes, and non-fiction trade books about perfect storms and climbers perishing on Mount Everest command huge sales. One significant feature of disaster narratives involving technology is that their public memories are often recorded in two stages. First, they are commodified in survivors' media accounts containing mixtures of facts, legends, and conspiracy theories. However, since modern societies usually seek to discover reasons for technological catastrophes, either to prevent recurrence or for legal purposes, there is a second stage of commodification: the reporting of 'official' inquiries, investigations, or trials. In this second stage, earlier memories may be amended or relegated to the status of legends to produce reports intended to become the codified, 'official' public memory of the event.

Much of the appeal of disaster narratives in general can be traced not only to the emotions induced by the catastrophes themselves, but also to representations of dramatic human reactions: dazed survivors exhibiting relief, heroic rescuers who risk their lives to save others. For the purposes of commodification, however, it is helpful if the disaster is not too horrific. Thus, unlike some larger-scale catastrophes (the Holocaust, Hiroshima) in which commodification is resented, the scale of the *Titanic's* sinking was limited enough to be disturbing without being too traumatic. In addition, the cultural, technological, and historical distance created by the differences between what happened in 1912 and more disturbing contemporary catastrophes – terrorist attacks, AIDS epidemics, Balkan war crimes – makes the travails suffered by *Titanic* passengers seem almost nostalgic by comparison. It might also be argued that an earlier, analogous sense of nostalgia in the 1950s – when the Cold War was flourishing and nuclear annihilation was becoming a grim possibility – contributed to the popularity of Lord's book and Baker's film.

Fourth, commodification thrives on what might be described as a process of problem solving minus critical thinking, on its ability to arouse and then to assuage the anxieties of consumers. On a humble, explicit level, this process can be seen in advertisements in which products 'solve' the problems of targeted audiences during prime-time television programmes. In the early evening, for example, advertisements for junk foods solve the problem of dealing with hungry children. On a slightly more complex level, this process can also be seen in disaster narratives in which the causes of an aeroplane crash or the reasons why so many people died in an earthquake are simplified and summarised. In the case of the *Titanic* narrative, the relatively simple steam-and-electricity technology of the 1910s and the common-sense solutions to the causes of that disaster also give it an additional nostalgia appeal: who could argue with the need to steam slower when entering ice fields or to have enough lifeboats for a ship's crew and passengers? This ability to assuage anxieties – particularly ones only obliquely or analogously related to the catastrophe itself – is, I believe, one of the most important reasons for the popularity of commodified cultural products such as disaster narratives.

In the first stage of the commodification process, immediately after the ship sank, there was a strong emphasis upon the ship's elite passengers. In the case of Bruce Ismay, the President and Managing Director of the White Star Line, there also was a keen interest in the extent to which he may also have contributed to the disaster by ordering Captain Smith to try to set a speed record. Many news stories were virtual roll-calls of the rich and famous who had died. Besides Astor and Guggenheim, the first-class passengers also included Major Archibald Butt, President William Howard Taft's military aide, and others whose fame now rests mainly on the fact that they died when the *Titanic* sank. This emphasis on the first-class passengers can be related not only to the fact that some of them were already celebrities but also to the way in which they (like the *Titanic*) were symbols of the conspicuous consumption, described by Thorstein Veblen in his *Theory of the Leisure Class*, that flourished in the late Victorian-Edwardian-Progressive era.[5]

The enormous concentration of wealth in the hands of individuals and families during that period due to laissez-faire capitalism and the rapid industrial development of the United States and Britain made millionaires the objects of awe, envy, admiration, and/or vituperation depending on the politics of the persons commenting upon them. As one of the millionaires' spokespersons, Andrew Carnegie, explained in an essay on

'Wealth', the 'free play of economic forces' and the law of the 'survival of the fittest' meant that human progress was caused by 'the concentration of business, industrial, and commercial [power] in the hands of a few'. These few would receive rewards for their efforts that were so enormous, said Carnegie, that 'it is inevitable that their income must exceed their expenditures, and that they must accumulate [great] wealth'.[6] For both the admirers and the detractors of Carnegie and other millionaires, such men seemed symbolic examples of social Darwinism and conspicuous consumption.

When these millionaires wished to travel, it was logical for them do so in a ship, like the *Titanic*, outfitted with a squash court and other amenities that led Joseph Conrad to comment tartly that it was really a floating hotel designed for 'people who can't spend five days of their life without a suite of apartments'; and therefore no one should have expected the *Titanic* to be very navigable.[7] For persons this rich, as Veblen reasoned, mere practicality could be scorned, since what counted was the ability to *display* wealth in ways that enabled one to compete with one's wealthy peers and awe one's economic inferiors. What better place or way to do that than on board an ocean liner where the rich could sleep in oak-panelled cabins or wash with Vinolia Otto 'luxury' toilet soap? Millionaires like those who sailed on the *Titanic* possessed so much wealth that they clearly belonged to a different caste than the rest of humanity. The question and anxiety that troubled the Edwardian and Progressive era was whether they were becoming, morally speaking, a different species: a race of pluto-crats who had evolved into beings who used their power to escape the tribulations of ordinary human existence and to threaten the security of people in other social classes who were less 'fit' or wealthy. Did survival of the fittest, in other words, really mean the survival of the richest?

In that context, the sinking of the *Titanic* might be considered good public rela-tions for plutocracy, since it demonstrated that millionaires could die as unselfishly as members of the other classes, thus showing that conspicuous consumption could be accompanied by conspicuous heroism. A few, most notably Ben Guggenheim, had illustrated this point by dressing in evening clothes and proclaiming, 'No woman shall be left aboard this ship because Ben Guggenheim was a coward.'[8] Hearing this story, one minister piously observed: 'People are better than we think they are . . . The mil-lionaires are not all bad men as it turns out'; and the *San Francisco Examiner* claimed the disaster showed that 'in the face of great emergencies' millionaires could die 'on an equality with the other brave men of humbler class[es]'.[9] The behaviour of heroic millionaires and 'other brave men' could also be contrasted in an adversarial way with the behaviour of the ship's less heroic male passengers. Major Butt, in particular, was believed to have kept cowardly steerage passengers from swamping the lifeboats by threatening them with a revolver.

Survivors' accounts and media comments upon the disaster emphasised other con-trasts between heroic and non-heroic male passengers. The most acceptable way for heroic men to survive, as Biel points out, was to go down with the ship, swim to the surface, and – by sheer luck – get a place in a lifeboat.[10] The next best way was to be ordered into a lifeboat by a ship's officer, presumably when there were no women on the deck still waiting to be rescued. Other surviving males were accused of cowardice or even cross-dressing in order to survive, thus revealing a symbolic as well as a moral lack of 'manliness'. The first-class, millionaire survivor who suffered the most was Ismay, who survived in the worst way by climbing into a lifeboat while 1,500 of his company's passengers and crew members died. In contrast to heroic elite passengers such as Butt, Ismay was stigmatised as a 'bad' millionaire who had used his status to survive rather than perish in a disaster that was caused largely by the shortcomings of his own company, the White Star Line. Since Captain Smith had gone down with the *Titanic*, Ismay also served as one of the disaster's chief scapegoats. At least one American newspaper accused him of manslaughter, and journalist Ben Hecht pillo- ried him in a ditty contrasting him with the *Titanic*'s seamen:

> To hold your place in the ghastly face
> Of death on the sea of night
> Is a seaman's job, but to flee with the mob
> Is an owner's noble right.[11]

The US Senate and British Board of Trade investigations influenced public mem- ories of the *Titanic* disaster by amending some of the more egregious legends that had surfaced in the survivors' memories and interviews or by replacing them with more credible reasons for the disaster. Ismay was partially exonerated of some of the charges against him, and Captain Smith was downgraded from a kind of nautical martyr to a pathetic victim of his own carelessness. The investigations also produced a symmetri- cal pairing of hero and scapegoat figures in the persons of Captains Arthur Rostron of the *Carpathia* and Stanley Lord of the *Californian*, the two ships that first reached the disaster scene. Even though Rostron arrived three hours after the sinking, he had risked the *Carpathia* by sailing it full-steam through an ice pack, and he was lionised as an implicit, heroic contrast to the *Titanic*'s feckless and/or inept officers. He was more explicitly contrasted to the hapless Lord, whose ship had been far closer to the sinking liner and might have saved some of its passengers – if Lord had not stayed in bed and ignored the *Titanic*'s distress rockets because of cowardice or negligence.

Captains Lord and Rostron were equally important figures in the next highly popular commodification of the *Titanic* story, Walter Lord's *A Night to Remember*, pub- lished in 1955, and Roy Baker's 1958 film of the same name. Although there might have been survivors still alive who had seen Guggenheim and Astor awaiting their doom, association and/or identification with dead millionaires had less appeal for audiences of the 1950s than they had earlier. That type of commodification is ridiculed in the opening scene of Baker's film in which a stuffy, middle-aged, middle-class couple on a train are offended when a younger man, also middle-class, reads the advertisement for Vinolia Otto Toilet Soap aloud in a mocking voice, shows it to his wife, and comments ironically, 'For the first-class passengers, mind you; the rest don't wash, of course'. The older man says these 'sneering remarks [are] in bad taste', since every patriotic Briton should be proud of the *Titanic*. The younger man's wife reveals that her husband is an officer from the *Titanic*, none other than Second Officer Charles Lightoller, played by Kenneth More. Everyone apologises, and Lightoller says his mockery was directed 'at the soap, sir, not the ship'. The *Titanic* and what it symbolises may be taken seriously, the scene implies, but the snobbery commodified by the soap advertisement deserves to be ridiculed.

For the *Titanic,* as portrayed in Lord's book and Baker's film, is not dominated by millionaires, even though Guggenheim and Straus make cameo appearances during the sinking. In an early sequence of the film, equal emphasis is accorded to each of the ship's three classes of passengers. First, a baronet and his wife leave their palatial country mansion accompanied by servants and eighteen pieces of luggage. Next, a young, middle-class, newly married, couple come out of a suburban church and depart in a motor car for their honeymoon on the *Titanic.* Third, a young Irish couple complete the social cross-section as they leave their village and depart to join the ship at Queenstown in a one-pony trap; it is obvious that they will be travelling steerage.

In the train compartment scene, it is significant that Lightoller is not wearing his uniform, but is instead dressed as a middle-class young man in a suit, so that he is identified as being in the middle-class stratum occupied by the ship's second-class passengers. Moreover, Kenneth More – with his rather ordinary good looks, stocky build, and brisk mannerisms – was the type of actor who was designed to play characters who were not millionaires or aristocrats. What Lightoller, as played by More, offers is not noble birth or wealth, but a great deal of brisk competence. Four decades earlier, many survivors' accounts and media reports, as well as the US Senate investigation, had strongly criticised the *Titanic's* officers, including Lightoller. After all, these were the men who, along with Captain Smith, had ignored a series of wireless messages warning that there was ice in the *Titanic's* path, and they had sent several lifeboats away from the ship only half-filled. In Lord's book and even more in Baker's film, however, Lightoller is a model of conscientious competence and professionalism. In what can be considered a rehearsal for the part that the actor played in Lewis Gilbert's 1960 *Sink the Bismarck!,* More's Lightoller is a pragmatic, no-nonsense character who does his job by relying on his own merits rather than flamboyant good looks or any kind of charisma. Analogously, *A Night to Remember* can be considered a kind of rehearsal for Walter Lord's later, more overtly patriotic popular history books about Pearl Harbor and the evacuation of Dunkirk.[12] In these later books, Lord successfully exploited a narrative format that he first developed in *A Night to Remember:* to blend dozens of survivors' stories into a narrative mosaic that mimics the uncertainty, fear, and confused activity that follow a disaster; to gradually emphasise the more competent and/or heroic responses and contrast them with inept reactions; and then to conclude the narrative with an implicit victory of good sense and organisation over the blunders that caused and followed the original disaster. In his Foreword to *The Miracle at Dunkirk,* Lord described this narrative as a 'series of crises' that had to be solved by the collective efforts of men who refused 'to be discouraged by this relentless sequence', and, therefore, 'Dunkirk remains, above all, a stirring reminder of man's ability to rise to the occasion, to improvise, to overcome obstacles'.[13]

What anxieties about social stratification, privilege, and social Darwinism were to reactions in 1912 to the sinking, focused on millionaires, anxieties created by the Second World War were to Lord's and Baker's 1950s narratives. For many middle-aged British and American readers and audiences of the 1950s, the most significant disasters in their lifetimes were those between 1939 and 1941. Many were, like Lord himself, Second World War veterans, and for that generation memories of the war had begun with a series of catastrophic defeats that included not only the fall of France but also Singapore and the Philippines. Yet the American and British military, along with their Soviet allies, had gone on to sink the *Bismarck* and win the battles of Britain, Midway, El Alamein, Stalingrad, and Iwo Jima. Therefore, much of the popularity of both Lord's book and Baker's film may be ascribed to the ways in which they implicitly create a parallel collective memory, enacted in 1912 and the north Atlantic, in which improvisation and organisation triumph over a 'series of crises' caused by a disaster. To phrase the issue slightly facetiously, in this interpretation the iceberg is Hitler and the Japanese military, Ismay and Captain Smith are Neville Chamberlain and the American isolationists, and Lightoller and Rostron are the thousands of lieutenants, commanders, and other ranks who won the war.

The virtues needed to achieve this kind of victory over disaster are implied in Lord's book and Baker's film by the behaviour of Lightoller and Captain Rostron of the *Carpathia*. Throughout the film, focusing as it did upon a far smaller cast of participants than the book, Lightoller is invariably depicted as the disciplined professional. He superintends the lowering of the lifeboats efficiently; when the passengers panic, he vigorously enforces the women-and-children rule, and he struggles heroically to maintain order so the last boats can be safely lowered. Other officers, including Captain Smith, the *Titanic's* engineers, and many of its seamen are depicted as equally competent as they meet their fates with stoic dignity or even wry humour: one of the engineers offers the men under his command a choice between praying or joining him for a cup of tea. Mildly comic relief and heroism are provided by a baker who gives up a place in a lifeboat and then gets drunk as he prepares to go down with the ship.

In contrast, many of the passengers behave fatuously until they realise the *Titanic* is sinking, and then they panic. Unlike the survivors' accounts of 1912 that blamed steerage passengers for panicking, Baker's film features a rabble possessing no particular class associations in its mob-the-lifeboats scenes. However, the ship's stokers, no longer under the control of the officers and engineers, become a chaotic, anarchic force. Identifiable by their white trousers and singlets, they run frantically around the ship trying to save themselves, but usually to no avail. Besides this implicit class contrast between the disciplined officers and frantic worker-stokers, there is an emphasis on differences in behaviour based on gender. With the exception of Molly Brown, the women passengers are prone to hysterics; they scream and shriek, and many have to be bodily heaved into lifeboats by seamen or male passengers. In the lifeboats, overdressed, first-class women make silly, insensitive comments while alongside them the cowardly Ismay, obviously unmanned by cowardice, weeps when he sees his liner sink.

Since heroes must be contrasted with incompetents or scapegoats, those roles in *A Night to Remember* are taken by Ismay and Stanley Lord. In many 1912 versions of the *Titanic* narrative, Ismay was a more problematical figure, a first-class passenger who had the bad morals to survive when women and children were dying, a rich capitalist who may have helped to cause the disaster by allegedly urging his captain to ignore ice warnings. In Baker's film, however, he is a stereotypical upper-class ninny

and coward who behaves foolishly during the sinking – in contrast to the stoic effi-
ciency of the officers, one of whom, Lightoller, shouts at him so that he does not
disrupt the lowering of the boats. Then, at a crucial moment when one boat is leaving,
Ismay sneaks into it. First Officer Murdoch sees him, momentarily stops the lowering of the boat, and then sneers and lets it reach the water. Officers are gentlemen
enough to stay at their posts, the scene implies, but such behaviour is not to be
expected of managing directors. But the main scapegoats in the film are Stanley Lord
and the officers of the *Californian*, who are too obtuse to understand why the liner
they see ten miles away is firing rockets – in fact, Lord is so unconcerned that he does
not get out of bed, even though the officers on watch report the rockets to him. In
contrast, in both Walter Lord's book and the film, Rostron of the *Carpathia* is alert
and well organised when he gives orders to prepare blankets and medical facilities as
his ship rushes to the scene of the sinking. Rostron, Lord wrote admiringly, 'symbolised the robust virtues' of the 1910s, because he 'was an experienced, respected ship-
master, known for his quick decisions and for his ability to transmit his own boundless
energy into those serving under him'.[14]

But the ability to manage and inspire collective action in a decisive, energetic way
was a virtue much prized in the 1940s as well as the 1910s. In both the book and film
versions of *A Night to Remember*, it is this ability that is seen as heroic through the
portrayals of Rostron and Lightoller. In the film, characters who struggle to survive
in an undisciplined way, such as the stokers, perish just as surely as those who are
passive or self-sacrificing such as the second-class newlyweds who decide to die
together and a first-class husband who nobly lies to his wife and children so they will
enter a lifeboat. On the other hand, it is the characters who are most skilful at impro-
vising solutions and managing the crises (or, in the case of the drunken baker, trust
their own dumb luck) who seem likely either to survive or to help others to survive.
Social Darwinism, in effect, has been supplanted by the type of disciplined, managed,
cooperative efforts that can be related to the ethos of the 1940s that was believed
responsible for the democratic nations' victories in World War II and was considered
vital in the 1950s if those nations were going to survive or win the Cold War.

This perspective is most clearly illustrated in Baker's film by the scenes that take
place after the *Titanic* sinks around the overturned collapsible B, one of the ship's
canvas lifeboats. As Lightoller swims toward it, stokers and passengers are standing on
the boat's keel, shouting and using oars to beat off other survivors. Lightoller scram-
bles aboard and takes command. 'Shut up and do what the officer says!' someone
shouts, and others call, 'Hear! Hear!' as Lightoller organises them so they trim ship by
leaning left and right to prevent swells from capsizing them. One of the men on the
collapsible dies, and the drunken baker, who was paddling alongside it, is taken on
board – presumably as a testimony to the powers of whiskey as well as discipline as a
means of survival. At dawn, Lightoller, the sober, chastened professional, summarises
the *Titanic*'s mistakes – acknowledging that the disaster would not have occurred if
the ship had not been steaming so fast and if lookouts had seen the iceberg seconds
sooner. But he is profusely praised by one of the passengers who tells him he has
nothing to reproach himself for, because 'you've done all any man could do and more,

Mr Lightoller. You're not [pause] God.' The film ends with a scroll of letters superimposed over waves informing the audience that the *Titanic's* victims' 'sacrifice' was not in vain since, after she sank, new regulations requiring more lifeboats and the establishment of an ice patrol had made it impossible for the disaster to recur. The sinking of the *Titanic* was tragic, but we have learned from it, the film implies, as order and discipline have replaced chaos; and a hierarchy based on merit and professionalism, rather than wealth and privilege, has been established.

Such rationality is notably not present in Cameron's immensely profitable and popular 1997 film. What it has instead, besides its digitalised special effects spectacles, is a hyperemotional shipboard romance and melodrama featuring two actors with immense appeal for young people – Leonardo DiCaprio and Kate Winslet. When Cameron's film is seen as a commodity, one of its most significant features is the timing of its release, since it is what is called in the United States, a 'summer movie', one of the 'blockbusters' appearing in June and designed to sell immense amounts of tickets and popcorn to American teenagers who have just graduated from high school and are swarming to malls with their dates. Once the importance of that market is recognised, it is obvious why Cameron chose nubile adolescents as main characters. DiCaprio's Jack Dawson is supposedly twenty, Winslet's Rose DeWitt Bukater is supposedly seventeen, and both behave as if they were fifteen years old. This also explains why – until the iceberg – the film is basically a 'coming of age' movie in which Jack's and Rose's main concern is escaping from assorted parental authority figures so they can consummate their love, and why the scene where they drink and dance in the steerage lounge is reminiscent of a hot date as seen in a Budweiser beer commercial.

What this interpretation does not quite so readily explain is the blatant melodrama of the post-iceberg portion of Cameron's film when the villainous robber baron Cal Hockley (wonderfully overacted by Billy Zane) and his henchman Spicer Lovejoy (David Warner) chase Jack and Rose around the sinking ship, firing shots at them because Jack has usurped the robber baron's *droit du seigneur*. What is politically striking about this sequence is the crude neo-populist polarisation of its main characters into, respectively, a stereotyped, poor-but-virtuous working-class youth and an equally stereotyped rich wastrel who battle for the love of a passionate young beauty desperate to escape from her supposed destiny as the wastrel's bride. These scenes, if made in black-and-white, with Cameron's dialogue displayed on intertitles, would have the quality of a 1912-vintage melodrama. To understand this better, it is necessary to analyse the anxieties, chiefly the economic anxieties, of the so-called X-Generation American young people (those raised during the Reagan, Bush, and early Clinton era), who were the film's main target audience.

During the 1990s, the American economy was described as the eighth wonder of the world in the mainstream media because of its booming stock market, low unemployment, and almost non-existent inflation. However, as many liberal and/or leftist economists have demonstrated, this 'boom' possessed certain significant structural inequities. To use an appropriate metaphor, this rising tide of wealth did not lift all boats equally, including those of people seeing Cameron's *Titanic*. For during the

1980s and much of the 1990s, what relevant statistics reveal is that rich Americans became substantially richer, many of the poor got poorer, and many members of the working and middle classes stagnated or 'lost ground' economically. 'Gap Between Rich and Poor Found Substantially Wider', said the *New York Times* in an article that pointed out that, by 1999, the richest 2.3 million (or 1 per cent) of American taxpayers would have as much to spend as the bottom 100 million and that that ratio had doubled since 1977.[15] Moreover, between 1977 and 1999, the incomes of the rich Americans in the top 1 per cent bracket had gone up by 119 per cent whereas the incomes of those in the bottom 20 per cent had declined by 12 per cent, those in the next lowest 20 per cent had declined by 9.5 per cent, and those in the middle 20 per cent had declined by 3.1 per cent, leading to assertions that America's working classes were becoming extinct and its middle classes were shrinking.

Among those most adversely affected by these changes were young people, particularly those in the working and middle classes. In another significant statistic, concerning the 44.3 million Americans who lacked or had lost health insurance in 1999, the *New York Times* revealed that the largest segment of that group, 30 per cent, were young people 18–24 years old.[16] In the view of Ted Halstead, writing in the *Atlantic*, many of the target audience of Cameron's film – Americans in their late teens or early twenties – were 'facing a particularly acute economic insecurity'. In contrast to the upward mobility experienced by the baby boomers, the median weekly earnings for men aged 20–34 had fallen by almost a third since 1973, a trend which had been sustained even through 'the said-to-be economically strong years 1989–1995'.[17]

This did not mean that America's political classes had entirely forgotten about young people, including those who were untalented or had received substandard educations in inferior school systems. As *The Onion* sardonically observed in its bogus 1990 news story about the Gulf War, 'Bottom 10 Percent of Last Year's Graduating Class Ready to Take on Saddam . . . President Bush has already deployed 5,000 19-year-olds with below-average maths and reading skills . . . and has pledged an additional 15,000 D-students if necessary.' It also claimed General Norman Schwarzkopf had described the United States Army as a 'defender of freedom' that is 'also a catch-all for those high-school seniors who don't want to work at a gas station but don't have the grades to get into their local technical college'.[18] Thanks to a flourishing economy in the mid-1990s, jobs pumping gas, as well as in the military, might be available; but these were rarely jobs with good pay that could lead to middle-class futures. Yet, at the same time, the young people facing such bleak futures were bombarded with media blitzes glorifying the fantastic incomes and wealth of sports stars like Michael Jordan and CEOs like Bill Gates.

Much of the appeal of Cameron's film, it can be argued, lies in the way it channels and commodifies the anxieties of X-Generation Americans, who were Cameron's prime audience, in the context of a 1912 disaster in which the rich and the powerful can at least be blamed and despised, rather than praised, for their selfishness and ruthlessness. Like Baker's film, Cameron's relegates most of the millionaires to the status of minor figures; but, unlike Baker, Cameron made an evil millionaire, Cal Hockley, a major character and depicted him as surviving, as he unscrupulously tries to bribe and then successfully lies his way into a lifeboat – while the heroic, working-class Jack dies so that Rose can live. Also unlike Baker, Cameron has no representative noble first-class passenger who is an equivalent to the husband in the 1958 film who stays on the sinking *Titanic* after putting his family into a lifeboat. Moreover, in contrast to the conservative depictions of millionaires in 1912, Cameron's film does not credit any of them with any virtues, including social Darwinian ones, much less any chivalrous values. Hockley survives because he is the sleaziest, not the fittest; for, like many millionaires depicted in the 1990s media, he is totally selfish and indifferent to the fates of persons in less privileged classes, including women and children.

Cameron also restored Bruce Ismay to his earlier role of villain (albeit a feckless rather than a malevolent one) by having him encourage Smith to steam faster so the *Titanic* might arrive sooner and receive more headlines. What is notable about Cameron's film is the virtually complete disappearance of the second- or middle-class passengers and the relegation of the ship's officers, particularly Captain Smith and First Officer Murdoch, to the status of lackeys for the wealthy. In Baker's film, these two groups were depicted as possessing capabilities for self-sacrifice or disciplined behaviour that enabled them to die with dignity (the newlyweds and the ship's engineers) or to survive with honour (Lightoller). Because Cameron almost completely eliminated such characters, the ship's final minutes in his film are a mixture of the technological sublime and a social cataclysm in which the officers, including Lightoller, are just as confused as everyone else; most of the passengers panic; and the steerage immigrants, again depicted as a rioting rabble, have to be held at bay by gunfire until one is killed by Murdoch, who then ingloriously shoots himself.

An even more significant exclusion from Cameron's version of the narrative is that of Captain Rostron. In both the US Senate and the British Board of Trade investigations, as well as in Lord's book and Baker's film, Rostron represented the dedicated, middle-class professional who was able to mitigate the consequences of the disaster through diligence and competence. In the 1958 film, in particular, when the *Titanic* is sinking, Baker cross-cuts to the *Carpathia* so that the confusion aboard the sinking liner is contrasted with the orderly professionalism of Rostron as he prepares his ship to take on survivors. In versions of the *Titanic* story in which his behaviour was praised and commodified, Rostron's behaviour could assuage the anxieties aroused by the disaster by encouraging hope that competence could rise above negligence, panic, and class distinctions by providing decisive, rational responses to a catastrophe. Commodification implies a certain degree of accessibility – at least imaginative accessibility – for consumers: the possibility that if they purchase a product they can possess the virtues associated with it, that they can become a little bit like Michael Jordan if they buy the right kind of sneaker. Thus, Rostron's absence and the diminution of Lightoller's role in Cameron's *Titanic* suggest that the values that they represented in the 1950s versions – and the membership in the middle classes that the possession of such values implies – are no longer available to Cameron's X-Generation youth audience.

Lacking a figure such as Rostron, the ending of Cameron's film can only offer and commodify the pathetic consolation of Jack dying heroically so Rose can survive – plus the even more pathetic spectacle of Rose's passivity, first as she floats on the north

Atlantic and then as she cowers on the *Carpathia* unwilling or unable to confront Hockley when he is searching for her. By his juxtaposition of Rose with the Statue of Liberty when she takes Jack's name in the next scene, Cameron presumably wanted to symbolise that this new name and identity gives her the freedom to become 'her own person', to use the argot of the 1980s and 1990s. In contrast, a 1912-vintage melodrama heroine would surely have exposed Hockley's dastardly behaviour so that he would have been stigmatised as a cowardly survivor. Disguised in a shawl aboard the *Carpathia*, Cameron's Rose tacitly accepts the *déclassé* status of the steerage passenger and immigrant who has no voice in society and thus is afraid to speak out against Hockley's abuse of his class privilege – until many years later, when she finally reveals the 'secrets' in her heart, but only decades after the evil robber baron and other survivors presumably have gone to their graves.

Notes

1 Scott Dikkers and Mike Loew (eds), *Our Dumb Century: The Onion Presents 100 Years of Headlines from America's Finest News Source* (New York: Three Rivers Press, 1999), p. 13.
2 Walter Lord, *A Night to Remember* (New York: Holt, Rinehart and Winston, 1955); *A Night to Remember* (1958), dir. Roy Baker, perf. Kenneth More, David McCallum, Jill Dixon; *Titanic* (1997), dir. James Cameron, perf. Leonardo DiCaprio, Kate Winslet, Billy Zane, David Warner.
3 Walter Lord, *The Night Lives On* (New York: William Morrow, 1986), p. 16.
4 Wyn Craig Wade, *The Titanic: The End of a Dream* (rev. edn, New York: Penguin, 1986), p. 322; Steven Biel, *Down with the Old Canoe: A Cultural History of the Titanic Disaster* (New York: Norton, 1996), p. 7.
5 Thorstein Veblen, *The Theory of the Leisure Class* (New York: Macmillan, 1912).
6 Andrew Carnegie, 'Wealth', in Robert Fossum and John Roth (eds), *American Ground* (New York: Paragon House, 1988), pp. 230–1.
7 Joseph Conrad, 'The loss of the Titanic', 'The Titanic inquiry', in *Notes on Life and Letters* (New York: Doubleday, Page, 1924), pp. 224, 234.
8 Wade, *Titanic*, p. 57.
9 *Ibid.*; Biel, *Down with the Old Canoe*, p. 53.
10 Biel, *Down with the Old Canoe*, p. 28.
11 Wade, *Titanic*, p. 45.
12 Walter Lord, *Day of Infamy* (New York: Bantam Books, 1963); Walter Lord, *The Miracle of Dunkirk* (New York: Viking, 1982).
13 Lord, *Miracle at Dunkirk*, pp. ix–x.
14 Lord, *A Night to Remember*, p. 155.
15 *New York Times* (5 September 1999).
16 *Ibid.* (10 October 1999).
17 Ted Halstead, 'A politics for Generation X', *Atlantic* (August 1999), 35–6.
18 *The Onion* (1990), p. 150.

Doctors and trauma in the First World War: the response of British military psychiatrists

One of the most personal and revealing accounts of treating soldiers in the First World War was written by Lt. Col. Charles Myers (1873–1946), consulting psychologist to the British army in France. Although based on his war diaries, *Shell Shock in France* was not published until 1940 when the outbreak of another conflict prompted him to recall his earlier traumatic experiences. His writing vividly revealed his frustrations, exhaustion, and final disillusionment. 'On the 31 March 1919,' Myers wrote,

> I was demobilised, not altogether unwillingly. For I was by now tired of the many diffi-culties and frustrations which had beset me in my four and half years' work. Before leaving the army, I appealed to the Director-General of Medical Services for some rec-ognition on behalf of certain junior medical officers of the neurological service who to my knowledge had done brilliant and strenuous work in a most unostentatious manner [but no distinctions were forthcoming] . . . With this farewell visit ended my medical work in the Army of the last Great War and . . . I returned to my psycholog-ical laboratory at Cambridge. The recall of my past five years' work proved too painful for me to accept the subsequent invitation either of the Medical Research Council to help in its historical and statistical work for the Army Council or of the War Office Committee on Shell Shock to give evidence before it. Indeed . . . the revival of these long-repressed memories – particularly those of certain experiences which I have refrained from mentioning – has been exceptionally unpleasant during the preparation of this volume.[1]

Why, then, did Myers end a victorious war feeling so dispirited? Was he alone in feeling this way, or was his response typical of those doctors who had enlisted in the Royal Army Medical Corps (RAMC) to treat the psychological casualties of war?

Before the First World War, there were few military psychiatrists in the British Army. Although the Royal Victoria Hospital, Netley, had a specialist psychiatric building, 'D Block', this was, in effect, an asylum for servicemen with psychoses or severe depression.[2] Soldiers who suffered from functional somatic disorders after combat, such as disordered action of the heart (DAH), or milder psychological states, such as neurasthenia or nervous exhaustion, were treated by military physicians with no specialist psychiatric training.[3] Indeed, the idea that a serviceman might suffer mental distress as a result of combat was barely considered.

Because of its scale and duration, the First World War drew large numbers of civilian doctors into the armed forces. The vast majority of RAMC physicians, therefore, were not regular officers but volunteers unschooled in military ways of thinking.[4] This influx of young and middle-aged men from diverse backgrounds helped to broaden the understanding and treatment of combat disorders. Although the epidemic of shell shock and other war-related psychiatric injuries has been widely documented, the effect on junior doctors of attempting to treat such cases is less well described. Under pressure to return soldiers rapidly to the front, RAMC officers had to listen to harrowing tales and to experience something of the fear and depression felt by these shell-shock casualties. Furthermore, doctors were presented with the dilemma that an effective therapeutic intervention might result in their patient's return to the front and subsequent death. Having been trained to save life, some found that they served as the state's instrument of enforcement.[5] As Freud remarked, military psychiatrists acted as if they were machine guns behind the front line, driving men back into combat.[6] Some were unnerved by the experience, while others, overzealous in their duties or driven by an exaggerated sense of patriotism, themselves became oppressors.

The military context

The army medical services were caught off guard by the scale and nature of the First World War. Dr Albert Wilson, who had worked in a French military hospital in the opening phase of the war, concluded, in November 1914, 'I do not think psychologists will get many cases'.[7] At first, military psychiatry was haphazard, relying on volunteers from civilian practice. William Aldren Turner (1864–1945), a distinguished neurologist at the National Hospital for the Paralysed and Epileptic, Queen Square, was rushed to France in December 1914 as a temporary lieutenant colonel when it became clear that psychiatric casualties were multiplying. Turner, who wished to return to London, handed responsibility for psychological cases seen in French base hospitals to Charles Myers. A medically qualified Cambridge psychologist, Myers had travelled to France shortly after the outbreak of war to work as a volunteer registrar in the hospital at Le Touquet funded by the Duchess of Westminster. Once there, he was offered a temporary commission in the RAMC by Sir Arthur Sloggett (1857–1929), the Director-General of Medical Services of the British Armies in the Field. In March 1915, Myers officially took over from Turner in Boulogne, touring medical units to offer a specialist opinion and gather data for a treatment policy.[8]

By March 1915, a rudimentary organisation had been established to manage psychiatric battle casualties.[9] In essence, soldiers diagnosed with shell shock were invalided to the UK, where a growing number of specialist psychiatric hospitals were opened by the military.[10] Yet this system of allocation soon broke down in the face of growing numbers and the decision to treat soldiers in France.

By the end of 1915, it was apparent that symptoms became increasingly entrenched the further a serviceman travelled from the front, and, if admitted to a UK hospital, he had little chance of ever being returned to a fighting unit. Having been made consulting psychologist to the British Expeditionary Force (BEF) in August

1916, Myers argued that specialist units should be set up 'as remote from the sounds of warfare as is compatible with the preservation of the "atmosphere" of the front'.[11] In November, in the aftermath of the Battle of the Somme and growing manpower shortages, Sloggett agreed that Myers could open specialist units in tented hospitals or casualty clearing stations (CCS) about ten miles from the trenches.[12] Four 'NYDN Centres' (meaning 'Not Yet Diagnosed Nervous' to avoid terms such as 'shell shock' or 'war neurosis') were established to serve the five armies of the BEF.[13] Admitted to these centres for about two weeks, soldiers were rested and given an encouraging message about recovery. This treatment strategy was described by Thomas Salmon, a US Army psychiatrist, sent to Europe in May 1917 to study British methods, and later given the acronym 'PIE' (Proximity, Immediacy, and Expectancy) by K.L. Artiss.[14]

Myers was allowed to set up these units only because the British army was desperate to stem the flow of psychiatric casualties leaving France. Sloggett mistrusted psychological methods and believed that the problem of shell shock could be addressed by military discipline and strict avoidance of the diagnostic term. He placed far more trust in Lt. Col. Gordon Holmes (1876–1965), consulting neurologist to the BEF, who shared his disdain for anything psychological. In January 1917, Sloggett transferred responsibility for shell shock and other psychiatric cases in the First, Second, and Third Armies to Holmes,[15] limiting Myers' authority to the Fourth and Fifth Armies.[16] Myers felt undermined and misunderstood. When Sloggett closed an experimental Advanced Sorting Centre that Myers had set up, he requested a posting to the UK, leaving France in November 1917.

Because of the structure of army medical services and the attitudes that dominated within the RAMC, military psychiatrists were inevitably marginalised and disregarded. Each of the forward units was run by one or two doctors working without the support of a protective peer group. Surgeons and physicians at base hospitals often found themselves in a close-knit group united by camaraderie and granted professional respect. By contrast, psychiatrists were regarded with grave suspicion by many of their medical colleagues. In October 1917, Harvey Cushing, an American neurosurgeon who visited the NYND Centre set up at No. 62 CCS at Haringhe for the Fifth Army, thought the atmosphere there 'very dismal . . . A dumping ground for MOs who can't wriggle out – none of them appear at all interested in, or acquainted with, psychiatry.'[17] If, indeed, psychiatry were a refuge for substandard doctors, those with a genuine interest and ability must have found military service a demoralising experience.

Shell shock in France

Traumatised soldiers presented in a variety of ways during the First World War, though the diagnosis doctors had the greatest difficulty understanding was shell shock. There was no accepted definition of the disorder, as patients suffered from a range of unexplained symptoms and disabilities. Typically, soldiers complained of fatigue, poor sleep, nightmares, and jumpiness, and had a variety of somatic symptoms such as palpitations, chest pain, tremor, joint and muscle pains, loss of voice or hearing, and functional paralysis. Captain Wilfrid Harris (1869–1960), a physician attached to the Springfield Hospital, Wandsworth, revealed the harrowing aspects of treating servicemen with shell shock. Men in this state, he observed, 'may break down in tears if asked to describe their experiences at the front. This is especially the case if the man's regiment has been severely handled, and numbers of his comrades and brother officers have been killed.'[18]

As regards causation, it was initially thought that there were two varieties of shell shock: commotional and emotional. Frederick Mott (1853–1926) hypothesised that the forces of compression and decompression, caused by proximity to an explosion, in turn led to microscopic brain haemorrhage.[19] He also believed that carbon monoxide released by the blast might lead to cerebral poisoning. By contrast, a psychological interpretation of shell shock came from other officers, many of whom had first-hand experience of war in France. Captain Harold Wiltshire, who until August 1915 had been responsible for the diagnosis of functional psychiatric cases at No. 12 General Hospital in Rouen,[20] observed that:

> Gradual psychic exhaustion from continued fear is an important disposing cause of shell shock, particularly in men of neuropathic predisposition. In such subjects it may suffice to cause shell shock per se. In the vast majority of cases of shell shock, the exciting cause is some special psychic shock. Horrible sights are the most frequent and potent factor in the production of this shock. Losses and the fright of being buried are also important in this respect.[21]

Myers himself experimented with rest and suggestion, sometimes supplemented by hypnosis, and found that some symptoms and bodily functions gradually recovered. Reliving the traumatic experience to master the strong feelings it evoked was regarded by some as a crucial part of the therapeutic process.

Doctors on active service

The doctors at greatest personal danger were regimental medical officers (RMOs) attached to fighting units in the front line. They shared the hazards of the infantry and were often casualties themselves. For example, Captain B.A. West, an RMO in Gallipoli and later attached to a siege battery in France, broke down in October 1916. After a year of treatment and convalescence, he returned to base duties in the UK but found that contact with patients revived his earlier experiences and admitted himself to St Andrews Hospital. On his last day of duty, he recorded in his diary: 'feeling thoroughly wretched and done up. Felt I could not continue . . . an hour of pure misery'.[22] Only in November 1917 was West able to return to work in a civilian hospital. RMOs were responsible for the initial diagnosis, though their understanding of psychiatric disorders varied widely. Field ambulance units conveyed men with shell shock to CCSs situated at a safe distance from the front.[23] If a soldier failed to respond to treatment at a CCS, he was evacuated to a base hospital either in France or the UK.

The shell-shock division of No. 4 Stationary Hospital, Arques, was run by Major Dudley Carmalt Jones (1874–1957).[24] A physician at St Mary's researching vaccines before enlistment, he found himself, without any training in military psychiatry, having to treat large numbers of servicemen.[25] Indeed, his clinical practice avoided psychological interventions. Carmalt Jones eschewed hypnotism because he believed that it conveyed a sense of occult power in the doctor. Under his treatment regime, soldiers were examined medically, allowed a short period of rest with medication to help them sleep, and put on a programme of graduated exercise, ending with route marches. Many physicians believed that 'rest, good food and encouragement' was all that was needed and that psychological interventions had little impact on outcomes.[26] At Arques, psychiatric input was provided by Captain A.E. Evans, who had worked as a civilian alienist before the war. Colleagues observed that Carmalt Jones was a 'gentle and kindly' doctor, who taught that 'patients were human beings to be treated with courtesy, kindness and patience'. He appears to have survived the experience, in part, because, as head of the medical division at the hospital, he was not tainted with the new psychiatric ideas. Nevertheless, he expressed some of the frustrations of those practising military psychiatry, concluding that RAMC doctors 'who know anything of nervous disease appear to have far the smallest numbers', and he 'put in a very serious plea for a thoroughly sympathetic and intelligent grasp of the problem on the part of the higher medical authorities'.[27] After the war, he practised as a physician at the Westminster Hospital before becoming professor of systematic medicine at Otago University, Dunedin, New Zealand.

In June 1917, Captain William Johnson (d. 1949), a neurologist, was seconded to Carmalt Jones's shell-shock division.[28] This was probably to gain clinical experience, as, in August, he was posted to No. 62 CCS, the NYDN Centre for the Fifth Army, at Haringhe. During the Battle of Passchendaele between August and October 1917, 5,000 patients were admitted with shell shock, about 1 per cent of the troops engaged.[29] Johnson also relied on rest, an atmosphere of cure, and words of reassurance, sometimes supported by vigorous massage to restore his patients to duty; he did not believe that psychotherapy was either needed or beneficial. He reported that of the 5,000 patients 55 per cent were returned to duty in the same units, though no record was kept of relapses.[30] Described as 'a reserved and modest man, rather shy, yet possessing a warm and friendly nature',[31] Johnson was not attracted to psychiatry after the war but practised as a general physician at various hospitals in Liverpool.

The NYDN centre for the Third Army was established by Captain Frederick Dillon at No. 6 Stationary Hospital, Frévant, though, in July 1917, with the redeployment of the Fifth Army, it moved to No. 3 Canadian Stationary Hospital in the citadel at Doullens.[32] Like Myers, he was familiar with psychoanalytical ideas, and appeared to have a particular interest in the works of Jung. He believed in abreaction to uncover unconscious conflict and also interpreted his patients' dreams.[33] The unit treated 4,235 patients in the 22 months to October 1918, and Dillon calculated that 63.5 per cent were returned to duty, mainly to fighting units, though no record was kept of relapses.[34]

Major William Brown (1881–1952), who commanded the NYDN centre for the Fourth Army at 21 CCS in Corbie on the Somme between November 1916 and February 1918, took a psychological approach.[35] In contrast to Carmalt Jones and

Johnson, he believed that shell shock could be treated by abreaction, often assisted by hypnosis. Brown argued that the memory of an unacceptable or terrifying event had been repressed at the expense of some form of physical functioning. Hence, it was necessary to persuade the soldier to recollect the frightening event so that it could be mastered and incorporated within his experience. Cure, therefore, required the doctor to relive the terrifying experience with his patient and to empathise with his suffering. Brown reported having treated from 2,000 to 3,000 soldiers, returning 70 per cent to combat units after an average of two weeks of therapy.[36] Between November and December 1917, at the time of the Cambrai offensive, he claimed a success rate of 91 per cent 'due to the number of exceptionally light cases that are sent down at the time of a push'.[37] In the light of other studies, these figures seem optimistic and took no account of relapses.[38]

Psychologically minded physicians who treated shell shock often encountered opposition to their ideas and methods in military hospitals.[39] Blindness to psychiatric ideas was often found in doctors characterised as 'the fire-eaters of the field ambulances' rather than those with actual experience of combat.[40] Henry Yellowlees (1881–1971), who worked as a 'mental specialist' in a French base hospital, recalled that 'many highly placed officials in the War Office made no secret of their belief that the whole thing [shell shock] was humbug from beginning to end'.[41] David Eder (d. 1936) gave up his post in a military hospital in Malta in 1916, claiming that 'the institutes of medicine have remained unshaken by the war'.[42] Arthur Osburn, a regular RAMC doctor who had served in the Boer War, recalled having to attend a lecture in 1917 given by a 'mental specialist':

> Shell-shock he sharply told us was a fable . . . His ruthless contempt for a doctor who let any man down to the base before he was mutilated was superb . . . His contempt for me was enormous, his asperity insolent, his acid sarcasm concerning my competence as a doctor covered an implied threat . . . I was reprimanded for being contumacious to an expert.[43]

The lecturer may have been Gordon Holmes, who was noted for his quarrelsome manner and disdain for psychological interpretations.[44]

Base hospitals in the UK

While shell-shock doctors may have found themselves isolated and unsupported in France, this was not always true in the UK, where specialist hospitals gathered together men of like-minded ideas. Maghull, taken over by the military in December 1914 to treat war neuroses, saw the gathering of a 'brilliant band of workers who at that time made it the centre for the study of abnormal psychology'.[45] In summer 1915, R.G. Rows (d. 1925), the medical superintendent, recruited Grafton Elliot Smith (1871–1937), professor of anatomy, and T. H. Pear (1886–1972), lecturer in psychology, both from Manchester University, who, in turn, were joined by William Brown and W.H.R. Rivers (1865–1922). Among the other tutors who worked at Maghull were Bernard Hart (1879–1966), William McDougall (1871–1938), Henry

Yellowlees, and T.A. Ross (1875–1941). With talented doctors drawn from different backgrounds and free to experiment, Maghull earned grudging respect from the military authorities and towards the end of the war was given responsibility for the postgraduate training of military psychiatrists. In all, 56 RAMC doctors, six Canadians, and five Americans attended the hospital's three-month course.[46]

Yet, not even Maghull could protect. Lt. Col. Rows was described as a shadow of his former self by the end of the war. The strain of running a major hospital, treating patients, and balancing the competing needs of his military masters and the demands of his staff and patients appear to have worn Rows down.[47] After the war, he began to research the psychogenesis of epilepsy and had just taken the post of pathologist at Prestwich Mental Hospital when he died at the age of 58.[48]

Craiglockhart Military Hospital, opened in October 1916 to treat officers with psychiatric disorders, also attracted a number of talented doctors. According to an anonymous contemporary account, the commanding officer, Major W.H. Bryce, 'had not got acclimatised to military etiquette [and] was apt to rush around the hospital without cap, Sam Browne, and spoke to many of his staff as equals'.[49] Rivers, who transferred to Craiglockhart when it opened,[50] was also described as unconventional, bowing 'courteously to VAD cooks instead of saluting', though he was 'very valiant if patients were tampered with in any way'. They were joined by an American, Major Ruggles, who 'worked on the same lines as Captain Rivers and was much liked'. Rivers believed that the symptoms of shell shock resulted when an adaptive form of repression failed to operate efficiently. Because most troops were not regulars but had volunteered or had been conscripted into the army and had been trained in great haste, they had not had the time to build up an effective mechanism to deal with strong emotions. Faced with 'strains such as have never previously been known in the history of mankind', he wrote, it was 'small wonder that the failures of adaptation should have been so numerous and severe'.[51] If symptoms were the result of a maladaptive attempt to deal with distressing memories and affective states, Rivers argued that catharsis and the reintegration of the event in a modified form was the appropriate treatment. He abandoned the primary role given to infantile sexuality by Freud and argued that it was the conflict between the soldier's sense of fear and duty that lay at the heart of war neurosis.[52] T.A. Ross, who had practised at Maghull in the latter part of the war, was convinced by his experience of working with traumatised soldiers that psychotherapy was the best treatment for neuroses. Fears brought to consciousness, he argued, 'may no longer be a source of stress and therefore symptoms'.[53]

Seale Hayne was the creation of Arthur Hurst (1879–1944), who had been drawn into military psychiatry from medicine. He had originally been sent to Salonica to work on the incidence and prevention of trench fever.[54] Ill health prevented him from proceeding to Mesopotamia as a physician, while Sir Maurice Craig encouraged him to work as a neurologist at Oxford. In the event, Hurst persuaded the War Office to set up a specialist rehabilitation unit for war neuroses in a newly built agricultural college at Seale Hayne, near Newton Abbot. Although he had encountered opposition from the Southern Command's Director of Medical Services, Hurst circumvented him with the help of Sir Warren Crooke-Lawless, the commanding officer of the Royal Victoria Hospital at Netley. The team that Hurst gathered, in contrast to Maghull or Craiglockhart, were largely physicians rather than psychiatrists, a point that concerned Myers. As a result, Dr R.G. Gordon was recruited to give weekly lectures on psychological medicine, though Hurst doubted that 'they had much effect on the practical work of the medical officers'.[55] After the war, Hurst returned to Guy's as a consultant physician, though his interest in functional somatic disorders endured; in 1921, he set up a small private hospital, New Lodge Clinic, near Windsor.

Not all military psychiatrists were disillusioned by their experience of war. Edward Mapother (1881–1940), for example, appears to have gained valuable experience.[56] A highly qualified doctor working at Long Grove Asylum, Epsom, he joined the RAMC in 1914 and served in Mesopotamia and France as a surgeon. Returning to the UK in April 1917, he completed the Maghull course before taking command of the neurological division of No. 2 Western General Hospital, Stockport. In August 1919, he was appointed by the Ministry of Pensions to run their special hospital for war neuroses in the buildings at Denmark Hill constructed to house the Maudsley. When it transferred to the London County Council for civilian use in 1923, Mapother became the medical superintendent, and later the first professor of clinical psychiatry at London University.[57] He continued to treat veterans with shell shock as psychiatric adviser to the Ex-Services Mental Welfare Society and helped to organise a series of conferences on war syndromes in the late 1930s when hostilities threatened.[58]

Captain Millais Culpin (1874–1952) had practised as a surgeon in France before entering the field of military psychiatry. Shell shock captured his interest, and when he was on leave in London, in November 1917, Aldren Turner encouraged him to undertake further training at Maghull.[59] Although Culpin found the course inspiring, his tutors 'gave no warning about hostility to the new [psychiatric] views'.[60] At short notice, he and another trainee were transferred to a hospital in Birmingham to treat 250 shell-shocked servicemen transferred from London because of air raids. Fellow doctors regarded them with disdain and thought their patients either insane or malingerers. Myers was called to address the crisis. Culpin's colleague was invalided out of the RAMC, while Culpin was ultimately moved to Ewell Military Hospital, where he found a more congenial atmosphere.

Not all doctors who worked in base hospitals were convinced by the new psychological treatments. Mott, based in the Maudsley Wing of King's, argued that hypnosis and psychoanalysis were not 'necessary or even desirable'. He believed that a quiet and recuperative environment was sufficient to enable servicemen to forget their traumatic experiences. Mott argued that 'diversion of the mind from the recollection of their terrifying experiences is essential for successful treatment' – a very different approach from the abreaction advocated by other doctors, including Rivers, Brown, and Dillon. This treatment had the advantage that Mott himself would not have to listen to harrowing experiences and was, in part, protected from the horrors of the battlefield. A period of distracted convalescence was the solution proposed by Mott: 'only common-sense and interest in the comfort, welfare and amusement of these neurotic patients are necessary for their recovery'.[61]

Doctors as instruments of the state

Having been invalided from France, Siegfried Sassoon described a medical assessment in London at which a temporary captain in the RAMC appeared to derive pleasure from tormenting officers with threats of a rapid return to action. 'I was told afterwards,' Sassoon recalled,

> that officers had been known to leave the doctor's room in tears . . . I prefer to think of him as a man who craved for power over his fellow men. And though his power over the visiting patients was brief and episodic, he must have derived extraordinary (and perhaps sadistic) satisfaction from the spectacle of young officers sobbing and begging not to be sent back to the front.[62]

Dr Lewis Yealland (d. 1954), a Canadian registrar in neurology at Queen Square, achieved prominence for his use of 'faradism' (the application of an electric current to various parts of the body) to cure functional aphonias and paralysis. Electricity was popularly believed to be beneficial, and machines that gave a mild shock were common among fairground amusements. Yealland used faradism to increase the power of suggestion, believing that soldiers with functional symptoms suffered from a weakness of will that required rigorous methods to begin the process of re-education. 'It must be remembered, however,' Yealland wrote, 'that faradism employed without suggestion and persistence in otherwise intractable cases will fail to produce recovery'.[63] He claimed a high success rate, which from his own descriptions of cases, appear in part to have been driven by fear. One serviceman was

> strapped in a chair for twenty minutes at a time while strong electricity was applied to his neck and throat; lighted cigarettes had been applied to the tip of his tongue and 'hot plates' had been placed at the back of his mouth.[64]

The patient had been warned that he could not leave the room until cured and, according to Yealland, four hours of electric shocks removed all symptoms. He published a detailed account of his cases to demonstrate the efficacy of his methods, though the book brought criticism from some, including Myers, who condemned such physical treatments in a letter to the *Lancet* on 27 December 1919:

> During the war, there were certain physicians who could explain to a patient suffering from functional hemiplegia that the cortical cells on one side of the brain were out of order . . . And they would proceed to tone up the disordered cells by painful faradism . . . I have always been convinced that such measures are not only needless, but also dangerous.[65]

Others, such as Taylor, also adopted faradism, though an analysis of 200 case notes at Queen Square showed that only 33 had been treated with electricity.[66] Yealland left the National Hospital after the war to become a consultant neurologist at the West End Hospital for Nervous Diseases, though his reputation had been somewhat tarnished by these controversial methods. His personality stood curiously at variance with his treatments, he being described in an obituary as a 'delightful personality' and by his daughter-in-law as 'a sweet little man'.[67]

Doctors in the aftermath of World War One

Having been exposed to traumatic and novel experiences during the war, how, then, did doctors cope with the return of peace? Despite having advanced the understanding of psychiatric disorders, many RAMC physicians were disillusioned by their experiences. Myers, for example, went back to Cambridge, but, in 1920, he left his academic post to join a London businessman, H.J. Welch, in setting up the National Institute for Industrial Psychology.[68]

William McDougall, who had worked at Netley and the Littlemore Hospital, returned to Oxford as Wilde Reader in Mental Philosophy after demobilisation from the RAMC, but, feeling unwanted, he emigrated to Harvard and a chair in psychology. He confided in a friend that 'I have done my best to serve my country during the war. I have returned to have my laboratory taken from me.'[69] Rivers returned to Cambridge in 1919 as prelector in natural sciences. However, he appeared to have abandoned clinical work, and even research, when he accepted the nomination as the Labour Party candidate for the University of London constituency. He died unexpectedly of a strangulated hernia in June 1922 before the election took place.[70] William Brown was one of the few to continue seeing patients in an academic context after the war. In 1921, he succeeded McDougall as Wilde Reader in Mental Philosophy at Oxford and founded the Institute of Experimental Psychology there; from 1925 to 1931, he also practised as a consultant psychotherapist at King's College Hospital.[71]

To what extent was this disillusionment (few RAMC psychiatrists seem to have wanted to remain in the forces once the war was over) a result of their own experience of trauma, both at first-hand and through the accounts of their patients? Unless they were in special psychiatric hospitals like Maghull or Craiglockhart, doctors such as Myers seem to have had little opportunity to share their ideas and casework. They were regarded with suspicion by the military and often scorned by other medical specialists. Although army medical services had generally become better organised by 1917,[72] reforms were resisted or blocked, and psychiatrists cannot have felt valued or even wanted. Understandably, most chose to deal with their experiences by trying to forget them and returned to civilian practice.

Repression of memory

Military psychiatry had been tolerated so long as it was needed to support the war effort. Once peace had returned, the new discipline was put to one side almost as if it were viewed as a necessary but unseemly aspect of battle. The 1922 *Report of the War Office Committee for Enquiry into 'Shell-Shock'* recommended that 'special instruction should be given to RAMC officers in the psycho-neurosis and psychoses as they occur in war, and selected officers should be encouraged to specialise in the study of these disorders'.[73] Deficiencies in training had been identified during the war, but it appears that little was done to address them after the armistice.[74] Culpin later observed that few doctors with any regard for their reputation would mention an interest in psycho-analysis during the 1920s 'without the verbal equivalent of spitting three times over the left shoulder, and even to speak about the revival of war memories carried the risk of being accused of advocating free fornication for everyone'.[75]

After the armistice the British army returned to its pre-war professional origins and largely dispensed with the service of its psychiatrists. The few that remained appear to have undertaken traditional hospital and outpatient roles, treating servicemen with psychosis and depression. In the period 1920 to 1936, for example, the *Journal of the Army Medical Corps* published only five papers on shell shock and other war neuroses. Why was this the case when they had demonstrated a role for themselves on the battlefield? Many RAMC doctors and senior commanders believed that properly trained troops, well led and with high morale, were virtually immune from psychological injury. Giving evidence to the Southborough committee, Lt. Col. Lord Gort suggested that shell shock was practically non-existent 'in first-class divisions' and that prevention was a matter of 'training . . . strong morale and *esprit de corps*'.[76] If Gort were correct, there was little need for military psychiatry. Elliot Smith and Pear, having urged that the new treatments inspired by shell shock should be more extensively applied 'not only for our soldiers now, but also for our civilian population for all time', were justifiably pessimistic even in 1917.[77] Yet, not all the gains of the First World War had been lost. In 1920, for example, Hugh Crichton-Miller (1877–1959), who had treated cases of shell shock in Alexandria and London, was instrumental in founding the Tavistock Clinic, while Mapother was one of the driving forces behind the reopening of the Maudsley three years later. Memories of the experience of shell shock were repressed or muted but remained available for recall if circumstances demanded.

The threat of war in the late 1930s and the possibility of a new epidemic of shell shock in soldiers and a civilian population subjected to aerial bombardment forced the government and the armed forces to look again at the lessons of the First World War. Experienced specialists, who had largely been ignored during the interwar years, were suddenly needed to advise on treatment and prevention.[78] The *Journal of the Royal Army Medical Corps* published three papers in 1937–38 on war neuroses, including one commissioned from Edward Mapother.[79] Holmes, Mapother, and Bernard Hart (who had worked at Maghull) served on the Horder committee set up in July 1939 to devise a strategy to deal with 'war neuroses' and any related claim on the state for financial compensation. News of the Ministry's initiative spread, and John McCurdy, C.S. Myers, George Riddoch, and T.A. Ross, who had not been included in the discussions, produced their own memorandum, which advocated the psychological vetting of recruits, the rapid treatment of combat stress, and a clear public statement that there would be no war pensions for psychological disability.[80]

Wishing to put their experiences to effect, others rejoined the RAMC, encouraged by its new director of army psychiatry, J.R. Rees, recruited from the Tavistock Clinic and himself a First World War veteran. Among those with earlier military service were G.W.B. James, Emmanuel Miller, and Henry Yellowlees, while E.A. Bennet and Wilfrid Bion had both been decorated while serving with combat units.[81] Although he did not volunteer, Myers was prompted to record his memories in a book, while others contributed through the medical journals. Thus, the crisis of survival created an environment in which it was acceptable to retrieve experiences of war-related psychiatric injury and to think about vulnerabilities and the impact of combat on psychological well-being.

Conclusions

A small but significant group of psychologically minded doctors who had volunteered for the RAMC were responsible for important advances in psychiatric diagnosis, psychopathology, and treatment. The enlistment of experienced specialists sometimes shook established military traditions. In some cases, these temporary officers were better qualified than the regular officers under whom they served.[82] Although this gave them the confidence to circumvent established procedures, it also created tensions and conflicts. Gains in psychiatric knowledge were often won at a cost to its practitioners. Although not usually required to risk their lives in the trenches, military psychiatrists in France often operated alone without the protective comradeship of men in combat units, and indeed often without the professional respect enjoyed by physicians and surgeons. In addition, they often found themselves faced with complex and sometimes competing demands. They had to try to ensure that those susceptible to stress and who would probably break down in the trenches were removed from active service, while ensuring that such cases were kept to a minimum. At the same time, for their own psychological well-being, they had to attempt to make some sense of what they were witnessing.

Psychiatrists at base hospitals did at least have colleagues with whom they could discuss cases, though the RAMC hierarchy did not offer them much professional recognition and respect. Because they were not subjected to the terrors and real danger of the RMO at the front, Mapother believed that this led them to exaggerate their therapeutic successes in part to justify their safe existence in the UK.[83] To some extent, the aggression of Holmes, Yealland, and others may have been an attempt to deal with any guilt they may have felt at having secure, non-combatant roles. A few disillusioned military psychiatrists, including Myers, Rivers, Brown, Elliot Smith, Pear, and Ross, turned to writing as a way of coming to terms with their experiences. Sadly, little of what had been discovered was incorporated in civilian psychiatry once peace had returned. Society and the military, by contrast, preferred to turn their backs on their observations and interpretations.

In his 1940 account of shell shock, Myers concluded:

> No members of the Royal Army Medical Corps had worked harder, spending the whole morning and a large part of each afternoon, year in and year out, in the wards, engaged in a task of treatment far more trying and exhausting than that of ordinary operating, fracture-setting, wound-cleaning, palpation or auscultation. But neither in France nor the UK, so far as I was aware, had a single mention or other distinction been up to that time conferred on any medical officer in the British Army for this work.[84]

Failing to mention his own CBE for war services, Myers had perhaps been overly sensitive to the slights and difficulties he had faced. Some officers coped and were not deterred from pursuing or taking up a career in psychiatry once the hostilities had ended. For too many others, however, this was not the case.

Notes

1 C.S. Myers, *Shell Shock in France 1914–1918, Based on a War Diary* (Cambridge: Cambridge University Press, 1940), pp. 139–40.

2 Philip Hoare, *Spike Island, The Memory of a Military Hospital* (London: Fourth Estate, 2001), pp. 217–23.

3 Edgar Jones and Simon Wessely, 'The origins of British military psychiatry before the First World War', *War and Society*, 19 (2001) 91–108.

4 Ian R. Whitehead, 'The British medical officer on the Western Front: the training of doctors for war', in R. Cooter, M. Harrison, and S. Sturdy (eds), *Medicine and Modern Warfare* (Amsterdam: Rodopi, 1999), pp. 163–84.

5 Ian R. Whitehead, *Doctors in the Great War* (Barnsley: Leo Cooper, 1999), pp. 254–5.

6 Quoted from Hans Binneveld, *From Shell Shock to Combat Stress, A Comparative History of Military Psychiatry* (Amsterdam: Amsterdam University Press, 1997), p. 135.

7 Albert Wilson, 'Notes on 150 cases of wounded French, Belgians and Germans', *British Medical Journal* [hereafter *BMJ*] (1914) 2: 807.

8 Myers, *Shell Shock in France*, pp. 14–17.

9 Edward Mapother, 'Discussion on the functional nervous disease in the fighting services', *Proceedings of the Royal Society of Medicine*, 29 (1936), 61.

10 Initially, two clearing hospitals were opened for assessment: the Royal Victoria Hospital, Netley, and the 4th London General (King's College Hospital, Denmark Hill, including from 1916 the Maudsley Wing). In addition, a growing number of treatment centres were set up including the Red Cross Military Hospital, Maghull; Springfield War Hospital, Wandsworth; the National Hospital for Paralysed and Epileptic, Queen Square, London; No. 2 Western General Hospital, Stockport; and Slateford Military Hospital, Craiglockhart.

11 Lord Southborough, *Report of the War Office Committee of Enquiry into 'Shell-Shock'* (London: HMSO, 1922), p. 124.

12 Ben Shephard, *A War of Nerves, Soldiers and Psychiatrists 1914–1994* (London: Jonathan Cape, 2000), pp. 47–8.

13 William Johnson and R.G. Rows, 'Neurasthenia and war neuroses', in W.G. Macpherson *et al.*, *History of the Great War Based on Official Documents, Medical Services, Diseases of the War, Volume 2* (London: HMSO, 1923), pp. 10–11.

14 Thomas Salmon, 'The care and treatment of mental diseases and war neuroses ("shell shock") in the British Army', *Mental Hygiene*, 1 (1917), 522–5; Edwin G. Zabriskie *et al.*, 'Division, corps and army neuropsychiatric consultants', in Thomas W. Salmon and Norman Fenton (eds), *The Medical Department of the United States Army in the World War, Volume X, Neuropsychiatry* (Washington, DC: US Government Printing Office, 1929), pp. 313–17; K.L. Artiss, 'Human behaviour under stress: from combat to social psychiatry', *Military Medicine* 128 (1963), 1011–15.

15 Shephard, *War of Nerves*, p. 47.

16 Myers, *Shell Shock in France*, pp. 19–20.

17 Harvey Cushing, *From a Surgeon's Journal 1915–1918* (London: Constable, 1936), p. 234.

18 Wilfrid Harris, *Oxford Primer on Nerve Injuries and Shock* (Oxford: Oxford University Press, 1915). This book was designed to fit into the tunic pocket of a medical officer on active service.

19 Frederick W. Mott, 'The effects of high explosives upon the central nervous system', *Lancet* (1916), 1: 331–8, 441–9.

20 Public Record Office (PRO), WO95/4081, War Diary, No. 12 General Hospital, 13 August 1915.

21 Harold Wiltshire, 'A contribution to the etiology of shell shock', *Lancet* (1916), 1: 1212.

22 Imperial War Museum (IWM), Diary of Captain B.A. West, 3 March 1917; see also Harold Deardon, *Medicine and Duty, a War Diary* (London: William Heinemann, 1928), p. 196.

23 F.S. Brereton, *The Great War and the RAMC* (London: Constable, 1919), p. 7.

24 PRO, WO95/4099, War Diary, 4 Stationary Hospital, 11 March 1917.

25 Obituary, *BMJ* (1957), 1: 649–50; obituary, *Lancet* (1957) 1: 591.

26 Sir Wilmot Herringham, *A Physician in France* (London: Edward Arnold, 1919), p. 135.

27 D.W. Carmalt Jones, 'War-neurasthenia, acute and chronic', *Brain*, 42 (1919), 212–13.

28 PRO, WO95/4099, War Diary, No. 4 Stationary Hospital, 29 June 1917, 26 August 1917.

29 Southborough, *Report*, p. 80.

30 Johnson and Rows, 'Neurasthenia and war neuroses', p. 41.

31 Obituary, *BMJ* (1949) 1: 593.

32 PRO, WO95/4100, War Diary, No. 6 Stationary Hospital, 11 July 1917; WO95/4109, War Diary, No. 3 Canadian Stationary Hospital, 3 July 1917.

33 F. Dillon, 'The analysis of a composite neurosis', *Lancet* (1919), 1: 57.

34 Frederick Dillon, 'Neuroses among combatant troops in the Great War', *BMJ* (1939), 2: 66; Colin Russel, 'The management of psycho-neuroses in the Canadian army', *Journal of Abnormal Psychology* 14 (1919), 29.

35 William Brown, 'The psychologist in war-time', *Lancet* (1939), 1: 1288.

36 William Brown, 'The treatment of cases of shell shock in an advanced neurological centre', *Lancet* (1918), 2: 197.

37 William Brown, 'War neuroses', *Lancet* (1919), 2: 833.

38 Edgar Jones and Simon Wessely, 'Psychiatric battle casualties: an intra- and interwar comparison', *British Journal of Psychiatry*, 178 (2001), 243–5.

39 Martin Stone, 'Shellshock and the psychologists', in W.F Bynum, R. Porter, and M. Shepherd (eds), *The Anatomy of Madness, Essays in the History of Psychiatry, Vol. II, Institutions and Society* (London: Tavistock, 1985), pp. 246–7.

40 E. Mapother, 'War neurosis', *Journal of the Royal Army Medical Corps*, 68 (1937), 13.

41 Henry Yellowlees, *Frames of Mind* (London: William Kimber, 1957), p. 154.

42 M.D. Eder, *War Shock* (London: Heinemann, 1917), p. i.

43 Arthur Osburn, *Unwilling Passenger* (London: Faber & Faber, 1932), p. 345.

44 J. Purdon Martin, 'Reminiscences of Queen Square', *BMJ*, 283 (1981), 1641; obituary, *BMJ* (1966), 1: 112; Shephard, *War of Nerves*, pp. 48–9, 181.

45 Ben Shephard, 'The early treatment of mental disorders: R.G. Rows and Maghull 1914–1918', in H. Freeman and G.E. Berrios (eds), *150 Years of British Psychiatry, Volume 2* (London: Gaskell, 1996), pp. 440–2.

46 Johnson and Rows, 'Neurasthenia and the war neuroses', p. 49.

47 Shephard, 'Maghull', p. 455.

48 D. Orr, Obituary, *Journal of Mental Science*, 71 (1925), 350–1; obituary, *BMJ* (1925) 1: 433–4.

49 IWM, Siegfried Sassoon, Vol. 2, 'Notes on the Staff of Craiglockhart War Hospital', 297.

50 Richard Slobodin, *Rivers* (New York: Columbia University Press, 1978), pp. 59–66.

51 W.H.R. Rivers, 'An address on the repression of war experience', *Lancet* (1918), 1: 173.

52 Denise J. Poynter, 'Regeneration revisited: W.H.R. Rivers and shell shock during the Great War', in Matthew Hughes and Matthew Seligmann (eds), *Leadership in Conflict 1914–1918* (Barnsley: Leo Cooper, 2000), pp. 238–9.

53 T.A. Ross, *The Common Neuroses, Their Treatment by Psychotherapy* (London: Edward Arnold, 1937), pp. 131–2.

54 Arthur Hurst, *A Twentieth Century Physician, Being the Reminiscences of Sir Arthur Hurst* (London: Edward Arnold, 1949), p. 138.

55 *Ibid.*, p. 152.

56 Obituary, *BMJ* (1940), 1: 552–3.

57 Obituary, *Lancet* (1940), 1: 624–6.

58 Ex-Services Mental Welfare Society Minute Book, 9 (3 June 1937), 61; 10 (7 September 1939), 78.

59 Millais Culpin, 'An autobiography', *Occupational Psychology*, 23 (1949), 145.

60 *Ibid.*, p. 146.

61 Mott, 'The effects of high explosives', p. 553.

62 Siegfried Sassoon, *The Complete Memoirs of George Sherston* (London: Faber and Faber, 1937), pp. 459–60.

63 Lewis R. Yealland, *Hysterical Disorders of Warfare* (London: Macmillan, 1918), p. 3.

64 *Ibid.*, pp. 7–15; see also Binneveld, *Shell Shock to Combat Stress*, pp. 111–14.

65 C.S. Myers, 'The justifiability of therapeutic lying', *Lancet* (1919), 2: 1213–14.

66 Peter Leese, 'Why are they not cured?', in Paul Lerner and Mark S. Micale (eds), *Traumatic Pasts, History, Psychiatry and Trauma in the Modern Age, 1870–1930* (Cambridge: Cambridge University Press, 2001), p. 217.

67 Obituary, *Lancet* (1954) 1: 578; letter to the author from Dr Sue Yealland, 29 October 2001.

68 Cyril Burt, 'An autobiographical sketch', *Occupational Psychology*, 23 (1949), 17.

69 Obituary, *BMJ* (1938) 2: 1232.

70 Obituary, *BMJ* (1922), 1: 977–8.

71 Obituary, *Lancet* (1952), 1: 1073.

72 Geoffrey Keynes, *The Gates of Memory* (Oxford: Clarendon Press, 1981), p. 145.

73 Southborough, *Report*, p. 191.

74 James W. Barrett, *A Vision of the Possible, What the RAMC Might Become* (London: H.K. Lewis, 1919), p. 154.

75 Millais Culpin, 'A criticism of modern trends in the treatment of psychoneurosis', *Medical Press*, 228 (1952), 71–3.

76 Southborough *Report*, p. 50.

77 Grafton Elliot Smith and T. H. Pear, *Shell Shock and Its Lessons* (Manchester: Manchester University Press, 1917), p. 108.

78 Ben Shephard, 'Pitiless psychology: the role of prevention in British military psychiatry in the Second World War', *History of Psychiatry*, 10 (1999), 505–10.

79 E. Mapother, 'War neurosis', *Journal of the Royal Army Medical Corps*, 68 (1937), 38–48.

80 Shephard, 'Pitiless psychology', p. 509.

81 H.V. Dicks, *Fifty Years of the Tavistock Clinic* (London: Routledge & Kegan Paul, 1970), pp. 102–7.

82 Philip Gosse, *Memoirs of a Camp Follower* (London: Longmans, Green & Co, 1934), p. xiii.

83 Mapother, 'Functional nervous disease', p. 66.

84 Myers, *Shell Shock in France*, p. 140.

Commemorations of the siege of Leningrad: a catastrophe in memory and myth

From the moment that the German armies crossed the frontier into the Soviet Union in June 1941, the Soviet media and Soviet citizens themselves represented the 'Great Patriotic War' as an 'epic' event of vast historical import. Likewise, the nearly 900-day siege of Leningrad that began in September 1941 immediately became mythologised. Understood as a 'historic event' even as it occurred, the siege rapidly became the subject of commemorations. From the first months of the war, besieged Leningrad became what historian Pierre Nora has defined as a *lieu de mémoire* (realm of memory) – one of those 'events . . . that are immediately invested with symbolic significance and treated, even as they are unfolding, as if they were being commemorated in advance'.[1] In its official commemorations of the siege, the state deployed evocations of personal trauma as a means of establishing the emotional authenticity of the national struggle. At the same time, individuals wove state-sponsored images and narratives into their 'personal' stories as a means of investing their wartime experiences with historic significance.

The drama and tragedy of the nearly two million Leningraders trapped by the blockade easily lent itself to myth making. For nearly three years, Leningraders endured sufferings that defy the imagination. In the worst period of the siege, they faced bitter cold in a city without heat, electricity or public transportation. During the deadly winter of 1941–42, the daily bread ration fell to a low of 125 grams. Temperatures dropped to forty degrees below zero. As many as 8,000 people died of starvation in a single day, and corpses piled up in streets and courtyards. The opening of the so-called 'Road of Life' across frozen Lake Ladoga in late 1941, and the re-establishment of a rail connection with the 'mainland' in 1943, helped to alleviate the starvation conditions. However, the city remained subject to often heavy German artillery attacks until the siege was fully broken in January 1944. Conservative official estimates put the total number of dead at 670,000, or nearly one-third of the city's pre-war population.[2] While post-Soviet accounts of the siege suggest that the city's starving, freezing inhabitants were less uniformly stoic, heroic, and courageous than the Soviet myth and some survivors claimed, Leningraders nonetheless remain, even in the most balanced recent accounts, remarkably strong and selfless.[3]

The examination of wartime memory projects illuminates the meanings and complications of the impulse to represent contemporary life in the language of history and myth. In its official commemorations, the state worked to co-opt and contain the emotional power of personal memory. Official commemorations ranging from museums to documentary films celebrated individual acts of heroism and invited Leningraders to recognise themselves as actors in the Leningrad 'epic'. The mythic narrative of the 'heroic defence' of Leningrad often distorted the realities of the besieged city, notably by downplaying or completely ignoring the extent of deaths due to starvation. Still, the state's images and narratives resonated with Leningraders seeking to find meaning in the personal tragedies of the siege. In the project under-taken by a group of Leningrad librarians to commemorate the siege, personal stories became entwined with public narrative.[4] Commemorations offered both sites for ritual mourning and a means of sanitising and politicising the trauma of the siege.

'Life becomes history'

The Soviet propaganda machine responded more quickly and more effectively than did the Soviet military to the invasion that began 22 June 1941. In the first issue of *Pravda* after the invasion, the press gave the war what became its official name: 'The Great Patriotic War' (*Velikaia Otechestvennaia voina*).[5] Just two days after the Germans crossed the border, the newspaper *Smena*, the organ of the Leningrad Young Communist organisation (Komsomol), reported that efforts to chronicle the war and to connect it to the glorious military history of Russia and the Soviet Union had already begun. At the State Public Library, workers planned an exhibition on the orig-inal 'Great Patriotic War' of 1812 that would also include material on the German invasion during the Civil War. At the same time, the Lenfilm studios announced plans to begin producing short war documentaries. The studio promised that the first five or six films would be released in ten or twelve days.[6]

In commemorating the present, state-sponsored exhibitions merged the personal and the public and pictured the war as a formative event in the life of the nation and in the lives of individuals. Family photographs, diaries, letters, commendations, and blood-soaked Komsomol cards documented individual lives and the national war effort. In December 1942, *Komsomol'skaia pravda* reported the opening of 'The Komsomol in the Patriotic War'.[7] The newspaper provided no account of the organ-isation of the exhibit, instead detailing its displays and emphasising the importance, if not necessity, of immediately commemorating 'life that becomes history'. The exhibit represented the war as an unexpected and momentous break in the lives of individuals and in the life of the nation. It began with photographs of 'recent peace-ful days' – the Dnepostrovskii dam, a soccer match, a physical culture parade in Red Square, the pavilions of the All-Union agricultural exhibition – and with newspapers from 22 June that betrayed no hint of the coming invasion. 'And then – a sharp fault (*sdvig*), a rupture changed the whole mode of life', a break commemorated by the 'slogans of those memorable days': 'Everyone to arms! Everyone to the defence of the Motherland!' Displayed alongside the official slogans, and putting a smiling human face on mass mobilisation, stood photographs of the 'cheerful faces of our remarkable girls, who, when it was required, replaced [their] comrades and brothers, mastering male professions'. Such photographs, along with the other personal effects on display, worked to suggest fundamental connections between the national and personal dimensions of the war.

Commemorating an ongoing reality, the exhibit aimed to inspire viewers to join the young people 'who look at us from the photographs'. The report reminded visitors that while the exhibit 'broke from life', life continued. The student metal workers immortalised in the exhibit, for example, were now teachers. Even more significantly, 'when the doors to the exhibit open, many of the visitors will see themselves, will see their own labour on these stands', and ask themselves 'why isn't my portrait hanging alongside the portraits of Gastello and Zoia Kosmodem'ianskaia?'[8] Such questions, the report concluded, led to the path of 'real eternal life that goes down in history'. Visitors were encouraged to think of their own lives in historic, if not mythic, terms.

Not only individuals, but also cities became the subjects of wartime commemorations. While family photographs helped to personalise heroism, local landmarks brought the struggle close to home. Certain cities, notably Moscow, Leningrad, and Stalingrad, had clear national resonance, yet wartime propaganda and wartime commemorations emphasised the local loyalties involved.[9] The emphasis on the war as a defence of the hometown was particularly pronounced in the case of Leningrad, a 'city front', where, according to official pronouncements, there was no line between the front and the rear. Posters created for the Baltic Fleet called sailors to 'Avenge native Leningrad!' (*Mstite na rodnoi Leningrad!*), and placed the unmistakable Leningrad skyline in the background of battle.[10] In June 1943, the Political Administration of the Leningrad Front sponsored the 'first exhibition of front artists'. Works depicting battle scenes and portraits of heroes, especially flyers, dominated the exhibition. Yet, the artistic 'documents of the defence of Leningrad, which the future historian of our great times will consult often', also included representations of the everyday life of the besieged city.[11] The show's catalogue noted a number of artists who employed typical 'Leningrad motifs', and whose work was 'imbued with the love of their native city'.[12]

The overlap of the city and the front constituted a key element in representations of the siege as both particularly poignant for natives of Leningrad, and as particularly 'historic'. Official wartime accounts of the city conflated personal and historic events. Writing in the spring of 1942 in *Literatura i iskusstvo*, Il'ia Gruzdev described an 'oral album', a public reading, that occurred in late January, 'during the most difficult period of the blockade'.[13] Addressing a roomful of writers, who, gathered in an unheated room in the depths of a brutal winter, were 'wearing everything that it was possible to wear', Gruzdev took it upon himself to offer inspiration, since 'not all the comrades were equally steadfast in enduring the difficulties of those days'. Gruzdev saved the shorthand minutes of his opening speech in which he emphasised the monumental historic importance of literary work in the besieged city. Five months later, he presented the text of his speech 'as a document of those days':

> Comrades! Think about what *luck* (or happiness, *schast'e*) it is to live in Leningrad, about the writer's good fortune that in these days puts us not in the backwoods (*zadvorkakh*) of history, but at the front of history, face to face with awesome events, in a great city, whose bleak days will go down in the history of the millennium. And if we have ears

that hear, and eyes that see, think about the fact that to us falls the luck of engraving
that which we see and hear. Not a single person in the world can replace us. Every day
in the city of Lenin is *unique*, not in the banal calendar sense, but in the sense that for
seven months, every day has changed the historical aspect of our city. Who examines
more avidly and passionately than a writer these swift years of history?[14]

Clearly meant to inspire cold, hungry writers with the vision of living 'in a great place
on earth', Gruzdev's speech represented the city as a place where each day and every
action carried profound historical significance.

Looking back on the same period, the poet Ol'ga Berggol'ts, who lived through the
entire siege, emphasised – in less bombastic, propagandistic terms – a similar sense of
living through a remarkable time in a place with a new 'historical aspect'. She captured the uncanny experience of seeing the familiar streets of her native city transformed into a wasteland. Making a difficult trip across the city on foot in February
1942, Berggol'ts saw

> a line of trolley buses, iced-over, snow-covered, also dead – like dead people. One after
> the other, rows, dozens. Stopped. And on the tracks near the [Alexander Nevsky]
> Monastery, rows of trams, with the glass broken out, with snowdrifts on the seats. Also
> stopped . . . Did we really once travel on these? Strange! I walked past the dead trams
> and trolley buses in some other century, in another life. Whether I was living one-
> hundred years before the present or one-hundred years after, I had no idea. It was all the
> same to me.[15]

Rupturing, without completely destroying, the familiar landscape of the city, the
blockade made the everyday strange, distorted both time and space. As Lydia
Ginzburg noted in her memoir of the siege, 'A new reality came into being, unprecedented, but still resembling the former one more than seemed possible.'[16]

For Berggol'ts, the sense of living in a familiar city deformed by war made the siege
a powerful personal and national experience. Visiting her childhood neighbourhood
during an air raid in October 1941, Berggol'ts surveyed the well-known landmarks
under attack, 'and my entire life suddenly shot before me, and with inconceivable
speed . . . pictures of my whole life and of the life of my motherland, and memories
about things that had happened even before my memory, rushed across my soul'.[17]
Without endorsing Gruzdev's contention that to live in a city under siege constituted
a piece of good luck for the writer, Berggol'ts and Ginzburg suggested that the experience stimulated a sense, or at least an expectation, of the momentousness of everyday events.

Official wartime commemorations played on this sense of the epic nature of the
city's present as a means of endowing the most mundane details of everyday life with
national significance. Berggol'ts, who was one of the best-known voices of Leningrad
radio throughout the war, told her listeners as early as the winter of 1941 that their
daily concerns were the raw material of history: 'And maybe, comrades, we will see
our daily bread ration, this poor little piece of black bread, behind the glass in some
kind of museum.'[18]

In 1943, with the siege not yet broken, an exhibition dedicated to the 'heroic defence of Leningrad' did in fact display the 125-gram ration of November 1941. Alongside Soviet military hardware and captured German tanks and artillery, the museum displayed not only the starvation ration of the winter of 1941–42, but also diaries, letters, and personal possessions that suggested the local and familial dimensions of the city's experience. The poet Vera Inber, who lived through the siege, recalled the bread, installed in a diorama behind the iced-over window of a bakery, as one of the most moving parts of the siege museum. The bread hardly constituted the centrepiece of the massive 20,000 square metre exhibition space organised by the military authorities to celebrate Soviet might. Still, its inclusion, and the powerful response of visitors to it, underscores the process of commemorating the national emergency in terms accessible and memorable to average citizens. The siege museum established on the site of the wartime exhibition (and shut down in 1953), and the reconstituted museum organised on the same site in 1989, continued the practice of juxtaposing the artefacts of battle and of everyday life, as a means of writing the tragic tale of the city into the grand narrative of Soviet military victory. The journalist Harrison Salisbury recognised this dynamic in his complaint that by situating the mock-up of the bakery among exhibits devoted to the heroic dimensions of the battle for Leningrad, the wartime exhibit 'had not captured the simplicity and triviality of real life', but instead had 'romanticised' civilian suffering.[19]

Looking back on the war in the 1950s, Berggol'ts argued that the blurring of the boundary between the personal and the public, the intimate and the national, the everyday and the heroic, constituted a general feature of life during the siege. In her memoirs, she explained:

> I've read many blockade diaries, written by the dark of home-made oil-lamps [*koptilka*], in gloves, with hands almost too weak to support a pen (more often – a pencil: the ink froze up); the entries in some diaries were cut short at the moment of the author's death. Singed and icy, the triumphant Leningrad tragedy breathes from the many, many pages of these diaries, where a person writes with total candour about his or her own relatives and friends [*svoikh*], everyday cares, efforts, sorrows, joys. And, as a rule, his or her 'own', the 'deeply personal', is at the same time more universal, or more general, the national [*narodnoe*] becomes deeply personal, indeed humane. History suddenly speaks with a living, simple human voice.[20]

Berggol'ts suggests that in besieged Leningrad the line between personal and national history blurred because individuals were living an epic. What she obscured was the degree to which the 'simple human voice' of history spoke in spaces, like the siege museum, that were controlled by the state. State control does not necessarily rule out the sort of personal sense of living through a moment of profound historical significance described in Berggol'ts's memoir and in the official wartime press. However, it does suggest that the blended personal and public stories that survivors perhaps found comfort in, also operated as propaganda. Leningrad's status as a 'realm of memory' grew in large part out of the state's efforts to appropriate powerful emotions by inscribing personal tragedies into a narrative of national unity and eventual triumph.

History becomes life

While state memorials worked to transform everyday reality into historical epic, unofficial memory projects used official representations of the siege to structure personal memory. In its official commemorations of the siege, the state used personal stories and emotionally resonant images to encourage Soviet citizens to recognise themselves as part of a larger national struggle. The work of 'front artists' and the exhibition of 'the heroic defence of Leningrad' aimed to mobilise and inspire the city's inhabitants in part by casting the national cause in personal terms as a defence of hometown and family. On the other side, commemorations of the siege undertaken by individual Leningraders drew on state-sponsored images and narratives.

Leningraders' use of official representations as a means of structuring their own memories suggests that, despite the distortions inherent in the myth of 'heroic Leningrad', survivors recognised themselves in the productions of the state. Ales' Adamovich and Daniil Granin, the editors of an important collection of oral histories and diaries published in 1982, emphasise that Leningraders literally saw themselves in the state's commemorations of the siege. In a chapter entitled 'Something unknown about a well-known photograph', the editors, Second World War veterans themselves, presented an interview with the subjects of a famous 1942 news photograph of a mother and two very thin daughters out for a walk in the spring sunshine. The photograph of survivors trying to get back to normal had become a part of official commemorations of the siege, exhibited at 'the Leningrad Museum, in the museum of Piskarevskoe Cemetery [the cemetery dedicated to siege victims], and in books and albums of the blockade'. In Veronika Opakhova's flat in central Leningrad, 'that blockade photograph, known throughout the world, is a family memento'. While Opakhova and her daughter began their stories of the siege with the photograph, they could not remember exactly where or when it was taken. For them, the powerful memory was recognising themselves in the photograph displayed in the Museum of the Heroic Defence of Leningrad and 'remembering all that!' Despite the fact that the photograph is 'terrible, of course, and frightening, and is always disturbing and brings one to tears', Opakhova kept it in her family album.[21]

The wartime memory project undertaken by a small 'brigade' of workers at the State Public Library provides a particularly illuminating and well-documented example of how the state's propaganda could become a feature of individual memory. Initiated neither by the party nor the state, the collection grew out of the desire of the library's workers to undertake meaningful work in the besieged city. The librarians hoped that their collection of official posters, pictures, and texts would stimulate survivors' memories. In a paper presented in 1945, the collection's director, Vera Karatygina, argued that 'for those who lived through the blockade in Leningrad, who along with everyone defended our city, each document, each scrap of paper will be a memory, will make it possible to realise the whole past'.[22]

Workers at the Public Library began collecting the published artefacts of the siege almost immediately after the Germans blockaded the city in autumn 1941. As air raids and artillery attacks disrupted the work of the library's branches – closing reading rooms, forcing the evacuation of rare volumes, and damaging buildings – two librarians who found themselves without work to do, M.A. Briskman, the head of the acquisitions department, and IU.A. Mezhenko, the head of the bibliographic department, developed the idea of collecting everything published in the besieged city.[23] Initially, the only criterion for inclusion in the proposed collection was the place of publication: blockaded Leningrad. The idea was to preserve the publications that constituted, and therefore would help to re-conjure, the material and intellectual milieu of the city. Karatygina, who took over the collection in autumn 1942, remembered that it initially included the edition of Stendhal's *The Red and the Black* that was a ubiquitous fixture in the windows of Leningrad bookshops, *War and Peace*, and a primer of fairytales for children, along with 'war orders-of-the-day, appeals, instructions for citizen conduct during air raids' – all works considered 'extremely characteristic of blockaded Leningrad'.[24] As originally conceived, the collection enshrined the published materials that Leningraders saw and held in their hands in these difficult days.

A year later, when the collection became the responsibility of Karatygina, whose prewar work had included the management of the library's 'St Petersburg, Leningrad' collection, the emphasis shifted toward an effort to compile an exhaustive catalogue of published materials pertaining to the siege, regardless of their place of publication. Karatygina emphasised the distinctiveness of her 'thematic' approach, but it, too, allowed the collection of materials of a 'general' nature. *The Red and the Black* had to go. Still, Karatygina deemed most interesting those objects in the collection that captured the look and feel of the city at a particular moment. She emphasised the importance of leaflets, posters, slogans, and ephemera (*melkii material*) – labels, tickets, ration coupons – in the reconstruction of the experience of the siege in memory and in history.[25]

Under Karatygina's leadership, the siege collection's 'brigade' became one of the library's most active and visible groups. When Karatygina became director of the collection in autumn 1942, she had only one associate, Elena Kots, the head of the library's Branch (*filial*) V, the Dom Plekhanova. Karatygina herself was the head of Branch II. By 1945, the collection employed seventeen women and two men. Karatygina remembered that 'it was absolutely natural that all of GPB's (the State Public Library's) best workers, left without work in connection with the evacuation of materials (*fondov*) or the temporary interruption of their job, drifted to us'.[26] This 'small collective', undertaking what Karatygina characterised as the task, 'unprecedented for GPB', of cataloguing a wide variety of materials, quickly came to occupy an 'absolutely exceptional position' in the library.[27] The British journalist Alexander Werth concurred. When he visited in September 1943, the collection, in contrast to the rest of the library, was 'buzzing with activity'. He found fifteen 'old ladies – most of whom looked like rather decrepit old gentlewomen who had seen better times . . . up to their ears in cuttings and posters and bills and . . . so absorbed in their work that they scarcely seemed aware of our existence – any more than of the shelling that was continuing outside'.[28]

For its members, the brigade was an 'oasis' that provided both refuge and support. The librarians created a physical space that suggested both the warmth of home and the historical importance of their work. They furnished their large room in the library's main building with furniture brought from the temporarily closed Branch II – portraits, rugs, a mirror, showcases, vases – and a rug from Branch V. Karatygina remembered that 'our room looked beautiful, elegant, even imposing, and it happily stood out from the rest of the building'.[29] They kept objects from the collection 'artistically' on display, and hung posters on the walls.

In an account of the 'brigade' put together in 1964, Karatygina noted that 'our work supported many of us, and helped many of us to bear all the severity of the blockade and the sorrow of loss'.[30] Many involved in the work of the collection lost a husband, child, or parent during the siege. Karatygina's mother died in November 1941.[31] Kots's mother died in the summer of 1942.[32] The collection's artist Z.N. Kosichkina-Bogoslovskaia lost her only daughter and later her husband.[33] Yet only the most extreme circumstances kept the librarians away from their work. In a description of Karatygina's wartime work included in her personnel file, the library's director claimed that 'During the time of the Great Patriotic War, work was not interrupted for a single day. When the room in the branch was without light – she brought work home; when she was sick, she worked lying in bed'.[34] In March 1942, a month in which thousands died of starvation, Mariia Zinov'eva asked for two weeks off because severe malnutrition made it impossible to walk to the library from her home on the Petrograd side, a district roughly three to four kilometres from the library. Recurrent poor health occasionally forced 55-year-old Zinov'eva to work shorter hours or take brief sick leaves, but she always returned to full-time work. The librarians missed few days of work.[35]

The work of collecting and cataloguing everything from newspaper clippings to postcards became a means of coping with catastrophe. As Karatygina noted, 'it was easier to live, having before you a clear aim, devoting all your strength to work, and living with a harmonious, united collective'.[36] An architect who spent the famine winter of 1941–42 preparing blueprints of the city's historical buildings echoed her sentiments. He told Werth that the blueprint project had been 'a double blessing'. With the city under air attack, the task itself 'had now become really vital'. The sense of the overriding importance of the work 'was the best medicine that could be given us during the famine . . . The moral effect is great when a hungry man knows he's got a useful job of work to do.'[37] Work helped individuals to cope with trauma by helping to restore a sense of internal control, and by connecting individuals to both co-workers and a larger purpose.[38]

In discussing the collection, Karatygina merged personal memory and public commemoration. In a talk at a library conference in autumn 1942, Karatygina catalogued the slogans of the posters that had covered the walls of the city: 'All for the defence of Lenin's city against the fascist barbarians' and 'Youths of Leningrad! Volunteer to go to the front! Stand up for the defence of your freedom, your honour, your Motherland!' She concluded that 'everyone of us has seen these posters and slogans, and in each of us they rouse the same feelings'. This shared response effectively turned each poster into an 'exact representation of how Leningrad lived in those heroic months'.[39]

For Karatygina, the power of propaganda to stimulate the personal memory of survivors, rather than its ability to provide an 'exact representation' of the blockaded city to outsiders, warranted its preservation. She noted, 'I don't know how it is with others, but for me, seeing the matchbook covers of that time, there rises up before my eyes the long, dark, sleepless nights of the winter of 1941–42, without light and heat, interrupted by air-raid sirens and the explosions of bombs.'[40] The matchbook covers that Karatygina claimed so forcefully brought back the experience of the siege featured the simplest sorts of propaganda. They carried patriotic slogans demanding 'All strength to the front', or more locally oriented messages proclaiming 'Glory to heroic Leningrad' and drawings of the city's most beloved landmarks.[41] Whereas the siege museum collected diaries, photographs, and other personal artefacts – a piano, a home-made oil lamp – to endow its largely military story with a human dimension, Karatygina suggested that individual stories could be evoked by the language of propaganda posters and matchbook covers. Even the state's seemingly most banal propaganda touched living memory for survivors.

For Karatygina, officially sponsored artistic representations of the siege in photographs and poetry also expressed the personal experiences of Leningraders. She argued that the endlessly reproduced photographs from the winter of 1941–42 that showed corpses being transported on a child's sled, people lining up for water, or the 'characteristic faces of the malnourished (*distrofikov*)' spoke 'better than any words of the unprecedented sufferings of Leningraders'.[42] At the same time, she was willing to grant that 'the terrible blockade winter was excellently represented by Vera Inber in "Pulkovo Meridian", by Ol'ga Berggol'ts and by other Leningrad writers and poets, who lived through those black days together with all Leningraders'.[43] Less literally but not less fully than Veronika Opakhova, Karatygina recognised her personal story in the public, state-sponsored pictures and words that everyone in the city saw and knew – from straightforward propaganda to literary representations.

When it came time for the librarians to commemorate their own efforts to commemorate the siege, the album they produced, *Leningrad v blokade* (Leningrad under blockade), constructed a memory of the siege out of news photographs and the words of Leningrad's siege poets, primarily Berggol'ts and Inber.[44] Mentioning neither Lenin, Stalin, nor the party, the album focused on the destruction of the city and the shared suffering of Leningraders. With its emphasis on the siege as a clear break in the lives of those who lived through it, and its preference for images over sustained narrative, the album gave concrete form to well-documented characteristics of traumatic memory. At the same time, the album's use of poetry suggests an effort to establish the sense of collective solidarity and purpose that can provide a means of working through trauma.[45] The librarians' siege album began with Berggol'ts's affirmation:

> Now I will not be torn away from you.
> By one unprecedented battle,
> One unique fate,
> We all are marked. We are Leningraders.

Suggesting that the siege divided the lives of all who lived it through it into 'before' and 'after', and that all who lived through the siege were now 'Leningraders', Berggol'ts's poem represents the blockade as a shared, collective struggle. As all Leningraders suffered a 'unique fate', the poet could speak for all of them, and the librarians could structure their own memories around the poet's words. Berggol'ts's verses set an appropriate tone for an album that commemorated not only the siege, but also the efforts of a small group of library workers to survive by making the public and mythic narratives of the siege a part of their everyday lives.

The state tried to inspire sacrifice and mobilise the population by displaying personal artefacts in the context of exhibitions designed to emphasise the historic dimensions of the war. Leningraders often recognised themselves in the state's official representations. Doing so could provide a means of coping with personal suffering by endowing it with meaning. The librarians found a heroic, collective context for their sufferings in the newspaper clippings, posters, and poetry that they so carefully catalogued. Of course, the meanings that Leningraders found in state images may not have always been those intended by the state. Opakhova's photograph operated in museums and official histories as an emblem of the renewal of the city in the spring following the first starving winter of the blockade. For her, it evoked the horrors of the winter preceding the photographs and the difficulty of recovery. Still, the state-sponsored artefact provided the starting point for her own story and its most dramatic moment – the moment of recognition. In Leningrad, there were no clear lines between myth and memory.

Notes

1 Pierre Nora, 'General introduction: between memory and history', in Lawrence D. Kritzman (ed.), *Realms of Memory: Rethinking the French Past*, (trans. Arthur Goldhammer, 3 vols, New York: Columbia University Press, 1996), I, p. 18.

2 On the events leading up to the siege, see Harrison E. Salisbury, *The 900 Days: The Siege of Leningrad* (New York: Harper and Row, 1969), pp. 142–270. More scholarly accounts include Richard Bidlack, 'Survival strategies in Leningrad during the first year of the Soviet-German war', in Robert W. Thurston and Bernd Bonwetsch (eds), *The People's War: Responses to World War II in the Soviet Union* (Urbana, IL: University of Illinois Press, 2000), pp. 84–107; Richard Bidlack, 'The political mood in Leningrad during the first year of the Soviet-German war', *The Russian Review* 59:1 (2000), 96–113. Salisbury concludes that 'an overall total of deaths, civilian and military, of the order of 1,300,000 to 1,500,000, seems reasonable', Salisbury, *900 Days*, p. 516.

3 Bidlack, 'The political mood in Leningrad', p. 112.

4 On the relationship of 'personal' memory to public narratives, see Andrew Lass, 'From memory to history: the events of November 17 dis/membered', in Rubie Watson (ed.), *Memory, History, and Opposition Under State Socialism* (Santa Fe, NM: School of American Research Press, 1994), p. 97.

5 John Barber, 'The image of Stalin in Soviet propaganda and public opinion during World War 2', in John Garrard and Carol Garrard (eds), *World War 2 and the Soviet People* (New York: St Martin's Press, 1993), p. 41.

6 'Vystavka "Otechestvennaia voina"', and 'Novye voennye fil'my', *Smena* no. 146 (24 June 1941), 4.

7 S. Alekseev, 'Zhizn', kotoraia stanovitsia istoriei: Segodnia otkrytie vystavki "Komsomol v Otechestvennoi voine"', *Komsomol'skaia pravda* (hereafter *KP*) (20 December 1942), 3.

8 Zoia Kosmodem'ianskaia and Captain Gastello were among the most systematically

publicised of Soviet war heroes. Gastello crashed his burning plane into a German army division; Kosmodem'ianskaia was a partisan caught and executed behind German lines. See Richard Stites, *Russian Popular Culture: Entertainment and Society since 1900* (Cambridge: Cambridge University Press, 1992), p. 99; Rosalinde Sartori, 'On the making of heroes, heroines, and saints', in Richard Stites (ed.), *Culture and Entertainment in Wartime Russia* (Bloomington, IN: Indiana University Press, 1995), pp. 176–193.

9   Lisa A. Kirschenbaum, '"Our City, Our Hearths, Our Families": local loyalties and private life in Soviet World War II propaganda', *Slavic Review* 59:4 (2000), 825–47.

10 The Red Baltic Fleet (KBF) posters are held at the Russian National Library (RNB), L3–310 p/7/2.

11 V. Saianov, 'Na vystavke khudozhnikov-frontovikov', *Leningradskaia pravda* no. 127 (1 June 1943), 4.

12 Politicheskoe upravlenie leningradskogo fronta, *Pervaia vystavka khudozhnikov-frontovikov: katalog* (Leningrad: Voennoe izdatel'stvo Narodnogo Komissariata Oborony, 1943), pp. 7–8, and reproductions following p. 47. See also Ven. Vishnevskii, '"Boevoi karandash": Na vystavke leningradskikh khudozhnikov', *Trud* no. 242 (13 Oct. 1943), 4; Bor. Brodianskii, 'Khudozhniki nashego fronta', *Na strazhe Rodiny* no. 304 (29 December 1943), 4.

13 Il'ia Gruzdev, 'O Leningrade', *Literatura i iskusstvo* no. 20 (16 May 1942), 3.

14 *Ibid.* (emphasis in original).

15 Ol'ga Berggol'ts, *Dnevnye zvezdy* in *Stikhi-proza* (Moscow: Gosudarstvennoe izdatel'stvo khudozhestvennoi literatury, 1961), pp. 126–7.

16 Lydia Ginzburg, *Blockade Diary* (trans. Alan Meyers, London: Harvill Press, 1995), p. 6.

17 Berggol'ts, *Dnevnye zvezdy*, p. 95.

18 Berggol'ts, 'Govorit Leningrad', in *Stikhi-proza*, p. 377.

19 S. Kara and A. Mikhailov, 'Zhivaia istoriia', *Na strazhe Rodiny* (30 April 1944), 2; *Vystavka 'Geroicheskaia oborona Leningrada': Ocherk-putevoditel'* (Leningrad: Iskusstvo, 1945), pp. 65–6. The museum organised in November 1945 on the basis of the exhibition was almost 40,000 square metres; V.P. Kivisepp and N.P. Dobrotvorskii, 'Muzei muzhestva, skorbi i slavy', *Leningradskaia panaroma* no. 8 (August 1991), 24; *Muzei oborony Leningrada: putevoditel'* (Leningrad: Iskusstvo, 1948), p. 44; Vera Inber, *Leningrad Diary* (trans. Serge M. Wolff and Rachel Grieve, New York: St Martin's Press, 1971), p. 207; Salisbury, *900 Days*, p. 571.

20 Berggol'ts, *Dnevnye zvezdy*, p. 33.

21 Ales' Adamovich and Daniil Granin (eds), *Blokadnaia kniga* (Moscow: Sovetskii pisatel', 1982), pp. 10, 16.

22 V.A. Karatygina, 'Rabota Gos. Publichnoi bibilioteki nad kollektsei i bibliografiei "Leningrad v Velikoi Otechestvennoi voine", 1945', Arkh. RNB, f. 12, t. 517, l. 7.

23 On the life of the library during the siege, see L. Frankfurt, 'Na bibliotechnoi vakhte', in A.F. Volkova, *et al.* (eds), *Zhenshchiny goroda Lenina: Rasskazy i ocherki o zhenshchinakh Leningrada v dni blokady* (Leningrad: Lenizdat, 1944), pp. 104–11; 'Biblioteki goroda Lenina v dni voiny', *Bibliotekar'*, nos 2–3 (1946), 24–39; Alexander Werth, *Leningrad* (New York: Alfred A. Knopf, 1944), pp. 138–44. On the origins of the collection, see Karatygina, 'Leningrad v Velikoi Otechestvennoi voine', *Trudy*, 253; Karatygnia, 'Rabota', Arkh. RNB f. 12, t. 517, l. 5–6. A fuller description may be found in the album, *Brigada Kollektsii 'Leningrad v Velikoi Otechestvennoi voine' Gosudarstvennoi publichnoi biblioteki k 20-letiiu sniatiia blokady Leningrada, 1944 27 I 1964* (Leningrad, 1964), and a part of the siege collection is currently held at the Public Library (now the Russian National Library) branch on the Fontanka.

24 Karatygina, Arkh. RNB, f. 12, t. 517, l. 6.

25 *Ibid.*, l. 7; Karatygina, 'O "Kollektsii Peterburg-Leningrad": Istoriia goroda po materialam kollektsii: Doklad V. A. Karatyginoi na Nauchnoi Sessii Gos. Publichnoi Biblioteki imeni Saltykov-Shchedrina, 2 i 3–XI-1942 goda', Arkh. RNB, f. 12, t. 297, l. 22.

26 Karatygina, *Brigada*, p. 14.

27 *Ibid.* The collection also attracted a fair amount of attention in the press, attention the librarians themselves catalogued in their file on the Leningrad press, 'Leningrad v Velikoi Otechestvennoi voine', *Izvestiia* no. 154 (2 July 1943), 3; *Leningradskaia pravda* no. 208 (3 September 1943), 3; S. Vinogradova, 'Peterburg-Leningrad', *Trud* no. 226 (24 September 1943), 4.

28 Werth, *Leningrad*, pp. 143, 144.

29 Karatygina, *Brigada*, p. 15.

30 *Ibid.*, p. 21.

31 Karatygina lichnoe delo, Arkh. RNB f. 10/1 (1949), 13.

32 Kots lichnoe delo, Arkh. RNB f. 10/1 (1959), 1, 8.

33 Karatygina, *Brigada*, p. 21.

34 Arkh. RNB f. 10/1 (1949), l. 11. See also Kosichkina-Bogoslovskaia, lichnoe delo, Arkh. RNB f. 10/1 (1946), 78.

35 Zinov'eva lichnoe delo, Arkh. RNB f. 10/1 (1948), 29–36.

36 Karatygina, *Brigada*, p. 21.

37 Werth, *Leningrad*, p. 44.

38 The work of the librarians and the architects has much in common with the strategies of Vietnam veterans who effectively coped with trauma. They 'consciously focused on preserving their calm, their judgement, and their connection with others, their moral values, and their sense of meaning, even in the most chaotic battlefield conditions'; Judith Herman, *Trauma and Recovery: The Aftermath of Violence – From Domestic Abuse to Political Terror* (New York: Basic Books, 1997), p. 59.

39 None of the posters she listed included references to Stalin or the party; Arkh. RNB, f. 12, t. 297, l. 22–3. She presented a lengthier narrative based on posters and wartime poetry in her 1945 lecture; Arkh. RNB, f. 12, t. 517, 9–16.

40 Arkh. RNB, f. 12, t. 517, 12–13.

41 Handmade album *Etiketi kollektsiia Leningrad v Velikoi Otechestvennoi voine, 1941–44 gg,* RNB, II L-3–304/5/1–57.

42 Arkh. RNB, f. 12, t. 517, 11.

43 *Ibid.*, 13.

44 *Leningrad v blokade, 1941–44* [handmade album] (Leningrad, 1946), RNB, L3 3646. On the importance of the albums that are part of the collection, see Arkh. RNB, f. 12, t. 517, 22; Arkh. RNB, f. 10/1 (1946), 78; Karatygina, *Brigada*, p. 13.

45 Herman writes that 'Traumatic memories lack verbal and narrative context; rather they are encoded in the form of vivid sensations and images', and argues that 'The solidarity of a group provides the strongest protection against terror and despair, and the strongest antidote to traumatic experience'; *Trauma and Recovery*, pp. 38, 214.

9   Donald Bloxham

The missing camps of *Aktion Reinhard*: the judicial displacement of a mass murder

Introduction

This essay concerns the establishment of a representation – or more precisely a non-representation – of the 'Holocaust'. The historical context is the crucible of the imme-diate post-war world, and specifically the Allied trials of Nazi criminals. The analysis stands in opposition to the position of Michael Marrus, who maintains that the Nuremberg trial effectively revealed the murder of the Jews to the post-war world, and to that section of Jeffrey Herf's *Divided Memory*, which suggests that the trial contrib-uted to a pre-Cold War 'interregnum' period of openness about the Nazi past in western Germany.[1]

The focus is upon the representation of one aspect of the 'final solution of the Jewish question': the '*Aktion* [operation] *Reinhard*'. *Aktion Reinhard* was the Nazi name for the process that ultimately encompassed the murder of all of the Jews of the *Generalgouvernement* – the mass of occupied central and south-western Poland not directly incorporated into the Reich, which expanded after the invasion of the USSR to include the district of Galicia in the east. Jews from other parts of Poland also per-ished in the *Reinhard* camps Belzec, Sobibor, and Treblinka, as did some smaller number from western Europe. In excess of 1,700,000 Jews in total were killed in the *Reinhard* gas chambers (at least 600,000 in Belzec, approximately 250,000 in Sobibor, and perhaps 900,000 in Treblinka – the total of Jews killed by gas at the latter camp may have been greater than that at Auschwitz-Birkenau), and the campaign was con-ducted within more-or-less distinct territorial and chronological limits, with the first killings occurring at Belzec in March 1942, and the last at Sobibor in October 1943. It also met with near complete success. It seems, then, that *Aktion Reinhard* can be seen as an early expression of the totality of Nazi intentions towards the Jews. More importantly, it was perhaps the clearest such expression.

This thesis is in contrast to that implicit in Martin Gilbert's *Auschwitz and the Allies*, which posits that Auschwitz was the prime signifier of the Holocaust.[2] The kill-ings in Poland, particularly in the Lublin and Galicia districts, were key stages in the development of the European-wide 'final solution'.[3] *Aktion Reinhard* was also a killing model on which Auschwitz-Birkenau could build; the former commandant of that camp complex, Rudolf Höss, could comment at Nuremberg on the improvements he had made in the killing process over those techniques used at Treblinka.[4] Necessarily, therefore, Auschwitz developed into a centre for the extermination of Jews over time; it achieved major importance in this sphere only from 1943.

Alongside Chelmno in the Warthgau region of western Poland, the *Reinhard* camps were three of the four 'pure' Nazi extermination centres. Functioning in tandem and under the same authority (that of the Lublin SS and police leader Odilo Globocnik, commissioned by Heinrich Himmler for the task), these three camps were unique even within the Nazi apparatus of murder. They were clearly of a different nature from the German concentration camps, which were designed for the incarceration and brutalisation of political opponents of Nazism. Nor did they have the confusing dual identity of the Auschwitz and Majdanek complexes as extermination and concentration facilities – a duality that has, for instance, recently and malevolently been exploited by David Irving. Lacking the facilities to support streams of labourers, the only purpose of the *Reinhard* camps was to expedite mass murder. Indeed, Belzec, Sobibor, and Treblinka were not really 'camps' at all, a fact which is critical because, as we shall see, that appellation was problematic in the post-war era in the representation and understanding of Nazi genocide.

An appreciation of the unique totality of Nazi anti-Jewish intentions, and a realisation that the 'ordinary' concentration camps – with which almost everyone in Germany and many in the liberal democracies were acquainted by the end of 1945 – were not the zenith of Nazi repression, requires a consciousness of the history of *Aktion Reinhard.* Yet Belzec, Sobibor, and Treblinka were scarcely investigated in the immediate post-war era. A number of reasons can be adduced for this oversight – some simply endemic to the confused post-war world; others the result of the explicit and implicit aims of the Allied legal and political authorities in Germany.

This essay does not purport to be a full explanation of the remarkable ignorance of *Aktion Reinhard* both then and now (the first academic monograph on the camps appeared as late as 1987), nor is it a criticism of the Allies or an *ex post facto* venture in showing 'how the trials should have been conducted'. Rather, it is an attempt to illustrate, with reference to a case study concerning nearly one-third of the Jews murdered during the Second World War, the role of the war crimes trials in the refraction of the history and memory of the Nazi years.

The final introductory note concerns the trials themselves. First and foremost was the trial of Hermann Göring and his co-defendants, including six indicted German organisations considered to be criminal, before the International Military Tribunal (IMT), composed of judges from the USA, USSR, UK, and France, at Nuremberg in 1945–6. This was the case of chief importance both for Germany and the Allies, the flagship trial of the leaders of the defeated state. It sought to lay bare the actions of Nazi Germany to the world, thereby justifying the Allied occupation, while simultaneously helping to 'democratise' the German people by illustrating the beneficial replacement of tyranny with Allied justice, and providing an indelible record of Nazi criminality for posterity.

We will also touch very briefly on one other case: the so-called 'Pohl' trial – that of SS-Obergruppenführer Oswald Pohl and his subordinates, members of the SS

Business-Administration Head Office (Wirtschafts-Verwaltungshauptamt; WVHA). The WVHA was responsible for the running and staffing of the regular concentration camps as well as Auschwitz and Majdanek (though the authority for the mass gassings at these camps came from the Reich Security Head Office – RSHA – under Reinhard Heydrich and then Ernst Kaltenbrunner), but not for the *Reinhard* camps. The 'Pohl' case was tried at Nuremberg after the IMT case by American judges and American prosecutors acting under similar legislation to the IMT trial. The American connection is an important one, for the United States provided most of the impetus of the IMT trial and, as we shall see, shaped its character.

The methods and preconceptions of the Nuremberg prosecution

What, then, were the peculiar features of this American trial venture? According to the leader of the American prosecution, Supreme Court Justice Robert H. Jackson, his task was:

> to try in two phases the question of *war guilt*. The first phase [was] to establish the existence of a general conspiracy to which the Nazi party, the Gestapo and other organisations were parties. The object of the conspiracy was to obtain by illegal means, by violation of treaties, and by wholesale brutality control of Europe and the world. When this plan should be proved, the second phase [was] entered upon which would consist of the identification of individuals who were party to this general conspiracy.[5]

Contrary perhaps to popular understanding, aggressive war was understood as the supreme crime, and the other criminal acts of the Nazis were considered ancillary – indeed pursuant – to it. The evidence on the so-called conspiracy and on acts of aggressive war was presented first at the trial, and consumed the opening months of the proceedings – the very time when most public attention was focused on Nuremberg. By the time, for instance, that the Soviet prosecution got around to placing a Treblinka survivor on the stand as a witness at the end of February 1946, reportage of the proceedings was a fraction of what it had been at the opening and would be at the judgment.

The question of witnesses brings us to the next consideration – namely, how the lessons of Nazism were to be taught. Despite opposition from within his own team, Jackson determined that the case would be conducted as far as possible from captured Nazi documents, which, he argued, would make the sounder 'factual' foundation, particularly when the record was examined by the historian. The approach owed a debt, as did the whole 'conspiracy' approach, to the highly complex and technical anti-trust trials that had been a feature of pre-war American commercial life. In practice, Jackson's approach discounted a substantial body of evidence that was not available on the printed page.

The prosecution made another important decision on the production of evidence. As the fundamental aim was to show how war crimes and 'crimes against humanity' derived from a conspiracy to aggression, establishing the link became, in practice, more important than charting the multitude of crimes. The story of the murders and privations was reduced, in the prosecutorial lexicon, to the presentation of 'representative examples' of atrocity, for fear that – to quote Jackson – the tribunal would become lost in a 'wilderness of single instances'.[6] The selection of these 'representative examples' was entirely loaded in one direction, however – the atrocities with which the prosecutors were acquainted. To illustrate the wider relevance of this point, and to return to the earlier contention about the confused use of the camp system in the 're-education process', we should consider what 'camps' the Allies were best acquainted with in 1945.

The 'concentration camps': symbols of repression and resistance

After its 'liberation' (by British troops), Bergen-Belsen became emblematic in British representations of Nazi persecution policy.[7] Dachau and Buchenwald fulfilled a similar function in the United States. While in some way 'representative' of concentration camps in Germany (though Belsen had, in fact, for most of its existence occupied a unique role as an 'exchange camp' for 'privileged' Jews), these institutions were by no means the most extreme product of Nazism, as we have seen. Nevertheless, they continued to be represented as epitomes of Nazi atrocity. Thus, for instance, though it was to be expected that in 1945–46 in its immediate vicinity Belsen would be utilised as a didactic tool and a stick with which to beat the locals,[8] two years later the only licensed book from Britain in the Hamburg region dealing directly with the Holocaust still concerned that camp alone. This selectivity served simply to perpetuate the circumscribed British memory of the recent past.[9] Regarding Western occupation policies more generally, it is evident that while the early policies of forcing the native populations to visit and clean the German concentration camps, and publicly displaying photographs of those places, confronted German civilians with the depravity of their erstwhile society,[10] the public screenings in the midst of the IMT trial of the American-made film *Todesmühlen* did not encourage differentiation between the institutions or the objects of oppression.

The twenty-minute-long *Todesmühlen* ('the mills of death': 1946) consisted in the main of a compilation of images of death from institutions in western and eastern Europe alike. It was hugely problematic in that concentration camps were equated with extermination centres – mass gassings, it was wrongly claimed, occurred at Dachau – and because at no point in the narration were Jews, or any other victim group, singled out.[11] Indeed, the film ended with an unfortunate reference to a Calvary of the murdered. Equally deficient were the hour-long OCCPAC production *Nazi Concentration Camps* (1945), prepared for the IMT, and the short documentary culled therefrom, entitled *KZ* (*'Konzentrationslager'*: 1945) and tested in Erlangen. A similarly titled edition of the occupation newsreel *Welt im Film*, shown in June 1945,[12] dwelt entirely on concentration and labour camps, erroneously describing the Hadamar 'euthanasia' institution in this category, and describing victims only in terms of their nationality. This type of visual imagery was recognised early as being particularly influential in proving the existence of the concentration camps per se.[13] The dearth of photographs of Auschwitz, and the poor pictorial presentation of Majdanek in the illustrated Allied press, when compared with, say, Belsen, also contributed towards keeping the extermination centres in obscurity in the Western mind.[14]

None of the foregoing is intended to belittle the concentration camps, nor the fate of non-Jewish peoples. Nor should it support German apologia of ignorance by suggesting that the majority were anything but acutely aware of the brutal Nazi repression of the Jews.[15] It is, however, testament to the poor quality of the information available on the grades of camp which may have obscured the differences between persecution of various groups, individual murders, and genocide; between the fate of German Jews and the wider destruction of European Jewry. Besides, most Germans knew of 'the concentration camps', if only as a concept enforcing civil obedience (the very reason they were instituted); educationally, the eastern extermination camps were more important, for they had been somewhat veiled by distance, secrecy, and rumour.

Even the proliferation of inmate memoirs encouraged by the Allies in 1945 and 1946 constituted an imbalanced picture of camp life. The vast majority were penned by political prisoners of various sorts, and again related chiefly to camps from within the Reich. Only three of the forty-two released in the British and American zones concerned Auschwitz; none, unsurprisingly, described the pure extermination centres. Of these three, only one was written by a Jew – a German Jew – and he had spent comparatively little time at the camp and was, in any case, an overtly political prisoner. The others were again written by political prisoners, one by an exiled German. All three writers had been incarcerated at Auschwitz I, the original concentration camp, as opposed to Auschwitz-Birkenau, the extermination facility.[16] Likewise, we have the study of the Nazi camp system written by Eugen Kogon, a non-Jewish camp inmate, and commissioned by the American authorities as an historical record and a re-educational device. His study of the camp system, *Der SS-Staat*, first published in 1945, was based substantially on extrapolation from his own experience of Buchenwald. Though it engages somewhat with the complex institutions of Auschwitz and Majdanek, it only touches on Treblinka, and omits reference to Belzec, Sobibor, and Chelmno.[17]

How do we tie these disparate representational phenomena together into an analysis of the occupation of Germany? Given that the 're-education' programme was an imposition of Allied views of 'the German', or at least 'the German of the recent past', it was logical that Germany's victims should be assigned only a secondary, subjective role. 'Representative' crimes against humanity were seen as almost interchangeable in establishing the base outcome of aggression and racism in which the vast majority of German people were seen by their silence to be at least tacitly complicit. Such had been the intention of the founders of occupation policy – particularly the Americans – from before the 'liberation' of the concentration camps; these places served simply to confirm beyond all doubt the necessity of a redirection of German society, and to provide the most vivid illustrations of that need.

Concentration camps were to be used to show what it was to be a German, or at least a German of the recent past, rather than to show precisely what Germany had done. Put differently, as the 'collective guilt' charge of the early post-war era was not specific to victim individuals or groups, neither was the evidence marshalled to support it. As the Allies gathered this evidence and developed their own general ideas of Nazi criminality, they were quite happy to transmit these perceptions back to the Germans. Occupation officials, who may have been less well informed about their subject matter than the population which they were supposed to be informing, chose the symbols with which they were most familiar, regardless of how unrepresentative these totems actually were. They thereby perpetuated – indeed perhaps helped to create – the enduring myths surrounding that most complex of entities, the Nazi 'camp' system.

To portray predominantly regular, western concentration and labour camps was not only inadequate in itself, it was actually problematic in the context of the Allied guilt accusations. That large numbers of the inmate populations of these camps were themselves German was seized upon by all opponents of collective measures.[18] It was an obvious inconsistency, and encouraged by the confused nature of early occupation policy. For instance, a report produced in April 1945 by the Psychological Warfare Department of the joint military command SHAEF on the making of a documentary on the concentration camps aimed to 'promote German acceptance of the justice of the Allied occupiers by reminding Germans of their past acquiescence' and, therefore, their 'responsibility'. However, it also aimed to show specific crimes committed in the German name to rouse the populace against the Nazis. The latter was to be accomplished specifically by focusing upon German victims of atrocities, and, if possible, establishing their individual identities.[19] The special June 1945 edition of *Welt im Film* duly pinpointed German resistance fighters in the camps. Jews were not mentioned at all.

So the German concentration camps could serve as symbols of resistance to Nazism as well as repression by it; and as Allied policy gradually shifted from 're-education' to the far milder 're-orientation', and Germany became not so much a 'collectively guilty nation' as a 'misled nation', the focus on this duality was given official sanction. What, though, of the 'camps' that were entirely unambiguous symbolically – the eastern killing centres? Here we return to the question of the representation of *Aktion Reinhard.*

The evidence on *Aktion Reinhard*

Compared to the German concentration camps, the cloak of official secrecy had been drawn particularly tight around *Aktion Reinhard.* The chief perpetrators were either dead or had escaped, the camps themselves had been dismantled and farms laid out on the sites, and only fragments of relevant documentation survived. Thus, any investigation of it was heavily dependent upon eyewitnesses. Despite the fact that only one inmate of Belzec outlived that camp, only thirty Jews survived Sobibor, and only sixty-seven survived Treblinka, there nevertheless remained sufficient material to build up a realistic picture of the camps from survivor testimony. As we have seen, however, the Nuremberg prosecutions preferred to rely on 'hard' Nazi documentary evidence rather than what were seen as unreliable and possibly exaggerated eyewitness accounts.

Paradoxically, prior to the trials, there was a considerable amount of at least anecdotal evidence on the *Reinhard* camps; David Cesarani claims that, by 1943, readers of the *Jewish Chronicle* had 'learned the approximate meaning of Treblinka, Sobibor [and], Belzec'.[20] This was certainly true of readers of most organs of the British Jewish press or publications dealing with Poland,[21] and would seem to be a fair summary of the state of knowledge concerning these camps of anyone interested in the Jewish situation.

In the latter half of November 1942, a report from Jan Karski, a courier for the exiled Polish government, was relayed to Western leaders. It included details of the killing methods at Belzec. At the end of November, the report was made public, and the information was relayed that, on the basis of a Himmler order, *Generalgouvernement* Jews were being deported to 'special "exterminating camps" near the townships of Treblinka, Belzec and Sobibor where they were murdered in wholesale massacres'. And, to quote David Engel, 'since the story of the deportations [to Treblinka] from the Warsaw ghetto had now broken in the West, and Jewish circles had begun finally to absorb the notion that Polish Jewry was being subjected . . . to a deliberate program of total biological annihilation, the [Polish Government-in-exile] had to take some official cognizance of events'.[22]

This 'cognizance' took the form of a note, dated 10 December 1942, by the Polish government to the governments of the United Nations concerning the extermination of the Polish Jews. The note elicited a speedy response from the Allied nations in the form of a joint declaration condemning Germany's 'policy of cold-blooded extermination' and naming Poland as 'the principal Nazi slaughter-house'.[23] For the purposes of this study, the important element of the Polish government's note was its reiteration of the report naming Belzec, Sobibor, and Treblinka together as extermination camps in Poland.

The Black Book of Polish Jewry: An Account of the Martyrdom of Polish Jewry Under the Nazi Occupation, published in New York in 1943, was an example of what could be made of the information coming out of Poland. Pulling together various Polish reports, this publication, which was sponsored by Eleanor Roosevelt and Albert Einstein among others, included a chapter on Treblinka. The report contained only one substantial error, involving the method of murder at Treblinka – it described the use of steam rather than the actual carbon monoxide (a common error in eyewitness accounts, being a matter that required expert knowledge of the workings of the gas chambers).

At Nuremberg itself, the re-formed Polish government submitted a symbolic indictment to the IMT listing evidence under all four counts pertaining to that country. It contained extensive details on the extermination camps, including their Jewish specificity.[24] Polish war crimes commission reports, compiled in much the same way as *The Black Book*, were the chief repository of survivor and bystander testimony on the *Reinhard* camps at the trial of the major war criminals. The most relevant such report was an indictment by the Polish government of the former civil chief of the *Generalgouvernement*, Hans Frank, which was again accurate as to the scope of operations of Belzec, Sobibor, and Treblinka except, again, as regards the methods of killing in the gas chambers.[25] Indeed, during the IMT trial, the Soviets adduced eyewitness evidence on Treblinka from such a report.

The need for expert testimony – for instance, concerning the means of killing –

might have been satisfied at Nuremberg by the contribution of two SS men who by various means had gained first-hand experience of the extermination camps. The first witness was an SS investigator, Konrad Morgen, whose wartime investigations had led him on one occasion to Auschwitz, and on another occasion to an encounter with Christian Wirth, inspector of the *Reinhard* camps, whereupon Wirth had boasted of his management of the Lublin killing centres.

The second witness to the *Aktion Reinhard* killing process contributed his testimony to the trials posthumously. This was Kurt Gerstein, head of the 'Technical Disinfection Services' of the SS, and expert on Zyklon B, the gas used in the murder process at Auschwitz. He was qualified to report on the *Reinhard* camps because, in August 1942, as part of a mission to research the possibility of using Zyklon B instead of diesel-exhaust fumes in the murder process, he visited the camps of Belzec and Treblinka, and a construction site at Majdanek. His comprehensive report on the mission, written in May 1945, included mention of the location of each *Reinhard* camp. His report on Belzec covered every aspect of the killing process in agonising detail, and has become perhaps the most oft-cited account of that horror.[26] As Saul Friedländer points out, the Gerstein report was accurate in every respect except those that Gerstein could only surmise, such as a large overestimate of the number of victims of the camps.[27] Moreover, in order to add greater weight to his statement, Gerstein handed over to the Allied troops to whom he had surrendered himself a series of bills for the large-scale purchase of Zyklon B (the lethal cyanide compound used at Auschwitz and Majdanek) by the RSHA, which were written in his name.

In the event, however, almost none of this evidence was followed up at Nuremberg. The IMT judgment, penned at length explicitly to act as an historical pronouncement on Nazism as well as for the contingent verdicts on the defendants, had only this to say about the extermination camps in its statement about the murder of the Jews:

> Part of the final solution was the gathering of Jews from all German occupied Europe in *concentration camps*. Their physical condition was the test of life or death. All who were fit to work were used as slave labourers in the concentration camps; all who were not fit to work were destroyed in gas chambers and their bodies burnt. Certain *concentration camps* such as Treblinka and Auschwitz were set aside for this main purpose.[28]

Otherwise, the only other mention of Treblinka in the judgment occurred out of context in the pronouncement on Hans Frank. It concluded that 'the concentration camp system was introduced in the Government General by the establishment of the notorious Treblinka and Midanek [*sic*] camps'; this statement was in a paragraph dealing with the repression of the Polish population, rather than with the extermination of the Jews.[29] To put these few references into context, the judgment should be broken down in simple proportional terms: the examination of the conspiracy and aggressive war charges considerably outweighed that on war crimes and crimes against humanity; as much time was devoted to Flossenbürg and Mauthausen as to Auschwitz (the only extermination camp accorded much attention at the trial); and nearly as much space went to summing up the evidence on the pillaging of private and public property as to the persecution of the Jews.

The Polish war crimes commission report on Hans Frank was used once by the American prosecution in an introductory presentation on the persecution of the Jews,[30] but not in the direct case against him. This was an indication of its supposed general but not specific value – indeed, victim and bystander testimony as a whole were used, if they were used at all, simply to 'add colour', as Jackson put it. Presumably, the IMT viewed the eyewitness testimony employed by the Soviets on Treblinka in much the same way. More surprisingly, though, given that they were provided by SS men, neither Morgen's nor Gerstein's evidence was used by the IMT or any other Nuremberg tribunal to establish a more general picture of crimes in the *Generalgouvernement*.

The Gerstein report was not even brought to the attention of the IMT. The Allied prosecutors knew of it, but the Americans opted not to use it,[31] and the French, to whom Gerstein's information was initially entrusted, chose only to emphasise the invoices for Zyklon B which, it will be remembered, were attached by Gerstein to his statement to add authority to the latter.[32] A small industry has grown up around the question of why the report was not allowed more attention, given not only its importance, but the extent to which Gerstein and his associates, and the French authorities after them, had gone to establish his credentials.[33] Some of these have been linked with Gerstein's own wartime experience, which was in many ways as remarkable as his testimony. At one extreme, there is the conspiratorial suggestion that French Catholics were keen to obscure his story, and thus the fact of his failed attempt to bring a reaction from the Papacy to the detail of the ongoing Holocaust.[34] Adalbert Rückerl has suggested alternatively that the report was dismissed as 'gross exaggeration, if not entirely the fabrication of a sick mind'.[35] It is possible that the French simply did not observe the correct procedure for entering a document into the record;[36] however, this could have been attempted again. Whatever the reason for the episode, it is clear that the Gerstein report, with its ostensibly incredible revelations, could be dismissed because it was eyewitness testimony. Conversely, the Zyklon B invoices, though no less remarkable in their own way, were accepted as a matter of course.

While there is some evidence that the limitations of what Tony Kushner has called the 'liberal imagination' affected the presentation of the Gerstein testimony, that evidence is conclusive in the case of Konrad Morgen. Serious doubts were cast over the veracity of Morgen's testimony before the IMT as a defence witness for the SS. Though he went on to testify in some of the subsequent Nuremberg trials, his words continued to arouse scepticism. These doubts arose chiefly from his attempt to differentiate the management of the extermination centres from those of the orthodox concentration camps. He, of course, had his own agenda for making these distinctions, and that was probably to dissociate the main body of the SS from the crimes of *Aktion Reinhard*. But the detail and nuances of Morgen's testimony were lost because he spoke truths which no one was yet ready to hear. He described visits to Dachau and Buchenwald in the course of his duties, and his relatively pleasant depiction of these camps, which had since their liberation been established in the Western mind as examples of the worst of Nazi atrocity, cast all of his testimony into the shade of doubt. The British prosecutor David Maxwell-Fyfe declared, with vitriol, to the IMT: 'On the face of it, the evidence which has been given by almost all the witnesses called [in the organisation cases] is untrue . . . The witness Morgen described the variety theatre, the cinema, the bookstalls, and the other amenities of Buchenwald. Dachau, he said, was a recreation camp.'[37]

Yet, it is evident that Morgen visited the camps long before they descended into the state of complete disrepair and depravity in which they were discovered by Allied troops. Besides, we know from the evidence of as unimpeachable a witness as Eugen Kogon, the former Buchenwald inmate, that that camp did indeed have such 'leisure' facilities, though for privileged inmates and for a restricted period.[38] Furthermore, it is not surprising that the camp administration would have attempted to give as favourable an impression as possible to an investigating judge.

At the 'Pohl' trial, Morgen also expanded on the differences between Auschwitz I and Birkenau, as between a concentration camp per se and an extermination facility. Asked by the judge whether he would apply the same reasoning to Dachau, 'where the gas chamber was actually within the compound of the concentration camp', he denied the existence of a gas chamber at Dachau. The judge responded with the claim that 'we know about the false shower bath, and we know about the crematoria, so don't . . . try to tell us there were no exterminations at Dachau . . . There is not any question about it.' Morgen could only point out, before he was ignored and the defence told to move on, what we now know to be true, namely, that 'the presence of a crematory does not necessarily prove that people were being gassed before being taken to [that] crematory'.[39] We now know that no mass gassings occurred at Dachau and any use of that murder method was small and experimental.[40]

On the same question, as in the Pohl trial, the ignorance of both the IMT and the Allied prosecution of the nuances in the system of Nazi atrocity, and its grades of cruelty, led to utter scepticism as to the value of the whole of Morgen's testimony.[41] Counsel for the defence was instructed not to waste time, and the final statement of the prosecution on the indicted organisations labelled Morgen a 'famous perjurer'.[42] As easily as that, this man's evidence was discounted, and the eastern killing centres located more securely in obscurity. This episode illustrates better perhaps than any other the peculiar circularity of an Allied re-education policy that set out, itself unsure, to recreate a past for political purposes.

Conclusions

The popular record of the 'camps', as created by the Allied occupiers, consisted of a mixture of inflated accounts of the better-known establishments and, in as far as the extermination centres were described, uncertainty about the numbers killed there, the identity of the murdered, and the ways in which they differed from, say, Dachau and Buchenwald. Hence differentiation was rendered difficult between murderous persecution and outright genocide; between the Nazi oppression of political opponents, many of whom were themselves German, and the destruction of European Jewry.

Even in the one arena specifically created for a detailed analysis of German criminality, these problems remained. Many factors contributed to the non-representation of *Aktion Reinhard* at the trials. However, it is clear that in the absence of the explicit documentation and the physical evidence which existed to inform about other parts of the killing process, the Nazi prediction that no one would listen to the survivors proved accurate. Given Western preconceptions of Nazi atrocity, there was no chance that any of the *Reinhard* camps would be accepted as 'representative examples'.

In considering these matters, it is important to understand what the Allies were trying to achieve with trial and occupation: German introspection. They wanted Germans to think about what Germany was. In essence, the enforced focus was on the criminal and not the crimes; it was certainly not on the victims, and thus the human cost of what the Allies thought of as 'Germanism'. As the war had been about defeating the Axis, and at no point specifically about halting mass murder, so the peace was all about reforming Germany. To the extent that this required recourse to the 'facts' of Nazism, these were supplied, but only in an attempt to mould the Germans into the image the Allies wished of them. As these policies were entirely perpetrator-centric, it is not surprising that they engendered a sort of narcissism. As they were more accusatory than explanatory, they engendered defensiveness.

The average German was confronted only by a series of confusing newsreel images and photographs, unrepresentative literature, and conflicting and inadequate press reporting – and by blanket guilt accusations followed by contradictory efforts to distinguish between 'Nazis' and 'Germans'. This had repercussions for Germany's examination of its past and the extent to which even committed leftist and liberal organs and intellectuals concerned themselves almost exclusively with 'the German crisis' – again with the perpetrators but without the victims. The connection should not be overplayed because, clearly, many factors came into play in the gradual displacement of the past that occurred in post-war Germany. However, it is apparent that these more-or-less sterile considerations of German guilt were amply facilitated by an Allied occupation and trial regime that removed the focus from the very worst crimes that the Nazis had committed.

A philosophical question also emerges here: namely, whether any one crime or institution in itself can be truly representative of the murder of the Jews, as the Nuremberg prosecutors thought. Auschwitz – that which has entered the popular consciousness as metonym for the Holocaust – could not be representative of anything other than itself, for the simple reason that nothing was the same as Auschwitz. Majdanek was perhaps the most similar institution, combining aspects of the extermination centre and the labour camp, yet it was not a place of primarily Jewish suffering. Auschwitz probably consumed more victims than any other individual camp, but this should not suggest that the death of a Jew at Auschwitz was in any way typical of the deaths of Jews in other extermination camps. This untypicality was not simply because the number of Jews murdered in *Aktion Reinhard* was in total much greater than the one million of Auschwitz. The consideration of the murder of approximately 1.8 million Jews in shooting massacres is another matter again. If anything, the 'pure' extermination camps of Belzec, Sobibor, and Treblinka (and Chelmno) were, as Pierre Vidal-Naquet has argued, an even closer approximation to 'absolute negativity'.[43]

Moreover, while Auschwitz became the epicentre of the genocide after 1942, before then that dubious distinction belonged to the western areas of Soviet territory and then the Lublin district of Poland. This leads us on to a sociological consideration of greater representational importance than the simple topography of the killing process: a consideration that can be roughly equated with the dichotomy 'Auschwitz versus the remaining killing sites'. The vast majority of Holocaust victims (five-sixths) were not Westernised, assimilated Jews, transported half-way across Europe; they were not Anne Frank, or the German Weiss family from the Hollywood soap opera *Holocaust*, nor were they the Americanised Hungarians carefully selected for Steven Spielberg's film *The Last Days*; they were primarily Yiddish speakers from the Pale of Settlement who were murdered in the lands of their birth. It was of such people that Gerald Reitlinger, one of the earliest historians of the Holocaust, wrote the following: 'the Eastern European Jew is a natural rhetorician, speaking in flowery similies . . . sometimes the imagery [thus conjured] transcends credibility'.[44] This unfortunate remark could have come straight from the mouth of Robert Jackson himself. It is also a suitable epitaph to the displaced memory of the catastrophe of Polish Jewry.

Notes

1 Michael Marrus, 'The Holocaust at Nuremberg', *Yad Vashem Studies*, 26 (1998), 5–41; Jeffrey Herf, *Divided Memory: The Nazi Past in the Two Germanies* (Cambridge, MA: Harvard University Press, 1997); Jürgen Wilke, 'Ein früher Beginn der "Vergangenheitsbewältigung": Der Nürnberger Prozess und wie darüber berichtet wurde', *Frankfurter Allgemeine Zeitung* (15 November 1995); Jürgen Wilke, Birgit Schenk, Akiba A. Cohen, and Tami Zemach (eds), *Holocaust und NS-Prozesse* (Cologne: Böhlau, 1995).

2 Martin Gilbert, *Auschwitz and the Allies* (London: Michael Joseph, 1981).

3 Dieter Pohl, *Nationalsozialistische Judenverfolgung in Ostgalizien 1941–1944* (Munich: Oldenbourg, 1966); Bogdan Musial, *Deutsche Zivilverwaltung und Judenverfolgung im Generalgouvernement. Eine Fallstudie zum Distrikt Lublin 1939–1944* (Stuttgart: Harrassowitz, 1999).

4 Wiener Library Nuremberg Document Collection, Nuremberg Document PS-3868.

5 Library of Congress, Washington, DC, Papers of Robert Jackson, container 191, 'Justice Jackson's story', fos 1046–7. Emphasis added.

6 *Trial of the Major War Criminals Before the International Military Tribunal* (hereafter *IMT*), 42 vols (Nuremberg: IMT, 1947), 2, p. 104.

7 Tony Kushner, *The Holocaust and the Liberal Imagination* (Oxford: Blackwell, 1994); Joanne Reilly, *Belsen: The Liberation of a Concentration Camp* (London: Routledge, 1998).

8 Rainer Schulze, 'A difficult interlude: relations between British military government and the German population and their effects for the constitution of a democratic society', in Alan Bance (ed.), *The Cultural Legacy of the British Occupation in Germany* (Stuttgart: Hans-Dieter Heinz, 1997), pp. 67–109, here 70–2.

9 The book concerned was Derek Sington's, *Belsen Uncovered* (London: Duckworth, 1946); see Rhys Williams, '"The Selections of the Committee are not in accord with the requirements of Germany": Contemporary English literature and the Selected Book Scheme in the British Zone of Germany (1945–1950)', in Bance (ed.), *Cultural Legacy*, pp. 110–38, here 126–34.

10 See, for example, Karl Jaspers, *Die Schuldfrage: von der politischen Haftung Deutschlands* (Munich: Piper, 1987), p. 29.

11 For the failure of the film in instilling a sense of collective responsibility, see Brewster Chamberlin, 'Todesmühlen: ein früher Versuch zur Massen "Umerziehung"', *Vierteljahreshefte für Zeitgeschichte* 29 (1981), 420–36.

12 Imperial War Museum film archive.

13 Chamberlin, 'Todesmühlen'; David Culbert, 'American film policy in the re-education of Germany after 1945', in Nicholas Pronay and Keith Wilson (eds), *The Political Re-Education of Germany and Her Allies After World War II* (London: Croom Helm, 1985), 173–202.

14 On the extermination camps, Ute Wrocklage, 'Majdanek und Auschwitz in der internationalen Bildpresse 1945', in Yasmin Doosry (ed.), *Representations of Auschwitz* (Oswiecim: Oswiecim State Museum, 1995), pp. 35–44; also Dan Diner, 'Massenverbrechen im 20. Jahrhundert: über Nationalsozialismus und Stalismus', in Rolf Steininger (ed.), *Der Umgang mit dem Holocaust* (Cologne: Böhlau, 1994), pp. 468–81, here 468–9.

15 See, for instance, Werner Bergmann, 'Die Reaktion auf den Holocaust in Westdeutschland von 1945 bis 1989', *Geschichte in Wissenschaft und Unterricht*, 43 (1992), 327–50, here 328.

16 Helmut Peitsch, '*Deutschlands Gedächtnis an seine dunkelste Zeit': zur Funktion der Autobiographik in den Westzonen Deutschlands und den Westsektoren von Berlin 1945 bis 1949* (Berlin: Edition Sigma, 1990), pp. 101–2, 173–7; the books penned by the regular political prisoners were Emil de Martini, *4 Millionen Tote klagen an! Erlebnisse im Todeslager Auschwitz* (Munich: von Weber, 1948); Zenon Rozanski, *Mützen ab . . . Eine Reportage aus der Strafkompanie des KZ Auschwitz* (Hannover: Verlag des Andere Deutschland, 1948); that by the sole Jew was Rudolf Weinstock, '*Das wahre Gesicht Hitler-Deutschlands'* (Singen: Volksverlag, 1948).

17 Eugen Kogon, *Der SS-Staat: Das System der deutschen Konzentrationslager* (Frankfurt am Main: Europäische Verlagsanstalt, 1961). Belzec is reduced to 'Belze', and cited as the graveyard of 50,000 Lemberg (Lvov) Jews (p. 216). This was true, but hardly the full story of Belzec.

18 Alfred Grosser, *Germany in Our Time* (New York: Praeger, 1971), p. 41; Victor Gollancz, *What Buchenwald Really Means* (London: Gollancz, 1945).

19 University of Warwick, Modern Records Centre, Crossman Papers, MSS154/3/PW/1/1–211, SHAEF PWD report, 25 April 1945.

20 David Cesarani, *The Jewish Chronicle and Anglo-Jewry, 1841–1991* (Cambridge: Cambridge University Press, 1994), p. 179.

21 For a list of relevant newspaper articles, see Donald Bloxham, *Genocide on Trial: War Crimes Trials and the Formation of Holocaust History and Memory* (Oxford: Oxford University Press, 2001), p. 116.

22 David Engel, *In the Shadow of Auschwitz: the Polish Government-in-Exile and the Jews* (Chapel Hill, NC: University of North Carolina Press, 1987), p. 198.

23 Kushner, *Liberal Imagination*, pp. 168–9.

24 Bodleian Library, Oxford, Goodhart Papers, reel 30, fos 83 onwards.

25 In a second Polish commission report, Nuremberg Document USSR-93, fos 41–5, the camps, including Belzec, Sobibor, and Treblinka, were separated into two categories under the title 'execution camps' (*Hinrichtungslager*).

26 Nuremberg Document PS-1553.

27 Saul Friedländer, *Counterfeit Nazi: The Ambiguity of Good* (London: Weidenfeld and Nicolson, 1969), p. 114.

28 *IMT*, 22, p. 466. Emphases added.

29 *Ibid.*, pp. 497–8.

30 *Ibid.*, 3, pp. 566–9; on presentation of this document, Major Walsh failed to cite the paragraph claiming that 'the erection of [Treblinka] was closely connected with the German plans aiming at a complete destruction of the Jewish population in Poland', and also that sentence coupling Belzec with Sobibor and Treblinka. His coverage focused mainly on concentration camps rather than extermination centres.

31 University of Connecticut Archives, Papers of Thomas J. Dodd, box 321, file 'Board of Review Documents 1945 October', shows that the US prosecution had considered using the affidavit.

32 *IMT*, 6, pp. 332–3, 363.

33 For some of the verifications and the history of the report, see Leon Poliakov, 'Le Dossier Kurt Gerstein', *Le Monde Juif*, no. 36 (1964), 4–20; Georges Wellers, 'À propos d'une thèse de doctorat "explosive" sur le "Rapport Gerstein"', *Le Monde Juif*, no. 121 (1986), 1–17.

34 For this theory, and others, see Pierre Joffroy, *A Spy for God: The Ordeal of Kurt Gerstein* (London: Collins, 1971), pp. 267–71.

35 Adalbert Rückerl, *NS-Vernichtungslager im Spiegel deutscher Strafprozesse* (Munich: DTV, 1977), p. 14.

36 This can be deduced from a study of Joffroy, *A Spy for God*, and the Francis Biddle Papers (University of Syracuse Archives), box 3, notes on evidence, vol. II, fos 47–51.

37 *IMT*, 22, pp. 175–6.

38 Kogon, *Der SS-Staat* pp. 131–7.

39 (Subsequent) Nuremberg Military Tribunal papers, trial IV, fos 6687–9.

40 Eugen Kogon, Hermann Langbein, and Adalbert Rückerl (eds), *Nationalsozialistischen Massentötungen durch Giftgas: Eine Dokumentation* (Frankfurt am Main: Fischer, 1983), pp. 277–80.

41 For the dismissive reaction of the American judge, see Francis Biddle, *In Brief Authority* (New York: Doubleday, 1962), p. 464.

42 *IMT*, 22, p. 323.

43 Pierre Vidal-Naquet, *Assassins of Memory* (New York: Columbia University Press, 1992), p. 97.

44 Gerald Reitlinger, *The Final Solution* (London: Vallentine, Mitchell and Co., 1953), p. 531.

Memory and authenticity:
the case of Binjamin Wilkomirski

Binjamin Wilkomirski's camp memoir *Fragments* was, when it appeared in 1995, acclaimed as one of the most fascinating representations of the Holocaust since Primo Levi's *If This Is a Man*. The discovery and subsequent confirmation of the author's true identity in 1998 has, in its turn, exposed a story so bizarre that it probably made the book known even more widely. In the Anglo-American world, where the book had been hailed by scholars of Holocaust history and literature, two major articles trying to explain the 'affair' appeared in prominent journals. In 1999, Elena Lappin's essay 'The man with two heads' was published in *Granta*, and Philip Gourevitch's 'The memory thief' in the *New Yorker*.[1] In the same year the BBC documented the story of *Fragments* in a film, *Child of the Death Camps*, broadcast in early November. This was preceded earlier that evening by a short discussion of the case by the historian David Cesarani and the writer Anne Karpf on BBC Radio 4. The film also identified another fraudster, a Canadian woman who claimed to be a survivor and whom Wilkomirski pretended to recognise as a child he had met in Auschwitz.

The academic profession, too, has begun to analyse the case, most notably, so far, in a half-day seminar organised by the Wiener Library in London.[2] At this event two speakers in particular made important points about the reception of *Fragments*.[3] My aim in this essay is to explore that subject in the light of reception and narrative theory, to show why Wilkomirski, by employing certain narrative techniques, was able to invite the kind of reception the book originally received, and to illuminate the way in which *Fragments* can, despite the fraudulent claims of its author, nevertheless be considered an authentic text.

The facts

In 1995, in its 'Jewish Library' series, the prestigious Frankfurt publishing house Suhrkamp brought out *Bruchstücke* by the hitherto unknown Swiss author Binjamin Wilkomirski.[4] It is the story of the narrator's survival of various concentration camps as a very young boy of Polish-Jewish descent, and of his subsequent integration into post-war Swiss society, a story which is told with a degree of detachment absent from previous survivors' accounts.

Harrowing details, amassed by the narrator without much of a narrative frame, both shocked and attracted readers. The book quickly appeared in several translations (in English as *Fragments*, 1996), and its author was awarded important prizes (including one from the *Jewish Quarterly* in 1997), and showered with invitations to be interviewed and to appear at conferences.[5] Nobody doubted the authenticity of the text until, in late summer 1998, the Swiss journalist Daniel Ganzfried, himself the son of an Auschwitz survivor, wrote an article in a Swiss weekly that questioned not only the authenticity of the story but also the identity of its author.[6] His research showed that Wilkomirski was the son of an unmarried Swiss woman, Yvonne Grosjean, and had later been adopted by a wealthy childless Zürich couple, Dr Kurt and Mrs Martha Dössekker, who gave him their name. How Bruno Dössekker subsequently came to conceive the book he has written has since occupied the minds of reviewers, historians, and literary scholars alike. What is known, mainly through Elena Lappin's and, more recently, Stefan Mächler's research, is that he seems to have had a long-standing fascination with the Holocaust, manifest in a sizeable personal collection of books on the subject.[7] Moreover, friends report that already as a young man Dössekker had an urge to make himself more interesting by inventing an exotic childhood for himself. Finally, what sounds like a severe midlife crisis, together with some unexplained physical ailments, prompted him, encouraged by his psychotherapist friend Elitsur Bernstein, to identify with the plight of the Jews, which he did to such a degree that he eventually assumed a Jewish identity.

Examples of identification with the persecuted Jew are known in creative literature, where the Holocaust is sometimes used as a metaphor for severe psychological pain, as in Sylvia Plath's poetry and, more recently, in *Das Judasschaf* by the German feminist writer Anne Duden. *Fragments*, however, belongs to an altogether different category, as Dössekker was able to convince his readers of its autobiographical character. Indeed, in *Fragments*, the Holocaust is not employed as a metaphor, as some reviewers have claimed.[8] Dössekker does mean what he says – he identifies completely with the character he has created for himself.

Why did nobody question the text?

My own reading experience before I knew of the author's false identity was such that I accepted the autobiographical identity of the text even though I was aware of various doubtful elements. First and foremost among these, the survival of such a small child was contrary to my knowledge of similar survival stories and historical probability.[9] I was, moreover, irritated by the ostensibly unchanged attitude of the narrator to food even after he must have had a chance of different experiences: in the Swiss children's home, following a period in a Krakow orphanage, he still treats cheese rinds and bread as if he had just come from the camps. I explained my doubts about the possibility of the narrator's survival to myself by reference to the chaos of the Holocaust, which might have permitted such a miracle. Moreover, the young age of the narrator at the time when the events took place could well have had an effect on the chronology in the text.

Indeed, I perceived the apparent lack of logic as proof of authenticity. This is how the narrator remembered the course of events. He did not try to change this subsequently by subjecting it to a logic that was not part of the experience itself.[10] I came to accept that, for Wilkomirski, memory was more important than the actual event. His constructed memory could, for example, have been a defence against the destructive potential of the remembered experience. Other survivors are known to have done this. In fact, in some cases, the shaping, or reshaping, of memory began in the camps themselves. Individual experiences entered the collective memory, especially where they could be assigned a symbolic meaning. Certain significant events, such as the suicide of Mala Zimetbaum in Birkenau or the shooting of the SS man Schilling by a young Jewess in one of the Auschwitz gas-chamber changing rooms, could thus not only assume legendary status but could also be narrated by survivors as if they themselves had witnessed them.[11] In Wilkomirski's text, however, memory was also employed to help construct, or reconstruct, an identity which, for reasons of war, persecution, and consequent uprooting, had not been allowed to develop in a normal way in the child and young adult.

This judgement was echoed by other scholars, most notably by Elena Lappin, who, as the editor of the *Jewish Quarterly*, met Wilkomirski when he came to London to receive his prize. In her sixty-page essay 'The man with two heads', she traces her own journey from reading the book as a genuine memoir to eventually – after weeks of meticulous research – coming to accept its inauthenticity. Her text shows graphically how much she resisted this process.

What were the reasons for readers' willingness to accept *Fragments* as an authentic text? I would like to concentrate here on three categories of reasons: psychological, historical, and textual.

Psychological reasons

In Germany, the denial of the Holocaust is a criminal offence. Moreover, there is still a residue of collective guilt feeling, which becomes manifest occasionally in a public debate.[12] This curious German masochism, which was noticeable in discussions about Daniel Goldhagen's book *Hitler's Willing Executioners* and later in the debate about the Berlin Holocaust memorial, is periodically replaced by the demand for a 'normalisation' of the German nation.[13] This happened in the historians' debate in the late 1980s, where the question was aired whether it was time to study the Holocaust in relation to other contemporary events rather than insisting on its singularity.[14] More recently, the eminent German writer Martin Walser, in his acceptance speech for the *Friedenspreis des Deutschen Buchhandels*, called for a scaling down of public memorialisation of the Holocaust in Germany. However, these attempts at emancipation from national history are usually swiftly quashed by the political and cultural establishment as politically incorrect. Guilt feelings are by no means unique to Germany. In the United States, too, they inform the present-day discussion of the Holocaust to a certain extent, based, for instance on the argument that the United States' restrictive immigration policy and the refusal to bomb railway lines and crematoria were detrimental to the fate of the Jews in Europe.[15] Moreover, some narratives of survivors' experiences have been treated as Holy Writ.[16] This attitude was criticised a few years ago by the political philosopher István Deák because, he argued, it rendered an accurate record of the Holocaust impossible.[17]

Historical reasons

Since the end of the war, the image of Holocaust survivors has changed. Their initial struggle for recognition has given way to memorialisation on a large scale. Holocaust museums and memorials outside Israel, such as those in Washington and Berlin, have been and are still being built, prompting sarcastic remarks from their critics, of which the most notorious is, 'There is no business like Shoah-business'.[18] In the wake of the increasing empowerment of the American Jews during the past two or three decades, memorialising the Holocaust has almost become a *raison d'être*.[19] This led Philip Gourevitch to remark that 'remembrance of the Holocaust, which was until recently held to be the special burden and sacred duty of Jews, [thus] has evolved into a common civic rite in much of Western culture'.[20]

This eruption of memory of the Holocaust fits into a wider context of late twentieth-century Western society to such an extent that even recent philosophical and textual theories have taken account of it. In their book *Literatures of Memory*, Peter Middleton and Tim Woods identify memory as a postmodern phenomenon, assuming that 'perhaps all literary texts . . . are forms of textual memory; all memory is ultimately memory of trauma because its aftershocks easily dominate the psyche'.[21] Using Freud's trauma theory as a point of departure, they demonstrate that traumatic experiences are at the heart of most literature, irrespective of genre. Dössekker's text both manifests and satisfies this interest in memory. If all literary texts are forms of sublimated trauma, a text that offers memory of the Holocaust has a trauma of a very specific kind at its centre. So much has been said and written about it that it has became part of our collective memory to the extent that the term is frequently used as a metaphor to describe other horrific events. And it is with an awareness of this collective memory that the author of a Holocaust testimony would present his text. Like an interviewee whose story is guided by the expectation of the listener, the author of *Fragments* is thus influenced by and responds to societal needs.[22] In choosing the Holocaust as a frame for his own traumatic life story, Dössekker thus treated the metaphor as fact.

Closely connected with the new interest in memory is the changed attitude towards authenticity. Historically, authenticity has evolved from an ethical ideal of sincerity.[23] For Adorno, authenticity was still synonymous with truthfulness and the opposite of all negations of art, but his contemporary, Walter Benjamin, in a famous essay on the impact of reproduction techniques on the work of art, challenged this view. Finally, in postmodernism, authenticity becomes an obsolete concept: it is not the message that is now perceived as authentic, as Marshall McLuhan says, but the medium.[24] According to Stefan Mächler, the media played a central role in turning Wilkomirski into a camp victim.[25] Authenticity has become 'the way in which we deal with the various dependencies that condition our existence.'[26] But whereas cultural theorists are sceptical about authenticity, there is in general a renewed yearning for it among 'ordinary' people; hence the enthusiastic reception of books like *Fragments*.

Textual reasons

How is this aura of authenticity created in Dössekker's text? The story is grippingly written from a relatively consistent child perspective, which pretends to offer the unmediated presentation of perception – a direct access to the former self of the narrator. The narrator is modelled here as the archetypal victim, being at once a Jew and an innocent toddler. The child perspective in Wilkomirski's text, Lappin suggests, is 'both a shield and a weapon: the author can effectively hide behind its imprecision and its vulnerability, and, at the same time, disarm a potentially sceptical reader with its emotional power.'[27] In addition, the child perspective can also be interpreted as a literary device. Other survivors have, in recent publications about their camp experiences, resorted to this narrative perspective in order to cast fresh light on the Holocaust, whose representation has come to be saturated with certain images.[28] In his text, Wilkomirski shows the impact of his 'first memories' on his later life.[29] Sometimes he even makes this explicit, as when an encounter with a rat emerging from a dead woman's body is related to the birth of his first child. With his 'archetypal story of deliverance', Wilkomirski presents what the narrative psychologist would call a 'good story'.[30]

This point becomes obvious if, for example, we look at the contextualisation of another such story: in Buchenwald, a three-year-old Jewish boy was hidden and saved by the communist camp cell. Bruno Apitz, himself one of the communists involved in this episode, later wrote a novel about it called *Nackt unter Wölfen*.[31] Zacharias Zweig, the father of the boy, also told his story and before his death in 1972 asked his son to publish it.[32] These two texts give us the rare opportunity to study which elements of an event trigger literary imagination and what exactly differentiates the contextualisation of the same event as an authentic report and as a novel.[33] While Apitz exploits strategies of writing fiction, including the modification of events and their historical chronology, in order to create suspense, Zweig, like other survivors, is at pains to narrate the event as objectively as possible. The difference between the two ways of contextualising the same event is brought out by the reception. While *Nackt unter Wölfen* went into several editions and a film of the book helped to make its author famous, not many people have read Zweig's authentic report.

Dössekker managed to combine both strategies and thereby achieve an even greater effect. Like Apitz's novel and Zweig's survival text, there is the miracle of a child's survival at the centre in *Fragments*; however, it is told neither as an adventure story nor as a mere factual report. The nineteen loosely connected events, each of which is assigned its own dense narrative, leave gaps between them that stimulate the reader's imagination. Deliberate structuring is not used here for the creation of suspense. The reader's attention is secured rather by the accumulation of similarly structured incidents arranged in a loose chronological order. It is not surprising that, after

Wilkomirski's true identity became clear, these literary devices were criticised as misleading. Philip Gourevitch, for example, suspects that the only function of the carefully structured plot of *Fragments* is to deceive the reader. Yet, structure is not necessarily in itself a sign of inauthenticity. Although most concentration-camp reports written by amateurs without claim to any literary quality display rather less forceful structures, some are very deliberately structured, yet these are not considered to be any less authentic. It is, however, worth mentioning that most of their authors either were already, or subsequently became, professional writers (Jean Améry, Imre Kertész, Tadeusz Borowski, Primo Levi, Ruth Klüger, and Fred Wander, to mention a few). What is significant about the structure of *Fragments* is that it is designed to exclude the reader, who may not view him/herself as one of the perpetrators, but will want to protect the child in the adult author and make up for the ordeal the toddler was made to suffer.[34] Indeed, the innocent child at the centre, together with the horrific events he claims to have witnessed, seemed to put the suffering of other survivors into a different perspective. However, the reader is also exonerated by the fact that the child, however hard and unjustified his suffering may have been, has survived to tell his story. It is clear that the victim/perpetrator opposition serves as the central channel of communication in the text.

Authenticity in *Fragments* is also achieved by the disjointedness of the text to which the title points as a kind of poetological programme. Both the title and the first section of the book refer to the impossibility of an integrated discursive representation of early childhood memory of the Holocaust. It is well known that memory is selective. We do not remember every event in the same detail and with equal intensity. For the survivors, the experience of the Holocaust is no exception. In order to give a full account of their camp experience, they typically have resorted to alternating summaries of longer periods which they do not remember so clearly with more detailed accounts of a few memorable events (for example, the arrival at the camp, and the floggings or hangings which they had to witness).[35] Some events, such as the daily roll-call, are narrated once in a durative fashion, with the implication that they were much the same on any other day. While most survivors contextualise their fragmented memory in this way, Wilkomirski, like some postmodern philosophers and historiographers, instead exposes the fragmentation; indeed, he makes it his narrative principle.[36] He limits himself to narrating the memorable events only. These, however, he relates in great detail. In order to distinguish between 'actual' and constructed, or reconstructed, memory, Wilkomirski frequently switches between the present and past tenses, thus giving the narrated events more depth and thereby making them more persuasive.[37]

It is the richness of detail in *Fragments* that may have persuaded many readers to believe Wilkomirski's story. It is the rhetorical mediation of these details which also facilitates the reader's emotional involvement. Cognitive psychologists know that vivid memories are taken to be 'signs of strong emotions' and are 'likely to be treated as accurate emotions, too', and thus 'we will be inclined to believe that it is a real memory'.[38] Yet, Dössekker did not only assemble a persuasive mass of details in his book; he was also keen to get them right. While he was opposed to using adult logic to structure his childhood recollections in retrospect, he did travel to places he 'remembered'. He did not just 're-enact his memory in tangible locations of space and time'; he actually visited places in Latvia and Poland in order to verify his supposed recollections, and managed to impress readers with the accuracy of his memory.[39] In 1993, he and his psychologist Elitsur Bernstein went to Majdanek, Auschwitz, Krakow, and Riga. Bernstein told Elena Lappin: 'before we went to Majdanek, Bruno prepared detailed maps of the camp from his memory. They were different from the maps in history books. When we got there, his maps turned out to be the correct ones, in all details and angles.'[40] Dössekker actually went a step further than treating 'textual memories as if they were personal memories', as Middleton and Woods allege; he tried to turn textual memories into personal ones by physically re-enacting them.[41] Dössekker's return to the alleged scenes of his suffering could be read as conforming with an insight which cultural theory gained from the work of the French philosopher Maurice Halbwachs on social memory. Halbwachs identifies the 'change of frame' as the single most important reason for forgetting. As the person departs from the scene of the event, the process of forgetting sets in.[42] Yet, by visiting Majdanek, Dössekker not only puts himself seemingly into the 'frame' which he expects to jolt his memory but also follows a literary tradition. At least since the Italian tours of the eighteenth-century gentleman-writer, the *genius loci* has been considered an important factor of literary imagination.

While child perspective, structure, fragmentation, and detail all convinced the reader of the authenticity of Wilkomirski's text, it is the autobiographical form of *Fragments* which indicates to the recipient most forcefully that she/he is encountering the personal story of a survivor. The author of an autobiography, according to the French theorist Philippe Lejeune, forms a 'pact' with the reader based on the identity of the names of author and first-person narrator.[43] The narrator in an autobiographical text therefore is not a medium, as in a fictional text, but an actual person with a known identity.[44] The identity of the author in its turn is usually verified by works he or she has published previously, and this guarantees the authenticity of the personal life story. In 1979, Paul de Man took issue with Lejeune's thesis of the 'autobiographical pact': the identity of names, de Man held, could not be taken as the exclusive tool to identify autobiography.[45] De Man did not perceive autobiography as a genre but rather as a construct that emerges in the process of a text's reception. In his view, it is more a prosopopoeia, a voice that calls from beyond the grave, which constitutes the autobiographical discourse and which can be detected in more than just the strictly autobiographical texts. This non-essentialist interpretation of the autobiographical text may sharpen our senses for the place of the author in the text. Yet, its refusal to take into account the autobiographical intention of the author limits its value as a tool to distinguish between autobiography, autobiographical novel, and fiction with autobiographical elements. In other words, de Man's definition of the autobiographical does not help us answer the question why we read *Fragments* as an authentic text.

However Lejeune's definition does, as it ties in with reception aesthetics, whose central concept is the 'horizon of expectations'. By this, we mean the collective of cultural assumptions and expectations, norms and experiences, that guide the reader's understanding and interpretation of a literary text in a given moment. The horizons are subject to historical change and thus constitute one factor responsible for the emergence of new evaluations of a literary work within time. In German philosophy, the term has an established tradition: Nietzsche, Husserl, and Heidegger have all used it. Hans Robert Jauß introduced it into literary theory. He developed the concept to designate the hermeneutic process taking place when we read. Jauß interprets the structure of expectation as a system of reference which informs reception of a text in terms of the laws or norms of genre, the relationship of the text to the literary environment known to the reader, its relationship to other texts, and the differential between fact and fiction. By drawing on the familiar, the text produces an expectation of norms in the reader, which can be reproduced, negated, parodied, varied, etc. Taking on board a concept of Russian formalism, Jauß identified the change of horizon, that is, the distance between expectation and text, as a measure of its literary quality.[46]

Both the subtitle of the English version of Dössekker's book – *Memories of a Childhood 1939–1948* – and the picture of the author at the age of 10 inside the book authenticate the personal story of the author. The title adds to this by suggesting a form that bestows credibility on the memory of early childhood. Thus, if readers believed the story, they were merely following guidelines laid down by the text, as, indeed, the first reviewer of the book, Klara Obermüller, suggested.[47] To elucidate this point, a glance at another novel published in the same year as the English translation of Dössekker's text may prove instructive. *Fugitive Pieces*, by the young Canadian woman writer Anne Michaels, gives a fictional first-person account of a male Polish Jew who, as a young child, was rescued and brought up by a Greek archaeologist and polymath.[48] Despite her title, which suggests a narrative strategy similar to that of *Fragments*, Michaels does not identify with the first-person narrator. A short epilogue names the most important archival sources that she had relied on in writing her book. There is no identity of names, nor even of gender. As if further to stress the lack of identity between author and narrator, the latter appears as two different people of different generations: Jacob or Jake, and Ben, who publishes the papers of the former and tells the story of looking for and finding him. Since the second and younger narrator, Ben – the son of two survivors with identity problems of his own – is not the author, the illusion created by the book is not even that of edited papers. Following Lejeune, we have to classify this text as a novel with a first-person narrator, a quasi-autobiography, a form that leaves the reader in no doubt that the account of the first-person narrator is not autobiographical.[49] A different case yet is another recent, successful text: *The Reader* by Bernhard Schlink.[50] Written in the first-person singular, it tells the story of a relationship in post-war Germany between a youngster and a former female Nazi camp guard. An abundance of autobiographical detail seems to identify the narrator with the author, and many readers have willingly followed this lead. While Schlink has never claimed autobiographical authenticity for his book, he has clearly and very effectively used verifiable personal data in order to satisfy a desire for the authentic emotion and experience in his readers.

Whereas we can now assume that the 'autobiographical pact' is an important pointer for the reader to determine the authenticity of a text, a problem arises in cases where, as with most Holocaust texts, the author has not been known through previous published work and thus his/her identity cannot serve as a guarantor. Although there was some early doubt over Wilkomirski's identity, his literary agent Eva Koralnik and the publisher Suhrkamp were convinced of the text's authenticity by Wilkomirski's explanation of the name of Dössecker in his birth certificate as being due to his adoption by a Swiss couple.[51] The dust jacket of the German original gives a short biographical sketch guided by the events narrated in the book.[52] The English version also points out that Wilkomirski is a well-known classical musician in his home country.

So how are we to resolve the question of authenticity? On the one hand, textual features suggest the genuineness of the Holocaust survival story; on the other hand, the true identity of the author proves this story to be flawed. If we follow Nicholas Davey, this paradox may be resolved.[53] Drawing on the philosophers Martin Heidegger and Hans Georg Gadamer, who had both concerned themselves with questions of hermeneutics, Davey suggests that there is not just one kind of authenticity but two: ethical and aesthetic. Ethical authenticity relies on the deliverance of the pact between author and reader, and is thus bound up with moral judgements. Aesthetic authenticity is concerned only with the text, and it is with the text that the reader establishes a relationship.

It is obvious from our discussion so far that *Fragments* lacks ethical authenticity. It is not a genuine document of the legal person Bruno Dössekker, as it does not relate to the facts and dates recorded about him in the public records. Aesthetic authenticity, however, can be claimed for *Fragments*. Its authenticity as a Holocaust text is rooted in its literariness and has been testified to by the reception it initially received. What 'Wilkomirski' relates, admittedly in a sensational fashion, does fit the experience of alienation attested by many survivors. Apart from the aesthetic authenticity of the text, there is also a kind of psychological authenticity. The story is a personal document of the figure 'Binjamin Wilkomirski', who constructs himself in and by it.[54] It is in this process of construction that he assumes a name.[55] Dössekker is also said to have told Bernstein that he himself remembers coming from Wilkomir.[56] Incidentally, constructedness of memory is not in itself a measure of authenticity, as even genuine memories are constructed to a certain extent. Memory does not ever seem to be an exact mirror of what happened, but is always shaped and influenced by events and experiences that come afterwards and is also guided by concerns the person who remembers holds at the time of remembering. Indeed, recent neurophysiological hypotheses suggest that memory is not contained in some sort of storage space. We rather have to see memory in connection with processes of perception and learning. Memory, in other words, seems – according to clinical studies – to have not only to do with the past but also a great deal to do with the present.[57]

Reception

When rumours about Wilkomirski's real identity first emerged, attention swiftly shifted from the book to its author. Daniel Ganzfried was the first to write a 'character assassination'. According to Elena Lappin, this was the reason why *Passagen*, the journal for which Ganzfried's article was originally commissioned, turned his piece down.[58] The aesthetic judgement of the book therefore was increasingly replaced by a moral judgement, leading to attacks on Dössekker as a person. Before Ganzfried's article appeared, it would have been deemed insensitive to question factual inaccuracies, for which readers (like myself) tried instead to find rational explanations.[59] Afterwards, however, everybody had a licence to call 'Wilkomirski' a liar. In November 1999, a Swiss solicitor gave the affair a farcical turn by bringing a court case against Dössekker, charging him with cheating the prosecuting party of the price for the book as well as part of his lifetime and also with gaining his sympathy by deceit.[60]

So, has the text changed since its first publication in 1995? Ruth Klüger, herself a child survivor, and whose memoir *weiter leben* appeared three years before 'Wilkomirski's' and, for different reasons, became equally acclaimed, alleged that the presentation of false suffering inevitably becomes kitsch.[61] But if we follow Saul Friedländer's definition of 'kitsch' in his study of Nazism, the term only partially fits *Fragments*.[62] While the text occasionally borders on the pornographic in its display of violence, and certainly exploits the theme of pureness and innocence with its child protagonist, it does not present the cheaper kitschy images and emotions; indeed, it deliberately avoids the sentimentalisation often found in connection with the representation of suffering children.[63] Nor is its language of the repetitive, redundant, and hypnotising kind that we associate with kitsch in its trivial form. Kitsch would have been manifest in the text even before *Fragments* was discovered to be a fraud. Klüger's allegation that the disclosure of the text's insincerity compromises its literary quality cannot therefore be accepted. The aesthetic value of a text does not change with the genre. Authenticity has nothing to do with literary quality. If there is any relationship at all between them, it is often perceived as problematic: genuine camp survivors have been at pains to avoid fictionalisation.[64] Before the author's identity came into doubt, *Fragments* was praised for its literary merits: not only was it accepted by several internationally renowned publishers, but it also received the Jewish Book Council's prize in America in the memoir category, and Dössekker's American publisher Arthur Samuelson went as far as to say that if the book did turn out to be fiction, 'Wilkomirski' would be an even greater writer.[65] In due course, *Fragments* is bound to be reclassified as a novel, and the next generation of readers will read it as a fictional text and judge it by its literary merits. Although it may no longer receive the attention it did when it was believed to be the story of a genuine survivor, it will continue to be a memorable text that captures certain truths about Jewish suffering in the concentration camps.

In other words, it is not the text that has changed since Ganzfried's disclosure, as Klüger alleges, but our attitude to it. Inga Clendinnen, accordingly, locates the difference between history and fiction in the difference of the reader's response to the text. With authors of authentic texts she engages differently, 'because I stand in a moral relationship with these people'.[66] In an essay on the author's sincerity published in 1983, Colin Lyas distinguishes between 'purely imitative imaginative' and 'non-imitative' works, and calls for 'a different kind of response' because 'non-imitative art adds to my empirical knowledge of human nature. This is why we are unable to be indifferent when we discover that what we took to be sincere expressions of an actual emotion is not so.'[67] Ruth Klüger is on the right track when she asserts that after the identity of its author became questionable *Fragments* became a 'different book although not a different text'.[68] The guidelines for the reception have changed. This is why we now notice elements in the text which have escaped us before or which we, for one reason or other, deliberately ignored.[69] We feel personally let down when we discover that the identity of an author, which we were led to believe was genuine, is false; and our disappointment is increased when our engagement with this text has been emotionally as highly charged as would be the case with an authentic Holocaust memoir, and especially with one that involves the survival of a child. The text had relieved us of too many of our guilt feelings as 'perpetrators' – had not a small child, against all odds, survived the most horrific events and remained seemingly human? And even managed to become a successful classical musician? It is thus not surprising that the reader's disappointment expresses itself in a rejection of the text and aggression against its producer.

Conclusion

There is no question that the historian has to consider the authenticity of sources and, in certain cases, it may even be useful for the literary scholar to do the same. It seems to me that the lesson we can learn from the so-called Wilkomirski affair is that a text by its literary strategies can command the interest of the reader. Hence, rather than condemning the author in an emotional outburst, it is probably more useful for the literary scholar to identify the strategies at work in the text – especially as the case of 'Wilkomirski' is more complex than one of mere deception. There is a certain truth to the story, as was recognised by its first readers and reviewers. The atmosphere of inescapable terror related by *Fragments* convinced even survivors and prompted them to welcome its author as their spokesman. What is more, the trauma at the centre of the text is authentic. It is the trauma of a small child's adoption in the Switzerland of the 1940s, which went terribly wrong, that gives the story additional credibility.[70] The geographical setting chosen by the author could thus convince readers that this trauma was associated with the Holocaust.

The narrative strategies, in particular the fragmentation, served as a guarantor of the authenticity of the trauma. However, the effectiveness of the fragmentation rests on the fact that it has been identified as a stylistic device employed to this effect by authors of postmodern novels. This dual purpose of narrative fragmentation makes the distinction between ethical and aesthetic authenticity in more recent Holocaust memoirs less straightforward. Yet, fragmentation and other more literary devices in those texts do not necessarily compromise their ethical authenticity. Child survivors, such as Ruth Klüger or Imre Kertész, do relate their personal experience in the camps. What the literary mode of representation signifies, however, is the utterly subjective angle from which they view and interpret their ordeal in retrospect. By offering an individual response which does not quite fit our collective memory, the aesthetic moulds more recently chosen by victims for personal memory are designed to challenge rather than confirm these collectively held views about the Holocaust.

Notes

1 Elena Lappin, 'The man with two heads', *Granta*, 66 (Summer 1999), 7–65; Philip Gourevitch, 'The memory thief', *New Yorker* (14 June 1999), 48–68.

2 The seminar took place on 26 March 2000.

3 The contribution by Sue Vice was published with the title, 'Fragments as fiction', in *Jewish Quarterly*, 178 (Summer 2000), 51–4. The other speaker was Anne Karpf, author of *The War After* (London: Heinemann, 1996).

4 Binjamin Wilkomirski, *Bruchstücke: Aus einer Kindheit 1939–1948* (Frankfurt/Main: Jüdischer Verlag im Suhrkamp Verlag, 1995).

5 Binjamin Wilkomirski, *Fragments: Memories of a Childhood 1939–1948* (trans. Carol Brown Janeway, New York: Schocken, 1996).

6 Daniel Ganzfried, 'Die geliehene Holocaust-Biographie', *Die Weltwoche* (27 August 1998).

7 Stefan Mächler, *Der Fall Wilkomirski: Über die Wahrheit einer Biographie* (Zürich: Pendo, 2000). Dössekker studied history at the University of Zürich. In the mid-1960s, he embarked on a doctoral thesis on the Jewish migration in middle and eastern Europe, which he never finished; Mächler, *Der Fall Wilkomirski*, p. 69.

8 See, for example, *Neue Zürcher Zeitung* (22/23 May 1999).

9 It is known that children did survive the camps even on their own and, after liberation, were cared for by organisations like the Communist Centralny Komitet Zydiwski in Krakow, but none seem to have undergone ordeals of the severity related in *Fragments*; Mächler, *Der Fall Wilkomirski*, p. 186.

10 Wilkomirski not only stressed this in his preamble but also reiterated it to his publishers; Wilkomirski, p. 4; Mächler, *Der Fall Wilkomirski*, p. 156, note 20.

11 Peter Burke, 'Geschichte als soziales Gedächtnis', in Aleida Assmann and Dietrich Harth (eds), *Mnemosyne. Formen und Funktionen der kulturellen Erinnerung* (Frankfurt/Main: Fischer, 1991), p. 290.

12 See Elisabeth Domanski: 'Die gespaltene Erinnerung', in Manuel Köppen (ed.), *Kunst und Literatur nach Auschwitz* (Berlin: Schmidt, 1993), pp. 178–96.

13 Daniel Goldhagen, *Hitler's Willing Executioners* (New York: Knopf, 1996).

14 Richard Evans, *In Hitler's Shadow: West German Historians and the Attempt to Escape from the Past* (London: Tauris, 1989).

15 Peter Novick, *The Holocaust and Collective Memory: The American Experience* (London: Bloomsbury, 1999), pp. 47–59.

16 See Alvin Rosenfeld, *A Double Dying. Reflections on Holocaust Literature* (Bloomington, IN: Indiana University Press, 1980). More recently, Peter Novick has written of the 'cult of the survivor as secular saint'; Novick, *The Holocaust and Collective Memory*, p. 11.

17 István Deak, *New York Review of Books*, 26 June 1997: quoted in Inga Clendinnen, *Reading the Holocaust* (Cambridge: Cambridge University Press, 1999), p. 188, note 27.

18 Richard Chaim Schneider, *Fetisch Holocaust: Die Judenvernichtung – verdrängt und vermarktet* (Munich: PUBL, 1977): quoted in Sigrid Lange, *Authentisches Medium. Faschismus und Holocaust in ästhetischen Darstellungen der Gegenwart* (Bielefeld: Aistesis, 1999), p. 16.

19 Novick, *The Holocaust and Collective Memory*.

20 Gourevitch, 'The memory thief', p. 66.

21 Peter Middleton and Tim Woods, *Literatures of Memory: History, Time and Space in Postwar Writing* (Manchester: Manchester University Press, 2000), p. 87.

22 See John Kotre, *Outliving the Self: Generativity and the Interpretation of Lives* (Baltimore, MD: Johns Hopkins University Press, 1984), p. 29.

23 Lionel Trilling, *Sincerity and Authenticity* (London: Oxford University Press, 1972).

24 Lange, *Authentisches Medium*, pp. 6ff.

25 Mächler, *Der Fall Wilkomirski*, p. 319.

26 Rüdiger Görner, *Homunculus in the Age of Simulation: Thoughts on Authenticity in Contemporary German Literature*, Inaugural Lecture, 10 June 1999, University of London, School of Advanced Study, p. 18.

27 Lappin, 'The man with two heads', p. 29.

28 See Andrea Reiter, 'Die Funktion der Kinderperspektive in der Darstellung des Holocausts', in Barbara Bauer and Waltraud Strickhausen (eds), *'Für ein Kind war das anders': Traumatische Erfahrungen jüdischer Kinder und Jugendlicher im nationalsozialistischen Deutschland* (Berlin: Metropol, 1999), pp. 215–29.

29 Kotre, *Outliving the Self*, p. 143.

30 *Ibid.*, p. 223.

31 Bruno Apitz, *Nacht unter Wölfen* (Frankfurt/Main: Röderberg, 1982). This was first published in 1958.

32 Zacharis Zweig, *'Mein Vater, was machst du hier . . .?' Zwischen Buchenwald und Auschwitz: Der Bericht des Zacharias Zweig* (Frankfurt/Main: dipa, 1987).

33 See Andrea Reiter, *Narrating the Holocaust* (London: Continuum, 2000).

34 This is indicated by the letters which Wilkomirski received from readers; Mächler, *Der Fall Wilkomirski*, pp. 304–12. One reviewer suggested that *Fragments* forces any reader into the position of the perpetrator: *Neue Zürcher Zeitung* (22/23 May 1999).

35 Reiter, *Narrating the Holocaust*.

36 Michael Roth, *The Ironist's Cage. Memory, Trauma, and the Construction of History* (New York: Columbia University Press, 1995), pp. 3ff.

37 See Reiter, 'Die Funktion der Kinderperspektive'.

38 Middleton and Woods, *Literatures of Memory*, p. 88.

39 *Ibid.*, p. 90.

40 Lappin, 'The man with two heads', p. 44.

41 Middleton and Woods, *Literatures of Memory*, p. 93.

42 See Jan Assmann: 'Die Katastrophe des Vergessens. Das Deuteronomium als Paradigma kultureller Mnemotechnik', in Assmann and Harth, *Mnemosyne*, pp. 346ff.

43 Philippe Lejeune, *Le pacte autobiographique* (Paris: Edition du Seuil, 1975).

44 See Jürgen H. Petersen, *Erzählsysteme: Eine Poetik epischer Texte* (Stuttgart: Metzler, 1993), p. 57.

45 See Paul de Man, 'Autobiographie als Maskenspiel', in Christoph Menke (ed.), *Die Ideologie des Ästhetischen* (Frankfurt/Main: Suhrkamp, 1993), pp. 131–46.

46 For a definition of 'horizon of expectation', see Ansgar Nünning (ed.), *Metzler Lexikon: Literaturtheorie und Kulturtheorie* (Stuttgart: Metzler, 1998), pp. 127ff.

47 Petersen, 'Gelenkte und freie Rezeption', pp. 36–41; Klara Obermüller: 'Spurensuche im Trümmerfeld der Erinnerung', *Die Weltwoche* (31 August 1995), quoted in Mächler, *Der Fall Wilkomirski*, p. 125.

48 Anne Michaels, *Fugitive Pieces* (New York: Vintage, 1998).

49 On the 'two-dimensionality' of the first-person narration in a fictional work, see Petersen, 'Gelenkte und freie Rezeption', pp. 55ff.

50 Bernard Schlink, *The Reader* (New York: Random House, 1999).

51 Lappin, 'The man with two heads', p. 32.

52 Ironically, the information on the dust jacket of *Fragments* thus does not verify the authenticity of the book's story, but is, in its turn, informed by the details given in this story.

53 Nicholas Davey, 'Art, religion and the hermeneutics of authenticity', in Salim Kemal and Ivan Gaskell (eds), *Performance and Authenticity in the Arts* (Cambridge: Cambridge University Press, 1999), pp. 66–93.

54 See Jeffrey Prager, *Presenting the Past. Psychoanalysis and the Sociology of Misremembering* (Cambridge, MA: Harvard University Press, 1989).

55 Lappin suggests Dössekker got the idea for the name 'Wilkomirski' from the picture of a rabbi on his study wall, whom his psychologist friend Bernstein identified to him as the last rabbi of Wilkomir before the Holocaust; Lappin, 'The man with two heads', p. 41. Mächler, however, asserts that Dössekker first came across the name in 1972, when, during a concert of the violinist Wanda Wilkomirska, an acquaintance of Dössekker noted a resemblance and suggested that they could be related; Mächler, *Der Fall Wilkomirski*, p. 283.

56 Lappin, 'The man with two heads', p. 41.

57 See Siegfried J. Schmidt, 'Gedächtnis – Erzählen – Identität', in Assmann and Harth, *Mnemosyne*, pp. 380, 384.

58 Lappin, 'The man with two heads', p. 24.

59 Even eminent historians such as Saul Friedländer are reported to have reacted in this way; Gourevitch, 'The memory thief', p. 55.

60 See *Tagesanzeiger*, Zürich (16 November 1999).

61 Ruth Klüger, *weiter leben. Eine Jugend* (Göttingen: Wallstein, 1992); Ruth Klüger, 'Kitsch ist immer plausibel', in *Süddeutsche Zeitung* (30 September 1998). Klüger has written on kitsch in relation to the Holocaust before, 'Missbrauch der Erinnerung: KZ-Kitsch', in Ruth Klüger, *Von hoher und niedriger Literatur* (Göttingen: Wallstein, 1996), pp. 29–44.

62 Saul Friedländer, *Der Kitsch und der Tod: Der Widerschein des Nazismus* (Munich: Hanser, 1984).

63 See Naomi B. Sokoloff, *Imagining the Child in Modern Jewish Fiction* (Baltimore. MD: Johns Hopkins University Press, 1992) and Reiter, 'Die Funktion der Kinderperspektive'.

64 Reiter, *Narrating the Holocaust.*

65 Lappin, 'The man with two heads', p. 49. Lawrence Langer was the first to notice similarities between *Fragments* and *The Painted Bird* (1965) by Jerzy Kosinski; Mächler, *Der Fall Wilkomirski*, p. 227. Mächler has verified that Dössekker read the book and was deeply fascinated by it. Wilkomirski's 'theory' of memory which he presented in various academic lectures could even have been informed by Kosinski; *ibid.*, pp. 226ff, 261ff.

66 Clendinnen, *Reading the Holocaust*, p. 170.

67 Colin Lyas, 'The relevance of the author's sincerity', in Peter Lamarque (ed.), *Philosophy and Fiction: Essays in Literary Aesthetics* (Aberdeen: Aberdeen University Press, 1983), p. 35; quoted by Alex Neill, 'Inauthenticity, insincerity, and poetry', in Salim Kemal and Ivan Gaskell (eds), *Performance and Authenticity in the Arts* (Cambridge: Cambridge University Press, 1999), p. 210.

68 *Süddeutsche Zeitung* (30 September 1998).

69 See especially Neill, 'Inauthenticity, insincerity, and poetry', pp. 197–214.

70 Mächler, *Der Fall Wilkomirski*, pp. 288ff.

Partition memory and multiple identities in the Champaran district of Bihar, India

Introduction

At the juncture of British withdrawal in 1947, British India was divided into two states: India and (East and West) Pakistan.[1] This division is commonly referred to as the 'Partition', capitalised to denote its uniqueness.[2] Unique though this case may have been, it was not the only territory to experience partition in the twentieth century: Turkey, Cyprus, Ireland, Palestine, and Bosnia are only a few of many examples. As in India, most of these partitions are remembered as catastrophes, as they were followed by often compulsory population exchanges and violence.[3]

Between 1946 and 1951, the Partition of India involved the movement of nearly nine million Hindus and Sikhs to India and about six million Muslims to Pakistan. Of the nine million arriving in India, five million came from what became West Pakistan, and four million from East Pakistan.[4] Most people left their place of birth due to a sense of insecurity. Many had experienced extreme violence during riots, others had suffered discrimination, and still others had undergone severe economic deprivation. The losses were such that Partition is described and remembered in India as a catastrophe.[5] If most historical accounts welcome the departure of the British, Partition narratives also recount the extreme violence and massive transfer of populations as an anticlimax to *azadi* (independence), and recall the religious or communal character of the flows of Hindus and Muslims accompanied by horrific sectarian and often gendered violence.[6]

Bharati Ray, for example, wrote about the 'trauma of Partition' and described it as 'a human tragedy of almost unimaginable proportions'. She recounted:

> For those of us who, whether as children or adults, lived during that period, the word Partition brings to our mind the streams of refugees entering India, the squatting colonies and pavement shanties, the inflation, the rationing and black-marketing, the nightmare that was Sealdah Station, the political agitation and extreme agony of the refugees. However, the most distressing aspect of Partition was the communal Holocaust that accompanied and followed it.[7]

Likewise, Kanti B. Pakrasi concluded in the first chapter of his book, *The Uprooted*: 'Terrific events took place in 1946–1947 to embitter Hindu-Muslim relations in undivided India and ultimately by making divisions of the Punjab and Bengal a *political solution was achieved at the cost of a social catastrophe.*'[8]

Partition, however, did not just result in the disintegration of people's lives; it also bequeathed communal identities often still at work in contemporary India.[9] This was particularly true for the people of Bengal. In the case of Punjab, the flows of people to and from east and west were huge but limited in time. Those between West and East Bengal, however, have been characterised by one scholar as 'delayed-reaction deterritorialization'.[10] Another has observed that in Bengal the event of Partition was not 'a crucial development on one particular day of a year', but 'a long drawn out and complicated process engrossing multiple vicissitudes of utmost importance'.[11] In Bengal, therefore, Partition was a 'political process which continued to unfold long afterwards, and indeed continues to unfold even today'.[12] For the narrators in this chapter, Partition was at times peripheral to their lives; at others, the dominant social reality. It was experienced both as an event and an unfolding process. Over time, their identities could be exposed to a multiplicity of forces, interests, and circumstances and subjected to change. The ways in which the Partition narratives of Bengal came to foreground one identity in place of another is the subject of this essay.

In the first section of this essay, I provide an analysis of the place of Bengali refugees in the Champaran district of Bihar. In the following sections, I examine the three stages of Partition experience narrated by these refugees; their lives before they crossed the international border between newly created India and East Pakistan; their lives after they had fled from their birthplaces and received 'shelter' in one of the refugee camps normally located in West Bengal in India; and, finally, their memories of Partition after they arrived in Bihar and were resettled by the government in so-called refugee colonies.

The attention given to these stages in the narratives depended on the interests of the narrator and the social context in which he or she was located, but they were always manifest. They did not necessarily appear in an orderly, chronological, fashion during the interviews. At times, the narrator kept switching between various stages (and identities), while, at other times, he or she elaborated on one rather than another. Nevertheless, for reasons of clarity, I have chosen to distinguish between these periods and order them chronologically. It will be shown that these stages reflect different identities that could compete with or complement the religious identity of being a Hindu. At times, these identities overlapped. In the conclusion, I will discuss how these narratives and the identities they reveal are linked to the present and may help predict the future.[13]

Bengali refugees in the Champaran district of Bihar

Like Bengal and Punjab, Bihar contains people for whom Partition is not a 'distant historical event',[14] but a daily reality, creating and shaping memories and therefore identities. This is particularly evident in Bihar's northern district of Champaran. The socio-economic scenario in West and East Champaran presents all the portents of a growing divide between the rich and the poor, a horrifying disparity in landholdings, exploitation of the poor, and caste conflict; but it has also witnessed the growing self-consciousness of the poorest classes, the so-called *dalits*.[15] At present, Champaran is far from peace and prosperity. The rich and the powerful classes have entered into a deep nexus with the various components of state machinery and with numerous criminal gangs operating in the region.[16] These elites are generally upper castes such as the *bhumihars* and *rajputs*, but now, increasingly, they also include the *yadavs*, the so-called Other Backward Castes (OBCs). Though the situation of poor landless peasants remains desperate, they are not, and never were, silent.[17]

In this environment live some 100,000 Bengali refugees from East Bengal. Most of them arrived in Champaran around 1964 due to a sudden rise in communal tension in East Pakistan. They often left their place of birth due to fear, economic hardship, or actual violence, though some had hoped for a better future in India. After they crossed the international border, many were sent to so-called relief camps generally located in West Bengal. Some were subsequently persuaded to cross state borders, and in this way came to be resettled in neighbouring Bihar. Those displaced people who 'opted' for the camps and now stay in colonies were identified as 'Bengali refugees'. This is how their offspring also identified themselves and how the so-called locals labelled them. The men and women narrating their (traumatic) pasts for this project were all living in one of the so-called refugee colonies in the Champaran District of Bihar, one of the poorest, most populous, and most underdeveloped states in India.[18] For the purpose of this essay, only first-generation refugees have been interviewed, yet it should be realised that the latter do transmit their narratives to other generations and therefore identities continue to be produced and reproduced.

Some of these Bengali refugees were politicians, advocates, engineers, doctors, and businessmen, but most were fishermen, agriculturists, rickshaw-pullers, servants, *bidi* (cigarette) workers, domestic helpers, mechanics, or beggars. Most of the inhabitants in the colonies in Champaran were illiterate. They sold fish and vegetables, were landless labourers, or had set up little shops and tea stalls. A few had land that was provided to them as a resettlement measure, but this land was subsequently divided between many family members, was often spread over various dispersed plots, and was not always fertile. Some had become teachers in primary Bengali-medium schools or were small traders. Others, especially among the younger generation, were unemployed or underemployed. Even though a few had been affluent, upper-caste *zamindars* (large landholders) while still in East Bengal, once they had crossed one of the border stations and registered themselves in the camps as 'refugees', they all had become vulnerable in more than one sense. In Champaran, most were of lower castes such as *namasudras, sahas, thakurs, burmans,* and *baris.* Whereas, in West Bengal, most of these caste groups were recognised as Scheduled Castes (SCs) by the government and (on paper) were entitled to preferential treatment in educational and job matters, in Bihar these castes were not included in the so-called reserved seat lists of government institutions.

As refugees, they apparently formed a separate group in the landscape of Champaran with their own interests, seemingly dissimilar to those of the 'locals', who consisted of upper- and lower-caste Hindus, non-refugee Bengalis, and Muslims. In one local newspaper, some 'prominent Bengali citizens' from Bihar's capital Patna 'expressed surprise' that, though almost forty-five years had passed, officials of the state government posted in East and West Champaran still did not treat the 90,000 refugees from erstwhile East Pakistan as citizens of the country. They were dubbed *ghuspaith* (infiltrators), and these refugees continued to be 'illegally evicted from their land plots and houses'.[19]

Yet, in different contexts or times, these refugees did share interests with some so-called locals if not with all. In fact, over time, these Bengalis had started to resemble the 'locals'. During our interviews, we found that most men and many women of the around 100,000 inhabitants of refugee colonies in Champaran could communicate in the local Hindi or Bhojpuri languages; could consume, cultivate, and sell 'Bihari' crops; and were living among 'caste or class fellows'. Yet, although at times language could 'unite' Bengalis in the area, non-refugee Bengalis sometimes commented on the class and often caste differences between the two Bengali-speaking communities. These local Bengalis regretted that the refugees had lost their identity, language, and self-respect. They complained that even the women had lost their morals and values.

Some poor locals (Hindus and Muslims alike) agreed that the sufferings of these inhabitants of the refugee colonies did not resemble those of the upper-caste or richer local Bengalis residing in the urbanised parts in the area. One low-caste and extremely poor *musahar* (literally, 'mouse-eater'; caste living on the margins of agriculture) explained: 'Actually, we share many of their problems. We also have difficulties in obtaining what we are entitled to get. We all want education, pensions, [red] ration-cards, caste certificates, loans, etc. They suffer in the same way. We do not have land and they have no caste certificates. Even these refugees have now become landless due to floods. Our fight is common and against the government. The officials are our enemies.'

In practice, however, harmonious class relations and/or caste solidarity did not always exist. Often there was no common struggle but rather competition over scant resources. At times, these inhabitants of colonies were 'refugees'; at times, 'Bengalis'; and, indeed, at times, 'Hindus'. In other social contexts or times, they were, rather, identified as caste, gender or class groups. They were not only 'Bengali-speaking Biharis' but also 'Hindi-speaking Bengalis', or even just 'Biharis'. They certainly were often identified with a region (for instance, East Bengal) but at other times with the nation (India). At times, they were 'locals'; at times, 'outsiders'. Again, they could be both simultaneously.[20] In this setting, narratives of displacement and settlement during the process of Partition both reflected and nourished these multiple identities and continued to inform refugees' relations with 'others'.

Memories of the exodus: leaving as Hindus

Though a few stated that Partition had promised them opportunities away from home, most residents narrated that the exodus from their place of birth had been a question of 'sink or swim'. 'Motherland is heaven', stated Satchuli Burman, adding rhetorically: 'Who likes to leave?'[21] The exodus had started well before the formal event of Partition in 1947, and it lasted long after. Most residents in the Champaran colonies highlighted the fact that they were Hindus and therefore had been forced to leave. Their Partition narratives certainly reflected or generated communal identities. In remembering the exodus, these refugees clearly felt they had left as Hindus, and they remembered communal violence as a motivation for departure. Kamala Bala Das, who was born in Noakhali, narrated that at first her family had left home due to floods. Subsequently, in their new locale, a 'big riot' had occurred: 'I saw hundreds of people, mostly Hindus, killed by Muslims. It was as if one banana tree had fallen down. The whole area was full of blood. We then discovered that the government of India provided facilities for those who had received their migration cards. The latter had to be used within three months. That is why we left.'[22]

Laxmi Rani Mondal came from a village situated, she related, in a 'Muslim-dominated area'. She recalled that in 1965 an order had been issued: 'We had to destroy our gods and goddesses by ourselves. It had also been forbidden to perform religious rituals and make the *ulu* sound [a religious act]. Married women were not allowed to wear conch bangles and vermilion. At first, I thought it was a kind of joke. Later they destroyed our temple, burned several houses, and broke *murtis* [religious artefacts]'. At the time, Laxmi was nine months pregnant and had to hide in the jungle. In the meantime, people had burned her house. After seeing such violence, she had been eager to leave the place: 'Thereafter, the Sikhs [that is, the Indian army] came, and we again had to wear our vermilion and bangles because they had said they would shoot all the Muslims. We left with the army and arrived in Sealdah Station, Calcutta.'[23]

Manindra Lal Bhattacharya had perceived there was no place any longer for rich, upper-caste Hindus like his family: 'Jinnah had declared that Pakistan was for Muslims. Nehru was secular and said India would not be a Hindu *rastra* [nation]. I have no right to comment on Nehru. I am a poor insignificant man and not like iron Nehru. Yet, Netaji Subhas was better. He did not support Partition'. Bhattacharya had first crossed the border and had wanted to settle down in West Bengal but returned to Pakistan due to 'unavoidable circumstances'. Yet,

> After two years, the riot started and Muslims surrounded me in Chittagong town. The problem was created by bad elements from outside who influenced local political parties and Muslims. We Hindus faced barbarism. I still get emotional. They raped women in front of husbands and children. They cut breasts and husbands kept mum. Yet though Nehruji sent launches and motor boats I did not leave. Local Muslims helped me but their houses were also burned. When after one year one major riot took place, I finally left my country. They had tried to kill me.[24]

Although people left because they were Hindus, religious identities were not always antagonistic. As Suresh Sharma has remarked, the religious dividing lines in Partition memories are often 'suffused and inherently blurred'. In his words, 'It was both things happening simultaneously – acts of kindness and acts of massacre. A clear manifestation of deep humanity as well as the perpetration of the most heinous kinds of crime – looting, murder, butchery, rape.'[25] Many residents thus recounted that they had had Muslim friends who had helped them and Muslim enemies who had attacked or betrayed them. At times, members of their own family had cheated them and Muslim neighbours had protected them. Others recollected that Muslim men had helped them, but Muslim women had not. Surya Kumar Ghosh had tears in his eyes while narrating the way in which he lost his father as well as uncle:

> On 2 February 1950, we witnessed a big riot in our village. I personally watched how Muslims killed my father and younger uncle. I was around twenty-three years old. I saw that incident and ran away like a mad person. I kept on running and running and then climbed a tree. Muslims came to me and tried to be friendly since they knew I had seen what they had done to my father. I never expected this to happen. On 1 February, we all had taken shelter in a house of a Muslim *zamindar*. He was a good man, but that same night some other Muslims had come who told us if we converted to Islam all our problems would be solved. The senior Hindus among us replied that they needed time to make up their minds, but actually just tried to gain time. Subsequently, Muslims provided food and we all fell asleep. The next morning, however, a rumour had spread that Hindus in Calcutta had started riots. Therefore, the Muslims decided not to give any chance any more to the Hindus and started killing them. In this way, I lost my father and uncle. Others lost close relatives too.[26]

Though, generally, lower-caste Hindus did not leave immediately after 1947, over time they, too, left their places of birth. Some mentioned that since all the upper castes had left, they had to leave too: 'Without them, how could we survive?' Nilmoni Das, a fisherman, added: 'First, local Muslims had told us that we, the lower castes, would be safe. But we were not.'[27] Harandra Chandra Sarkar narrated that he came from Kathar in Assam, which, after a plebiscite, had become part of Pakistan. Consequently, Harandra angrily declared, 'Though father had lots of land that was very fertile, they always snatched our crops, and slowly we lost all our civil rights.' He added, 'In their hearts, the Muslims wanted us to leave, but openly they were friendly.'[28]

Though often narrated in communalist language, which generated and reflected communal identities, memories of this stage of Partition also reveal elements of blurring, in which religious identities were not always antagonistic, nor always a readable guide to motivation and action.

Memories of the camps: arriving as (East) Bengalis

The narratives did not stop at the border. 'Hindus' crossed the border and became 'Bengalis'. The government had decreed that there was 'no further scope in West Bengal for the settlement of displaced persons'. After 1956, therefore, new camps were opened for them outside that state.[29] One of these was the Bettiah Camp in Champaran. People remembered how they had arrived in West Bengal and how, from there, they had been transported to the so-called refugee camps in Bihar. Gradually, the loss of place as well as efforts to recover that sense of place became much more prominent in their narratives than religious identities. People clearly remembered what happened after their arrival in Bihar and the difficulties they faced as a Bengali-speaking group in a Hindi-speaking environment. Time had brought forth new circumstances and demands, and the meanings the displaced bestowed on their memories changed along with their identities. As the narratives progressed, communal identity was exchanged for 'Bengaliness'.

For many it was this 'Bengaliness' that made them decide to 'desert' from the camps in Bihar and return to West Bengal. Anil Kumar Biswas narrated the activities of Sudhir Mondal, a well-known refugee leader who had urged him and 'hundreds of others' to leave the Bettiah Camp in Champaran: 'Mondal told us that we were Bengalis and we should return to Bengal. *Mar chele buke jabo* [mother's son should go to mother's lap]'.[30] The desire to return was intensified by the conditions in the so-called transit camps, where refugees stayed for as long as eight years before they were resettled. Improvements had been continually promised, but the camps remained unhygienic and overcrowded. Water was sometimes scarce, and the camp rules were strict, particularly after 1964. Hari Das Barui, who had been sent to the Bettiah Camp in 1955 and had stayed for five years, recalled his impatience:

> In the meantime, we protested. We wanted development and even went to the Writers' Building in Calcutta but the West Bengal Chief Minister, Bidhan Chandra Roy, who supported Congress, put us in jail. Women separate from men. We had to return and the Bihar Government was requested to arrange our rehabilitation. We signed that we would return to Bihar but while in jail others (non-refugees) had taken our names and occupied our places in Champaran illegally. Finally, however, those who could show original documents such as certificates, border slips, camp registration forms, etc., could get their legitimate places.[31]

Not all those displaced to Bihar, however, preferred to return. The attachment of some was to East rather than West Bengal. Many tried to ensure their legitimate places in India; Hindus sought to claim recognition as Bengali Biharis or, alternatively, Bihari Bengalis, declaring, 'East, West, Bihar best'. These sought to fight for their rights where they were. Manindra Lal Bhattacharya, for example, remembered his arrival at Bettiah station vividly and described the prevailing situation as 'very pathetic'. Being upper caste, he had requested another camp to stay in, as he could not eat with lower castes. He had hoped to share food with the upper-caste Bengalis residing near the *dak bangla* (government guest house), who might also offer him a job. As one of the very few educated displaced persons among the mostly illiterate masses of the displaced, he became president of the Bihar Provincial Refugee Welfare Council. He recollected:

> We protested against the local government. We believed they were misusing central government funds. The local officials (Biharis) wanted to construct barracks as a development programme but we wanted an industry. If government were to set up an industry we would get jobs and would no longer have to depend on cash doles. However, the local superintendent of police provoked the collector and government threatened us. We were arrested and put in jail. Others started movements against this. Then the minister of the Department of Revenue and Rehabilitation came, Mr. Mouni. He was a Muslim but kind hearted. He promised to free us from jail and to rehabilitate all the refugees. After one year this materialised

Yet, Bhattacharya concluded: 'We do not have all our rights even now.'[32] Although their campaigns were not always successful, it is significant that these Bengalis, realising that they could use the label to assert their rights, had begun to identify themselves as 'refugees'.

Memories after resettlement: staying as refugees

Most people residing in the refugee colonies were not satisfied with the way in which they were resettled. They complained that they had received smaller loans than promised, had received only part of the instalments, or had had to pay bribes to receive what they had been promised. Besides, though land had been given to them, the land rights had never been formally accorded to them. Consequently, many still faced problems in getting loans or other facilities from cooperatives or banks. Most of the colonies had no electricity or piped water, and some suffered from floods or drought. Many of the colonies were far away from towns and extremely isolated in the remote interiors of the district and raided by dacoits. Educational facilities were bad or altogether absent. Looting was common. Some complained that their land was captured, and crops confiscated, or that their land was scattered and infertile. Many were now without land, as the paternal land had been distributed among the many sons. Single women were worst off. What bothered these residents most was the fact that, though the Bihar government had at last directed officials to issue them caste certificates (only in the Annexture I list), only a few had actually obtained them, in return for bribes. Moreover, they wanted to be recognised in the Annexture II list, like the same caste groups in West Bengal.[33] According to the residents of most colonies, they belonged to the poorest of the poor. Most unfortunately, though most had now been resettled and often allotted plots of land and at times even had voting rights, they nevertheless wondered whether they were living in *nirbasan* (exile) or had been *punarbasan* (resettled).

In their narratives, the 'refugisation' of memories is clearly visible. Although they had identified themselves as Hindus and Bengalis (among others) in other contexts and other places, after resettlement they remembered themselves firstly as refugees. Nagendra Chandra Burman recollected that he had been extremely happy just after his resettlement. Yet, life took a different course:

> We were sent to the Ranaghat Transit Camp and then proceeded to Bettiah Station from where we were sent to camp no. eight. After some time, we were rehabilitated. The land we received was very fertile. The locals became friendly with my father since they had come to know he had brought some money. They looted him and some jewellery was stolen. To this day the locals try to rob us. It is all due to jealousy. They are mostly landless and labourers. They think that though they have lived here for the last fourteen generations, the Government has never provided them land and agricultural facilities and instead showed hospitality to us the Bengali refugees. After 1979, irrigation facilities were provided and locals advised us in growing maize, sugarcane, oil seeds, vegetables, and wheat because the soil here is not good for rice. Then they came overnight to cut our crops. Nevertheless, we have developed the area. They are now sharecroppers. Forty per cent of the total production goes to them if they work on our land.[34]

Partition had also not ended for Satchuli Burman. He remembered:

I lived for over three years in Bettiah Camp. Nevertheless, I did not leave. It was Government's duty to rehabilitate us. I did no work in the camp. Our occupation is agriculture. Sudhir Mondal, a leader, started telling us we should leave so nearly 100 to 150 Bengali families left and they travelled without tickets. His plan was totally wrong. Government's decisions had been made already. Finally, those who left also returned. For the last ten years we have faced problems, not during those days. Then there were only language problems. The river changed its course and has grabbed our land and houses. There is too much population and the dacoits are harassing us. They are cutting our land at night. We are afraid of the *deshwalis* (locals).[35]

These people remained 'refugees' not only in the eyes of the 'locals' but also in their own opinion. In part because some of them started using the label as their only weapon in their struggle for equality, they remained separate from people with whom they had so much in common.

Conclusion: can Partition memory help to overcome the catastrophe?

The inclusion of oral narratives of the past can produce a fuller knowledge system relating to catastrophes, such as the Partition of India, than those underlying earlier history writing. Narratives of displacement and resettlement, all part of the Partition process, continue to provide central symbols of identity and inform the residents' relations with other social groups. The narratives included in this chapter demonstrate that previous scholarly work on Partition memories has concentrated too much on religious identities. It often focuses on Muslim and Hindu identities that appear internally singular and absolutely exclusive. This essay shows that in Partition narratives people claim membership of multiple religious and social groups.[36] I have demonstrated that Partition narratives expressed antagonistically communal identities, fraternally communal identities, or entirely non-communal identities.[37] Some residents did indeed communalise their recollections of Partition to reflect pride in their religious identity and revulsion at that of another.[38] Yet, the narratives were also about class, regional, national, linguistic, gender, ethnic, and caste differences and related multiple identities. In addition, they provide evidence for the reintegration of community – a banding together for a common purpose – rather than just its catastrophic disintegration.

   These narratives are thus useful documents for examination because they directly link the past to the present. Partition memories derive primarily from the urge of these residents in refugee colonies to place themselves in time and space. But they also serve a contemporary social purpose – memories change according to the needs of the present, and Partition memories can be evoked to serve class, caste, regional, gender, linguistic, or religious interests. By invoking these narratives, residents can assume identities as Hindus, as Bengalis, as (poor, lower-caste) refugees, or as various combinations of these identities depending on the multiple shifting of social contexts.[39]

   It is this characteristic of memory, one scholar has argued, 'which makes the human species peculiarly prone to erratic irrational behaviour', yet it is the 'recasting of that memory that we see as the way out for the human species to behave in a rational, sane way'.[40] We have here assessed the memory of people living on the periphery of Partition. It is now important to discover the 'play between the memory of an individual and the making of collective identity', as it functions in the present and may function in the future.[41] This will help us to explain the present and to predict the future. Given that Partition narratives offer more than binary and opposed communal identities, invoking these memories need not necessarily play a role in fanning inter- and intrastate tensions.[42] Rather, this memory might offer these residents 'time-honoured modes of coping, adaptation and problem solving on a collective basis'.[43] As Suresh Sharma has argued: 'memory subsumes forgetting and remembrance, it means that everything need not to be remembered, that everything is not remembered and, that everything is not remembered all the time'.[44] If communal harmony and group unity are remembered, and violence and discord forgotten, it might offer these people a mode to overcome the trauma of catastrophe.

Notes

1 This essay is an offshoot of a larger project supported by the Indo-Dutch Programme on Alternatives in Development on 'Displaced Populations and Development in the South Asian Contexts', carried out between 1997 and 2000. This is a revised version of a paper presented at the international conference on 'The Memory of Catastrophe', Southampton, 14–17 April 2000. The revisions owe much to the work of Peter Gottschalk on the multiple identities of Muslims and Hindus in Bihar. Gottschalk demonstrates how various narratives express group memories of the past in the context of social relationships in the present. My analysis of narratives relating solely to Partition reveals the mutability of group identification as revealed through narratives. This is of great importance for the understanding of contemporary group relations in Champaran and prediction of future group alliances and conflicts. See P. Gottschalk, *Beyond Hindu and Muslim: Multiple Identity in Narratives from Village India* (Oxford: Oxford University Press, 2000).

2 See, for instance, S. Kaul (ed.), *The Partitions of Memory: The Afterlife of the Division of India* (Delhi: Permanent Black, 2001); C.E. Haque, 'The dilemma of "nationhood" and religion: a survey and critique of studies on population displacement resulting from the Partition of the Indian Subcontinent', *Journal of Refugee Studies*, 8:2 (1995), 185–209.

3 See, for instance, T. Triadafilopoulos, 'Lausanne, Potsdam, and after: reassessing the consequences of refugee incorporation in Greece and Germany', unpublished paper presented at the international conference on 'Refugees and the Transformation of Society: Loss and Recovery', organised by the Research School for Resource Studies for Development (CERES), Soesterberg, 21–24 April 1999.

4 *Hindu* (3 January 2002).

5 See M. Hasan (ed.), *Inventing Boundaries: Gender, Politics and the Partition of India* (Oxford: Oxford University Press, 2000); D.A. Low and H. Brasted (eds): *Freedom, Trauma, Continuities: Northern India and Independence* (New Delhi: Sage, 1998); P. Kumar, 'Testimonies of loss and memory: Partition and the haunting of a nation', *Interventions*, 1:2 (1999), 201–17.

6 See R. Menon and K. Bhasin (eds), *Borders and Boundaries: Women in India's Partition* (New Delhi: Kali for Women, 1998).

7 B. Ray, 'Women and Partition: some questions', in B. Bharati and A. Basu (eds), *From*

Independence Towards Freedom: Indian Women Since 1947 (Delhi: Oxford University Press, 1999), p. 3.

8 K.B. Pakrasi, *The Uprooted: A Sociological Study of the Refugees of West Bengal, India* (Calcutta: Editions Indian, 1971), p. 16. Italics in original.

9 See K. Sinha-Kerkhoff, 'The dangers of memory and endangered memory: Partition memory and memory of Muslims in Jharkhand, India', forthcoming in *In Review*.

10 N. Chatterjee, 'Midnight's Unwanted Children: East Bengali Refugees and the Politics of Rehabilitation', PhD dissertation (Brown University, 1992), p. 18.

11 Pakrasi, *The Uprooted*, p. 1.

12 J. Chatterji, 'The fashioning of a frontier: the Radcliffe Line and Bengal's border landscape, 1947–1952', *Modern Asian Studies*, 33:1 (1999), 242.

13 See, for this, also K. Sinha-Kerkhoff, 'Futurising the past: Partition memory, refugee identity and social struggle in Champaran, Bihar', *South Asian Refugee Watch*, 2:2 (2000), 74–92.

14 J. Alam and S. Sharma, 'Remembering Partition', *Seminar*, 461 (January 1998), 101.

15 *Times of India* (4 January 1997).

16 *Ibid.*

17 See J. Pouchepadass, 'Peasant protest in a global setting: the Champaran Movement reconsidered', unpublished paper presented at the international conference on 'Bihar in the World and the World in Bihar', organised by the Asian Development Research Institute (ADRI), Patna, 16–19 December 1997.

18 See, for instance, A. Das, *The Republic of Bihar* (New Delhi: Penguin, 1992).

19 *Times of India* (23 January 1997).

20 For an in-depth analysis of these residents, see my report submitted to IDPAD: K. Sinha-Kerkhoff, *The Making and Unmaking of Identities in Post-Partition Bihar: Relief, Refugees, Rehabilitation and Beyond* (New Delhi and The Hague, 2001).

21 All interviews were carried out by Mr Dipankar Mukherjee (my assistant) and me. They were taped and afterwards translated from Hindi or Bengali. Here I first refer to the name of the informant, their age, and the date of the interview in the following way: Satchuli Burman; age 70; 16 October 1998.

22 Kamala Bala Das; age 85; 16 October 1998.

23 Laxmi Rani Mondal; age 56; 16 October 1998.

24 Manindra Lal Bhattacharya; age 83; 26 October 1997.

25 Alam and S. Sharma, 'Remembering Partition', p. 100.

26 Surya Kumar Ghosh; age 74; 12 January 1999.

27 Nilmoni Das; age 65; 8 February 1998.

28 Harandra Chandra Sarkar; age 68; 15 October 1998.

29 Ministry of Rehabilitation, *Annual Reports* (New Delhi: Government of India Press, 1956–7), p. 4.

30 Anil Kumar Biswas; age: 58; 16 October 1989. For many Bengalis, the world, the earth, India, and Bengal are female. One is born of the earth and goes back to the earth; women are often regarded as Mother Earth, see L.M. Fruzzetti, *The Gift of a Virgin: Women, Marriage, and Ritual in a Bengali Society* (Delhi: Oxford University Press, 1990), pp. 24–5. For the social implications of this set of ideas for Bengali women and girls, see K.R. Kerkhoff, *Save Ourselves and the Girls! Girlhood in Calcutta Under the Raj* (Rotterdam: Extravert, 1995).

31 Hari Das Barui; age: 71; 8 February 1998.

32 Manindra Lal Bhattacharya; age: 83; 26 October 1997.

33 The central government as well as the state governments in India have adopted so-called reservation policies. Accordingly, a certain percentage of jobs and places in educational institutions are reserved for particular caste groups. One of these groups is the so-called Other Backward Castes (OBCs). The latter is again subdivided into subcastes either put into the Annexture I category or allotted Annexture II status. The latter provides a wider scale of privileges than the former.

34 Nagendra Chandra Burman; age: 54; 15 October 1998.

35 Satchuli Burman; age: 70; 16 October 1998.

36 Cf. Gottschalk, *Beyond Hindu and Muslim*, p. 174.

37 *Ibid.*, p. 124.

38 *Ibid.*, p. 162.

39 *Ibid.*, p. 134.

40 Alam and Sharma, 'Remembering Partition', p. 100.

41 *Ibid.*, p. 99.

42 Shail Mayaram challenges the theoretical terrain based on the binary categories 'Hindu' and 'Muslim', and suggests instead an alternative conception of liminal identity; S. Mayaram, *Resisting Regimes: Myth, Memory and the Shaping of a Muslim Identity* (New Delhi: Oxford University Press, 1997).

43 D. Summerfield, 'The social experience of war and some issues for the humanitarian field', in P.J. Bracken and C. Petty (eds), *Rethinking the Trauma of War* (London: Free Association Books, 1998), p. 22.

44 Alam and Sharma, 'Remembering Partition', p. 102.

Bodies do count: American nurses mourn the catastrophe of Vietnam

> I dreamed that night about Vietnam . . . It was a new dream: *Thousands of American mothers were walking in the streets of Saigon, carrying the bloody bodies of their dead sons. Above the wailing, screaming, and gnashing of teeth, one word was constantly repeated: Why?*[1]

This 'bloody' parade, recorded by Vietnam nurse veteran Lynda Van Devanter as her response to the end of the war, is an act of commemoration that challenges and subverts the way war is both remembered and forgotten. It enacts the dual themes of trauma and grief with which her autobiography, *Home Before Morning*, is centrally concerned. In the image of the mother carrying the mutilated body of her son, Van Devanter, like the other nurses whose writing I shall be discussing, brings together war stories usually explored separately: the world of combat and the world of home; the physical trauma to the combatant's body, and the psychological trauma of grief. Its context is a nurse's story that itself parades injured bodies in an act of remembrance and demonstrates the intimate connection between combatant and non-combatant experience of war.

The image of mothers literally 'taking to the streets' with 'the bloody bodies of their dead sons' makes public both the injury and the grief, and collectively challenges the state's appropriation of the bodies, asking the question, 'Why?' Judith Herman defines this coming together of private pain and the public telling of the trauma story as testimony: 'Testimony has both a private dimension, which is confessional and spiritual, and a public aspect, which is political and judicial.'[2] Van Devanter's dream suggests that she is handing back the broken bodies she nursed to their mothers, while at the same time her autobiography as a whole shows that she is unable to let them go: she must take on the burden of mourning, the mother's role of carrying and revealing these bodies to public view. This image of the mothers, whose 'wailing and gnashing of teeth' is, to borrow from Michael Bibby, 'the inchoate mourning and grief that defies words', conveys a wordless grief that allows Van Devanter to take us to a place of pain beyond the words she uses to describe it.[3] Van Devanter tells her own story to reveal and to grieve for the injury and death she witnessed as a nurse in Vietnam. In doing so, she collapses the narrow definition of war as combat. These mothers experience war in the deaths of their sons; the nurse veterans experience war as an endless parade of mutilated bodies.

Thus, the bodies that demand attention in the nurses' poetry and autobiography are mourned not only because they are dead, but also because, dead or alive, they have been mutilated and fragmented. This display of the mutilated body is a trope of Vietnam writing that belongs to combatant prose and poetry as well as to the writing of the nurses. As Samuel Hynes notes: 'Bodies are dragged through the narratives – maimed, dismembered, violated, hideous, stinking bodies. And body parts.'[4] For both nurses and combatants, such a revelation is a political act asserting Elaine Scarry's claim that 'the main purpose and outcome of war is injuring'.[5] For the American military in Vietnam, however, 'bodies' held meaning as numbers in a game that influenced strategy as well as the way the war was reported.

In his discussion of GI resistance poetry, Bibby examines the link between the role of the body count in Vietnam, and the discourse of mutilation that marks the writing from that war:

> The emphasis placed on the body count in military reward and advancement encouraged soldiers not only to produce needless slaughter to legitimate their role in Vietnam to the military managers but also to manufacture imagined numbers . . . Troops were eventually trained, as the body count became more important and the war progressed, to read a complex semiotics of body parts in order to produce numbers satisfactory to military management . . . Severed limbs signified a whole for body counting purposes. While military managers sought to represent the war as a set of abstract numbers falling into debit and credit columns, ground troops were made either to produce these numbers directly . . . or to infer these numbers from the macabre bits of bone and tissue cast aside by the war's destruction. Mutilation, in other words, was systemic in the discourse of the Vietnam experience for ground troops.[6]

The falsification of numbers also existed when counting American dead. American bodies only counted if they were killed directly by enemy action. Combatants who were evacuated to hospital and died en route or at hospital were labelled 'died of postoperative complications'. The whole system was thereby rendered meaningless.

For Bibby, these images of the trauma inflicted on the human body tell the combatant story of the Vietnam War. For the nurses caring for those bodies on a daily basis, mutilation was also systemic in the discourse of *their* experience. The bodies in their war zone, whether dead or alive, are bodies excluded from the official count. The nurses' re-counting connects their story as nurses with the combatant story, and at the same time connects Vietnam with 'the world', linking the fragmented bodies of the men with the women, particularly mothers, at home.

Van Devanter's account of her nursing experience in Vietnam, *Home Before Morning*, Winnie Smith's autobiography, *American Daughter Gone to War*, and nurses' poetry from the Vietnam War are all concerned with exactly the need Van Devanter's mothers display in their march through the streets of Saigon: to retrieve their 'sons' from the anonymity of the body count; to reveal the purpose of war as injury, and to put that injury on display while making a display of their own grief; to ask the question, 'Why?'; and to publicly mourn the deaths of the men whose lives (and deaths) are so intimately connected to their own. In particular, the image is a form of commemoration that refuses to allow the 'disowning of injury', as Scarry puts it; 'The perpetuation of war would be impossible without the disowning of injury.'[7]

Van Devanter's image of the mothers and their bloody sons demands that we question the processes of remembering and forgetting that take place both during and in the aftermath of war. As Daniel Sherman reminds us, 'commemoration privileges certain kinds of experience and excludes others, [and] deploys and organises not only memory but forgetting'.[8] Commemorating war, even the Vietnam War, often means appropriating terms such as 'sacrifice', 'honour', and 'service', wherein the state interposes the consolatory rhetoric of sacrifice between the body of the mother and the body of her dead and mutilated son, undermining or denying the pain and loss of war and disowning injury.

Although mothers are traditionally privileged mourners in the context of war, their privilege excludes them from participation in the politics of war itself; both their mourning and their relationship with their combatant sons is strictly regulated by the military and the state. Yet, as Nicole Loraux notes in her discussion of Greek tragedy, *Mothers in Mourning*, the image of the bereaved mother clinging to the body of her son mutilated in war is so poignant that it has the potential to undermine the stability of the state. The Greeks, therefore, imposed strict regulations on women's mourning in the aftermath of war. For Loraux, the power of the image of the grief-stricken mother is revealed through what she calls the *pathos* of the mother:

> The sight of the son's corpse is *pathos* in the highest degree . . . the grief and the memory of the intimacy of those bloody bodies produce excessive pain for the body-memory of mothers . . . To hold in their arms what is 'bloody, yet still the treasure of the mother', such is the wish of Euripides' suppliant mothers. But [in this particular case] as a good civic leader, Theseus will make sure that they do not *see* those bodies disfigured by blood . . . they will have a right only to the bones of the funeral pyre, pure abstraction of the beloved body[9]

The privileged relationship between the mother and the dead son lies behind the concept of the 'gold star' mother, which originated during the First World War in the United States. The women's section of the Committee of National Defence convinced many women to wear a distinctive gold star emblem to express their sacrifice of a son to the nation, an action wherein grief was purportedly allayed by the consolatory rhetoric of sacrifice, and the outer trappings of mourning, black, transmuted into the pride of the 'gold star'.[10] Private grief was thus controlled and pressed into public service, ultimately giving the government and the military control over the body of the mother as well as the son.

Like Theseus, in Euripides' play, who makes sure the mothers do not *see* the bloody bodies of their sons, and allows them only the abstraction of the body, the American military in twentieth-century wars covered up the bloody bodies and presented only the abstraction of the body given in service to the state, the flag, the gold star, or the medal. In each case, a transaction was performed wherein the physical body of the soldier was exchanged for a symbol of military honour and pride. The state therefore maintained control over the mourning for the dead combatant. Gloria Emerson in *Winners and Losers* describes how the language surrounding the official notification of death during the Vietnam War upheld such control: 'The Secretary of the Army has requested me to inform you . . . The idea was to convey regret – deep, official masculine regret – but not regret that sounded too regretful, too mushy, as if the death had been a waste.'[11] To reinforce the 'official masculine' ideology surrounding death in war, families are rewarded; yet such consolation for grief prescribes limits on mourning. Public display is controlled by the ritual of a military burial. The gun salute and taps create a context in which every sound and movement is exactly prescribed. Thus, commemoration of this particular death allows no room for individual grief, and certainly no overt display of 'wailing and gnashing of teeth'. Grieving mothers are thus prevented from putting their grief on public display, as Van Devanter's mothers do, and very importantly, distracted from the task of questioning the validity of death in war, of asking, 'Why?'

These mothers, and the writing of veteran nurses, subvert a ritual that is designed to silence their grief and to separate them from their sons' mutilated bodies. Refusing to relinquish these bodies, the mothers have 'undone' the military funeral and burial, and exhumed their dead sons to reveal their mutilation. This public act of grieving, in which the mother is reunited with her dead son, and holds him physically, as she had done in infancy, challenges the military ownership of the son, and subverts the military attempts to offer platitudes in place of the dead son. Even while the military returns the body of the son to the mother in America, it at the same time seeks to 'disown' the presence of injury in the literal and metaphoric act of covering the body with the flag. Van Devanter's mothers subvert the position they are relegated to by the military as passive receivers of their sons' bodies engaging in private grief; they become active rejectors of this position and revealers of the military conspiracy of 'disowning' injury, refusing the consolatory rhetoric and stripping away the flag.

The fragmented body that becomes a synecdoche for all the mutilated bodies that pursue Van Devanter on her return home from the war is the image of Gene. Van Devanter places Gene at the centre of her narrative, and his image links America and Vietnam both at the time she first encounters him and in his continuing presence in the intrusive post-trauma flashbacks she has after her return home.

Gene, the 'young bleeder', his face partially shot away, begins as another faceless, nameless boy who pumps blood out as fast as she can pump it in. For three pages he remains literally and metaphorically faceless until Van Devanter accidentally kicks aside some of his clothing, and

> A snapshot fell from the torn pocket of his fatigue shirt. The picture was of a young couple . . . on the back of the picture was writing, the ink partly blurred from sweat 'Gene and Katie, May 1968'. I had to fight the tears as I looked from the picture to the helpless boy on the table. Gene and Katie, May 1968 . . . This wasn't merely another casualty . . . He had been real. He was a person who could love and think and plan and dream.
>
> I wouldn't cry, I told myself. I had to be tough.[12]

It is in the context of this event that Van Devanter loses her own sense of security and her belief in the middle-American values represented in the image of Gene and Katie at the prom. A day later she recounts:

All I could see was Gene, Gene and Katie, May 1968. Then I began seeing all of them – the double and triple amputees, boys with brain injuries, belly wounds, and missing genitals . . . all the images came crashing back on me . . . I became a wild person, sobbing and shaking uncontrollably. '. . . I want to go home, Vietnam sucks, we don't belong here. This is wrong.'

After I awoke I felt numb, I threw away the rhinestone flag I had previously worn on my uniform and found myself feeling nothing.[13]

Gene becomes a person in the context of Katie, the woman he has brought to Vietnam in the photographic image. The image of the couple in the photograph – and the intimate connection between the two – is destroyed not just for Gene, but for both of them, in Vietnam. At the same time, Van Devanter's fragmentation of her own psyche and her ideological world takes place in the context of Gene's fragmented body. Like the mothers who would appear in her dream several years later, her own wailing and gnashing of teeth become part of the endless parade of mutilated bodies that disrupt her sleep – dreams that always end in the question, 'Why?' These begin the moment she arrives back 'in the world'. Sleeping in the plane on her return home from Vietnam, Van Devanter is awakened by the nightmare image of Gene's shot-away face. His image, a metaphor for the futility of Vietnam, is also a metaphor for the Vietnam she carries back to America. Until Van Devanter published *Home Before Morning* in 1983, these nightmares remained part of her private traumatised isolation. The writing and publishing of the book allow her to reveal the bloody bodies she nursed and to bring them home to America in a public as well as private sense.

Like Van Devanter, Winnie Smith in *American Daughter Gone to War* links the mutilated bodies of the combatants she nurses with an image of the America that sent them to fight. As a nurse telling her war story she, too, sees her role as revealing the mutilated body – bringing it back to America and presenting it in the context of the middle-American values, in this case the American game of football, the rhetoric of which is often confused with the rhetoric of war. In the following passage, Smith is concerned not just with revealing the injury that is war, but in revealing it in the context of American ideals of masculine prowess and heroism on the football field:

The soldier's face is deeply tanned, not discoloured like so many in death. The dirt of battle gives him the air of an athlete at rest after a workout. Sweat streaks outline helmet straps along his jaw. He could be a high school football player after a scrimmage in the mud [she pauses] – *except for the misshapen form under the sheet, flat where there should be arms and legs.*[14]

Smith begins with the image of the soldier as 'warrior', the description of helmet and straps lending the narrative a timeless quality, only to strip it ruthlessly away in the manner of a perverse conjuring trick, as she moves from the potentially consolatory image of the peaceful death to the nurses' story: the fragmented body.

While the daily working environment of the Vietnam nurse called for grief as a primary emotional response, at the same time nurses found it necessary to negate emotions in the interests of professionalism, often causing enormous psychological conflict. In one of the few discussions of military nurses' experience in Vietnam, Jenny

Schnaier defines three of the main stressors as follows: seeing the mutilation of young bodies, having a continual stream of casualties, and feeling the need to negate emotion.[15] As one nurse comments succinctly, 'If we broke down, they died.'[16] Such necessary negation of emotion resulted in feelings of guilt in women who internalised an ideal version of their role as nurses and women, which told them that they should both care for the casualties as professionals and grieve for them as women or mother substitutes. The dates on the poems collected in the anthology *Visions of War, Dreams of Peace*, show that most women could not confront the war experience and begin grieving until long after their tour of duty had ended. Moreover, many of the poems focus on the direct connection between the inability to grieve and the woman's guilt at not undertaking this particularly female burden. For example, it is not until 1990 that Penny Kettlewell, in 'The Coffee Room Soldier', can confront such negation of emotion and its legacy of guilt, and give a name to the anonymous broken body of twenty years earlier:

> I initially stepped casually over his shattered body
> laid out, unbagged, on the coffee room floor
> out of the way
>
> . . .
>
> Dispassionately I assessed his wounds
> and sipped from my cup.
> I then saw his face
> that of a child in terror
> and only hours ago
> alive as I
> or maybe I was as dead as he,
> because with another sip, a cigarette and a detached analysis
> I knew I could no longer even feel.
>
> I stepped out and grabbed a mop and pail
> so we would stop slipping in the blood on the R & E floor
> bagged the extra body pieces and the coffee room soldier
> re-stocked supplies, then went outside to watch the sunrise,
> alone and destitute of tears.[17]

Such negation of emotion during the war was reinforced by a necessary silence about the war experience on the veteran's return home. Both Van Devanter and Smith document their mothers' responses to the war as an overt silencing when they tried to tell of their experiences and show photographs. The silence imposed was exacerbated by their position as women. As one publisher she approached told Van Devanter: 'what could a woman possibly have to say about war, especially the Vietnam War'.[18] For the women veterans as well as the men, grief thus became what Chaim Shatan terms 'impacted', the result of a concerted effort to forget on the part of the nation as a whole. Laurence Kermayer reminds us, 'As remembering is a social act, so too is forgetting. The contemporary landscape of memory is created through the modern *ars memoria*, which involve not so much feats of hypermnesia as of strategic forgetting.'[19] For nurses, like combatants, social context often dictated their public memory: they recounted amusing anecdotes to their friends and family, while remaining silent about the disturbing, and thus less socially acceptable, memories.

Chaim Shatan's comments on combatants are therefore equally applicable to nurses in a war zone:

> The 'post-Vietnam syndrome' confronts us with the unconsummated grief of soldiers – 'impacted grief' in which an unending, encapsulated past robs the present of meaning. Their sorrow is unspent, the grief of their wounds is untold, their guilt is unexpiated. Much of what civilians view as cynical disillusionment is really the veteran's numbed apathy from an excess of death and bereavement.[20]

Van Devanter's story is the story of grief; it reveals her need to mourn with the mothers of her dream, for whom participation in a collective public mourning was denied, and at the same time to mourn herself for all the men and women represented in the image of Gene and Katie. Likewise, Winnie Smith's autobiography continues the process of mourning that is both private and individual and public and collective. Her title itself indicates that loss is at the centre of the book – her pre-war private self, as well as the public self, 'the American daughter', is 'gone', 'lost to' the war in Vietnam.

The most private writing of women who nursed in the Vietnam War is their poetry, most of which remained unpublished until Van Devanter and Furey edited the anthology *Visions of War, Dreams of Peace* in 1992. The poetry, what the editors call 'private writings hidden in the dresser drawer', was written between 1961 and 1991.[21]

Van Devanter's narrative is held together by the chronological framework of pre-Vietnam, tour of duty, and return home, yet the fragments that force the reader to participate in intrusive flashbacks or dream sequences are the most salient feature of the story. The poetry of nurse veterans often presents a further stage of fragmentation: a place where the external controls collapse and experience is expressed in incomplete, fragmented images and forms, as if the writers were unable to fit the parts into an organised whole. The dominant metaphor for such a breakdown in all these writings is the fragmented body. As Jane Marcus comments on First World War women's writing: 'The fragmented bodies of men are reproduced in the fragmented parts of women's war texts . . . Writers of war produce pieces of texts, like parts of a body that will never be whole.'[22]

That many of the poems in the collection *Visions of War, Dreams of Peace* were written as long as twenty years after the nurse's tour of duty, and most of them after the main site of mourning for the war, 'the Wall', provided a focus for grief, demonstrates the ongoing need to grieve for both the mutilated bodies they nursed and for the selves that were fragmented in the context of that experience. Intrinsic to the expression of this grief in many poems is an idealisation of the nurse/combatant relationship that sometimes borders on the sentimental and might initially appear to undermine the politically directed testimony of these poems. Yet, as the poetry shows even more than the autobiography, such idealisation coexists in a very uneasy relationship with the images of the shattered bodies designed to subvert any notion of idealisation or consolation. Thus, on the one hand, the writing reveals the procession of injury that undermined the ideologies the nurses had brought to the war, as we have seen in Van Devanter's narrative; on the other hand, it also reveals the necessity of psychological survival both during and after the experience; hence the clinging to an ideal, even when the failure to achieve the ideal engenders guilt.

Van Devanter's image of the grieving mothers carries a dual sense that she has handed the sons back to their mothers so that they can participate in her grief for their sons, but at the same time she *is* the mother carrying the dead son. The dream image of the mothers thus represents the nurses' role, as much as it does the real mother. The poetry struggles with the same burden of responsibility for the 'bloody bodies'.

While much of the poetry nominally privileges the position of mothers in relation to the dying soldier, the physically intimate act of nursing, wherein the nurse plays an idealised maternal role, often subverts and supplants the image of the real mother. Thus, the nurse, in place of the mother, participates in the *pathos* of what Loraux calls the 'body-memory' of the mother for her son. As one nurse affirms: 'There is nothing more intimate than sharing someone's dying with them . . . that act of helping someone die is more intimate than sex, it is more intimate than childbirth, and once you have done that you can never be ordinary again.'[23] In her poem 'Hello David', Dusty takes on a burden of suffering she refuses to communicate to the mother: she carries the real knowledge of the soldier's death, while providing the mother with conventional words of consolation. In doing so, she separates the mother from the mutilated body of her son and takes her place. Her one potential consolation is in privileging her intimate relationship with the soldier, and yet, paradoxically, the knowledge that relationship brings, condemns her to pain greater than either mother or dying son, in that she can accept neither consolation nor relief of pain.

> I will write to your mother
> and tell her you were brave
> I will write to your mother
> And tell her how much you loved her.
>
> . . .
> What I will not tell her
> is that you were wasted.
>
> Good-bye, David – my name is Dusty.
> I am the last person
> you will see.
> I am the last person you will touch.
> I am the last person
> who will love you.
>
> So long, David – my name is Dusty.
> David – who will give me something
> for my pain?[24]

As Marcus implies, the nurses experience their own fragmentation in the context of the fragmented bodies they nurse. Thus, Joan Furey's fragmented sense of her own body parts in her poem 'Vigil' reveals her psychological fragmentation:

> Legs ache, head throbs,
> Every muscle taut

> Every nerve on edge
> I want to scream but I can't
>
> Day after day, week after week
> A parade.

The term 'parade' here is an ironic comment on the image of the military parade. In Vietnam terms, it means an attack. Thus, the 'parade' leads to a parade not of men but of body parts:

> stumps where once
> there was a leg and arm. A face even
> adults will hide from
> . . .
> It could tear you to pieces
> giving them an identity
> of more than SOLDIER[25]

Eventually, for some nurses, intimacy itself is defined ironically as a relationship with body parts:

> I knew you better than most.
>
> It was your arm, leg, lung, brain, heart
> I knew most intimately[26]

When physical fragmentation becomes a metaphor for psychological fragmentation, it reveals Kermayer's hypothesis that the narrative of trauma breaks down because 'narrative is an insufficient container or organiser for traumatic experience'.[27] Kettlewell's 1990 poem, 'Sister Mary', is an act of contrition for the sin of what she has not done, but at the same time it reveals the burden of carrying an impossibly idealised role, so that what once appeared to be firm beliefs now become fragmented questions:

> Each new being she tenderly enfolds
> Within her nurturing eldest sister heart
> Caring without ceasing, praying for hope,
> Yearning for strength and yet with shadows of guilt regretting
> There's just not enough for them and her too
> 'Mea culpa'?
>
> Oh, she would know then, and again and again and again
> That somehow she 'should have done more', but could she?
> Yes, she learned well that each soul was as the broken body of Sister Mary's
>   Jesus.
> But now could she see beyond the pain of all the unfulfilled dreams,
> theirs, hers and Sister Mary's.
> 'Mea maxima culpa'?[28]

Again, Mary Brunner's 'To My Unknown Soldier Boy', also written long after the war, enacts the grief that was necessarily suppressed at the time:

> I regret I didn't take your
> dying, broken dirt covered body
> into my arms for her,
> for you,
> for me.
>
> Your wounds,
> your crying for help,
> your pleading eyes,
> will haunt me until
> my own death.[29]

Both Brunner's and Kettlewell's poems reveal their own feelings of inadequacy in the context of the broken bodies: an inadequacy born of their inability to enact an idealised role. Their act of contrition, then, is to take on the burden of mourning, of keeping faith with the dead and commemorating them; revealing the broken bodies is necessary to that remembering. On publication, that private act becomes what Herman calls 'testimony', and takes on the political and judicial role of holding up the bodies to public view.

While these poems are written to mourn the dead, there is no sense that this mourning provides consolation or closure. Rather, like the endless parade of bloody bodies in Van Devanter's dream, the outpouring of grief is never-ending. As Dusty writes:

> I go on
> seeing the wounded when I hear a
> chopper, washing your blood from my hands,
> hearing your screams in my sleep, scrubbing
> the smell of your burned bodies from my clothes,
> feeling your pain, which never eases,
> fighting a war that never ends.[30]

While Dusty's poem deals with the private nightmare of grief, Dana Schuster's 'My Dead Are Not Silent' is a very public refusal to accept parameters on her grief, rejecting the state-sanctioned bureaucratic amnesia that 'sanitizes' injury: 'My dead will not be shelved/numbered/catalogued/straightened into sanitized rows.' The image of 'shelved and numbered rows' is an image of two kinds of burial: the military burial of the body that imposes rigid order on the actual process and place of burial – military graves are 'sanitized rows' – and the burial of individuals in bureaucratic rows and numbers of statistics, filed away from view and hence forgotten.

Bibby sees 'the tropes of mutilation in GI poetry as resistance to the master narratives of the war'.[31] The nurses' prose and poetry likewise employ mutilation in the way Bibby describes, as resistance to and subversion of master narratives. But their resistance is demonstrated not only in the image of the mutilated body, but also in the connection between that male body and the body of a woman. They collapse entirely the idea that war is the combatant story; they return meaning to the fragmented male body by retrieving it from the master narrative and by positioning it in an intimate relationship with the female body. This combined narrative of injured combatant and nurse is as essential to the story told by the Vietnam Women's Memorial as to the poetry and prose. Glenna Goodacre's sculpture, like the poetry and prose, remembers war not in terms of its dead, as the Wall does, or as supporting a masculine ideology of combat, represented by Frederick Hart's *Three Fighting Men*, but war as an experience that can be defined as 'a world of hurt'.

While the image of the nurse holding the injured soldier undeniably evokes the idealised image of the nurse mother, best exemplified in the well-known Red Cross poster from the First World War, 'The Greatest Mother in the World', and the Pietà, at the same time it subverts precisely the idealism represented by such images. Thus, the statue captures the ambivalence nurses had about their role, caught between the ideal version of the role they should play and the impossibility of enacting that role in a real situation. Moreover, the image at the centre – the nurse holding the wounded and dying soldier – tells a very different story from that of the Red Cross Mother, completely in control, effortlessly holding the securely bound wounded soldier. In Goodacre's memorial, the nurse can barely support the weight of the soldier. The other women, calling out or praying, go on calling or praying, but none of them can bring an end to the suffering.

Commemoration, for the mothers carrying their dead sons through the streets of Saigon, for the nurse mothers who try but cannot fulfil the obligations of the idealised Pietà, but who forever mourn the dying soldier, is a process of mourning. Mourning as the manifestation of grief is enacted in the nurses' autobiographies, poetry, and the women's memorial. But it is not a process that suggests closure. As Don Ringnalda points out, the monument 'shows care and commitment, but it also shows pain and anguish without the conventional redemptory compensations'.[32] Van Devanter's mothers continually walk the streets of Saigon, wailing and gnashing teeth and asking, 'Why'? To quote Ringnalda again: '[the memorial] has no "finish". At whatever point one decides to walk away from it, there is a sense of having left things undone.'[33] The inclusive image of the woman holding the fragmented body, whether in prose, poetry, or sculpture, claims trauma, both physical and psychological, as the dominant motif of war – owning the injury that is 'the main purpose and outcome of war'.

While Van Devanter's publication of her war experience and its traumatic aftermath gave many of the returned women veterans permission to speak publicly of their own experiences, the primary sanctioning of these war memories came with the placing of the women's memorial in the context of the other sites of Vietnam commemoration, after years of lobbying by the Vietnam Women's Memorial Project. This public recognition of the women's, particularly nurses', experience in Vietnam is important not just because it acknowledges that the women had a legitimate claim to a place in the larger site of remembering the war, but also because their war is remembered through trauma, injury, and pain. Moreover, while the Wall remains the primary site of memory and mourning for the war in Vietnam, it cannot, as one nurse articulates, convey the experience of dying or of holding the dying that is central to the nurses' war story:

It was almost too neat, almost too precise, almost too lined up. It somehow can't reflect the horror of holding a young man while he dies. It just can't. It's not the same . . . Mr and Mrs America, Mr and Mrs Congresspersons . . . it was terrible watching your children die. You have no idea what it looks like. If you did, you wouldn't have another war.[34]

To exclude women from the war story is to avoid watching the dying. In spite of a growing public acceptance of women's memories of the war in the larger American cultural memory, and an increasing body of fiction, poetry, and autobiography, also available in the 'unofficial' form of web sites, exclusion from the academy, by historians and literary critics, means that the memory of the war these women carry is still marginalised, while the combatant experience of war continues to dominate conferences, critical discussion, and the academic classroom. Unlike women's writing from the First World War, which has made its way into the mainstream by efforts from within the academy, the woman veteran's voice from Vietnam has yet to receive such validation.

The importance of an academic engagement with forms of commemoration that destabilise the master narratives of war is affirmed by Geoff Eley's comments on war and memory:

A willingness to engage with the unstable and indeterminate interrelationship of 'history' (in the professional and disciplinary sense of the term) and 'memory' (as a general name for the construction of the past's cultural meanings and the associated representational archive) has become a pressing necessity for historians of the contemporary world.[35]

To ignore a body of work that demands the war be remembered primarily as a site of injury and mourning, the academy participates in those forms of privilege and exclusion wherein acts of remembering can become acts of selective forgetting. We would do well to note Carolyn Forché's claim in her introduction to *Against Forgetting: Twentieth Century Poetry of Witness*, 'These [writings] will not permit us diseased complacency.'[36] They provide a crucially important locus for rereading, redefining, and challenging the hegemonic structures that influence the memory not only of the particular catastrophe of the Vietnam War, but of all wars.

Notes

1 Lynda Van Devanter (with Christopher Morgan), *Home Before Morning* (New York: Warner Books, 1983), p. 316. Emphasis in original.

2 Judith Herman, *Trauma and Recovery* (New York: HarperCollins, 1992), p. 181.

3 Michael Bibby, *Hearts and Minds: Bodies, Poetry and Resistance in the Vietnam Era* (New Brunswick, NJ: Rutgers University Press, 1996), pp. 154–5.

4 Samuel Hynes, *The Soldier's Tale: Bearing Witness to Modern War* (London: Penguin Books, 1997), p. 191.

5 Elaine Scarry, *The Body in Pain: The Making and Unmaking of the World* (Oxford: Oxford University Press, 1985), p. 63.

6 Bibby, *Hearts and Minds*, p. 163.

7 Scarry, *Body in Pain*, p. 64.

8 Daniel Sherman, 'Monuments and masculinity in France after World War One', *Gender and History*, 8:1 (April 1996), p. 84.

9 Nicole Loraux, *Mothers in Mourning* (trans. Corinne Pache, Ithaca, NY: Cornell University Press, 1998), p. 35.

10 For a full discussion, see Kurt Piehler, *Remembering War the American Way* (Washington, DC: Smithsonian Institute Press, 1995).

11 Gloria Emerson, *Winners and Losers* (New York: Random House, 1976), p. 143.

12 Van Devanter, *Home Before Morning*, pp. 197–8.

13 *Ibid.*, p. 202.

14 Winnie Smith, *American Daughter Gone to War: The True Story of a Young Nurse in Vietnam* (New York: Warner Books, 1992), p. 121. Emphasis added.

15 Jenny Schnaier, 'A study of women Vietnam veterans and their mental health adjustment', in Charles Figley (ed.), *Trauma and Its Wake*, Vol. 11 (New York: Brunner Mazel, 1985), p. 107.

16 Elizabeth Norman, *Women at War: The Story of Fifty Military Nurses Who Served in Vietnam* (Philadelphia, PA: University of Pennsylvania Press, 1990), pp. 34–5.

17 Lynda Van Devanter and Joan Furey (eds), *Visions of War, Dreams of Peace: Writings of Women in the Vietnam War* (New York: Warner Books, 1991), p. 47.

18 *Ibid.*, p. xxi.

19 Laurence Kermayer, 'Landscapes of memory: trauma, narrative and dissociation', in Paul Antze and Michael Lambek (eds), *Tense Past: Cultural Essays in Trauma and Memory* (New York and London: Routledge, 1996), p. 191.

20 Chaim Shatan, 'Stress disorders among Vietnam veterans: the emotional content of combat continues', in Charles Figley (ed.), *Stress Disorders Among Vietnam Veterans: Theory, Research and Treatment* (New York: Brunner Mazel, 1978), p. 51.

21 Van Devanter and Furey (eds), *Visions of War*, p. xxii.

22 Jane Marcus, 'Corpus/corps/corpse: writing the body in/at war', in Helen M. Cooper, Adrienne Auslander Munich, and Susan Merrill Squier (eds), *Arms and the Woman: War, Gender and Literary Representation* (Chapel Hill, NC: University of North Carolina Press, 1989), p. 128.

23 Van Devanter and Furey (eds), *Visions of War*, p. 121.

24 *Ibid.*, pp. 43–4.

25 *Ibid.*, p. 35.

26 *Ibid.*, p. 45.

27 Kermayer, 'Landscapes of memory', p. 185.

28 Van Devanter and Furey (eds), *Visions of War*, p. 37.

29 *Ibid.*, p. 107.

30 *Ibid.*, p. 117.

31 Bibby, *Hearts and Minds*, p. 172.

32 Don Ringnalda, *Fighting and Writing the Vietnam War* (Jackson, MS: University of Mississippi Press, 1994), p. 235.

33 *Ibid.*

34 Interview with Judy Hartline Elbring in Ron Steinman, *Women in Vietnam: The Oral History* (New York: TV Books, 2000), p. 153.

35 Geoff Eley, 'Foreword', in Martin Evans and Ken Lunn (eds), *War and Memory in the Twentieth Century* (Oxford and New York: Berg, 1997), p. xi.

36 Carolyn Forché, 'Introduction', in Carolyn Forché (ed.), *Against Forgetting: Twentieth Century Poetry of Witness* (New York and London: Norton, 1993), p. 32.

'Not much of a place anymore': the reception and memory of the massacre at My Lai

On the morning of 16 March 1968, the men of Charlie Company, 11th Light Infantry Brigade, Americal Division, US Army, entered the village of Son My, on the coast of central Vietnam.[1] The company was led by Captain Ernest Medina. In charge of the company's First Platoon was Lieutenant William Calley. The company encountered no enemy forces, no opposing fire of any kind. Its only casualty was self-inflicted. Nevertheless, by early afternoon, over 400 villagers lay dead. Those killed were – almost exclusively – women, old men, and small children. For some of the women, rape had preceded death. Other victims had been tortured and mutilated, and then killed. Much of the killing, though not all, had occurred in the collection of hamlets known by the Americans as My Lai 4. Much of the killing, though not all, had been conducted by First Platoon.

Through the 11th Brigade up to divisional headquarters, senior military officers were aware that a large number of civilians had been killed at My Lai. Contrary to Army regulations, however, the divisional command allowed the 11th Brigade to investigate itself. In the subsequent report, to the extent that civilian casualties were acknowledged, they were asserted to have been small scale and accidental, primarily the result of long-range artillery fire. Rumours and allegations of deliberate mass killings were dismissed as enemy propaganda.

For a year thereafter, the official record remained silent on the subject of My Lai. In April 1969, however, Ronald Ridenhour – a young GI who had served in the 11th Brigade – wrote a letter to the Chairman of the Joint Chiefs of Staff, the Secretary of Defense, the President, and several congressmen and senators, describing what had happened at My Lai and requesting an investigation. Ridenhour himself had not been present at the massacre, but his account was compiled from detailed conversations with soldiers who had witnessed and, in some cases, participated in the killing. Quietly, the Army's Office of the Inspector General began to investigate the allegations. In early September, William Calley was charged with six specifications of murder, including the deliberate shooting of 109 Vietnamese civilians.

Although brief details of the charges against Calley were released to the press, it was only in November – following the appearance of a news story by Seymour Hersh – that the massacre at My Lai began to attract serious media and public attention. In the same month, it was announced that Calley would be court-martialled. Eventually, four officers and nine enlisted men were charged with major crimes relating to the massacre. Many of these charges, however, were subsequently dismissed. Of the handful of cases that went to court martial, all but that of Calley resulted in acquittal. Convicted of murdering twenty-two villagers at My Lai, Calley was sentenced in March 1971 to life imprisonment with hard labour. That sentence was swiftly commuted to twenty, and then ten years. In November 1974, Calley became eligible for parole and left military custody. In 1976, he married and took over the management of his father-in-law's jewellery store in Columbus, Georgia.

Throughout the period that the massacre at My Lai featured prominently in American public discourse – from the initial media revelations to the immediate aftermath of Calley's court martial – commentators were rarely inclined to understate its historical significance. As evidence accumulated in November 1969, a *New York Times* editorial declared that the atrocities 'may turn out to have been one of this nation's most ignoble hours'.[2] Concluding an ABC television news broadcast towards the end of that month, anchorman Frank Reynolds sombrely concluded that, as a consequence of the allegations, 'our spirit as a people is scarred'. The massacre, he believed, offered 'the most compelling argument yet advanced for America to end its involvement in Vietnam, not alone because of what the war is doing to the Vietnamese or to our reputation abroad, but because of what it is doing to us'.[3] After Calley had been convicted, the theologian Reinhold Niebuhr suggested that the episode had caused a rupture in modern American consciousness: 'This is a moment of truth when we realize that we are not a virtuous nation.'[4] *Time* magazine agreed, asserting that 'the crisis of confidence caused by the Calley affair is a graver phenomenon than the horror following the assassination of President Kennedy. Historically it is far more crucial.'[5] In these renderings, the massacre at My Lai was a pivotal event not just in the history of the Vietnam War, but also in the history of the American nation as a whole.

More than thirty years on, however, the status of the massacre as historical pivot is unclear, not so much because it is explicitly contested, but because of the apparent mutedness of its memory. Commonly, if somewhat paradoxically, those who write about My Lai reflect upon the silence that surrounds it in contemporary American discourse. According to the authors of the most detailed recent account of the killings, the massacre 'is now almost completely forgotten, erased almost entirely from the national consciousness. What was once an image of incandescent horror has become at most a vague recollection of something unpleasant that happened during the Vietnam War.'[6] Christian G. Appy comments that My Lai 'has virtually disappeared from public debate or memory'. During the 1980s, very few of his students 'even recognized the name'.[7] In the view of David Anderson, meanwhile, 'Answers to disturbing questions about My Lai remained difficult to fashion because the event itself was so painful to recall. For many years Americans sought to repress the entire Vietnam War experience in both their own minds and the nation's collective memory.'[8]

As Anderson's assertion indicates, the status of the My Lai massacre within American collective memory cannot be considered in isolation from the content of national memories of the Vietnam conflict as a whole, or from the political and cultural contexts in which those memories have been and continue to be produced. Over the course of the last two decades, the practices of cultural representation and public commemoration, which are generally regarded as constituent of national memories of the war, have stimulated a succession of critical and historical studies. In many of these studies, individual acts of memory are allocated an ideological value on the basis of their compatibility with American tradition and myth; commonly thereafter, the authors chart the changes in the mean ideological coordinates of these memory acts over time, from the immediate aftermath of the war when responses to Vietnam existed in a condition of tension with long-standing cultural assumptions through progressive stages of convergence as the nation's centre of political gravity shifted to the right during the 1980s.[9] In their assessment of ideological content, these studies frequently place particular emphasis upon the way in which representations and commemorations of the conflict engage in attributions of victimhood and guilt. Evidence of the conservative drift of national memory is thus found in the silence that apparently surrounds the subject of American wartime atrocities and in the ethnocentricity with which politicians, film-makers, and writers dwell upon the human costs of the war. Fred Turner states that representations of 'the American soldier as executioner', which he considers to have been pervasive in the national culture during the late 1960s and early 1970s, had entirely disappeared from public discourse twenty years later; various tropes of the veteran as victim stood in their place.[10] Similarly, Andrew Martin argues that, insofar as the national conscience continues to be exercised by the conflict in Vietnam, its principal concern has been the treatment of US military veterans, not the violence inflicted upon the Vietnamese.[11] According to Jim Neilson, even the war literature sanctioned by more progressive critical forces has tended 'woefully [to] misrepresent the heroism and the vast suffering of the Vietnamese and consistently view the war through the narrow prism of American history and culture'.[12] Philip H. Melling, meanwhile, asserts that the peripheral place of Vietnamese suffering in American representations of the war reflects a deeply rooted cultural solipsism stretching back to the autobiographical conversion narratives offered up by the Puritans in colonial New England, a solipsism which encouraged Americans in the mid-twentieth century to see their activities in Southeast Asia as another errand in the wilderness, and which led them subsequently to adopt combat strategies and tactics unsuited to the conditions. It is no surprise, therefore, to find a similar self-absorption evident in post-war narratives, in which the tragedy of the war resonates primarily in its consequences for Americans, not for the people of Vietnam.[13]

It is not the case, however, that the sorts of pathologies that characterised the massacre at My Lai have entirely disappeared from cultural representations of the Vietnam experience. Even while they develop their overall arguments about the conservatism and ethnocentricity evident in national memories of Vietnam, many of these writers acknowledge that the ideological project of reincorporating the war within American tradition and myth has not gone uncontested. Andrew Martin, for example, identifies in a number of memoirs and novels a rejection of official political renditions of the conflict as a 'tragedy without villains', of 'those contrivances that would displace war and death onto historical myths of a politics of inadvertence, or that condense two decades of killing and maiming into the metaphor of the quagmire'.[14] Indeed, in the view of some critics, the canon of Vietnam War literature in particular has functioned very effectively as a counter-hegemonic cultural force; both Thomas Myers and Tobey C. Herzog contend that many of the most widely read literary works on Vietnam have sought to disrupt and challenge the erasure of the moral problematic from the nation's memories of the war.[15] Myers considers the writings of Vietnam veterans to have been an especially valuable resource in the struggle against conservative revisionism: 'Mixtures of rage and regret, guilt and expiation, their reports point steadfastly to the complexity and to the continuing influence of the historical configuration in which the American soldier was both brutal agent and endangered species.'[16]

Atrocity, it seems, is not quite the unspeakable and unspoken memory of the Vietnam War. To read many of the published oral-history testimonies and memoir accounts of American veterans is to engage with a world in which civilians were routinely killed, tortured, and mutilated for no reason of military logic; in which the rape of women and the desecration of bodies were mundane, everyday occurrences; in which atrocity was a banal and unremarkable fact of life in the field.[17] In the last decade, the massacre at My Lai has been a central drama in novels by Tim O'Brien and Norris Church Mailer, while the mass slaying of children in a Vietnamese village triggers the plot of Peter Straub's best-selling 1988 thriller *Koko*.[18] Scenes in which American soldiers brutalise Vietnamese civilians have been a feature of many of the most significant films about the conflict, including *Apocalypse Now* (1979), *Platoon* (1986), *Born on the Fourth of July* (1989), and *Casualties of War* (1989). In *Platoon*, indeed, a massacre on the scale of My Lai is averted only at the final moment. In March 1998, as the thirtieth anniversary of My Lai approached, all four major television news shows reported on a medal ceremony honouring three former servicemen who had intervened during the killings to rescue inhabitants of the hamlet, and the CBS programme 'Sixty Minutes' accompanied two of the men on a journey back to the site of the massacre to meet its survivors.[19] In 1999, Susan Faludi's *Stiffed: The Betrayal of Modern Man* – a dissection of the condition of contemporary American masculinity – devoted a chapter to the thesis that the massacre resulted from the failure of senior military officers in Vietnam to provide ethical leadership to the men under their command; to fulfil the role of surrogate fathers.[20] That same year, the atrocities at My Lai once again emerged as a referent in public discourse after the Associated Press revealed that during the Korean War members of the US Army's 7th Cavalry Regiment had killed hundreds of civilian refugees near the village of No Gun Ri.[21] The massacre also flickered briefly across the national consciousness in the spring of 2001, when former Senator Bob Kerrey admitted involvement in the killing of at least 13 unarmed women and children during a raid on Thang Phong, a Vietnamese hamlet, in February 1969.[22]

The massacre at My Lai, then, has not been entirely forgotten. Nevertheless, there is a somewhat incidental and insubstantial quality to these instances of remembrance; on the basis of such evidence, it is difficult to assert with confidence that the crimes committed in the village have a secure and permanent place within the American collective memory. Furthermore, the stories of which they form a part are almost exclusively stories about America and Americans, rarely dwelling for very long upon the toll of lives, limbs, health, families, communities, resources, and history experienced by the massacre's actual victims. The fragile, intermittent, and partial character of the massacre's hold on the nation's consciousness, once again, cannot be explained in isolation from the process by which the memory of the Vietnam War as a whole has been detoxified over the course of the last three decades. Students of that process of detoxification, however, often disagree on the question of where agency lies. Criticising the failure of American films about the war to engage seriously with the moral issues that it raised, Peter Marin abstains from more complex articulations of cultural authorship and simply blames the film-makers themselves.[23] Philip H. Melling attributes the indifference with which American memory regards the fate of the Vietnamese to the revitalised condition of evangelical Christianity in the late 1970s, when the literary testimonies of Vietnam veterans became subsumed within the popular but solipsistic genre of spiritual autobiography, the conversion narrative of Puritan New England revived for another troubled age.[24] He also ascribes a role to critical postmodernism, which has tended to commend to the attention of the culture texts that ultimately disarticulate the war experience for their readers, fracturing perspective, disrupting narrative, and asserting all knowledge – even knowledge of violence and its consequences – to be local and thereby unreliable.[25] Fred Turner, meanwhile, argues that the responses of the wider American society to the Vietnam War replicated those of the traumatised veteran, passing from a state of memory repression through spasms of recollection and denial to an attempt to reconcile the past with the national sense of self.[26] The originality of his study lies in the sustained development of that central metaphor, but it is in the nature of metaphors that the phenomena that they link are essentially distinct: the individual's struggle for recovery from trauma and the efforts of a complex capitalist society to adapt to the consequences of a lost war are surely charged from very different sources.

A more forceful explanation of the place of Vietnam in American cultural discourse is offered by Andrew Martin, who connects the operations of collective memory to 'the historically specific structures of power and production'.[27] In this respect, Martin declares allegiance to the British tradition of cultural studies, which he considers more sensitive to the work of hegemonic forces in the field of language and text than either the pluralist American Studies movement of the 1950s or the more recent attempts by some postmodernists to reduce historical conflict and change to the self-referential play of signs and symbols across the surface of contemporary culture. In the case of Vietnam, he suggests, hegemonic interests had not been able entirely to sublimate the divisions that the war had engendered in American society, but some strategic silences had been imposed upon cultural memory. In Martin's view, cinematic and televisual depictions of Vietnam consistently borrow from the generic conventions of domestic melodrama: in accordance with these conventions, the war becomes primarily a tale of sibling tensions within the American family. The devastation that it wrought upon the Vietnamese people is a marginal element in these renderings, and, thus excluded from mainstream representations, issues of national morality are cast into the dark, unexplored recesses of American cultural memory. Despite his emphasis upon the role of hegemonic structures in the creation of such silences in popular discourses, however,

Martin's account of their operation in specific historical instances seems rather attenuated, limited largely to the observation that many publishers in the 1970s were unwilling to consider works about the war, and to a brief discussion of conservative attempts to intimidate both Hollywood studios and television networks during the Reagan presidency.[28] In Martin's analysis, the interplay of diffuse popular desires and hierarchical cultural forces in the erasure of images of national pathology from the American memory of Vietnam remains suppositional; it is not empirically demonstrated.

For Jim Neilson, as for Andrew Martin, the cavities that have developed in the nation's consciousness of what was done in its name during the war in Vietnam cannot be understood without reference to the role of material forces and the ideological alignments they have generated and sustained within hegemonic institutions. Neilson asserts that the increasing dominance of media conglomerates within the publishing industry, together with the emergence of a complacent liberal-pluralist paradigm within academic literary studies, has led to the marginalisation of any text that engages in more than a very modest moral critique of American actions in Indochina, or that attempts to explain those actions in terms that could also implicate existing structures of power. Those literary works which have advanced radical condemnations of national conduct, Neilson suggests, have tended to be either ignored or castigated for their ostensible crudity, or else commended primarily for their aesthetic qualities, with their political content attributed little significance at all. Neilson's analysis, like that of Andrew Martin, identifies few instances of direct institutional manipulation of literary discourses concerning Vietnam, but it is, of course, in the nature of hegemonic forces that they do not have to operate through such means. Instead, by examining the canonising process, Neilson establishes on the part of the gatekeepers of literary culture a pattern of behaviour – in particular, a persistent reluctance to interrogate the relationship between the pathologies of the American war effort and the exploitative practices and counter-revolutionary logic of the capitalist system – which serves to corroborate his argument about the investment of the American political and economic elites in the ideological rewriting of national memories of Vietnam.

What the nation now remembers about the Vietnam War, however, cannot be entirely explained by the constellation of ideological interests within the sphere of cultural production, as Neilson himself acknowledges.[29] The readership of literary texts about Vietnam was often rather modest, while students of filmic and television representations of the war can rarely make wholly confident deductions about the capacity of these fleeting sensory experiences to permanently refashion the historical consciousness of their audience. Although cultural critics have often quite rigorously illuminated the explicit and implicit ideological assumptions of the Vietnam texts that they have studied and lucidly mapped the broader political world through which these texts passed, none of their analyses have yet provided a completely convincing historical explanation of the radical transformation in memory that they assert has occurred: either the identified agents are too diffuse for their activities to be effectively scrutinised, or they operate in cultural arenas too local to produce the ecumenical effects for which they are said to be responsible. The problem may lie in an interpretative overstretch: the critics have magnified the dimensions of the phenomenon, and thus their analyses of its causes, seeking to explain too much, subsequently fall short by explaining too little. Jim Neilson, for example, begins his investigation with the following enquiry: 'how, against the best efforts of so many, did a war once perceived as a nearly genocidal slaughter to perpetuate American neocolonialism come to be viewed as an American tragedy?'[30] In addition, reflecting upon the indifference of American public opinion to the violence perpetrated against the people of Iraq during the Gulf War of 1991, Neilson asks: 'How did a nation that had once had a mass antiwar movement and had once responded with outrage to U.S. atrocities become oblivious to such horrors?'[31] There seems to be a paradox here: the departure point for the rightwards march of memory was a period of popular enlightenment which apparently occurred some time in the late 1960s, even though, at the very same moment, the nation was implicated in a collective moral catastrophe. It is an interpretation that exaggerates the contradictions existing between national policy and national conscience at the height of the war, and also therefore the distance travelled by that conscience in the years since.

In December 1969, a few weeks after the initial media revelations about the killings in My Lai, researchers from the Wright Institute in California conducted a survey of Oakland residents and found a sizeable proportion unwilling to accept that American soldiers had been to blame. One of those interviewed asserted: 'Our boys wouldn't do this. Something else is behind it.'[32] In Columbus, Georgia – close to Fort Benning where William Calley was being held – the mother of a soldier who had been killed in Vietnam told a reporter for CBS television news: 'Our men are calm soldiers. Our men are brave soldiers – that's the way they're trained. We don't have bad soldiers.'[33] Around the same time, 43 per cent of Minnesota residents polled recalled that their first reaction to the massacre stories had been to consider them untrue.[34] The origins of such responses may lie, as one Wright Institute psychologist suggested, in the self-centred refusal of individuals to assume moral responsibility for actions undertaken in their collective name and in a concomitant reluctance to commit themselves to a campaign for a political accounting; simple ignorance, however, may also have played an important role.[35] Before the massacre revelations, very little of the casual, random violence that characterised the US military campaign in Vietnam had been reported in the news media at home, certainly when compared with accounts that appeared in foreign newspapers or the emphasis placed by American reporters upon atrocities committed by the other side.[36] With only a handful of exceptions, these reporters and the institutions for which they worked chose to maintain a silence over the darkest aspects of the national war effort. Just how much had not been told became evident in the wake of the My Lai exposures which, as *Time* magazine recorded, 'started a flood of other horror stories. Dozens of journalists, soldiers and visitors to Viet Nam have begun to recall other incidents of U.S. brutality. Individual acts of senseless – sometimes gleeful – killing of civilians apparently happened often enough to be deeply disturbing.'[37] In view of what hitherto had and had not been admitted about the ethical content and human consequences of the nation's war-fighting methods, it was perhaps not surprising that when the grim details of American atrocities in My Lai were finally revealed, many in the United States initially experienced a kind of cognitive dissonance and sought refuge in denial.

As the weeks passed, however, the incredible became credible. Media coverage of the My Lai story had gathered momentum during the second half of November, as news reporters collected compelling first-hand testimonies from those who had witnessed the killings as well as admissions of involvement from some of the participants. On 20 November, one major newspaper in the Midwest – the *Cleveland Plain Dealer* – published graphic monochrome images of the victims of the massacre which it had obtained from Ronald Haeberle, a former army photographer; Haeberle had accompanied Charlie Company into My Lai on the day that the massacre occurred.[38] For over a minute that evening, in complete silence, CBS television news panned a camera slowly across these images, which were subsequently reprinted by a number of other newspapers in the following days and then sold for colour reproduction in *Life* magazine in early December.[39] On 22 November, the *New York Times* published its first editorial on the subject, asserting that reports of the atrocity were 'so shocking, so contrary to principles for which this country has always stood, as to be beyond belief. Yet the evidence mounts daily that something horrible did take place.'[40] Two days later, CBS radio and television networks broadcast an extended interview with Paul Meadlo, a member of Charlie Company, in which Meadlo admitted killing 'just too many' civilians at My Lai, among them women and children.[41] In late November, US Secretary of State William Rogers privately told John Freeman, Britain's ambassador in Washington, that he personally 'had no doubt that disgraceful and almost certainly criminal actions had taken place' in the village.[42] On 8 December, in a nationally televised news conference, President Nixon himself commented: 'What appears [*sic*] was certainly a massacre, and under no circumstances was it justified.'[43] By this time, it had become unsustainable to deny, at the very least, that large numbers of Vietnamese civilians had indeed been killed by American troops that day in My Lai.

At that moment, it seemed possible that the nation would then embark upon a fearless accounting of what had happened at My Lai – the sort of accounting, indeed, that might generate a realistic and tenacious consciousness of the pathology of the Vietnam War as a whole. The *New York Times* was not alone in calling for a full Congressional investigation of the massacre.[44] In the wake of the revelations, a group of eminent lawyers and law professors wrote to President Nixon proposing an impartial commission to examine more generally whether US military operations in Vietnam were consistent with the laws of war.[45] Within the US military establishment, General William R. Peers was instructed to head an official investigation into the initial brigade- and divisional-level enquiries into events at My Lai, an investigation that was subsequently extended to include a study of the massacre itself and its causes.[46] Moreover, it was not unreasonable to expect, following the army's announcement that Lieutenant Calley would be court-martialled, that a whole series of legal proceedings against those others implicated in the killings might ensue, thus precipitating a process of public education about the true nature of the wider war in Vietnam.[47]

Certainly, what seemed at the time to be a painful and comprehensive national debate subsequently did take place. Over the course of the next year and a half, a vast array of different actors – politicians from Left and Right, radical and traditional veterans' groups, intellectuals, and ordinary Americans – joined with the military and news media to discuss the causes of the massacre and where responsibility lay. In April 1971, after the court martial of William Calley, 91 per cent of respondents to a Harris poll said they had closely followed the trial proceedings in the press and on the radio and television.[48] By 13 May, the White House had received well over 300,000 letters, cards, and telegrams from members of the public concerning the Calley case, with more than 15,000 still arriving each week; it was expected that the task of acknowledging this correspondence would not be completed until August.[49] The influx of mail, declared one television news reporter, had established an 'all-time Washington record'.[50] Even for this turbulent era of American history, the public response to the outcome of Calley's court martial still exhibited a rare intensity.

Although collective memory is constantly subject to change, early conceptualisations of a particular experience must receive special attention from scholars seeking to comprehend the way in which it has subsequently been remembered within the culture. The medieval historian Patrick J. Geary has asserted that much of our current understanding of the early Middle Ages has been largely determined by the refashioning of historical memory undertaken by writers in the eleventh century.[51] As James Fentress and Chris Wickham have noted, the process of conceptualising an experience – the ordering into narrative sequence, the selecting of what is relevant and irrelevant, and the assigning of social meaning – serves to make its memory tenacious.[52] Thus, if we are to fathom – with respect to My Lai – how an ambiguous quiet has been conjured from the babble of voices three decades before, it is necessary to examine the implicit and explicit conceptualisations offered by that babble, not least because it is in those conceptualisations that silences first occur.

On the critical issues of causation and culpability, three distinct interpretations emerged. In the opinion of some Americans, the killings were simply an aberration, the only meaningful explanation for which lay in the specific criminality of Charlie Company, with the actions of Ernest Medina, William Calley, and the men they led into My Lai that day. Testifying before the Senate Armed Services Committee in the wake of the revelations, Secretary of the Army Stanley Resor asserted that the massacre was 'wholly unrepresentative of the manner in which our forces conduct military operations in Vietnam'.[53] Calley's conviction, indeed, was ensured by the failure of his defence to weave the events of 16 March 1968 into a wider canvas and to erase the impression left upon the court by a succession of prosecution witnesses who testified to the lieutenant's personal enthusiasm for the grim task of slaughter.[54] As Pentagon officials advised the White House in the wake of the verdict: 'Calley is not a scapegoat, nor a poor lieutenant singled out to bear the entire burden of a difficult war. His act stands alone in infamy among known atrocities by U.S. Forces in the war.'[55]

Others, however, judged that the massacre could not be explained without reference to the broader culture of American war-making in Vietnam; if the soldiers of Charlie Company had butchered civilians at will, they asserted, it was only because they had considered their conduct consistent with the attitudes and practices of their GI peers, with the policies of the military command, and with the conscience of the political nation at home. Reading the first news revelations about My Lai in November 1969, the psychiatrist Robert Jay Lifton experienced an epiphany of anger and shame: 'The rage was directed partly toward the warmakers in power, and partly toward myself for not having personally done more to confront or resist American slaughter of Vietnamese.'[56] Responding to the verdict against Calley, Ohio Governor John J. Gilligan stated: 'The guilt assigned by the court must be shared – by his superiors, by members of Congress, by the Administration and, in truth, by all of us who have tolerated the continuation of this awful war.'[57]

A number of those contributing to the debate, however, drew the circle of responsibility more broadly still, as broadly, perhaps, as it could be drawn: in their view, atrocity, like war, was an eternal recurrence in human affairs, an expression of the unchanging primal essence of man. Writing in the *New York Times*, Tom Wicker proposed that the massacre had proved 'nothing specific about Vietnam; it only shows once again what man is capable of once he lets loose the beast within himself'.[58] Though it acknowledged that wrongdoing on the scale of My Lai was 'not to be shrugged off with easy references to human nature', *Time* magazine concluded that 'to ignore the persistent dark element in man can be as misleading, and intolerant, as to see only the dark'.[59]

The national discussion about the massacre at My Lai, then, engaged the active attention of perhaps unprecedented numbers of Americans; it reflected upon compelling questions of national morality and the human character; and it encompassed many different expressive styles: dry institutional discourses, emotive jeremiads, existential ruminations. The energy and eclecticism of the debate, however, was not sufficient to secure the place of the massacre in the American collective consciousness, for a variety of reasons. Firstly, the debate was never truly resolved: the three competing conceptualisations of causation and culpability were never to cohere in a way that would produce a single, simple memory of the killings that the national culture could carry into the future. That was not perhaps surprising. A small group of eminent moral philosophers, commissioned to consider the constellation of responsibility for the massacre, diverged widely in their opinions; how much harder it would have been, then, for a whole country to achieve consensus.[60] A national survey conducted two months after the conclusion of Calley's court martial, when the initial intense public reaction to its outcome had died down, found that 46 per cent of respondents believed that higher officers should have been prosecuted along with the lieutenant, 11 per cent asserted that higher officers alone should have been held to account, while 28 per cent took the view that no legal proceedings were justified at all.[61]

The administration of Richard Nixon was also divided in its attitude towards the Calley conviction. The President decided to release the lieutenant from the stockade and confine him instead to his quarters at Fort Benning, pending an appeal, and announced that he would personally review the case at the end of the judicial process. At that time, he asserted, he would make a statement 'setting the whole thing into perspective', and letting 'the American people know, and the world know, why such a prosecution did take place and why it was upheld, or why it is not upheld'.[62] These actions were taken, however, against the advice of some senior aides, including Secretary of Defense Melvin Laird, national security adviser Henry Kissinger, and White House counsel John Dean.[63] Both Laird and Dean believed that the verdict had been basically just, and that there should be no executive intervention at least until the judicial process had run its full course. Following the President's announcement, they continued to caution against any further involvement while the case remained within the military justice appeals system, not least because such involvement might be judged to prejudice not just proceedings against Calley, but also those against others implicated in the massacre, as well as ongoing and future unconnected war crimes prosecutions.[64] When the prospect of executive intervention was raised again in early 1973, following the affirmation by Calley's conviction by the Court of Military Review, Nixon himself expressed an inclination to wait until the appellate procedure had been fully completed: the American people, he asserted, were now 'primarily interested' in the return of US prisoners of war from Vietnam.[65] In the event, Nixon made no further public statement on the case and, when reviewing powers were ultimately exercised by the executive, with Calley's sentence reduced to ten years, it was on the authority of the Secretary of the Army, Howard H. Callaway, not the President. Already established by that time, it seems, was the convention of presidential silence on the issue of US atrocities in Vietnam, according to which the rhetoric of the executive could acknowledge only the sufferings that American military personnel had endured, not those that they had inflicted.[66] The Nixon administration thus contributed little to the moral and historical education of the American people on the subject of My Lai; it proved unable to negotiate the political and legal complexities of the case in a manner conducive to the inculcation of an enlightened and sustainable national memory of the massacre, its causes, its consequences, and its lessons.

In addition, even as the killings at My Lai and their judicial aftermath dominated news headlines, the conditions for the ethnocentricity of later memories of the massacre were already in place. Fentress and Wickham note that, though essential for the past to become the remembered past, the process of conceptualisation also involves forgetting – the filtering out of aspects of the experience that are either difficult to accommodate or do not seem immediately compelling at the moment of memory creation.[67] So it was with My Lai, the story of which – for nearly all those energetically debating the issue of causation and culpability – progressively evolved into a story about Americans, about the burden of guilt carried by Calley, Medina, and their men; displaced from the centre of concern, the actual victims of the massacre were subsequently rendered powerless to make their claims upon American memory and conscience stick.

This was not, however, an entirely deliberate design, expressive of a culture determined from the outset to drive those at the raw end of the atrocity to the margins of its consciousness. For the most part, US government officials and mainstream media commentators did not seek to legitimise the killings in the village by describing its inhabitants as Vietcong sympathisers, nor did they denounce survivor testimony as enemy propaganda or allege that it was motivated by a hope for financial compensation; such assertions were more evident in South Vietnamese official responses, in the comments made to news reporters by lawyers of the accused, and occasionally in the reactions of ordinary Americans recorded by the press and other interested researchers.[68] More informed than most of the public about the damning details of Calley's

actions in My Lai, the reporting and editorial staff of national and regional news journals were also more inclined to commend the eventual verdict in the court martial as
just, and to remind their readers precisely of the reasons why.[69] *Life* magazine declared
that 'acquittal would have been a disaster: here was a responsible officer, not even in
the position of being fired upon, who callously mowed down women and children'.[70]
Enlightened media commentary was evident even in the American South, the heart-
land of popular sympathy for the convicted man. The *Atlanta Constitution* editorial-
ised: 'War does not excuse the murder of unarmed men, women and children in a
noncombat situation no matter how many people say so or how many similar incidents may be cited. And My Lai, by the weight of evidence, was such a situation.'[71]
If, ultimately, the American media were unable to establish an empathetic connection
between their audiences and the villagers of My Lai, and thus were unable also to
inculcate a sustainable consciousness of what the massacre had actually meant for its
victims, practical problems of access and the inadequacies of journalistic style were
probably as much to blame as lack of compassion and a failure of moral will.

Within a few days of the first massacre revelations, television bulletins and national
newspapers began incorporating survivor accounts into their reports, though – as a
result of military operations in Quang Ngai province between the time of the killings
and their public exposure – many former inhabitants of My Lai had been scattered
around a variety of different villages and refugee camps, and were initially not easy to
locate.[72] One correspondent also asserted that survivors who were otherwise willing
to talk to the American media were being intimidated by local officials into keeping
quiet.[73] The Vietcong, moreover, continued to operate within the now largely
deserted village, and it was thus inaccessible to reporters without a military escort.
Americans having visited the moon for a second time only a week or so before, aerial
pictures of the massacre site implied a remoteness more profound than even that of
outer space. 'This is as close as anyone can get safely to My Lai,' noted one ABC
newsman in late November 1969, 'a quick low pass in a helicopter.'[74] Only occasionally were journalists able to perambulate around the scene of the killings and to shoot
film of destroyed buildings or the graves of those who died. To television audiences in
the United States, watching constant images of Fort Benning and its courthouse
where William Calley was being tried, the landscape of My Lai itself and the physical
legacies of the massacre were to remain largely unwitnessed and obscure. It was difficult for these audiences therefore to weigh the losses suffered in the village in terms
less abrupt than those offered by Ronald Haeberle's pictures of bodies lying on a road;
in terms of the family homes, neighbourhoods, and farms that once structured the
rich, complex lives of their inhabitants; in terms of a human community now cast into
desolation. Nor was the void filled by the words – however well intentioned – of correspondents on the scene. Conditioned by their professional convention of 'objectivity', reporters generally eschewed the sort of language that might have helped to
communicate the scale of the human cost, favouring instead ironic, stylised, and often
abstracting strokes of the journalistic pen. CBS newsman Don Webster, describing
his location as 'what used to be My Lai', commented on the failure of Charlie
Company to destroy bunkers in the village – a standard military procedure: 'If the

allegations are correct, the soldiers may have been too busy on other chores'.[75] In April 1970, Richard Threlkeld, also of CBS, reported from a nearby refugee camp: My Lai, he asserted, was 'not much of a place anymore, just a few ruined huts and at night it's the home of a few Vietcong'. Echoing his ABC colleague, Threlkeld noted, 'Now, two years after the massacre, this is about as close as anyone can safely get.'[76]

If the material evidence of massacre lay in a kind of no man's land, the American news media did at least have access to oral testimonies from villagers who had survived the killings. Once again, however, journalists seem to have been unable to use such testimonies effectively to convey the human dimensions of what had happened in My Lai to their audience at home. Some of the survivor accounts that appeared in the news journals and on television were undoubtedly horrific; even the most jaundiced and numbed of readers and viewers may have been shocked by the frankness with which they communicated how those killed really died. While describing the way in which the inhabitants of the village had been lined up and shot, one survivor interviewed by CBS imitated with his hands how the men of Charlie Company had held their machine guns, and then dramatically rocked and twisted his body as if to demonstrate what happened to the bodies of those upon whom they had opened fire.[77] More usually, however, the stories of survivors were mediated by interpreters or simply summarised by the reporters themselves; if, for an English-speaking audience, intelligibility was achieved, something of the communicative power of personal testimony told first-hand was inevitably lost. In addition, these accounts were often rendered complete with editorial annotations – 'they say', 'they explained' – that, intentionally or unintentionally, served to intimate the subjectivity and provisionality of what was being recalled. Ultimately, the villagers of My Lai had little control over the use of their testimonies by the US press or their prominence more generally within American discourses on the massacre. Their hold upon the attention of the American people was conditioned by the ability of the American media, looking increasingly for new developments towards a military courthouse in Georgia, to remember where it was that the essential story of the massacre lay. Such vigilance could not always be assumed. It was not a survivor of the atrocities whose ghost-written memoir came to be serialised in *Esquire* magazine and published by Viking Press, but that of William Calley.[78]

That the sufferings of the victims of the massacre were swiftly displaced from the centre of national concern was also in part a function of the endeavour to bring the perpetrators to justice. It is in the nature of a court martial to focus on questions of causation and culpability, and, after the fact of the atrocity had been established in late 1969, it was this judicial process, the courtroom arguments about who was to blame and the ultimate legal fate of Calley, Medina, and their men, that provided the day-to-day news content of the My Lai story, not the immutable reality of the dead and the distant ongoing struggles of those who had survived. Moreover, as Donald Bloxham has established with regard to war-crimes trials in post-war Germany, it is not inevitably the case that the perspectives of victims are well represented in efforts to attain a judicial accounting of the crimes committed against them. Reservations concerning the likely objectivity of their testimony and fears of an anti-Semitic backlash as well as ethnic prejudice on the part of one or two trial-planners had served to limit the role played by Jewish witnesses in the Nuremberg proceedings.[79] Similar factors may have been at play in the various My Lai courts martial. Although members of the Peers commission and, later, defence and prosecution counsel visited Quang Ngai province and interviewed a number of local people, no Vietnamese witnesses were ever called to testify in any of the massacre trials.[80] When two Vietnamese interpreters did submit depositions in the court martial of Captain Medina, the defence attorney attempted to have them declared inadmissible because, he argued, it was uncertain whether either of the men understood English.[81] In correspondence with the White House, one senior Pentagon official explained that few of the civilians interviewed in Vietnam 'could contribute anything that would have qualified as relevant evidence', a statement that was perhaps rather less obtuse than it initially appeared.[82] That Calley, for example, had killed innocents was never really in doubt, and in any event was to be amply revealed in the court testimonies of his men; on the issues most pertinent to his legal guilt, however – whether he had been ordered to engage in mass slayings and whether he should have known that such orders, if given, were wrong – Vietnamese witnesses probably had nothing to contribute. Overall, therefore, a sad irony pertained: the judicial process intended at least in part to secure justice for the villagers of My Lai provided them with little opportunity to graft their stories into wider American narratives of the war. In diverting public attention to the fate of the perpetrators, moreover, the massacre prosecutions may even have been instrumental in the effacing of victim perspectives from American cultural discourse.

For many Americans, therefore, an empathetic identification with the war experiences of the Vietnamese was not easily achieved even at the moment when the pathologies of the conflict were being most forcefully exposed. Indeed, if there were discernible concentrations of popular sentiment on the subject of the My Lai massacre, they seemed expressive as much of dismay that Calley and his men should have been held legally responsible for their deeds as of disquiet at what these soldiers had actually done. Although a majority of Americans came to accept that the killings merited some form of judicial response, the perception that blame was being assigned disproportionately to junior officers and ordinary GIs, combined with a certain innocence as to the wantonness of his conduct in the village, appears to have converted William Calley into a kind of populist symbol, making him the object of sympathy that might otherwise have been directed towards his victims.[83] In the immediate aftermath of his conviction, 69 per cent of those polled agreed that the lieutenant and the others indicted had been 'singled out unfairly as scapegoats'.[84] Many survey respondents who disapproved of Calley's trial apparently came from demographic backgrounds consistent with the expectation that rules of social behaviour would be set by others, that an individual was to follow these rules, and that if he or she did so, they would not be held personally accountable for any adverse consequences. As such, they identified strongly with Calley's defence that he was only following orders, perhaps much more so than they could with the experience of those who had suffered at his hands.[85]

Although American debates about the massacre at My Lai were impassioned and inclusive of much of the national community, they were not sufficient to force the country to conscience. Most probably, indeed, they represented the first stage of forgetting. This was not an entirely deliberate design; the process abounded with ironies and unintended consequences. The discordant responses to the massacre precluded its easy absorption into the nation's usable past. Meanwhile, desirable though it was, the pursuit of a judicial reckoning, functioned to direct public attention to the origins of the atrocities rather than their effects; to the perpetrators rather than the victims. That many Americans came to express sympathy for those indicted was as much a reaction to what they considered the maldistribution of criminal guilt as it was a reflection of ethical myopia. Similarly, the failure of the American media to engage the home front in the ordeals of the My Lai villagers cannot be attributed simply to a culture-wide ethnocentricity; practical problems of access to both survivors and the massacre site, together with professional journalistic convention and, occasionally, a facile reporting style, reduced the potential of the coverage to generate empathy within its audience.

It is perhaps only those who have suffered who can effect a full accounting, by flinging the visceral experience of atrocity and loss in the path of glib summation and casual sentiment; by insisting that the wounds they bear are not wounds that can heal; by making the memory of those responsible truly traumatic. This did not happen with My Lai. Even as the massacre dominated public discourse within the United States, the sufferings of the victims became neutralised as a source of national anxiety and remorse, and their presence within the culture was reduced to half-remembered images of what the narrator in Tim O'Brien's novel baldly calls 'Dead human beings in awkward poses'.[86] The cause was probably lost by the end of Calley's court martial; that the murderer could be cast as victim, as Calley briefly was, indicated the extent of the displacement that had already occurred. The displacement continued through the 1970s and 1980s, as what remained of American empathy for the Vietnamese dissolved almost entirely in the wake of withdrawal and the fall of Saigon, as the plight of the boat people revised the ethical indices that had earlier condemned the United States for its efforts to prevent the communist regime from coming south, as American veterans claimed for themselves the status of victims of war, and as the country's ideological orientation took a conservative turn. Commonly, the failures of national memory over Vietnam are perceived to have originated in the wake of these developments. With My Lai, however, we must look much earlier, in particular to the complex, diffuse operations of culture and politics at the time when the massacre first broke upon the American scene.

Notes

1 For comprehensive accounts of the massacre at My Lai, see Michael Bilton and Kevin Sim, *Four Hours at My Lai* (London: Penguin, 1992); Joseph Goldstein, Burke Marshall, and Jack Schwartz, *The My Lai Massacre and Its Cover-up: Beyond the Reach of Law? The Peers Commission Report with a Supplement and Introductory Essay on the Limits of Law* (New York: The Free Press, 1976); Richard Hammer, *One Morning in the War: The Tragedy at Son My* (New York: Coward-McCann, 1970); Seymour Hersh, *My Lai 4: A Report on the Massacre and Its Aftermath* (New York: Random House, 1970).

2 *New York Times* (22 November 1969).

3 ABC News (28 November 1969), Vanderbilt Television News Archive (hereafter VTNA).

4 *New York Times* (4 April 1971).

5 *Time* (12 April 1971).

6 Bilton and Sim, *Four Hours*, p. 4.

7 Christian G. Appy, *Working Class War: American Combat Soldiers and Vietnam* (Chapel Hill, NC: University of North Carolina Press, 1993), p. 277.

8 David L. Anderson, 'What really happened?', in D.L. Anderson (ed.), *Facing My Lai: Moving Beyond the Massacre* (Lawrence, KS: University Press of Kansas, 1998), p. 12.

9 Examples include Keith Beattie, *The Scar That Binds: American Culture and the Vietnam War* (London: New York University Press, 1998); Walter H. Capps, *The Unfinished War: Vietnam and the American Conscience* (Boston, MA: Beacon Press, 1990); Michael Clark, 'Remembering Vietnam', in John Carlos Rowe and Rick Berg (eds), *The Vietnam War and American Culture* (New York: Columbia University Press, 1991), pp. 177–207; Andrew Martin, *Receptions of War: Vietnam in American Culture* (London: University of Oklahoma Press, 1993); Robert J. McMahon, 'Contested memory: the Vietnam War and American society, 1975–2001', *Diplomatic History*, 26:2 (Spring 2002), 159–84; Philip H. Melling, *Vietnam in American Literature* (Boston, MA: Twayne Publishers, 1990); Jim Neilson, *Warring Fictions: Cultural Politics and the Vietnam War Narrative* (Jackson, MS: University Press of Mississippi, 1998); Marita Sturken, *Tangled Memories: The Vietnam War, the Aids Epidemic, and the Politics of Remembering* (London: University of California Press, 1997); Fred Turner, *Echoes of Combat: The Vietnam War in American Memory* (New York: Anchor Books, 1997).

10 Turner, *Echoes of Combat*, p. 11.

11 Martin, *Receptions of War*, pp. 157–8.

12 Neilson, *Warring Fictions*, p. 7.

13 Melling, *Vietnam in American Literature*, pp. 17–33, 85–95.

14 Martin, *Receptions of War*, pp. 70–1.

15 Thomas Myers, *Walking Point: American Narratives of Vietnam* (New York: Oxford University Press, 1988); Tobey C. Herzog, *Vietnam War Stories: Innocence Lost* (London: Routledge, 1992).

16 Myers, *Walking Point*, p. 193.

17 See, for example, Mark Baker, *Nam: The Vietnam War in the Words of the Men and Women Who Fought There* (London: Abacus, 1982), pp. 131–53; Myra McPherson, *Long Time Passing: Vietnam and the Haunted Generation* (London: Sceptre, 1988), pp. 567–603; Philip Caputo, *A Rumor of War* (New York: Ballantine Books, 1977), pp. 290–320.

18 Tim O'Brien, *In the Lake of the Woods* (New York: Penguin, 1995); Norris Church Mailer, *Windchill Summer* (New York: Fourth Estate, 2000); Peter Straub, *Koko* (New York: Signet, 1989).

19 ABC News (6 March 1998); CBS News (6 March 1998); NBC News (6 March 1998); CNN (6 March 1998), VTNA. See also Trent Angers, *The Forgotten Hero of My Lai: The Hugh Thompson Story* (Lafayette, LA: Acadian House, 1999).

20 Susan Faludi, *Stiffed: The Betrayal of Modern Man* (London: Vintage, 2000), pp. 291–358.

21 See, for example, *Washington Post* (30 September 1999), and Charles J. Hanley, Sang-Hun Choe and Martha Mendoza, *The Bridge at No Gun Ri: A Hidden Nightmare from the Korean War* (New York: Henry Holt, 2001), pp. 224–6.

22 See Gregory L. Vistica, 'One awful night in Thanh Phong', *New York Times Magazine* (25 April 2001).

23 Peter Marin, 'Coming to terms with Vietnam: settling our moral debts', *Harper's* (December 1980), 41–56.

24 Melling, *Vietnam in American Literature*, pp. 49–64.

25 *Ibid.*, pp. 3–7.

26 Turner, *Echoes of Combat*, pp. 12–16.

27 Martin, *Receptions of War*, p. 8.

28 *Ibid.*, pp. 75–6, 121–3.

29 Neilson, *Warring Fictions*, p. 6.

30 *Ibid.*, pp. 5–6.

31 *Ibid.*, p. 4.

32 Edward M. Opton, Jr., 'It never happened and besides they deserved it', in Nevitt Sanford, Craig Comstock & Associates (eds), *Sanctions for Evil* (San Francisco, CA: Jossey-Bass, 1971), p. 62.

33 CBS News (16 December 1969), VTNA.

34 *Minneapolis Tribune* (21 December 1969).

35 Opton, 'It never happened', p. 61.

36 William M. Hammond, *Public Affairs: The Military and the Media, 1968–1973* (Washington, DC: Center for Military History, 1996), p. 223; Daniel C. Hallin, *The 'Uncensored War': The Media and Vietnam* (Berkeley, CA: University of California Press, 1989), pp. 156–8.

37 *Time* (5 December 1969).

38 *Cleveland Plain Dealer* (20 November 1969).

39 CBS News (20 November 1969), VTNA. Newspapers that reprinted Haeberle's pictures included the *New York Post* (21 November 1969) and the *New York Times* (22 November 1969). *Life* published the colour images in its 5 December issue, available at news-stands from 1 December 1969.

40 *New York Times* (22 November 1969).

41 CBS News (24 November 1969), VTNA. A transcript appeared in the *New York Times* (25 November 1969).

42 Freeman to Greenhill, 2 December 1969, Public Records Office, Kew, PREM 12/3552.

43 'The President's News Conference of December 8, 1969', *Public Papers of the Presidents: Richard Nixon, 1969* (Washington, DC: US Government Printing Office, 1971), p. 1003.

44 *New York Times* (22 November 1969).

45 Goldberg *et al.* to Nixon, 5 December 1969, '[cf] ND18–4 War Crimes – Trials [1969–70]' folder, box 43, Confidential Files, Subject Files, White House Special Files (hereafter WHSF) Nixon Presidential Materials Project (hereafter NPMP) National Archives at College Park, MD (hereafter NACP).

46 Westmoreland and Resor to Peers, 'Directive for Investigation', 26 November 1969, Westmoreland and Resor to Peers, 'Son My Investigation', 2 February 1970, in Goldstein *et al.*, *My Lai Massacre*, pp. 33, 43.

47 On 22 November, the *New York Times* reported that 26 individuals were currently being investigated in connection with the massacre. The announcement concerning Calley's court martial was made two days later.

48 Harris to Higby, 'Harris Survey', 5 April 1971, 'Calley' folder, box 16, John D. Ehrlichman Alphabetical Subject File, Staff Member and Office Files (hereafter SMOF), WHSF, NPMP, NACP.

49 Smith to Wilson, 13 May 1971, 'Calley Corr.' folder, box 14, John W. Dean III Subject File, SMOF, WHSF, NPMP, NACP.

50 CBS News (1 April 1971), VTNA.

51 Patrick J. Geary, *Phantoms of Remembrance: Memory and Oblivion at the End of the First Millennium* (Princeton, NJ: Princeton University Press, 1994), p. 7.

52 James Fentress and Chris Wickham, *Social Memory* (Oxford: Blackwell, 1992), pp. 72–4.

53 *New York Times* (27 November 1969).

54 For an account of the trial, see Richard Hammer, *The Court-Martial of Lt. Calley* (New York: Coward, McCann & Geoghegan, 1971).

55 Untitled document, 3 April 1971, enclosed with Haig to Ehrlichman, 'My Lai', 7 April 1971, 'Calley-April–May 1971' folder, box 14, John W. Dean III Subject Files, SMOF, WHSF, NPMP, NACP.

56 Robert Jay Lifton, *Home from the War: Vietnam Veterans: Neither Victims nor Executioners* (London: Wildwood House, 1974), p. 16.

57 *New York Times* (4 April 1971).

58 *Ibid.* (2 December 1969).

59 *Time* (5 December 1969).

60 Peter A. French (ed.), *Individual and Collective Responsibility* (Rochester, VT: Schenkman Books [1972], 1998).

61 Herbert C. Kelman and Lee H. Lawrence, 'Assignment of responsibility in the case of Lt. Calley: preliminary report on a national survey', *Journal of Social Issues*, 28:1 (1972), 177–212.

62 'Panel Interview at the Annual Convention of the American Society of Newspaper Editors. April 16, 1971', *Public Papers of the Presidents: Richard Nixon, 1971* (Washington, DC: US Government Printing Office, 1972), pp. 537–9.

63 See 'statement on the Calley trial recommended by Secretary Laird', 31 March 1971, 'Calley case 160' folder, box 18, Ronald L. Ziegler Numerical Subject File, SMOF, WHSF, NPMP, NACP; handwritten notes, 1 April 1971, 'April 1, 1971–May 19, 1971 [Part 1]' folder, box 43, H.R. Haldeman Notes, SMOF, WHSF, NPMP, NACP; Dean to Ehrlichman and Haldeman, 'Presidential Response – Calley Court-Martial Case', 1 April 1971, 'Chronicle – April 1971' folder, box 1, J. Fred Buzhardt Chronological Files, SMOF, WHSF, NPMP, NACP.

64 Untitled document, 3 April 1971, enclosed with Haig to Ehrlichman, 'My Lai', 7 April 1971, 'Calley-April–May 1971' folder, box 14, John W. Dean III Subject File, SMOF, WHSF, NPMP, NACP; Dean to Ehrlichman, Haig and Krogh, 'Request for Clarification on Confinement of Lieutenant Calley', 23 July 1971, 'Calley – later devs' folder, box 14, John W. Dean III Subject File, SMOF, WHSF, NPMP, NACP.

65 Kehrli to Dean, 'Decision by the Court of Military Review in the Calley Case', 19 February 1973, 'Calley – later devs' folder, box 14, John W. Dean III Subject File, SMOF, WHSF, NPMP, NACP.

66 For a valuable discussion of this convention as observed in the public statements of Presidents Ford, Carter, Reagan, G.H.W. Bush, and Clinton, see McMahon, 'Contested memory'.

67 Fentress and Wickham, *Social Memory*, pp. 73–4.

68 See, for example, the remarks of George Latimer, Calley's attorney, to the *New York Times* (13 November 1969); the comments of the Quang Ngai province chief and South Vietnamese northern province commander reported, respectively, on CBS News (18 November 1969) and NBC News (24 November 1969), VTNA; and a number of responses recorded in the Wright Institute's survey, in Opton, 'It never happened', pp. 49–70.

69 For one contemporary analysis of the divergence between media and public reactions to the verdict, see Joseph Kraft, 'Lt. Calley no media hero', *Washington Post* (4 April 1971).

70 *Life* (16 April 1971).

71 *Atlanta Constitution* (2 April 1971).

72 ABC News (17 November 1969); CBS News (17 November 1969); NBC News (17 November 1969), VTNA; *New York Times* (15, 17 November 1969).

73 ABC News (1 December 1969), VTNA.

74 ABC News (26 November 1969), VTNA. Reporting from the village in March 1971, NBC reporter Tom Streithorst stated it was 'now officially listed as pacified, but it's ranked in the lowest category of pacification. You still hear firing, there are mines and booby-traps reported; it's not advised for outsiders to remain here at night.' He continued: 'The government authorities weren't too happy about us coming here. The United States Americal Division refused to accompany us. As one South Vietnamese civilian said: "My Lai is like a piece of filth. Nobody wants to touch it."' NBC News (19 March 1971), VTNA.

75 CBS News (25 December 1969), VTNA.

76 *Ibid.* (24 April 1970).

77 *Ibid.* (18 November 1969).

78 'The confessions of Lieutenant Calley', *Esquire* (November 1970); 'The continuing confessions of Lieutenant Calley', *Esquire* (February 1971); 'The concluding confessions of Lieutenant Calley', *Esquire* (September 1971); John Sack, *Lieutenant Calley: His Own Story* (New York: Viking Press, 1971).

79 Donald Bloxham, *Genocide on Trial: War Crimes Trials and the Formation of Holocaust History and Memory* (Oxford: Oxford University Press, 2001), pp. 63–9.

80 Goldstein *et al.*, *The My Lai Massacre*, pp. 30–2; Wallace to Hughes, 'Vietnamese Witnesses in My Lai Prosecutions', 17 September 1971, 'My Lai Cases – General' folder, box 15, John W. Dean III Subject Files, SMOF, WHSF, NPMP, NACP. Richard Hammer notes that no Vietnamese attended the Calley court martial even as spectators; Hammer, *The Court-Martial of Lt. Calley*, p. 73.

81 Mary McCarthy, *Medina* (London: Wildwood House, 1973), p. 29.

82 Wallace to Hughes, 'Vietnamese Witnesses in My Lai Prosecutions', 17 September 1971, 'My Lai Cases – General' folder, box 15, John W. Dean III Subject Files, SMOF, WHSF, NPMP, NACP.

83 In a survey conducted by the Roper Organization two months after the end of Calley's court martial, 59 per cent of respondents agreed that, with respect to My Lai, legal proceedings of some kind had been necessary; Kelman and Lawrence, 'Assignment of responsibility', p. 188.

84 Harris to Higby, 'Harris Survey', 5 April 1971, 'Calley' folder, box 16, John D. Ehrlichman Alphabetical Subject File, SMOF, WHSF, NPMP, NACP.

85 Kelman and Lawrence, 'Assignment of responsibility', pp. 204–6.

86 O'Brien, *In the Lake of the Woods*, p. 48.

Remembering Vukovar, forgetting Vukovar: constructing national identity through the memory of catastrophe in Croatia

The catastrophe of Vukovar

During the 1980s a surge in overt nationalism within the Federation of Yugoslavia produced increasing disaffection between Croatian and Serbian communities within the Republic of Croatia.[1] The situation worsened when, in April 1990, the Croatian electorate chose the nationalist Croatian Democratic Union Party (HDZ), headed by Franjo Tuđman, to form the next Croatian government. The HDZ immediately began to implement a range of nationalist policies, including the creation of a new Croatian-only police force. These actions deepened the rift between Croatians and Serbs in Croatia and exacerbated Croatian-Serb feelings of exclusion.

In August 1990, the Croatian-Serb community of Knin, in the Krajina area of south-eastern Croatia, severed links with the rest of Croatia and announced that it would hold a referendum on whether to declare independence. A detachment of the new loyalist police was sent by the Croatian government to seize Knin, but this was intercepted by the Federal Yugoslavian air force. The Knin communities continued their rebellion, which soon spread to the Croatian-Serb communities in the north-east of Croatia. The tensions between Croatian-Serbs and Croats escalated throughout the winter of 1990 and the spring of 1991. There were outbreaks of fighting in the eastern regions of Croatia. Croatian-Serbs, aided by paramilitaries from Serbia, sought to expel Croatians from predominantly Serb areas. As a result of these actions the town of Vukovar became cut off from the rest of Croatia.

In May 1991, the HDZ held a referendum on whether Croatia should secede from the Federation of Yugoslavia. Croatian-Serb communities withheld their vote. On 25 June 1991, the republics of Croatia and Slovenia announced their secession from the Federation of Yugoslavia. A few weeks later, formal hostilities began in Croatia. The Yugoslavian People's Army (JNA) and Serb paramilitaries laid siege to Vukovar. On 18 November, after three months of sustained shelling that razed much of the town to the ground, Vukovar fell to Serbian forces. The non-Serb population was expelled, and fled to Croat-held areas in Croatia. These refugees brought with them tales of extreme brutality by Serbian forces, including rape, torture, arbitrary killing and disappearances.

In 1992, Vukovar became a United Nations Protected Area (UNPA). In 1995, Croatia signed the Dayton Agreement and agreed to end hostilities with other entities within the former Yugoslavia. In 1998, the town was officially returned to the Croatian nation as a fulfilment of the terms of the Dayton Agreement. In 2001, Amnesty International reported that 'over 600 people' were 'still listed as missing in the Vukovar-Srijem region'.[2]

Shifting catastrophes, memories, and identities

This chapter began its life in 1999 as an essay entitled 'Remembering Vukovar: constructing national identity through the memory of catastrophe in Croatia'. It drew on recently completed fieldwork in Croatia and Bosnia-Herzegovina to examine the place that the fall of the town of Vukovar in 1991 held in the Croatian national consciousness. It argued that Croatia's right-wing government was using the memory of the fall of Vukovar to construct a Croatian national identity that was framed around its heroic suffering and victim status during the recent conflicts. At the same time, the government was denying and eliding the role of Croatians in the perpetration of recent (1991–95), and not so recent (1941–45), war crimes.

However, while this essay was being written, political events within Croatia forced a change in focus. In December 1999, Franjo Tuđman died, leaving vacant the post of Croatian president and leader of the HDZ. In national elections held in January 2000, the Croatian electorate voted overwhelmingly for the removal of the HDZ government. In its place, they appointed a new coalition government, headed by the Social Democratic Party (SDP). The new government began its term of office by rejecting the nationalist values of the previous government. Instead, it embraced a Western European economic and political model, promoting industry and commerce, and favouring a method of governance that could be seen as open and transparent. This rejection of old values and the adoption of new styles of governance had a transformative effect on the construction of Croatian cultural memory and national identity. The dominant reading of the fall of Vukovar changed, producing shifts also in public perceptions and collective memory. Drawing on personal observations, and on local and international media reportage of events in Croatia, this chapter takes into account these later developments and examines the mutations of Croatian collective memories of the conflicts between 1993 and 2002.

Personal observations: Croatia, 1993

My first impression of Zagreb, the capital of Croatia, was that the city appeared to be traumatised both by the economic effects of the war (Croatia was almost bankrupt) and by the government that had been in power for the last three years. As a geographic space the city was turned in on itself. The shops were empty, but there was a thriving, alternative economy in the form of a relatively unseen black market. The breadth of the area that represented the city centre of Zagreb was very small. The people occupying this space seemed introverted, depressed, frightened, and subdued. This sense of anxiety was acknowledged by some of the people that I spoke to, but they tended to ascribe it to a fear that war would reach the city. What most did not voice was that they were also frightened of each other – frightened that their behaviour, speech, and attitudes were being monitored by the government and secret police, continuing a Tito-esque policing of the thoughts and deeds of the body politic.[3] The discovery in Croatia, in February 2000, of secret police files on a large number of people and organisations bears witness to the legitimacy of this fear.[4]

The Feasts of All Saints and All Souls, 1993

My visit coincided with the celebrations of All Saints and All Souls Days (31 October–2 November), when Croatian Catholics commemorate the dead. Although this is ostensibly a religious festival, it is observed by most ethnic Croatians regardless of whether they are practising Catholics; many are atheists with a cultural background of Catholicism. The tradition is to visit the grave of dead relatives and friends, and to light candles in remembrance of those who have died.

Accompanied by four British colleagues, I went to the Mirogoj, the main Zagreb cemetery – a huge plot of land where the majority of city dwellers are buried when they die. The masses of people visiting the cemetery were very silent, and their mood was extremely sombre. Although we respected the silence, there was a distinct feeling that our presence as outsiders had been noted, and that it had been intrusive and inappropriate for us to attend.

Although the anniversary of Vukovar almost coincides with the Feast of All Saints, I was not aware during this visit of any pronounced attempt to commemorate this event. Perhaps this was because Vukovar and other parts of eastern Slavonia were still contested territories. Although they lay within the UNPA, they were still held by local Serb militias. Croatia was experiencing defeat and a downturn in morale at this point during the war. Vukovar had not yet become a public icon manipulated by the government.[5]

The initial impressions that I carried back to Britain was that the city of Zagreb was dominated by the right-wing nationalists in power. Its people were frightened and uncertain of their government and of the war that they were fighting, but they also manifested a strong Croatian national identity. This was evident even among some of the anti-war activists that I met. It was also often articulated in terms of hostility towards the 'other' – that is, Serbs and, increasingly, Muslims. This attitude was nurtured by Tuđman's party and reinforced by the Croatian experience of a 'defensive', ethnicised war, which Croatia then appeared to be losing. People were forced to stick together as Croatians. For many, this also meant supporting government policy. Zarana Papić, a Serbian activist and academic in Belgrade, noted a similar phenomenon during the 1999 NATO bombing of Serbia during the Kosovo conflict: 'The pro-fascist collectivization of Serbians under the NATO bombs becomes an overall phenomenon, reaching in its scope further than ever even among the previously declared democrats, anti-nationalists or pacifists, and [which] therefore [has created] an indifference to the destruction of the Other, the most dominant, political, cultural, public and private, fact of today's Serbia.'[6] During Croatia's war in 1993, it was a sense of collective Croatian solidarity in the face of adversity that kept Tuđman and his party in power. In many ways, Tuđman became a scaled-down Tito, an authoritarian Croatian father figure, who had replaced the Yugoslav ideal with a Croatian ideal, while, like Tito, policing the fringes of society.

Personal observations: Croatia, 1998

I was also in Croatia in between August and November 1998 – three years after the official end of the conflicts in the former Yugoslavia. During this visit, I spent several weeks living in Zagreb, which had changed markedly since 1993. The city appeared to be thriving economically, though this observation was contested by my respondents. They argued that many of the retail outlets were run by those who had been involved in the wartime black market, while the people spending money represented a new social class of war profiteers, whom my respondents labelled 'criminal'.[7] The state-run television was broadcasting a lot of footage of the recent conflicts, including a slot on the war just before the national evening news. I asked a Croatian colleague why this was happening. Her opinion was that the state-run media were 'fanning the flames of nationalism'. She felt that the government was concerned about its performance in the forthcoming elections in the following year and was attempting to manipulate public feeling.[8]

The Feast of All Saints, 1998

On Saturday, 31 October, I attended a fair of non-governmental organisations (NGOs), organised by the United Nations High Commissioner for Refugees (UNHCR) to raise the profile of Croatian NGOs and to help these organisations to attract international funders. A variety of Croatian NGOs from different political backgrounds were represented at the fair. Among these were a number of right-wing and paramilitary organisations, including a group called *Apel*. Representing relatives of the Vukovar 'disappeared', *Apel* campaigned for the identification and exhumation of mass war graves which they believed contained the bodies of those missing.

Although Saturday, 31 October was one of the days on which Croatians expected to commemorate their dead, the Croatian government had decreed that the following day, Sunday, 1 November, All Saints Day, was a national holiday and would be the day when public commemorations of the dead would take place. Thus, the UNHCR decided that it would be reasonable to hold the NGO fair on the Saturday. However, before the fair began, several NGOs complained to the UNHCR that its timing was inappropriate, and warned that right-wing groups and paramilitary organisations might stir up trouble. These fears were well founded. On Saturday afternoon, a woman from *Apel* approached the stall of the Serbian Democratic Front (SDF), and publicly accused one of its male representatives of torturing people at the Ovčara concentration camp.[9] In what seemed like a carefully orchestrated manoeuvre, members of various paramilitary organisations sealed the exits and then encircled the SDF's stall. Several people screamed abuse at the SDF, such as, 'We have had enough of foreigners and Četniks who are one and the same anyway.'[10] Those screaming abuse then physically assaulted several representatives of the SDF. There was a palpable atmosphere of hate in the room. The group that I was with quickly left the building at this point, concerned about their safety. We heard later that officials from the UNHCR had summoned the Minister of Interior and the police, and that the para-militaries handed the SDF representative over to the police, who subsequently let him go, satisfied that he was not a war-crimes suspect.

The following day, I decided to revisit the Mirogoj cemetery. In contrast to the terse silences of 1993, the cemetery was alive with activity. Television cameras located at the entrances to the cemetery were filming all the mourners as they arrived. Another camera, located at the centre of the cemetery, alongside a Croatian flag and a bleed-ing Christ on a cross, was filming the ritual filling of the central space with thousands of candles. Clearly conscious of the cameras, many mourners appeared eager to perform their rituals in their presence. They allowed me, as an outsider, to observe this activity openly, and to feel that my presence was quite acceptable, in a way that I had not at the same event five years previously.

When I returned to my hotel, I switched on the television to watch the reportage of All Saints Day. Images of the mourners that I had just left were being broadcast to the nation. These were interspersed with other clips of film. There was footage of a ceremony that morning, when President Tuđman had laid a wreath on 'the Altar of the Homeland' at Medvedgrad, in remembrance of all those that fell for Croatia in the 'Patriotic War'.[11] There was graphic and disturbing footage of the fall of Vukovar, including lingering images of dismembered bodies. The broadcast also included film of a vigil being held by relatives of the Vukovar 'disappeared' and members of *Apel,* which had taken place at the 'Vukovar Wall'/'Wall of Pain'. This was followed by inter-views with relatives of the Vukovar 'disappeared'.[12] This last clip of film was inter-spersed with sweeping camera shots of displaced relatives of the 'disappeared' going about their daily business, in high-quality accommodation (eliding the reality that most displaced persons from Vukovar were living in extremely poor accommodation in very rundown ex-hotels).[13] Accompanying every visual reference to Vukovar was an eerie and unsettling choral-dirge sung to the percussive accompaniment of a single bass drum.

On my return to Britain, my experience at the NGO fair, the trip to the cemetery, the television reportage of the Feast of All Saints, and the constant televised remin-ders of the war throughout that autumn, kept resurfacing as the most significant memories of my visit to Croatia and started to merge together as a mnemonic para-digm of my observations on Croatia and the data that I was collating from interviews. The cultural signifiers employed by the state media and the right-wing nationalists during the Feast of All Saints and elsewhere seemed to exemplify the way in which the state was imposing a dominant collective memory of the war and victimisation onto the nation. This imposed memory was not being projected as something past; rather, it was being maintained as something ongoing, something in the present. Forgetting, writes Jonathan Boyarin, is the 'free-association counterpart of remem-bering', but such forgetting seemed difficult for Croatians at this time.[14] The govern-ment was seeking to ensure that the virtual spaces – television, radio, and newsprint – around those remembering provided no opportunity for forgetting to begin.

Time, space, and memory

My readings of the Croatian memory may, of course, have been framed by my own cultural experience and beliefs, and by hegemonic Western tropes of remembrance inappropriately projected onto the western Balkan region. That there are particularities to Croatian customs surrounding death, bereavement, and remembrance is indicated by the work of the anthropologist Andrei Simić on Serbian and Croatian family life:

> the Yugoslav tends to view the family not as an entity isolated in one moment in time but rather diachronically as one stretching endlessly backward and forward, the generations flowing almost imperceptibly one into the next without sharp ruptures or discontinuities. Therefore, regardless of the actual composition of a given household at any moment in time, ideologically and conceptually its developmental cycle is a very long one, one that is, in fact, theoretically infinite. In this way, for example, households may symbolically contain members who are physically absent, even dead.[15]

This concept of the family as existing within diachronic time places the absent and the dead of the family firmly in the present. It is a concept relevant to discussion of Croatian collective memory. One of the figurative devices employed by Tito when he came to power was the notion of the family as the embodiment of the nation, with the statesman as the father of the nation, and it was a notion maintained by ex-Yugoslavian statesmen after Tito's death. When elected, Tudman swiftly constructed a place for himself as father of the Croatian state. Ethnic Croatians were the children of the state. Thus, in diachronic family time, it was conceivable that Vukovar and the ethnic Croatians killed in the fighting in 1991–95 should have existed in the present for the Croatian nation in 1998.

It seems unlikely, however, that diachronic time could have existed at this juncture of Croatia's history. Simić describes the conditions for diachronic time as being where the generations flow 'almost imperceptibly one into the next without sharp ruptures or discontinuities'.[16] The rise to power of a new nationalist leader, the secession and creation of a new nation state, followed by a war, would have created a discontinuity in the fabric of Croatian time that would have been impossible to ignore, forcing some recognition of this event and a suspension of diachronic time.[17] It would seem to follow, then, that post-war repair or restoration of this time system, in the form of forgetting, was required.

In Croatia, however, forgetting was impossible because of the state's insistence on reminding people of the catastrophe that had taken place. The state's intervention thus prevented a resumption of diachronic (or any other type of) time. Instead, by emphasising the fate of Vukovar and the ethnic Croatians killed in the fighting, the state media helped to produce a mood of absence and loss and thus created a time and memory paradox. Symbolically, the state asked the nation to forget its lost ones, to place them in the past, but it simultaneously insisted that the memory of loss stay in the present. In so doing, the state made it difficult for Croatians to place the catastrophe within any secure time frame; the memory of Vukovar, therefore, condemned the nation to a condition of stasis.

Those present at Mirogoj cemetery in Zagreb during the televised Feast of All Saints in 1998 may have been aware of the paradox. The iconography employed in the cemetery evoked the concepts of sacrifice, nation, and commemoration. The presence of the television camera next to these icons of remembrance and commemoration disrupted any such signification. The camera extended an invitation to the mourners to perform for an audience. Those that took up this invitation thus appeared complicit with the camera crew in enacting remembrance rather than meaning it. The commemoration became a spectacle and perhaps also a façade.[18]

The performative character of the commemoration assumes additional significance when one considers the geographic spaces onto which this remembrance was mapped. The interlinking of images of Zagreb mourners with footage of bloody, dismembered bodies in Vukovar fulfilled a number of political objectives. It connected the relatively unaffected city of Zagreb and its inhabitants with the areas most affected by the war, suggesting a communal, national sympathy (but not necessarily empathy).[19] At the same time, it urged the public to recall Vukovar as an especially brutal event within the defensive homeland war. The clear aggressors and perpetrators of these war crimes were the Serbs. Events at the NGO fair also slotted into this strategy. The effect on those watching and those performing was to bring the war back into the present, to remind the Croatian nation of its ongoing trauma, and, of course, to blame the Serbs.

In 1998–99, therefore, the Feast of All Saints was not a unique event, but part of a broader government- and media-imposed policy of framing Croatian national identity around a celebration of the recent war. This was usually achieved through media reportage that dwelled on the brutalities that had been inflicted on Croatians in this war, constructing them as victims, while at the same time eliding any mention of the brutalities that Croatians may have inflicted on others.[20] Yet, although, in 1998, the Croatian government appeared happy to identify many of the needs of those civilians who had experienced Serbian brutalities, it seemed unwilling actually to address most of these needs. For example, the state was prepared to construct Vukovar as a symbolic, monumental icon of Croatian trauma and suffering, but it was unwillingly to invest in relocating people from Vukovar, or to invest in an adequate reconstruction of the city. In this way, the concept of Vukovar represented a continuity of suffering that was located both in the past and the present. The relatives of the Vukovar 'disappeared' and the members of *Apel* were vital in maintaining Vukovar as a symbol of suffering. They represented an extremely useful cog in the state-propaganda machine. The reward for this group's complicity appears to have been the high-quality, but clearly temporary, accommodation that was filmed and broadcast to the nation during the Feast of All Saints.

Using memory to stay in power

The failure of the Croatian government to address the needs of those who were still genuinely traumatised by the war seems to have been part of a deliberate policy of maintaining the status quo by also maintaining a national identification with the experience of war and trauma. Ironically, however, this discourse of continued war – while illusory in the city of Zagreb – was a reality actually elided by the government with regard to former front-line communities in other parts of Croatia, such as Pakrac, Vukovar, Osijeck, parts of Dalmatia, and Karlovac. In 1998 and 1999, in many of these communities, physical and emotional violence still intersected many parts of society, public and private.

My fieldwork observations also indicated that, in other Croatian communities relatively unaffected by the war, some form of ending/closure to the war was being sought. But closure/forgetting was consistently contested and resisted by the government, with the complicity of many ordinary citizens. Several respondents identified this as a strategy intended to combat a perceived lull in public support for the government and its identification with nationalism and war.[21] For a government whose power base was predicated on a collective national identity constructed around the politics of Croatian-ness and a defensive war, this lull represented a threat to its hold over the country. This was not simply a threat to political power, but a threat to a network of financial corruption woven among a small circle of politicians and their friends since the government first came to power.

The finances of this cadre (whose power extended into the unofficial Republic of Herceg-Bosna, in south-western Bosnia-Herzegovina) were generated during the Croatian and Bosnian wars through a variety of means: the syphoning of money out of government funds; black-marketeering; the secretive buying up and asset-stripping of privatised industry and retail sectors (many of these industries have subsequently collapsed because of a failure to reinvest in them); the use of the army as an unofficial workforce by individual politicians; and the collaboration of church, army, and individual ministers in specific personal financial investments, such as the setting up of a massive tourist centre at the shrine of the miraculous weeping statue of the Virgin Mary at the village of Marija Bristica, which hosted a visit from the Pope in 1999.[22] The beneficiaries of this war exploitation represented a new social class of the 'nouveau riche' in Zagreb. Their houses, high on a hill overlooking the city, were or are the homes of rich ex-communists ousted from power in the late 1980s and early 1990s. The Croatian government and its elite group of close supporters thus had a lot to lose should they fall from power.

System change

The reasons behind the government's fall from grace, in the elections of January 2000, are numerous and complex. One clear cause of this change in voting patterns, however, was the highlighting of the endemic corruption of the government and its elite supporters during late 1998 and 1999.[23] Tudman's death was another: it created a void in power that allowed people to release themselves from the pull of his Tito-esque statesmanship and from a particular era and style of politics. Tudman's death thus represented a catalyst for change.

After the elections and the creation of a new liberal coalition government, the news from Croatia suggested that there had been a swift transition in collective national identity and in attitudes towards the war. From being a nation immersed in the trauma of war, Croatia became a nation that began to see the war as an historical event. Interestingly, the methods used by the government to effect this change were similar to those used by Tuđman and the HDZ.

The dominant 'reading' presented to Croatians by the new government was that Croatians were the victims of the HDZ, duped by their underhand, bellicose policies. A classic example of this new spin-doctoring was the sensationalised story of Tuđman's hotline to Milošević. Croatia's newly elected president Stipe Mesić, as reported by Drago Hedl in March 2000, invited journalists to his offices to show them the 'black telephone' which allegedly allowed his predecessor to bargain with Milošević for control of former Yugoslav territory. Having noticed that several of the telephones on his desk never rang, Mesić apparently called in the Croatian secret service, which revealed that one line was directly linked to Milošević's Dedinje office in Belgrade. A search ensued for any transcripts of conversations between Tuđman and Milošević. These reports seemed to add weight to the speculation of both the media and opposition politicians in Croatia that 'two military campaigns code-named Flash and Storm – which saw Croatia reclaim a large part of its occupied territories from the Serbs – were in fact sanctioned by Milošević'.[24] The current government also alleged that secret state documents concerning Tuđman's role in the war were removed by Miroslav Tuđman, Franjo Tuđman's son and former head of the Croatian intelligence services.

Distancing itself from the war, the new coalition government demonstrated its cooperation with The Hague by delivering the alleged Bosnian-Croat war criminal, Mladen Naletilić, to the International Criminal Tribunal for Former Yugoslavia.[25] Repudiating its links with war criminals, the government also severed its financial links to the Republic of Herceg-Bosna, and the president, Mesić, drew attention to the vast sums of money paid by the previous government to the renegade nationalist politicians of the HDZ in that region.[26] The new government also sought to discredit the HDZ and its leaders by drawing attention to instances of corruption: two prominent HDZ politicians were arrested and accused of embezzling state funds.[27]

These revelations cast Tuđman and the HDZ in the role of national scapegoats while eliding Mesić's possible complicity with the deeds of the HDZ (he joined the party in 1990 and was speaker in the Croatian parliament until he fell out with Tuđman in 1994, a year before the war officially ended). The new government's spin, in its first few months of power, sought to contrast Mesić's moderation with Tuđman's nationalist excesses, projecting Mesić as a respectable and responsible Europe-aligned politician, and since 2000, Mesić's actions have continued to promote this public persona. For example, he went to The Hague 'to give secret testimony' against Croatian war criminals; and on a state trip to Israel, on the Feast of All Saints in 2001, he apologised for the Croatian persecution of Jews during the Second World War.[28] Mesić's personal reinvention has created a role model for the nation at large, buttressing – and embedding into the collective memory – the argument that Croatians were led astray by Tuđman and duped by the HDZ.

Thus, the Croatian collective perception of catastrophe has shifted from a focus upon Vukovar to the HDZ's dirty war and its betrayal of the trust of ordinary Croatians. According to this new model, Croatians once again became victims. Responsibility for the war and the perpetration of violence lay with a clearly identified set of now-repudiated political actors, and not with the nation at large – the identity of which has become sanitised and Europeanised. This new Croatia courts Western Europe and the United States in pursuit of trade and inward economic investment. Croatia's reinvention of itself in many ways reprises that of West Germany in the post-Second World War years, when collective memory was imposed from above and predicated upon the 'suppression of the past', deploying the concepts of 'bad Germans' and 'good Germans' and supplanting traditional forms of national identity with the communal pursuit of and pride in economic success.[29]

There are similarities also with Tito's policy in post-Second World War Yugoslavia. Immediately after the war, fascism was suppressed and criminalised, in favour of communism. By the mid-1960s, however, Yugoslavia had reinvented its national ideology as market-driven socialism. Like West Germany, it was focusing on trade and industry.[30] The difference between West Germany and Yugoslavia was that West Germany was being monitored and was monitoring itself, so that national identity could not be framed through territory or a sense of its divided self. In contrast, despite Tito's legislation against fascism and nationalism, Yugoslavian national identity emphasised its united republics and provinces (the notion of 'Brotherhood and Unity') while calling to mind their previous separateness, their history of division, nationalism, and fascism, and focusing in particular on Croatia's role in this history.

'Brotherhood and Unity' in the time of Tito

Dubravka Zarkov observes that Tito's insistence on the concept of 'Brotherhood and Unity' drew attention to what it purported to replace – its absent, darker side of internecine rivalry and hate: 'The self-glorification of socialism needed the narrative of a perpetual bloodshed in the past in order, by way of contrast, to glorify its victorious present. It needed the "pre-socialist history of ethnic hatred" in order to create and sustain the "socialist history of brotherhood and unity"'.[31] A constant reminder of Croatia's 'bad past', the policy of 'Brotherhood and Unity' retained nationalism within the Yugoslav collective memory as an absence: a symbolic but unspoken void. Nationalism did not disappear; though excluded from the public sphere, it nevertheless continued to exist as a private, cultural, contested memory, subject to local and individual strategies of remembering and forgetting.

These elisions of nationalism are noted by Dubravka Ugrešić in her autobiographical novel *The Museum of Unconditional Surrender*. Ugrešić constructs these elisions as paradigms of the inherent oppositional tensions within Croatian collective and cultural memory and of the way in which the collective consistently intersects the private. She describes the experience of a male friend, whose mother doctored and crafted her son's memories of his father after the Second World War, informing him that 'his father had vanished in the whirlwind of the war'. What survived the whirlwind of war was a little faded photograph of his father.

Later his mother died too; later he founded a family. One day quite by chance he discovered that his father had been executed after the war, he had been one of those 'on the wrong side'. He took another look at his father's little photographs, and for the first time noticed that the picture was not only old but had been carefully touched up (in all probability by his mother's hand). A little line here, a little smudge there and his father's hated uniform blurred into an indistinct suit.

Ugrešić contrasts this family's secret with her mother's fear, as war broke out in 1991, that her own dead husband's partisan war history would be remembered, and his family denounced and threatened, by the right-wingers who had now come to power:

> Although she was racked by the icy fever of fear – my mother despite everything kept tenaciously to her dogged ritual visits to my father's grave. I believe it was then that she looked for the first-time at the moist gravestone and suddenly noticed the five-pointed star (although it had always been there at her own request) and perhaps for the first time she had the thought, feeble and exhausted as she was, that she might be able to paint out the five-pointed star carved into stone.[32]

Using these examples, Ugrešić traces the process by which alternative realities, truths, and memories have been adopted by former Yugoslavians, while a dominant collective memory is imposed upon them from above.

Respondents who worked during the Tuđman era in NGOs that tried to challenge the cultures of racism and violence within Croatia endorsed Ugrešić's observations on private memory. Through anecdotes, they indicated that many Croatians appeared to have rewritten their individual personal histories to conform to the public memories being imposed on them at the time. But they also noted that when these new histories were challenged, people were forced to retrieve their older, written-over memories, demonstrating that private memories were made up of transient, shifting emphases, determined by state propaganda. The boundaries between public and private memories were, then, essentially blurred. There was a grey zone between public 'collective' memory and private memory. The dominant fictions of public memory affected public representations and manifestations of private memory.

Croatian public and private memory in 2002

The state-led imposition of the latest version of national identity and collective memory on the Croatian people resonates with – and invites – rewritings, elisions, and hierarchies of memory similar to those employed at the time of Tito, the coming to power of Tuđman, and the ending of the Croatian war. What, then does the future hold for Croatia, in terms of institutional power and its relationship to memory?

Although the nation has shifted ideologically, affecting collective readings of the war, the present government has not silenced extremist voices. In November 2001, the BBC's Alix Kroeger reported that extreme nationalists had jeered at President Mesić when he arrived at a memorial march in Vukovar.[33] Other news reports from Croatia consistently refer to public demonstrations by the Right. There are still members of the HDZ representing the opposition in the Croatian parliament.

This all suggests that Croatia is not currently a mono-ideological nation, as it has been during previous manifestations of state power. Although public memory is being altered, it is not being altered under threat. It is possible that the legitimisation of public voices of opposition will allow private memory to become less transient, less moulded by public memory, less suppressed. However, there is still a brittleness to democratic political culture in Croatia, and a sudden swing back to a right-wing majority could return the nation to more rigid model of public and private remembrance.

Recent comment on the political situation in Croatia observes that there is a distinct possibility of a swing back to support for the HDZ. The coalition government is experiencing a decline in support because of economic problems, resulting in chronic unemployment and soaring food prices. With regard to the possibility of the HDZ being returned to power, Dominic Hipkins, writing from Zagreb in March 2002, reports:

> Political pundits no longer treat that prospect with ridicule. 'The HDZ will win the next election,' said the outspoken columnist and human rights lobbyist, Ivan Zvonimir Ćicak. Though a long-term critic of Tudman's party, he now believes the population has lost patience with the government . . . The next parliamentary elections are scheduled for 2004. However a collapse of the ruling coalition could trigger an early poll.[34]

Hipkins states: 'Ivo Sanader . . . the current HDZ president claims his efforts to create a mainstream conservative alternative to [Prime Minister Ivica] Račan's five party coalition are winning support from fellow right-wingers in western Europe. "We are close to the German Christian Democrats," he said.' The HDZ are hoping to exploit the rise in fortunes of the Western European Right, and to exploit the pro-Western policy that helped the coalition government to come to power.

The effects of an HDZ re-election on public and private memory would probably be formative, with a swift reversion to enforced suppressions, elisions, and revisions of the past. In the view of Jacques Lacan, 'What is refused in the symbolic order returns in the Real': if the existence of a memory is denied in language and lived experience, it must emerge in psychosis, a place of nightmare where reality and rules are suspended.[35] For Croatia, this would be another catastrophe. The suppression of public and private memory would have a hugely detrimental effect on the collective mental health of the nation. Further elision, denial, suppression, and shifting of blame might well create a national psychosis that perhaps could only re-emerge in the future as violence against those who are outside the collective – those who are 'not Croatian'.

Notes

1 For general texts on Croatia and the wars in the former Yugoslavia, see Laura Silber and Alan Little, *The Death of Yugoslavia* (London: Penguin Books/BBC Books, 1995); Marcus Tanner, *Croatia: A Nation Forged in War* (London: Yale University Press, 1997); and Mark Thompson, *A Paper House: The Ending of Yugoslavia* (London: Vintage, 1992).

2 Amnesty International News Service No. 203, Amnesty International On-line, 2001, web.amnesty.org/ai.nsf/Index/EUR050022001, p. 1. Although these figures represent

Croatian missing persons from the Vukovar region, many Croatian Serb civilians from the north-east of Croatia are also listed as missing.

3 At the end of my visit, I was castigated by a Croatian acquaintance for expressing controversial political opinions in public, although I had not thought my comments to be particularly controversial. This acquaintance advised me to be careful about what I said in public spaces because my conversation was probably being monitored and could have detrimental affects on my Croatian contacts. Slavenkula Drakulić (vilified in the independent Croatian magazine *Globus* [10 December 1992], for suggesting that Croatian soldiers and men might also be raping women in the conflicts) refers to police intimidation of a political agitator. This man was finally arrested, imprisoned, beaten, and then fined by Croatian police for continuing to criticise government policies towards Vukovar refugees; S. Drakulić, *Balkan Express* (London: Hutchinson, 1993), p. 102.

4 Drago Hedl, 'Croatia's secret files', in Institute for War and Peace Reporting, *Balkan Crisis Report*, 119 (25 February 2000), 5–6.

5 As Drakulić shows in *Balkan Express*, the government was, in 1993, doing its best to ignore the catastrophe of Vukovar.

6 Z. Papić, 'Kosovo War, feminist politics and fascism in Serbia', email report from Belgrade Women in Black, 1999. Papić, an anti-war activist, knew the constructed links between conflict in Kosovo and the NATO bombing of Serbia, but presents here the dominant fiction in Serbia that these events were separate phenomena.

7 This is supported by J. Bugaksji, 'Organized criminality and economic security', read at the Capitol Hill Conference on Croatia, 1 March 2000, and subsequently published on the Internet by the Eastern Europe Project of the Center for Strategic and International Studies, Washington, DC: www.csis.org/ee/testimony03012000.html.

8 Interview in Zagreb, September 1998.

9 Ovčara was a concentration camp where people from Vukovar were taken by Serb soldiers and paramilitaries when the town fell. The exhumation of mass graves at Ovčara began in December 1992 and continued in the spring of 1996; see Eric Stover and Gilles Peress, *The Graves: Srebrenica and Vukovar* (New York: Scalo, 1998).

10 Quoted from email circular sent to international and local NGOs by V. Vidović two days later. This described this event as I had remembered it, and other witnesses later corroborated Vidović's account.

11 HRT Vijesti (state television network) evening news translated into English (1 November 1998): www.hrt.hr/vijesti/arhiv/98/11/02/. Medvedgrad is a medieval fort overlooking Zagreb; it was turned into a shrine to the Homeland/Patriotic War of 1991–95.

12 The Vukovar Wall, or Wall of Pain, outside the UN building in Zagreb, is an ad hoc structure erected by relatives of the Vukovar 'disappeared'. Each brick in the wall bears the name of someone who disappeared at Vukovar. The wall acts both as a memorial and a protest against the alleged UN uninterest in war crimes and in tracing mass graves.

13 Several respondents noted this. One has a close relationship with a doctor who treats this community of displaced people.

14 Jonathan Boyarin, *Storm from Paradise: The Politics of Jewish Memory* (Minneapolis, MN: University of Minnesota Press, 1992), p. 1.

15 A. Simić, 'Machismo and cryptomatriarchy: power, affect and authority in the traditional Yugoslav family', in Sabrina P. Ramet (ed.), *Gender Politics in the Western Balkans: Women and Society in Yugoslavia and the Yugoslav Successor States* (University Park, PA: Pennsylvania State University Press, 1999), p. 16.

16 *Ibid.*

17 There was also a rupture in terms of who was, figuratively speaking, family, and who was not. Croatian Serbs were disinherited/othered, removed from the symbolic genealogy of the national family.

18 Commemoration can begin only when it is commemorating something that is in the past or has been forgotten; see Boyarin, *Storm from Paradise*, and Michael Rowlands, 'Memory, sacrifice and the nation', in Erica Carter and Ken Hirschkop (eds), *New Formations: Cultural Memory*, 30 (Winter 1996), 8–17. The women of Srebrenica exemplify this thesis. At a talk in Brighton in 1995, representatives of these women were vehemently against the idea of a memorial to the men of Srebrenica. They felt it inappropriate: they had no bodies, no proof of death. However, as the bodies of the men and boys who were killed are being gradually identified, the women are now campaigning for a memorial; *Guardian* (15 April 2002).

19 The inhabitants of Zagreb lived in fear of the fighting reaching the city, although this never happened; most of the war violence witnessed by its inhabitants was imported via television and newspapers.

20 This policy was embodied in the Croatian government's reluctance to admit that any Croatians had committed war crimes, or to cooperate with the International Criminal Tribunal for the former Yugoslavia. It did, however, bow to pressure to extradite the Bosnian-Croat war criminal, Tihomir Blaskic, who was sentenced to a 45-year jail sentence for his role in the Ahmici massacre in April 1993.

21 Interviews, August and September 1998.

22 Dominic Hipkins, 'Croatia: HDZ confident of revival', Institute for War and Peace Reporting, *Balkan Crisis Report*, 22 (8 March 2002); source interviews; also Bugaksji, 'Organized criminality', and Zarko Modrić, 'Tuđman's dark secrets surfacing', in *Yomiuri Shimbun* (22 May 2000) also at: www.balkanpeace.org/cib/cro/cro10.shtml.

23 In November 1998, a female bank worker revealed details of Franjo Tuđman's wife's bank account to the Croatian media. Gospidina Tuđman had allegedly syphoned funds from charities that she was involved in. The bank worker was taken into custody by the police and endured a weekend of gruelling police questioning. At the time, this scandal appeared to cause a public backlash against the government. Campaigns by opposition parties in late 1999 also highlighted government corruption. The state's control of the television network meant that the opposition campaigns were run through independent newspapers, such as *Feral Tribune*, and through rumour.

24 Drago Hedl, 'Milošević's hotline', Institute for War and Peace Reporting, *Balkan Crisis Report*, 126 (21 March 2000), 4.

25 Naletilić had been indicted for alleged war crimes committed while commanding a convict battalion in Bosnia-Herzegovina; *Guardian* (22 March 2000).

26 Mirsad Behran, 'Balkan Berlin remains divided', in Institute for War and Peace Reporting, *Balkan Crisis Report*, 123 (10 March 2000).

27 Drago Hedl, 'Knives out for HDZ cronies', in Institute for War and Peace Reporting, *Balkan Crisis Report*, 114 (8 February 2000), 4–5.

28 Ian Traynor, 'Coup for war crimes tribunal but big fish go free', *Guardian* (11 January 2001); BBC News (31 October 2001).

29 Gerd Knischewski and Ulla Spittler, 'Memories of the Second World War and national identity in Germany', in Martin Evans and Ken Lunn (eds), *War and Memory in the Twentieth Century* (Oxford: Berg, 1997), pp. 239–54. See also Boyarin's assertion that 'the very fact that Germany shows itself to be morally concerned about its legacy of genocide helps smooth the way for current international commerce'; J. Boyarin, 'Space, time and the

politics of memory', in J. Boyarin (ed.), *Remapping Memory: The Politics of Timespace* (London: University of Minnesota Press, 1994), p. 12.

30 See Spyros A. Sofos, 'Culture, politics and identity in Former Yugoslavia', in Brian Jenkins and Spyros A. Sofos (eds), *Nation and Identity in Contemporary Europe* (London: Routledge, 1996), pp. 251–81.

31 Dubravka Zarkov, 'Gender, orientalism and the history of ethnic hatred in the former Yugoslavia', in Helma Lutz, Ann Phoenix, and Nira Yuval-Davis (eds), *Crossfires: Nationalism, Racism and Gender in Europe* (London: Pluto Press, 1995), p. 107.

32 Dubravka Ugrešić, *The Museum of Unconditional Surrender* (London: Phoenix, 1998), p. 26. The red, five-pointed star was the emblem of the Communist Yugoslav state.

33 Alix Kroeger, 'Croat town remembers fall', BBC News (18 November 2000): news.bbc.co. uk/hi/english/world/europe/newsid_1662000/1662896.stm.

34 Dominic Hipkins, 'Croatia: HDZ confident of revival'. See also Sanja Vukćevic and Branko Galić, 'Croatia: Serb property restitution held up', Institute for War and Peace Reporting, *Balkan Crisis Report*, 331 (17 April 2002).

35 Quoted in Judith P. Butler, *Bodies That Matter: On the Discursive Limits of 'Sex'* (London: Routledge, 1993), p. 187.

Who do you think you are kidding, Mr Sawoniuk? British memory of the Holocaust and Kosovo, spring 1999

In 1989, the doyen of Holocaust historiography, the Canadian scholar Michael Marrus, reflected on the past ten years and what he depicted as the Holocaust 'enter[ing] the bloodstream of North American popular culture, in striking contrast to its absence in previous decades'. Marrus, however, was unsure that this interest would continue in the future, concluding, 'In the long run . . . the passage of time seems likely to cool some of the passions associated with the Holocaust.' In itself, Marrus did not believe that a quiet period was a bad thing, hoping that in terms of popular representation of the Holocaust, the removal of an emotional response might lead to 'a more prudent, discriminating judgment of quality . . . govern[ing] what is to be shown in the future'. In particular, Marrus hoped that historians of the Holocaust would read more carefully, helping to demystify the subject and improve public discourse about it.[1]

Over a decade later, rather than diminishing, popular interest in, one might almost say obsession with, the Holocaust continues to grow in the Western world. Rather than taking the emotion out of the debate, some historians have added to it – one thinks in particular of the work of Daniel Goldhagen on the perpetrators,[2] William Rubinstein on the response of the liberal democracies,[3] and Peter Novick on the collective memory of the Holocaust.[4] Rather than the 'fundamental opposition' of history and memory, as theorised by Pierre Nora, widely consumed Holocaust polemics show that the former can become one articulation of the latter.[5] Books such as those of Goldhagen, Rubinstein, and Novick act as sites of memory in themselves. In these cases, publishers have put commercial success over sober scholarship in their decision to market what are at best uneven and at worst sloppy pieces of historical research.[6] To a lesser extent, this was true of Penguin's publication of Deborah Lipstadt's frequently shallow *Denying the Holocaust* (1993).[7] After the failure of David Irving's libel case in the British High Court, which concluded in April 2000, the head of Penguin Books UK acknowledged that it was unlikely that they would be able to recover their £2 million plus costs, but 'sometimes principles override financial considerations. How can you be a loss-maker when you win a case on such overwhelming grounds as these?'[8] Such a claim to moral integrity, buttressed by the decision to donate the royalties of Penguin's published version of Mr Justice Gray's verdict on the libel case to the Royal Marsden Hospital, ignores the initial impetus to produce a book that was clearly seen as a best-seller in a controversial area.

It is, of course, possible that in the long term Michael Marrus may be proved correct. For the foreseeable future, however, for better or worse, the Holocaust will be more present in the popular imagination than ever before. It is true that we are witnessing the last major stage of debate concerning Holocaust reparations in one form or another. Issues of compensation and justice were raised during and immediately after the war, but only recently has there been a concerted and, compared to the late 1940s, successful attempt to get property and assets returned to victims or their descendants, and compensation given to those often forgotten in Holocaust narratives, such as Jewish and non-Jewish slave labourers.[9] In terms of punishment for the perpetrators, countries such as the United States, Canada, Australia, and the United Kingdom have belatedly, to a lesser or greater extent, faced up to their responsibility in letting in after the war those who had been responsible for war crimes.[10] Nevertheless, Anthony (previously, Andrei) Sawoniuk was, in 1999, the first and last man in Britain to be tried under the War Crimes Act of 1991.[11] On an international level, the halt, in March 2000, of the trial in Vienna of the 84-year-old Heinrich Gross, accused of experimenting with children as part of the euthanasia programme, is perhaps symbolic of the end of such prosecutions relating to the Nazi era.[12]

The saying 'too little, too late' is appropriate for almost all issues of justice and compensation with regard to the Holocaust. However, it is still the case that, grudgingly, issues such as Nazi gold, involving assets stolen from the victims, and over which almost no Western country has been absolved of involvement, have led to an acceptance of some responsibility for past actions by those who have been labelled 'bystanders' to the Holocaust.[13] Aside from issues of compensation, however, it is significant that the response of the international community to the 'Swiss' gold controversy has been to pledge money and resources for Holocaust commemoration and education. The days of financial compensation relating to the Holocaust are nearly over. It was not simply, however, a matter of guilt that prompted the Stockholm conference in November 1999, the origins of which are linked to the original Swiss gold question, to demand Holocaust education/commemoration around the world. Perhaps of equal significance is the development of the Holocaust as the ethical measuring rod of the modern world. It has become a symbol of man's potential for inhumanity to man, an incontestable horror, in spite of the efforts of the deniers. In the provocative words of Jake Chapman, one of the *enfants terribles* of British modern art, the Holocaust is now 'a kind of moral potty training for adults'.[14]

Peter Novick suggests that it was American-Jewish organisations of the late 1970s who managed to give the Holocaust the prominence it now enjoys in the contemporary world.[15] Novick's somewhat conspiratorial 'top-down' model distorts the complex reality of how many American Jews increasingly connected to the Holocaust 'bottom up' in constructing their identities. Although American Jewry played a crucial role in popularising the Holocaust, it remains the case that it is non-Jews, the Tony Blairs of this world, who seem desperately in need of the certainties of absolute right and wrong, or what Jeffrey Shandler calls the 'master moral paradigm' apparently offered by the Holocaust model, and who evoke messages from it as we enter a new millennium.[16]

In this chapter, I will only touch upon issues specifically relating to the commemoration of the Holocaust, large and growing as they are, especially in the United Kingdom, with its new permanent exhibition on the Holocaust in the Imperial War Museum,[17] and the controversies generated by Holocaust Memorial Day, first implemented in January 2001.[18] Instead, I will discuss how the memory of the Holocaust has affected popular and governmental discourses, in response to contemporary affairs, in particular the NATO conflict over Kosovo in spring 1999.

Historians and others rightly demand more precision and rigour in the use of the term 'collective memory'. Some even argue that the term itself is nonsense, as memory is purely linked to an individual's psychology. This purist position is somewhat pedantic, as few would claim that the construction of memory takes place without societal and cultural influences. Indeed, here the focus will be on how individuals construct contemporary events in relationship to the memory of the past and how they do so in conjunction with, as well as in opposition to, collective global, national, and local mythologies.[19] The Holocaust has been at the centre of much debate about the nature of collective memory, concentrating on Continental Europe, the United States, and Israel. Little or no attention has been given to the United Kingdom, which has its own unique relationship to the Second World War.[20]

The years 1939 to 1945 are still clearly the major point of national reference in Britain, producing memories which, although far from uniform, are still of a very different nature from those in the rest of Europe.[21] The role of the Holocaust in the shaping and construction of these memories has been dynamic and continues to be contested in Britain. Immediately after 1945, in Britain and elsewhere, there were very few who saw the Second World War as representing a specific Jewish tragedy. The general trend, exemplified in Nuremberg and other post-war war trials, was to highlight the guilt of a Nazi elite, and, with regard to atrocities, to blame them on the criminal SS rather than the hundreds of thousands of Germans and others that we now know to have been involved in carrying out genocide.[22] In this elite approach, the enemies of the former Western allies have been portrayed as the new Hitlers, from Nasser in the 1950s through to Idi Amin in the 1970s and Saddam Hussein and Slobodan Milošević more recently. From the 1960s, especially after the Eichmann trial, the systematic murder of European Jewry gained a popularly recognised title, 'the Holocaust', and, more generally, was regarded as a distinct part of the Second World War. As it increasingly entered the public imagination and collective memory, references to the Holocaust became part of the moral armoury of those on the Left-liberal side campaigning against the Vietnam War, as well as the nuclear arms race, or on the religious Right campaigning against abortion.[23] In essence, however, this was use of the Holocaust against those who were deemed to be perpetrators or potential perpetrators.

More recently, Christopher Browning,[24] German scholars such as Götz Aly,[25] and, of course, Daniel Goldhagen have, in their different ways, argued against a top-down elite explanation of the implementation of genocide. On a popular level in Britain, the war crimes debates from the late 1980s and the trial of Anthony Sawoniuk in 1999 at the Old Bailey show how this has filtered through to a popular level. In Germany, the exhibition 'War of Extermination: Crimes of the Wehrmacht, 1941 to 1944', which started travelling around Germany and Austria in 1995, caused controversy and much soul-searching.[26]

In Britain, in spite of the popular anti-Germanism unleashed in politics, especially in relation to the European Community, economics (for example, the BMW/Rover jobs crisis in 2000), and, most blatantly, international football, there is still a strong myth of the good German soldier who fought an honest war, as against the evil, beastly SS that carried out unspeakable, but certainly not unreadable, crimes, as the success of lurid paperbacks such as *Scourge of the Swastika* in the 1950s and beyond illustrated.[27] There is also still general ignorance concerning the involvement of Nazi collaborators in the east. Not surprisingly, there was some resistance inside and outside Parliament to the creation of the war-crimes legislation, with the issue often crudely depicted as alien Jews demanding Old Testament-style revenge as against the British tradition of Christian forgiveness.[28] Nevertheless, those who had seen the material uncovered as part of the Hetherington Chalmers report of the War Crimes Inquiry, which highlighted the role of the ordinary man in carrying out the most horrendous atrocities, were converted to the essential need for the law to be changed in Britain and for investigations pending trials to begin.[29] It is perhaps testimony, as Jon Silverman has argued, to the power of those ignorant of the specific details and never convinced of the need for the legislation that prosecutions became so delayed that the almost inevitable resulted: few of the accused – in fact, in the end, only one, Sawoniuk – were found fit to stand trial.[30]

In this trial, Sawoniuk's defence counsel, William Clegg, attempted to revive the model of the Holocaust instigated by the few, and, in essence, the responsibility of Hitler alone. In defending the accused, he also invoked a mythical image of Britain at war. He did so by utilising the most successful and enduring cultural response to the conflict in the UK – the BBC television comedy *Dad's Army*. The film historian Jeffrey Richards has described *Dad's Army* as 'one of the phenomena of modern tele-vision history'. It ran from 1968 to 1977 but has been repeated almost constantly thereafter. But why, as Richards asks, 'does a series about a group of bumbling old men in a Home Guard unit in an out-of-season seaside resort continue to captivate?'[31]

Richards' answer is that *Dad's Army* not only encapsulates the essence of Englishness and celebrates it, but also taps into a 'nostalgia not so much for the war as a time of shortage, destruction and loss but as a period of shared effort and sacrifice, common purpose and good neighbourliness and justified struggle against a wicked enemy'.[32] He adds, 'Critics of *Dad's Army* claim it is a mythic rather than a realistic picture of wartime Britain. But that is not how its millions of fans would see it.'[33] In short, for its millions of viewers, young and old, both for those who experienced the war and those born after it, *Dad's Army* has become the actual, and peculiarly British, version of the conflict. The use of Bud Flanagan, one of the great comedians of the war, to perform the evocative title song, 'Who Do You Think You Are Kidding, Mr Hitler' (which, although sounding as authentic as Flanagan's recordings in the war such as

'Run, Rabbit, Run', was actually written in the 1960s for the series), added to the melding and confusing of past and present. *Dad's Army*, as the series' latest historian puts it, is 'England at its kindest, gentlest and most decent'.[34] It was this gentlemanly war that William Clegg wanted the jury to imagine in the Sawoniuk case rather than the killing fields of eastern Europe.

In what has been voted as the funniest moment in British television history, a 'fresh-faced youth', Private Frank Pike, insults a German prisoner of war captured by the heroes of *Dad's Army* – the Walmington-on-Sea Home Guard platoon. Pike recites a playground version of the war song 'Whistle While You Work', adding, true to his juvenile character, that 'Hitler is a twerp'. Infuriated, the German captain demands the youth's name for post-war retribution. 'Don't tell him, Pike!', orders the pompous leader of the platoon, Captain Mainwaring.[35] At the close of the trial, Clegg argued that Sawoniuk was

> just a boy of 20 or 21 who even the peasants described as poor. The jury had heard about Hitler and Himmler but that had nothing to do with the defendant . . . Do you think Hitler had got some hotline to a hut in Domachevo to discuss the policies with Sawoniuk? It's absurd. It's like comparing Churchill consulting Pike of Dad's Army. It's nothing to do with the real issue of the case.[36]

Clegg provided here a remarkable attempt to domesticate the history of the Holocaust. *Dad's Army* was filmed largely in East Anglia, especially Thetford, rich in associations of the myth of England as a village. It thereby buttresses the idea of rural England alone fighting the military might of the Nazis.[37] It was not Domachevo in Belarus in 1942, where Sawoniuk terrified and brutally murdered the local Jews.[38] Nor was Sawoniuk, in spite of being almost the same age, the somewhat pathetic but utterly harmless, thumb-sucking bank clerk Frank Pike, whose only acts of rebellion were to keep his sweet allocation all to himself and to threaten 'telling his mum on you' when requested to carry out orders which involved getting wet or cold in any way: 'stupid boy', as Captain Mainwaring often sighed in exasperation. Ultimately, however, the multicultural jury, who, critically, had visited the scene of the crimes in Belarus, which literally brought home to them the very ordinariness of the killing fields, rejected Clegg's attempt to summon up Englishness. They found Sawoniuk guilty of carrying out crimes that his fictional English contemporary could not have begun to imagine, let alone imagine carrying out.[39]

In 1990, a documentary on British attitudes to the war included the statement from one man that 'Auschwitz means a lot of very unpleasant things to a lot of people'. As a commentator suggested, he was 'so schooled in English understatement that he lacked a vocabulary which could embrace the subject. In this naive undefiled state the British are almost unique in Europe.'[40] But after several decades of Holocaust awareness in Britain, admittedly not on the same intensive level as the United States, such comments are less to the fore. Even Clegg admitted that hearing the graphic descriptions of the massacres was 'enough to make anyone's blood run cold'.[41] In his study of First World War memorials, Geoff Dyer relates the comments by British tourists recorded in a visitor's book at Tyne Cot in Belgium: 'We really showed those fascists a thing or two!' and, next to a Star of David, 'What about the six million Jews?' Underneath was the statement of another visitor: 'Wrong war, mate.'[42]

The strength of the dominant British war narrative and its related memories often interferes with understanding of the Holocaust – and the growing if still not respectable backlash against Holocaust commemoration in this country is part of that failure. Nevertheless, the situation is far from static, and there is greater comprehension than ever before that other things happened between 1939 and 1945 beyond the legendary world of Spitfires and Vera Lynn.[43] Thus, we have, perhaps not without some challenge and by no means completely, moved on to the 'Right war, mate', and one beyond that of the quintessentially English Private Godfrey and his sister Dolly maintaining genteel respectability in wartime Walmington-on-Sea.[44]

Indeed, not only has the possibility of different wars been embraced, but also the possibility of links between them. Just as it took much time to move on from the simplistic notion of perpetrators of the Holocaust being sadistic monsters, so it took many years for the concept of the bystander to develop.[45] In the United States, and to a far lesser extent in Britain, there has been an acceptance that, during the 1930s and even during the war itself, there had been opportunities for the democracies to rescue Jews, first from wholesale persecution and later from mass murder. It is partly that sense of guilt, justified or otherwise, that has led to the official commemoration of the Holocaust in countries, such as Britain and America, where no murder of Jews took place. In Britain, particularly, however, the added factor of guilt concerning appeasement – one that even now continues to shame the Conservative Party – has been added to the now popular sentiment that this country abandoned or was indifferent to the fate of the Jews during the war.

I am far from suggesting that this critical sentiment towards Britain's refugee policy during the Nazi era remains unchallenged. The remarkable support, largely from non-Jews, for William Rubinstein's *The Myth of Rescue*, a book which denies that one single additional Jew could have been saved by the democracies, suggests that there are those who were relieved that British war memory could return to its untarnished state.[46] Rubinstein's Jewishness also helped this process, removing all need to question whether the motives for such a response were really wholesome. Moreover, the canonisation of rescuers of Jews, labelled 'Britain's Schindlers', such as Nicholas Winton and Captain Foley, also suggests a desire to avoid less pleasant stories of British animosity towards Jewish refugees, as does the plaque unveiled in the House of Commons in 1999, 'in deep gratitude to the people and Parliament of the United Kingdom for saving the lives of 10,000 Jewish and other children who fled to this country from Nazi persecution on the Kindertransport 1938–1939'.[47]

Nevertheless, at present, the dominant idea on a popular, if not an official level, and whether fairly or unfairly, is that more could have been done to help.[48] This refocused memory of the past has had a discernible impact on public constructions of contemporary political crises. It was a heady moral mix of ingredients that was responsible for a significant amount of the popular support for the NATO action to help the Albanian Kosovans in spring 1999. First, there was an increasing awareness of and ethical concern with issues linked to the Holocaust. Second, there was an assumption of the failure of appeasement during the 1930s. Third, there was an awareness or belief that not enough was done during the Nazi era in this country to help the Jews. In the second half of this chapter, I want to outline initially how this manifested itself in both public and private discourse, and from there tease out the implications of what happens when the Holocaust becomes common currency in debates concerning international relations.

Discussion of the underlying reasons behind the NATO intervention will be limited to the way that rhetoric was used to justify the war. The conflict, rather superficially, has been referred to as 'Madeleine's War'; as President Clinton put it: 'Secretary Albright, thank you for being able to redeem the lessons of your life story by standing up for the freedom of the people in the Balkans.'[49] Clinton was referring to his secretary of state's family – as victims of both the Nazis and the communists.[50] Much has been made of Albright's until recently suppressed Jewish identity, including the murder of many of her family in the Holocaust, her confrontation with which, it has been suggested, has manifested itself in 'an aggressive moralism and idealism, pledging "never again" to let the world turn a blind eye to atrocities'.[51]

From a very different, less personalised perspective in Britain, the Labour Party's independent-minded Minister for International Development, Clare Short, shared what Clinton, speaking of Albright, referred to as having 'learned the lessons of Munich'. Short, three weeks into the height of the conflict, when public opinion in support of the war in the light of NATO blunders was beginning to wane, stated that 'This conflict and the arguments over it make me and many others think about the Nazis and Hitler . . . the arguments of some of my colleagues . . . make me ashamed and I feel they are the equivalent to the people who appeased Hitler.'[52]

In the summer of 1992, the Western media exposed images from the brutal Bosnian Serb camp for Muslims in Trnopolje. The *Daily Mirror* featured a photograph of the prisoners behind barbed wire, with one figure dominating the image, stripped and emaciated. It was headlined 'BELSEN 92' and subtitled 'Horror of the New Holocaust'.[53] In the early 1990s, as Yugoslavia collapsed and 'ethnic cleansing' developed, references to the Nazis and the Holocaust were frequently made. Later in the decade, however, instrumentalisation of Second World War memory developed much further. As Patrick Finney suggests, 'there was something striking about the intensity and the tenor with which participants, propagandists and observers insistently drew on the imagery and vocabulary of 1939–45 to frame the contingencies of the confrontation between NATO forces and Serbia over Kosovo'.[54] Even earlier in the conflict than the interventions of Clinton, Albright, and Short, direct references to the Holocaust had been made when roughly two thousand Kosovo Albanians were herded onto trains, having been hounded out of their homes from Priština and forced into Macedonia. The *Guardian's* correspondents Ian Traynor and Jonathan Steele, in an article entitled 'Nightmare of Sealed Trains Returns', started their piece by referring to what had happened as 'a chilling echo of the pogroms and camps of the Nazi era'.[55] Paul Harris of the *Daily Mail* was even more explicit, with photographs of the Albanians being forced without food or water onto the trains alongside another labelled 'Grim echo: Jews herded aboard trains by the Nazis in

1942'.[56] Most graphic, however, was Martin Samuel in the *Express*, who argued that was happening was

> Just a step away from the obscenity of Auschwitz: We see pictures of refugees. Behind
> them lie a mountain of unseen dead. Already, there are concentration camps. Already,
> civilians are shot at random, for being old, for being young, for being disabled . . . Serbs
> and Nazis are not comparable, it is said. The missing word is 'yet'.

Samuel, writing after visiting Auschwitz, imagined what those murdered in the gas chambers would say if they 'knew some people were prepared to let it happen again. Do what is right, they would ask of us. Do what is right.'[57]

The memory of the Holocaust, or rather the iconic representation of it, surrounded politicians' and commentators' discussion of the plight of the Kosovo Albanians, the role of their persecutors, and the response of the outside world. Emma Bonino, European Union Commissioner, when asked to describe Kosovo responded immediately: 'It's like *Schindler's List*.'[58] The *Mirror*, returning to the connection it had made seven years earlier, portrayed Kosovan refugees in locked trains with the headline, '1939 or 1999?'. It was, the photograph caption put it, 'a grim echo of the holocaust horror in *Schindler's List*.[59] There is a tension in the politicisation of Holocaust memory here, one that I will return to in the conclusion to this chapter. On the one hand, there is the danger of regarding the Holocaust as untouchable and sacrosanct, as beyond history, understanding, and comparison. On the other hand, those evoking its memory have often done so without subtlety or due care, falling back too easily on the moral certainties of right or wrong it superficially offers. The pitfalls of this dilemma were exposed in the well-meaning, but ultimately vacuous comments made by the maverick Labour figure, Ken Livingstone, a cautious supporter of the war effort in 1999: 'I was brought up to believe that the Holocaust was a unique evil surpassing anything before or since in human history. While I understand the pain and horror that has led [to this] claim, it is a myth that prevents us from understanding how easy it is for politicians and the people they lead to sink into genocidal evil.' Those objecting to comparisons often focus on the sensitivities of those who suffered during the Holocaust. It must be suggested that a much greater practical danger is that indiscriminate use of the Holocaust comparison as an ethical sledgehammer renders it insensitive in dealing with other, no less horrific, crimes against humanity which are simply different in their scope and execution. In short, it may lead to a simplistic and misleading diagnosis of other ills.[60]

What happened in Kosovo involved appalling atrocities, including mass murder, but it was not total genocide – the trains with the Kosovan refugees were not taking the victims to be slaughtered but to be removed from their homeland. This is not to belittle the horror of the actions of the Serbian forces and the local militias, but to suggest that the event's particular impact and nature were in danger of being misunderstood by a too easy comparison to what have become dominant Holocaust tropes that have percolated popular memory – especially the use of railways and concentration camps. The Serbs murdered thousands, maybe tens of thousands of Kosovan Albanians. But they also created a refugee population of nearly one million for which the West, including the United Nations High Commission for Refugees, was almost totally unprepared.[61] The appalling term 'ethnic cleansing' has been linked to the Nazis but was hardly a contemporary term of the 1940s – it has been dated to 1992 and the removal of Muslims from Bosnia.[62] Its logic and its impact are fundamentally different from that of a regime ultimately connected to a policy of mass extermination and the racial reordering of the whole map of Europe. To take another example, drawn from the work of Rose Lindsey, referring to the earlier part of the decade and the atrocities committed in Bosnia: the media's discovery of concentration camps there raised inevitable comparisons with the Holocaust. But because the latter, perhaps incorrectly, is not associated with mass, systematic rape, this possibility was never even considered until women's groups, local and international, forced this issue in former Yugoslavia onto the public arena.[63]

It is also of concern that mass murder or even genocide that does not fit the iconography of the Holocaust will not trigger the same Western concern: thus, the Hutu onslaught on the Tutsis hardly registered protest – it was in Africa and it was carried out with the minimum of technological sophistication. In fact, these deaths were not totally dissimilar to the murders carried out by mobile killing squads and local collaborators, such as those by Anthony Sawoniuk in Domachevo, which accounted for almost half the total of Jews murdered in the war, but which have received little attention in popular portrayals of the Holocaust. The result and indeed the speed of killing in Rwanda were appallingly similar, yet the absence of trains, concentration camps, and gas chambers in the destruction process meant that the connection to the Holocaust and the need for international intervention were avoided, even though television images showed exactly what had happened and how.[64] This was, after all, Africa, where the inhabitants tended to do that sort of thing anyway. Revealing such tendencies, one journalist, confronted with the misery of tens of thousands of Albanian refugees in spring 1989, commented, 'It was like a scene from Africa, not Europe.'[65] One writer from Mass-Observation, an organisation that we will turn to shortly, was acutely aware of the arrogant tendency to deny the reality of twentieth-century European history. Responding to news of the atrocities carried out in 1999, she wrote: 'People keep saying how can this happen in Europe, it has happened in other continents, think of Rwanda or the Kurds. Why do we think that other races are barbaric but Europeans are not? How arrogant we are. We have so quickly forgotten what happened in the Second World War. There are no depths to which Europeans will not sink.' She concluded, therefore, that 'NATO had to intervene to try to save the Kosovo Albanians from genocide, rape and expulsion'.[66] The comments of this woman, a further education lecturer in Yorkshire, are a reminder that the public, while of course, influenced by politicians and the media, are not solely conditioned by them. News and official proclamations are filtered down through a complex process of individual and collective responses in which the memory of the past is a critically important factor. What part, then, did the Holocaust and the Nazi era as a whole play in responding to the Kosovo crisis?

Mass-Observation was a unique organisation set up in Britain during the 1930s to provide an 'anthropology of ourselves by ourselves'. It was revived in the 1980s, with

hundreds of ordinary volunteers writing about their everyday lives as well as responding to the events around them, including the Kosovan crisis.[67] What follows is an analysis of several hundred Mass-Observers' diaries and general writings in spring and
summer 1999. It goes without saying that the usual qualifications about the representative nature of the Mass-Observation panel need to be considered. There are far more
women than men, more elderly than young, a shortage of working-class observers, and
an almost total absence of people of colour. These, of course, are not minor problems,
but they are an obstacle only if the material is used in a crudely quantitative way rather
than for its strength – providing detailed, subjective writing which reveals all the
contradictions and ambiguities of ordinary people in Britain responding to everyday
domestic issues as well as contemporary national and international crises. Moreover,
the material is enriched by the quality of those producing it. Mass-Observers tend to
be critically and independently minded, and the writing process is an important part
of their attempt to make sense of their place in the world. The life-story approach
adopted by many Mass-Observers also makes their directive responses an ideal source
to tease out the relationship between individual and collective memory.

Although I have argued against using the Mass-Observation material to make crude
generalisations, there were still some strong, underlying trends in the 1999 responses.
There was a tendency among the strongest supporters of NATO intervention to invoke
the memory of the Holocaust, and there was an absence of such references among those
who saw the action as motivated by factors other than humanitarianism. At one
extreme was the response of a woman author from Watford, who argued:

> it was absolutely right that Nato became involved . . . because atrocities were going on
> in Kosovo and to stand idly by and let it happen would have been absolutely wrong . . .
> I am generally pacifist, and when there was the Gulf War I was highly suspicious that
> the involvement of Britain and the USA was motivated by concerns about the oil supply,
> but in the case of Kosovo I think it is obvious that there were only humanitarian reasons
> for Nato going to war with the Serbs. The persecution of the Albanian Kosovans was
> totally unacceptable and can only be compared to the Nazi persecution of the Jews.[68]

Another respondent, critical, like Clare Short, of those opposed to bombing, argued
that the 'whole attitude [was] reminiscent of Neville Chamberlain and his pieces of
paper. Murdering butchers don't understand diplomacy. They mistake it for weakness
and at least our message to Milošević must be that we are not fools and we will not
stand by and allow him to mastermind another holocaust.'[69]

At the other end of the responses was a retired male nurse, who rejected British
involvement and concluded that this was an American venture: 'That grinning ASS
BLAIR would stand on his head if the USA said so.'[70] There was also a Socialist
Worker Party member with a rather generous interpretation of geography: '"We" have
been had right royally over Kosovo. And the press took the bait. Not one of them has
told us the truth' – an oil find under the Caspian Sea.[71] Apart from oil in the region,
general distrust of American imperialism and deep unease at the Americans' self-
appointed role as the 'world's policemen' were the major reasons given by those who
objected to the intervention. While the Holocaust tended to be written out of such

accounts, other genocides, in contrast, were often highlighted. As one Mass-Observer put it, quoting a letter he had written to Tony Blair: 'We let Tutsis and Hutus slaughter each other, we let the Sudanese do likewise, we stand aside when Turks slaughter Kurds, the Indonesians Timorese – the list is . . . endless' – so why intervention in this particular case, other than for potentially suspicious reasons?[72]

Others, however, while generally hostile to NATO intervention, were uneasy in their own minds because of the memory of the Holocaust. A typically honest and self-questioning Mass-Observation response came from a university administrator. First was the admission of ignorance: 'Where (or what) is Kosovo?' Because it was 'the first time we'd heard about it', it added 'to my feelings of the whole situation seeming a bit contrived'. Second, while she acknowledged the 'humanitarian need of saying "no" to the Serbs, I can't see really what it's got to do with *us*.' She drew a parallel with Northern Ireland as a British problem for the British themselves to sort out, but she conceded that 'equally, those who must have been aware of the Nazis' behaviour towards the Jews managed to pretend it wasn't happening and with appalling consequences'. Even so, she suspected that 'there was a much bigger agenda going on here', suggesting it might be Clinton and Blair both needing to prove themselves as statesmen.[73]

Some Mass-Observers invoked the memory of the Holocaust in a resigned way, arguing that the atrocities in Kosovo were part of a twentieth-century pattern and thus illustrative of man's destructive capacity, which no armed or diplomatic intervention could ultimately deter. For some, however, perhaps swallowing too literally the 'never again' slogan, there was incredulity: 'I just feel that after all the talk that has surrounded the holocaust and the horrors of the extermination of the Jews in the Second World War it is totally incredible that a similar thing has happened.'[74] Yet, although crass comparisons and naive statements of the type, 'why can't people just live together and be nice to one another', are far from absent in the 1999 responses, there is also evidence of a strong engagement in the horror – for some, at least in Britain, there was a proximity of genocide through television images. In contrast, few Mass-Observation diarists during the Second World War identified closely and intensively with the Jewish victims of Nazism, partly because the effort of imagining and connecting was so difficult.[75] Here, however, is a housewife from Bristol from the 1999 survey:

> To see on the television all the refugees being driven from their homes, the atrocities, the brutality, the sickness and despair is terrible . . . I just cannot begin to imagine what it would be like to be told to leave my home instantly and to leave so much that is precious behind. I also cannot imagine what it would be like to be separated from my family and the scenes on the television are heartbreaking.

This woman, in common with many other Mass-Observers and tens of thousands across Britain, was engaged in helping Kosovan refugees who came to this country and collecting goods and money for those abroad. She added:

> Perhaps this is about the only way at present ordinary folk can help, but I still feel inadequate when sitting in my comfortable, warm, room with a good meal cooking on the stove, hot water waiting for my bath etc. as we watch the appalling conditions the refugees, young and old, some very sick, are having to endure.[76]

Let us conclude – or rather open up questions that can be further explored rather than definitively answered. First, the engagement with the Holocaust has made it easier for people to accept the reality and possibility of mass murder and has helped, alongside instant satellite television reporting, an identification with the victims of genocide. Second, the engagement with the Holocaust is almost exclusively Eurocentric, and, perhaps, one might argue that the connection between earlier European-inspired murder in the form of slavery and imperialism and the horrors of the twentieth century needs to be made before the West will similarly engage with genocides such as those that occurred in Rwanda.[77] Third, using the Holocaust and the Nazi era as a moral weapon to demand intervention in contemporary crises has the advantage of bringing onto the agenda human-rights issues and especially the protection of persecuted and threatened minorities. Fourth, and as a qualification to the third issue, it has the disadvantage, at best, of not necessarily dealing with the actual threat posed by the perpetrators either to the stability of regions or to the minorities under attack, and, at worst, of minimising the suffering of the victims because their suffering does not measure up to the Holocaust.

Fifth, there are real dangers in engaging in ethical issues for both states and the public when evoking the memory of the Holocaust. The Holocaust can be used to self-question – why was not more done to help? – and also to strengthen self-congratulatory tendencies. Brave little Britain must take on the might of dictators and protect minorities from genocide, but not too many questions need to be asked about what is going on at home. Thus, the moral crusade of 1999 looks rather shabby when the treatment of asylum seekers in Britain and beyond, the largest number of whom are from former Yugoslavia, is taken into consideration. The late Hugo Gryn, in a speech about modern asylum seekers, was worried that nothing seemed to have changed since the incident of the *St Louis*, the ship, in 1939, carrying Jewish refugees which was sent back to Europe: 'half a century later, we, and by we I include our political leaders as well, we act as if nothing happened'.[78] It is remarkable, or maybe not so remarkable, that Jack Straw should be given awards for his contribution to community relations and to Holocaust education. As Home Secretary in Tony Blair's first Labour government, Straw was the major architect of Britain's current draconian asylum legislation that has banned, among other things, the right of refugee children to have toys, and through its policy of forced dispersal (against all advice from refugee organisations), has, in its first two years of implementation, led to 2,000 racial attacks on asylum seekers. The first Holocaust Memorial Day in Britain was promoted by Straw, who had introduced racist refugee restrictionism, and was thus ethically flawed from the start. Straw's claim to anti-racism comes from his being appalled by the Holocaust and by the racist murder of the black teenager, Stephen Lawrence. Here the standards of what anti-racism consists of are as low as can be imagined, and the dangers of confronting the Holocaust as a feel-good factor are exposed.[79] It is a British version of what Peter Novick cynically refers to, in relation to US Holocaust Museums, as 'the warm glow of virtue that such a vicarious identification [with the victims] brings'.[80]

If, then, it were concluded that our understanding of the Holocaust is still too flawed for it to be used in contemporary discussion – and the ease with which David Irving manipulated the British media, managing to find infinite space to put forward his views of denial even after his resounding defeat and dismissal by the judge as a racist and anti-Semite,[81] suggests few in power and authority are taking issues of representation very seriously – should we follow those, such as the author William Styron, who call for some 'quiet' with regard to the subject?[82] This, I fear, is a rather pointless request. The Holocaust genie is out of the bottle for better or worse, and it will continue to be used to confront a range of domestic and international moral dilemmas. What we can hope for and must demand is a more nuanced debate, which in turn will require a greater understanding of the history and nature of the Holocaust. Politicians, journalists, publishers, and those in the arts in particular need to examine carefully and truthfully their own motives for evoking the Holocaust. The Mass-Observation material suggests that, to some extent, this is already happening on a more popular level.

To sum up: there is the danger, on the one hand, of Holocaust preciousness, of its being regarded as too sacred for any comparison. The message from the Kosovan crisis in 1999, however, seems to be that the obscurity of the Holocaust – indeed, the fledgling status of Holocaust memory in the first decades following the end of the Second World War – is at a total end, and that the Holocaust has become a ready, perhaps too ready, currency for those in government and the public alike. On the other hand, there is the danger of its memory being used as a moral blunderbuss to discharge at a whole range of serious but very different problems in the contemporary world. Barbie Zelizer has examined the use of images from the liberated Nazi concentration camps 'side by side with depictions of more recent horror'. As she warns, such 'recycling of photos from the past not only dulls our response to them but potentially undermines the immediacy and depth of our response to contemporary instances of brutality, discounting them as somehow already known to us.'[83] Only connect, indeed, but surely in a self-reflective way: one that does not lead to paralysis of action or Rambo-like instant justice. While Slobodan Milošević was not Adolf Hitler, neither was Anthony Sawoniuk in 1942, nor a Kosovan Serbian militiaman in 1999, Private Frank Pike.

Notes

1 Michael Marrus, 'The use and misuse of the Holocaust', in Peter Hayes (ed.), *Lessons and Legacies: The Meaning of the Holocaust in a Changing World* (Evanston, IL: Northwestern University Press, 1991), pp. 108, 117.

2 Daniel Goldhagen, *Hitler's Willing Executioners: Ordinary Germans and the Holocaust* (London: Little Brown, 1996). See also Robert Shandley (ed.), *Unwilling Germans? The Goldhagen Debate* (Minneapolis, MN: University of Minnesota Press, 1998).

3 William Rubinstein, *The Myth of Rescue: Why the Democracies Could Not Have Saved More Jews from the Nazis* (London: Routledge, 1997). For a critique of Rubinstein's approach within the context of broader historiographical trends, see Tony Kushner, '"Pissing in the wind"? The search for nuance in the study of Holocaust "bystanders"', in David Cesarani and Paul Levine (eds), *'Bystanders' to the Holocaust: A Re-Evaluation* (London: Frank Cass,

2002), pp. 57–76, especially 71–2. For Rubinstein's response, see the introduction in the second edition (London: Routledge, 1999).

4 Peter Novick, *The Holocaust and Collective Memory: The American Experience* (London: Bloomsbury, 1999). For a critique, see David Cesarani, 'Memory, representation and education', in John K. Roth, Elizabeth Maxwell, and Margot Levy (eds), *Remembering for the Future: The Holocaust in an Age of Genocide* (Basingstoke: Palgrave, 2001), pp. 231–6, and David Cesarani, 'Is there, and has there ever been a "Holocaust Industry"?', in Latvian Commission of Historians (eds), *The Issues of the Holocaust Research in Latvia* (Riga: University of Latvia Centre for Jewish Studies, 2001), pp. 83–99.

5 Pierre Nora, 'Between memory and history: *les lieux de mémoire*', *Representations*, 7:26 (Spring 1989), 8.

6 In one case, I was told explicitly by a commissioning editor that the negative readers' reports were dismissed because it was known that the book would create controversy and hence sales.

7 Deborah Lipstadt, *Denying the Holocaust: The Growing Assault on Truth and Memory* (Harmondsworth: Penguin [1993], 1994). Lipstadt makes a crude attack on deconstructionism, linking it to the growth of Holocaust denial from the 1970s; for a more sophisticated approach also making the linkage, see Richard Evans, *In Defence of History* (London: Granta, 1997), pp. 238–43. Lipstadt's strength is in the field of American Holocaust denial, following her work on the American press and the Holocaust. She is much weaker on European, including British, denial.

8 Anthony Forbes-Watson quoted in the *Guardian* (12 April 2000). For the Irving trial, see *The Irving Judgment: Mr David Irving v Penguin Books and Professor Deborah Lipstadt* (Harmondsworth: Penguin, 2000); D.D. Guttenplan, *The Holocaust on Trial: History, Justice and the David Irving Libel Case* (London: Granta, 2001); and Richard Evans, *Lying about Hitler: History, Holocaust, and the David Irving Trial* (New York: Basic Books, 2001).

9 Christian Pross, *Paying for the Past: The Struggle over Reparations for Surviving Victims of Nazi Terror* (Baltimore, MD: Johns Hopkins University Press, 1998); Avi Beker (ed.), *The Plunder of Jewish Property During the Holocaust: Confronting European History* (Basingstoke: Palgrave, 2001).

10 See Allan A. Ryan, *Quiet Neighbors: Prosecuting Nazi War Criminals in America* (Orlando, FL: Harcourt Brace Jovanovich, 1984); David Cesarani, *Justice Delayed* (2nd edn, London: Phoenix Press, 2001).

11 David Cesarani, 'Getting away with murder', *Guardian* (25 April 2001). For the earlier failed attempt to prosecute Szymon Serafinowicz, when the jury decided he was unfit to stand trial due to senile dementia, see Alan Robinson, 'War crimes, old soldiers and fading memories: the Serafinowicz case', *Journal of Holocaust Education*, 8:1 (Summer 1999), 42–57, and Jon Silverman, 'War crimes inquiries', *History Today* (November 2000), 26–8.

12 *Süddeutsche Zeitung* (20 April 2000); *The Times* (22 March 2000); *Guardian* (22 March 2000).

13 For a critique of the term 'bystander', see David Cesarani and Paul Levine, 'Introduction' in D. Cesarani and P. Levine (eds), *'Bystanders' to the Holocaust*, pp. 1–8. On the controversy, see Jacques Picard, *Switzerland and the Assets of the Missing Victims of the Nazis* (Zürich: Bank Julius Baer, 1993); Jean Ziegler, *The Swiss, the Gold and the Dead* (New York: Harcourt Brace, 1998); Natasha Dornberg, *The Last Deposit: Swiss Banks and Holocaust Victims' Accounts* (Westport, CT: Praeger, 1999); and Foreign and Colonial Office, *Nazi Gold: The London Conference, 2–4 December 1997* (London: HMSO, 1997).

14 See, for example, Jonathan Glover, *Humanity: A Moral History of the Twentieth Century* (London: Jonathan Cape, 1999) and Richard Bernstein, *Radical Evil: A Philosophical*

Interrogation (Cambridge: Polity, 2002); Chapman quoted by Jonathan Jones, 'Shock treatment', *Guardian* (7 September 2000).

15 Novick, *The Holocaust and Collective Memory*, part 4.

16 Jeffrey Shandler, *While America Watches: Televising the Holocaust* (New York: Oxford University Press, 1999), p. xii.

17 Steve Paulsson, *The Holocaust: The Holocaust Exhibition at the Imperial War Museum* (London: Imperial War Museum, 2000); Tony Kushner, 'Oral history at the extremes of human experience: Holocaust testimony in a museum setting', *Oral History*, 29:2 (Autumn 2001), 83–94.

18 See the debate between Nira Yuval-Davis, Max Silverman, and David Cesarani in *Ethnicities*, 2:1 (2002), 107–33.

19 For a highly critical perspective, see Noa Gedi and Yigal Elam, 'Collective memory – what is it?', *History and Memory*, 8:1 (Spring/Summer 1996), 30–50, and the forum on 'History and memory' in *American Historical Review*, 102 (1997), 1371–1412.

20 See, for example, Iwona Irwin-Zarecka, *Frames of Remembrance: The Dynamics of Collective Memory* (New Brunswick: Transaction Books, 1994).

21 Patrick Wright, *On Living in an Old Country: The National Past in Contemporary Britain* (London: Verso, 1985).

22 See Donald Bloxham, *Genocide on Trial: War Crimes Trials and the Formation of Holocaust History and Memory* (Oxford: Oxford University Press, 2001).

23 Alain Finkielkraut, 'All German Jews?', in A. Finkielkraut, *Imaginary Jew* (Lincoln, NE: University of Nebraska Press, 1994), pp. 17–34, provides an autobiographical example of left-wing identification with Holocaust suffering.

24 Christopher Browning, *Ordinary Men* (New York: HarperCollins, 1992).

25 Götz Aly, *Final Solution: Nazi Population Policy and the Murder of the European Jews* (London: Arnold, 1999) and, for an excellent collection of the new research, Ulrich Herbert (ed.), *National-Socialist Extermination Policies* (New York: Berghahn Books, 2000).

26 *Eine Ausstellung und ihre Folgen. Zur Rezeption der Ausstellung Vernichtungskrieg, Verbrechen der Wehrmacht 1941 bis 1944* (Hamburg: Hamburg Institute for Social Research, 1999).

27 See Donald Bloxham, 'Punishing German soldiers during the Cold War: the case of Erich von Manstein', *Patterns of Prejudice*, 33:4 (1999), 25–45; Lord Russell, *The Scourge of the Swastika: A Short History of Nazi War Crimes* (London: Cassell, 1954).

28 Tony Kushner, *The Holocaust and the Liberal Imagination: A Social and Cultural History* (Oxford: Blackwell, 1994), pp. 265–6; Cesarani, *Justice Delayed*, ch. 10; Joseph Finklestone, 'Suspected Nazi war criminals in the United Kingdom: aspects of the controversy in Parliament', *British Journal of Holocaust Education*, 1:1 (Summer 1992), 25–46.

29 Sir Thomas Hetherington and William Chalmers, *War Crimes: Report of the War Crimes Inquiry* (London: HMSO, 1989).

30 Jon Silverman, 'Prosecuting Nazi war criminals – lack of will or lack of skill?', Parkes Centre Seminar, University of Southampton, March 2000.

31 Jeffrey Richards, *Film and British National Identity: From Dickens to Dad's Army* (Manchester: Manchester University Press, 1997), p. 353. For numerical indications of the series' success, see Graham McCann, *Dad's Army: The Story of a Classic Television Show* (London: Fourth Estate, 2002), pp. 3–5.

32 Richards, *Film and British National Identity*, pp. 358–61.

33 *Ibid.*, p. 364.

34 McCann, *Dad's Army*, pp. 8, 73; Richards, *Films and British National Identity*, p. 360.

35 *Ibid.*, pp. 3–4.

36 Clegg reported in *Guardian* (20 March 1999).

37 C. Henry Warren, *England Is a Village* (London: Eyre and Spottiswoode, 1940) was an immensely popular evocation of rural England set close to the location of *Dad's Army*. See also Richards, *Films and British National Identity*, p. 365.

38 For the crimes committed by Sawoniuk, see the widespread coverage in the British national press on 2 April 2002.

39 On their visit to the killing sites, see the *Guardian* (17 February 1999), and Cesarani, *Justice Delayed*, pp. 276–9, on the background to the case.

40 *The Media Show*, Channel 4 (14 October 1990) and comment by Mark Steyn in *The Independent* (15 October 1990).

41 *Guardian* (20 March 1999).

42 Geoff Dyer, *The Missing of the Somme* (London: Hamish Hamilton, 1994), p. 107.

43 See Angus Calder, *The Myth of the Blitz* (London: Jonathan Cape, 1991); Malcolm Smith, *Britain and 1940: History, Myth and Popular Memory* (London: Routledge, 2000).

44 Godfrey is the oldest of the platoon's soldiers; see McCann, *Dad's Army*, pp. 151–3.

45 See Kushner, '"Pissing in the wind"'.

46 Rubinstein, *The Myth of Rescue*.

47 Kushner, '"Pissing in the wind"', pp. 71–2; Michael Smith, *Foley: The Spy Who Saved 10,000 Jews* (London: Hodder and Stoughton, 1999); 'Britain's Schindler', BBC Radio 4 (7 June 1999); and Muriel Emanuel and Vera Gissing, *Nicholas Winton and the Rescued Generation* (London: Vallentine Mitchell, 2001); see *Jewish Chronicle* (18 June 1999) for the ceremony at the House of Commons.

48 This is supported by the Mass-Observation survey: 'Coming to Britain', summer 2000 directive, University of Sussex archive.

49 Walter Isaacson, 'Madeleine's War', *Time* (17 May 1999).

50 Ann Blackman, *Seasons of Her Life: A Biography of Madeleine Albright* (New York: Scribner, 1998); Thomas Blood, *Madam Secretary: A Biography of Madeleine Albright* (New York: St Martin's Griffin, 1999).

51 Isaacson, 'Madeleine's War'.

52 Clare Short on 'Woman's Hour', BBC Radio 4 (20 April 1999).

53 *Daily Mirror* (7 August 1992). See John Taylor, *Body Horror: Photojournalism, Catastrophe and War* (Manchester: Manchester University Press, 1998), pp. 60–5, for the controversy when *Living Marxism* journalists questioned that atrocities had been committed at the camp.

54 Patrick Finney, 'On memory, identity and war', *Rethinking History*, 6:1 (2002), 1.

55 *Guardian* (1 April 1999).

56 *Daily Mail* (2 April 1999).

57 *Express* (2 April 2002).

58 Bonino quoted by Isabel Hilton, 'We imagine war as a Hollywood film', *Guardian* (5 April 1999).

59 *Mirror* (1 April 1999).

60 Livingstone in the *Independent* (21 April 1999).

61 Tony Kushner, 'Kosovo and the refugee crisis, 1999: the search for patterns amidst the prejudice', *Patterns of Prejudice*, 33:3 (July 1999), 73–86; Ken Booth (ed.), *The Kosovo Tragedy: The Human Rights Dimension* (London: Frank Cass, 2001).

62 Tomasz Kamusella, 'Ethnic cleansing in Silesia 1950–89 and the ennationalizing policies of Poland and Germany', *Patterns of Prejudice*, 33:2 (April 1999), 52. Kamusella suggests the term was first used by *The Economist*.

63 Rose Lindsey, 'Nationalism and Gender: A Study of War-Related Violence Against Women' (unpublished PhD thesis, University of Southampton, 2000).

64 Linda Melvern, *A People Betrayed: The Role of the West in Rwanda's Genocide* (London: Zed, 2000); Philip Gourevitch, *We Wish to Inform You That Tomorrow We Will Be Killed with Our Families: Stories From Rwanda* (New York: Farrar, Straus and Giroux, 1998).

65 John Hooper, 'In the heart of Europe, a lost tribe fights for a loaf of bread', *Guardian* (3 April 1999).

66 University of Sussex, Mass-Observation Archive (hereafter M-O A), Spring 1999 directive, T842.

67 Dorothy Sheridan, Brian Street and David Bloome, *Writing Ourselves: Mass-Observation and Literacy Practices* (Cresskill, NJ: Hampton Press, 2000), which covers both the old and revived Mass-Observation projects.

68 M-O A: Spring 1999 Directive, A2212.

69 M-O A: E2836, a 48-year-old female working in freelance telemarketing.

70 *Ibid.*, T2150.

71 *Ibid.*, J2830, a 41-year-old female forensic phonetician.

72 *Ibid.*, R2065, a retired male medical administrator.

73 *Ibid.*, C2844, aged 39.

74 *Ibid.*, E2538, a 35-year-old female art student.

75 See Tony Kushner, 'Different worlds: British perceptions of the Final Solution during the Second World War', in David Cesarani (ed.), *The Final Solution: Origins and Implementation* (London: Routledge, 1994), pp. 246–67.

76 M-O A: Spring 1999 directive, D2585, a housewife in her fifties.

77 See the special issue of *Patterns of Prejudice*, 36:4 (2002), edited by Mark Levene, which makes comparisons and opens up such debate.

78 Hugo Gryn, *A Moral and Spiritual Index* (London: Refugee Council, 1996).

79 Straw's White Paper, *Fairer, Faster and Firmer – A Modern Approach to Immigration and Asylum* (London: HMSO, 1998) was the basis of the Immigration and Asylum Act of 1999. *The Independent* (25 March 2000) reported that 'Jack Straw . . . has outraged refugee support groups by ordering that toys should not be provided for the children of asylum-seekers.' For the impact of the dispersal of asylum seekers in terms of racial violence, including murder, see *The Independent* (16 September 2002).

80 Novick, *The Holocaust and Collective Memory*, p. 13.

81 This was particularly true of the BBC's flagship radio news programme, 'Today'.

82 Styron at a festival in Prague, quoted by Jonathan Freedland, 'Let's close the book', *Guardian* (12 April 2000).

83 Barbie Zelizer, *Remembering to Forget: Holocaust Memory Through the Camera's Eye* (Chicago, IL: University of Chicago Press, 1998), pp. 14–15.

Index

CPSIA information can be obtained
at www.ICGtesting.com
Printed in the USA
LVHW081622170921
698101LV00011B/580